THE STONE AGE

ALSO BY LESLEY-ANN JONES

Bohemian Rhapsody: The Definitive Biography of Freddie Mercury
Ride a White Swan: The Lives and Death of Marc Bolan
Naomi: The Rise and Rise of the Girl from Nowhere
Imagine
Tumbling Dice
Who Killed John Lennon?: The Lives, Loves and Deaths of the Greatest Rock Star
Hero: David Bowie
Love of My Life: The Life and Loves of Freddie Mercury

With David Ambrose:
How to be a Rock Star

With Phil Swern and Robin Eggar,
foreword by Bill Wyman:
The Sony Tape Rock Review

THE STONE AGE

SIXTY YEARS OF
THE ROLLING STONES

Lesley-Ann Jones

PEGASUS BOOKS

NEW YORK LONDON

THE STONE AGE

Pegasus Books, Ltd.
148 West 37th Street, 13th Floor
New York, NY 10018

First Pegasus Books cloth edition August 2022

ISBN: 978-1-63936-207-3

10 9 8 7 6 5 4 3 2 1

Printed in the United States of America
Distributed by Simon & Schuster
www.pegasusbooks.com

IN MEMORIAM

Christopher Robin Milne, 1920–1996
Ahmet Ertegun, 1923–2006
Ronald Schatt: Ronnie Scott, 1927–1996
Giorgio Sergio Alessandro Gomelsky, 1934–2016
Ian Andrew Robert Stewart: 'Stu', the 'Sixth Stone', 1938–1985
Charles Robert Watts: Charlie Watts, 1941–2021
Lewis Brian Hopkin Jones: Brian Jones, 1942–1969
Jimmy Miller, 1942–1994
Anita Pallenberg, 1942–2017
Robert Henry Keys: Bobby Keys, 1943–2014
Roger Scott, 1943–1989
Nicholas Christian 'Nicky' Hopkins, 1944–1994
Richard Roman Grechko: Ric Grech, 1945–1990
Ian Patrick McLagan, 1945–2014
William Everett Preston: Billy Preston, 1946–2006
James Aaron 'Jim' Diamond, 1951–2015
Meredith Curly Hunter, 1951–1969
Judy Elizabeth Totton 1952–2021
James 'Jimmy' McCulloch, 1953–1979
David Bolton, 1956–2020
Gavin Thomas Martin, 1961–2022
Laura 'Luann' Bambrough: L'Wren Scott, 1964–2014
Tara Jo Jo Gunne Richards, 1976

'Its mystery is its life. We must not let in daylight upon magic.'
WALTER BAGEHOT, 1826–77

'A new band of pierrots, "The Rolling Stones", came into existence yesterday at the Queen's Hall. Their entertainment is described as "A series of Pierrotical Fantasies". We understand that, in the main, it is intended for the benefit of children, but one or two of the items are likely to cause children a little surprise and their parents no little perturbation. The programme contains a dozen items, of which half are calculated to please the very best type of child, while the others are more suited to amuse sophisticated elderly men. Many of the more sophisticated items are extremely clever and all are amusing. The only criticism is that they do not somehow seem to have got into the right programme.'
THE TIMES, 28 DECEMBER 1921

CONTENTS

'It does get boring, people asking me, "Is this the last Stones tour?"
They've been asking that since 1964.'
MICK JAGGER

'Five strings, three notes, two fingers, one arsehole
and you've got it.'
KEITH RICHARDS

'Such psychic weaklings has Western civilisation made
of so many of us.'
BRIAN JONES

'I was listening to music long before rock'n'roll.'
BILL WYMAN

'I find it hard to get old and hard to say no.'
RONNIE WOOD

'That's our claim to fame, y'know. Carry on lads, regardless ... We're a
terrible band really. But we are the *oldest*. That's some sort of distinction,
innit? ... The only difference between us and Westminster Abbey is that
we don't do weddings and coronations.'
CHARLIE WATTS

Chapter One

KARMA

Saturday 5 March 2016

Translucent, triumphant, the pale-eyed bride wears the icy blue of a Disney *Frozen* princess. The Dress, an £8,000 silk and tulle Vivienne Westwood confection, is draped, layered and looped around her statuesque six-foot form. On the arm of her son who is giving her away, she glides the length of the marbled nave in flat Roger Vivier silver pumps, chosen to avoid towering over her shorter husband (she generally favours Manolo Blahnik heels). Her head nods like a sprung toy dog's on a parcel shelf. Her yellow hair hangs loose beneath a handkerchief of net. Never partial to professional make-up artists, she has painted her face herself. She smiles broadly, laughter lines crinkling, matte cranberry mouth framing the slightly crossed front teeth that she couldn't be bothered to fix. Clutching a white beribboned posy, she floats so closely past me that I smell her toothpaste. Her engagement ring dazzles. A little large on her finger, the huge stone, a cool £2.8 million worth of twenty-carat marquise-cut diamond, has slipped to one side.[1]

This is not a wedding, as such. The marriage itself took place yesterday at Spencer House,[2] followed by a fashionable lunch at Scott's of Mayfair. They have gathered here today to witness the blessing of the union of previously thrice-wed media mogul Rupert Murdoch,[3] eighty-four, and reformed rock chick Jerry Faye Hall, a quarter of a century his junior.

Though the full-lipped, fox-eyed features of love of her life Mick Jagger are everywhere you look, thanks to the presence of their four children, there is predictably no sign of the rocker himself. Delicious, then, the swishy arrival of his first wife Bianca, whom he left for the leggy Texan supermodel celebrating marriage today. Their differences long buried, Mick's glamorous exes are devoted friends.

Who else have we got? A hundred or so guests, including Cabinet minister Michael Gove and his columnist wife Sarah Vine; celebrity snapper David Bailey, who has come as a tramp, in trainers, plaid donkey jacket and knitted beanie hat, and who will be photographing the clan in due course; Rebekah Brooks, controversial Leveson Inquiry figure, infamous former editor of the *News of the World* and the *Sun*, now CEO of Murdoch's British newspapers, who is matronly on the arm of her husband Charlie; Sir Michael Caine and his exquisite wife Shakira, the Lord Lloyd Webber and Lady Madeleine, Bob Geldof and Jeanne Marine, unmade-bed artist Tracey Emin and playwright Tom Stoppard. There is also Karis Hunt Jagger, Mick's daughter with actress Marsha Hunt, paternity of whom he denied before giving in and coughing up, as economically as possible. She is a picture.

Bridesmaids? A frock of them. Come in The Daughters, in hues of blue. Dear Prudence, Murdoch's first-born, is elegant in teal. His second daughter Elisabeth blooms in bluebell. Mick's third daughter Lizzy, his first with Jerry, is sweetly wrapped in lazuline. Her sister Georgia May rocks delphinium. Flower girls Chloe and Grace, Rupert's offspring with his latest ex Wendi Deng, are coy in little-boy blue.

St Bride's Church is our location. The one with the wedding-cake spire at the Ludgate Circus end of Fleet Street, which has been a familiar landmark on London's skyline since 1703. It remains the spiritual home of the British media, despite the newspaper industry's exodus thirty years ago. I remember it well. I was stationed on the Street of Shame at the time, as a music and showbusiness journalist for the *Daily Mail*. It was Rupert Murdoch, the octogenarian groom at the altar today, who was responsible for the devastation. Damned if he was going to be held to ransom by print unions past their sell-by date and galvanised by Prime Minister Margaret Thatcher's stance against unions in general, he sacked 6,000 striking print workers, offloaded hundreds of journalists who refused to embrace his new technology, and moved his papers – the *Sun*, *The Times*, *The Sunday Times* and the now-defunct *News of the World* – to Docklands. Barbed-wired Fortress Wapping became the epicentre of hellish dispute, and 1986 concluded in mass demonstrations, bloody riots, the violent death of a teenage labourer and crushing defeat for the unions. Within two years, most of the nationals had followed suit, relocating to more accommodating postcodes and switching to computerised technology.

For nearly three hundred years, the Street had been the mecca of hacks and scribes. Pre-rolling TV news, pre-internet and social media, ninety per cent of information reached the public via newspapers. Thanks to the Murdoch revolution our vibrant village, the crucible of the childhood dreams of we who had grown up longing to be journalists, was decimated.

Those who remember what happened may be forgiven for wondering how Murdoch has the nerve to show his face in this holy place, known variously as the 'journalists' church', the 'cathedral of Fleet Street' and the 'parish church of journalism'. Some regard as 'a bit rich' his return to solicit the blessing of the street he destroyed. Others describe it as a 'laundering', a whitewashing of history, a bare-faced quest for absolution of his 'crimes'. The cynics weigh in with retorts that Murdoch has always been in the habit of thumbing his nose, so why would he stop now? 'This is comparable,' quips one, 'to Dracula getting married in a blood bank.'

Hours ahead of the service, security guards patrol the boundaries with sniffer dogs. Anti-News Corp protesters displaying offensive banners at the first-floor windows of a building opposite the church's North Door are thwarted when that entrance is closed and locked. The wedding party is re-directed via a side street, and enters the church through another entrance. Ladies and gentlemen, will you please stand.

*

It occurred to me at the time, and I still believe, that the conquest that day was not Rupert Murdoch's, but Jerry's, revenge being the dish best eaten cold. When she left Roxy Music star Bryan Ferry for Jagger in 1977, she did so for love. She gave the Stone four children and twenty-two years of her life. With a callousness bordering on reptilian, he cheated and lied his way through their relationship, taking women, dozens of them, and even the odd man, whenever and wherever he wanted, without sparing a thought for her indoors. Jerry, humiliated, hit back. Her brief 1982 affair with filthy-rich royal horse breeder Robert Sangster, the personal pal of Frank Sinatra whom she declared could have bought Mick out 'ten times over', gave the rocker a sip of his own serum. The boot was now on the other one. Mick, predictably, fought to win her back. 'It was the only time he ever picked me up from the airport,' she lamented, after the pair reunited.

They tied the knot in Bali in 1990 and lasted another nine years. When it emerged that he had fathered yet another child with yet another paramour – Lucas Morad Jagger with Brazilian model Luciana Gimenez Morad – only seventeen months after his apparent wife had given birth to their youngest child Gabriel, that was it. Jerry filed for divorce, suing reasonably for personal maintenance, child support and a share of his assets, only to discover to her horror that she had never been married in the first place.

Legendarily parsimonious, Jagger battled his way through court. His precious bank balance won. Their 'marriage', conducted in a Hindu ceremony, was found not to be legally binding in either Indonesia or Great Britain, and was declared null and void. So what were those beautiful wedding photos about, Mick? He seized on the verdict and screwed Jerry's settlement into the ground. Respect for seaweed-tongued, insouciant Jagger receded, even among diehard Stones fans for whom he walks on waves. The world had come a long way (with still a long way to go) since the heady days of rock'n'roll madness, when women were disposable and good only for one thing, when his rootless, macho, predatory lifestyle was a thing to which to aspire, at least according to the kind of hopeless, subcultural males who would one day acquire the epithet 'incels'.

Of all the debauched, shameful and selfish behaviour Mick had displayed down the years, this took the chocolate chip. The woman wore his rings, third finger left. She had birthed him a brood. His dismissal of Jerry caused catastrophic fall-out; their four cherished children were now branded illegitimate, and by their own father.

He lurks, the karma chameleon, red, gold and green. Creeping behind stone pillars and sliding under pews, he emits an insidious essence.

Invisible to the naked eye he skulks, the undetected life and soul. He barely stirs during the quiet contemplation of readings from 1 Corinthians and from the ancient Chinese text the *Tao Te Ching*, delivered by Rupert's son James and Jerry's son Gabriel. He agitates to the hymns – 'Amazing Grace', 'Jerusalem', the soaring sounds of William Walton's 'Set Me as a Seal Upon Thine Heart', swishing his tail. He pauses, lies still, waits patiently. In another life, pleased to meet you, he was a man of wealth and taste. As we sow, so must we reap. The last laugh is Jerry's. Look at her now, sticking it to the Stone. Not only for herself but for every Stones woman chewed and spat out without a backward glance. This is Jerry getting her own back, even if revenge is the last thing on her mind. He is here for her. Hope you guess his name.

*

When Rupert Murdoch acquired the *News of the World* in 1969, he inherited a feud between the scandal- and crime-touting rag and the Rolling Stones that had been raging unabated for years. Colluding with corrupt police officers, the title's hacks targeted the drug-swilling group as architects of degeneracy and scourges of society, whose influence over impressionable youth must be eradicated. The newspaper was prurient and hypocritical, pouring disapproval and disbelief over their law-breaking 'antics' and 'debauched', 'depraved' behaviour while dedicating seventy-two-point headlines and endless column inches to Stones coverage. Titillation and condemnation went hand in hand. An undercover reporter scooped Brian Jones using illegal substances in a club, but mistook him for Mick Jagger (accidentally on purpose?) in his published exposé. Jagger sued. The infamous ensuing drugs bust at Redlands, the West Wittering (West Sussex) home of guitarist Keith Richards, during which Jagger's fur rug-clad girlfriend Marianne Faithfull was alleged to have been found serving confectionery from an unusual receptacle was, as it were, tit for tat. When the *News of the World* folded in 2011 as a result of the phone-hacking scandal,[4] at a cost of more than two hundred jobs, Mick must have raised a cup to good riddance. Little could he have known that his old adversary would return to haunt him in the form of former proprietor Murdoch, the ghost of arrests and porridge past, who would not only serve as a funnel for the re-splashing of gloriously scurrilous old Stones editorials but who would yank him down a peg or two in the most public of ways, by taking his beautiful woman scorned as his own wife. Taunting Jagger with the very commitment he himself had resisted made Murdoch the victor and a mockery of the loser. Money talks. In Jagger's world, it's the only voice worth hearing. Rupert's net worth is estimated at around $20 billion. Mick curls up at night with a mere $500 million. Take that.

*

I had anticipated Jerry's wedding as a Stones-free zone. Sure enough, no Charlie and Shirley, no Ronnie and Sally, no Keith and Patti, no Ronnie's pretty, bubbly ex-wife Jo. But there can be no barring the doors to phantoms. Here they stand, a collective link to a less than blissful past that Jerry has mostly contrived to leave behind. I had managed to miss their arrival, and spot them just as the last guests make to leave: a better-days blonde in blue floral dress, green shoes and black coat with deep fur collar, on the arm of an elderly male in inky suit, grey V-necked sweater and open-necked shirt. Not very wedding-y. They pause for the waiting press photographers and exchange a few mind-how-you-gos. The old man blinks behind black-rimmed specs. He is paunchy and jowly. He seems both vague and vaguely familiar. His sparse grey hair and moustache could use a trim. I know him from somewhere. Our eyes meet under the arch, and we recognise each other. More than thirty years earlier, when I was a young television presenter and tabloid newspaper columnist, I became embroiled by default in a scandal that shocked the world. It rendered this man an alleged paedophile. The suspicion has stuck like stench. It led eventually, whatever they say, to his resignation from the Rolling Stones.

Bill Wyman was once the band's bassist. The better-days blonde is his wife Suzanne. The former object of his affections was a schoolgirl, Mandy Smith. They began dating when she was thirteen years old. I was there the night they met, at an awards event at London's Lyceum ballroom. I spent the evening with Bill and Midge Ure of Ultravox, with whom I had worked at Chrysalis Records. Unbeknown to me at the time, I was used as a clueless cover-up, drawn into Bill's mixed-age friendship circle assembled to conceal his and Mandy's burgeoning relationship. They began sleeping together, she said, when she was only fourteen. They married four years later.

I am invited to spend the afternoon at Spencer House, where the marital celebrations continue. Fuelled by crates of Moraga Bel Air wine from Rupert's own Californian vineyard, they have, by all accounts, a fine old time. I leave them to it. I repair instead with dear friends and fellow guildsmen to Two Brydges,[5] a small members' club in WC2. Our modest lunch and conversation restore perspective. The day is ended. Darkness falls.

*

Jerry's association with the greatest rock'n'roll band in the world was finally over. Although it can never be fully said and done, can it, when one's name has for so long been linked to a rock superstar's and when one shares children and grandchildren with the man, causing the rest of your lives, whether you like it or not, to overlap. Even when stretched to the max, bio-elastic never breaks. Long fascinated by the Stones' influence and culture, I found myself looking back over their lives as their sixtieth anniversary approached. I had not been around to witness their genesis, which prompted me to venture back ... to the first-ever gig at the Marquee Jazz Club on London's Oxford Street, on 12 July 1962. Mick Jagger sang lead vocals, Brian Jones and Keith Richard played guitar, Ian Stewart was the pianist and Dick Taylor was on bass. The drummer? They are still arguing about that. While some insist that Tony Chapman wielded the sticks, Keith was adamant in his 2010 autobiography *Life* that his friend and future Kink Mick Avory did so: 'not Tony Chapman, as history has mysteriously handed it down.'

Whoever it was, the fledgling group bagged the gig when Alexis Korner's Blues Incorporated – the club's Thursday night regulars fronted by Jagger, who would turn nineteen a fortnight hence – were asked to perform for a BBC live broadcast. Mick wasn't included in the airing, so Brian persuaded the Marquee's owner Harold Pendleton to let their new group stand in. They borrowed cash from Jagger's father to rent equipment for the night. When Brian phoned local listings paper *Jazz News* to advertise the occasion, so the legend goes, the copy taker asked for the name of the band. They didn't have one. Anxious Jones's eyes fell to a pile of records lying on the floor, and to the title of the first track on

The Best of Muddy Waters: 'Rollin' Stone'.

Which twinkles, like a fable. Nobody cares whether or not the story is true. They spent the summer gigging around the capital's clubs and dives. Mick, Keith and Brian soon moved in together. Their new home was a squalid, unfurnished second-floor flat at 102 Edith Grove, Fulham, two beds between three. Filthy crockery and cutlery were flung from the kitchen window rather than washed up. Drummer Charlie Watts soon joined them, and Bill Wyman was hired. The classic line-up, set in Stones.

Sixty years later and three founders down, they are still at it. No group attracts greater legend, not even the Beatles. With the exception of the Who, who are now reduced to two original members, no other rock act has lasted that long. The Stones are veterans of more than two thousand concerts and counting, and are one of the most popular live acts in entertainment history. Their 2005–07 A Bigger Bang tour was then the highest-grossing tour of all time. Their 18 February 2006 free one-nighter on Rio de Janeiro's Copacabana Beach, experienced by more than two million people on the sand and in the surrounding streets, broke records as the largest rock concert ever staged.

They are also songwriting and recording superstars, with estimated sales of more than 240 million units. They have won three Grammy Awards and a Lifetime Achievement Award. They have been inducted into the Rock and Roll Hall of Fame (1982) and the UK Music Hall of Fame (2004). They came tenth on the US Billboard Hot 100 All-Time Top Artists Chart in 2008. Eleven years later, they made it to second place on *Billboard* magazine's Greatest Artists of All Time list, reflecting American chart success, behind the Beatles and ahead of Elton John, Mariah Carey, Madonna, Barbra Streisand, Michael Jackson, Taylor Swift and Stevie Wonder. By the Greatest Artists of All Time reckoning of *Rolling Stone* magazine, they rank fourth behind the Beatles, Bob Dylan and Elvis Presley, eclipsing Chuck Berry, Jimi Hendrix, James Brown, Little Richard and Aretha Franklin.

In September 2020, they broke the UK's Official Charts record when they beat twenty-one-year-old singer-songwriter Declan McKenna to No. 1 with *Goats Head Soup*. It was that album's second seizing of the sweet spot, having debuted at the top on its original release in 1973. It set the

Stones a new record, making them the first band in official chart history to score a No. 1 album in six different decades. They now have thirteen No. 1 albums, including the reissues of *Exile on Main St*, considered by many to be their finest, and *Goats Head Soup*, thus equalling the record of Elvis Presley and Robbie Williams. Only the Beatles achieved more No. 1 albums in the UK. They have 18 million followers on Facebook and 3.5 million on Twitter. One of the most streamed acts on Spotify, they net close to 20 million monthly listens. Nearly 2 million subscribers follow their YouTube channel, with more than 650 million views. Although the global pandemic pressed pause on the American leg of No Filter, their latest tour, and despite the sad but not unexpected death of eighty-year-old Charlie Watts, business resumed during autumn 2021 when the band hopped back on the road. They started hinting at a new album, their first since 2016's *Blue & Lonesome*, which was in turn their first for eleven years.

With a combined age of 232, the band's core line-up – Mick, 'Keef' and 'the new boy' Ronnie, who took over from Brian Jones's replacement Mick Taylor in 1975 – continue to wield vast influence. This despite the rise of cancel culture, regarded by many as an important tool of social justice but by others as a senseless form of social media mob rule. In October 2021, faced with a barrage of hostility (not for the first time) for their song 'Brown Sugar' – which critics claim is 'gross, sexist and sickeningly insulting towards black women', with lyrics described as 'some of the most stunningly crude and offensive that have ever been written' – the band backed down, deleting it from the set list of their resumed tour. Their second most frequently performed song behind 'Jumpin' Jack Flash' was placed on hold. 'I don't know,' pondered Keith Richards. 'I'm trying to figure out with the sisters quite where the beef is. Didn't they understand this was a song about the horrors of slavery? But they're trying to bury it … At the moment, I don't want to get into conflicts with all of this shit, but I'm hoping that we'll be able to resurrect the babe in her glory somewhere along the track.'

'We've played "Brown Sugar" every night since 1970,' commented Jagger, in defence of the band's 1971 No. 1 hit. 'Sometimes you think, "We'll take that one out for now and see how it goes." We might put it back in.' Will they?

Piers Morgan demanded its reinstatement. The ubiquitous journalist and television presenter, who is now a global star and who was once my editor, branded the Stones 'cowards' for caving in to the 'woke bullies' and dropping the song, which includes references to a Gold Coast slave ship and a slave owner whipping women. 'There is nothing racist about "Brown Sugar",' raged Morgan, pointing out that the song defends and supports black women, and that it does not make light of slavery. Calling out rap songs featuring lyrics that *are* deeply offensive to females, he warned: 'The woke-filled narrative will now be that the song IS racist, so the Stones are therefore racist, and they've abandoned performing it because they accept these assertions. What utter nonsense.'

'I'll tell you how racist the Rolling Stones are,' says Bernard Fowler, the acclaimed recording artist and backing vocalist who has worked with a string of A-list artists throughout his long career, and who has served the Stones devotedly on stage and in the studio for around thirty-five years. 'I'm a black man from the Queensbridge Projects [New York, named after the Queensboro Bridge which sits just north of the site, once described as 'literally hell on earth']. Death, the Devil and drugs were all over Queensbridge. I wanted to be a professional basketball player so I could get the hell out. Instead, I found music.

'Mick? I love him. There's only one Mick Jagger, and he's a freak of nature. He has a lot more time to rock before he gets to quit. As long as he has a voice and can still perform the way he does, he should do it. He's out-performing people a third of his age. Who else can do that? He's a consummate pro, and it's an amazing thing to see. Are we friends? Oh, yeah. I would say so. I would hope so. I've spent my life with these guys. They are like family to me. I've watched their children grow, and I love them all.

'We were on a tour, might have been the Voodoo Lounge or the Urban Jungle, and we were in Austria. Before the gig, I went to do a little shopping. I walked a few blocks, went into a store, and noticed a guy standing outside. I was heading back out of the store to go to the hotel when I noticed that the guy was walking behind me. All of a sudden he starts yelling. I don't speak German, so no idea, right? He's looking at me. Oh boy, I'm thinking, here we go, he's a crazy. I'm from New York, I'm ready to confront him, but I'm thinking, probably not a good idea. The lady behind the counter in the store has a funny look on her face. "I'm so sorry," she says sadly, "I can't repeat what he's saying.'"

Over at the venue late that afternoon, Bernard borrowed a little motor scooter and took himself off to meet some friends.

'I'm inside the gate of the gig, I'm watching people walk by, and suddenly a guy sees me and starts yelling. A different guy. What the fuck? Two cops with submachine guns appear, and they speak to him. "This guy says that you stole his ticket," says one of the cops. What? I show them my laminate to prove that I'm with the band. But instead of going the right way, they go the other way. They take me off to some trailer and hold me for forty-five minutes. I kid you not. Finally a guy comes in and just says to me, "You can go." No explanation, no apology, nothing. I go backstage, I get dressed, I go visit Ronnie and then I go visit Keith. Keith and I sit down, we're talking, we're listening to some music, just chilling. "Brother B.," says Keith pleasantly, "how was your day today?"

"'I had the weirdest fucking day today," I told him. "I went shopping, I was detained at the gig ..." He stops. This is who Keith is. He says, "What? They fucking did *what*? Where's Tony Russell?" [Keith's personal assistant since 1988, whom Bernard calls 'Keith's Man Friday'] "Fucking cops!" says Keith. "Go get JC!" [that's Jim Callaghan, the head of our security]. "Bernard, don't go nowhere!" Callaghan comes in. Keith tells him the story. "I want those two motherfuckers *here*!" yells Keith. He starts pacing. He has a certain way he walks when he's pissed (off). JC comes back, he can't find the cops. Keith is now *hot*.

'It's an outdoor show, you've got the mayor there, you've got the governor, all the dignitaries. The show is supposed to have gotten started, but it gets held up. "I want their balls *here*!" Keith is demanding, raging like an animal. "I want the chief of police!"

'Half an hour goes by. An hour and a half. Almost two hours. I'm in my dressing room, lying low. Mick's getting an earful, and he comes to talk to me, wanting to know from me what happened. I say, "Mick, Keith only asked me how my day was. How was I to know he was gonna go and do *this*?"

'Tony Russell comes in. I walk outside with him, to find that Keith has the head of police, the deputy head, the mayor, the promoter of the gig, all standing in a line, like a firing squad. "You motherfuckers detain him because he's *black*?" Keith is screaming. "Those two fucking cops, where are they?" And then he said to them all, pointing at me, "*Apologise!* You're gonna fucking apologise to him. *Right. Now!*" And every one of them did.

'That's a stand-up cat. I will never forget it. When Keith Richards calls me, I answer. When he calls from wherever he is, maybe London or LA, and goes, "Bernard, where are you?" I go, "I'm in New York, I'm in the studio, I'm coming!"'

*

Mick and Keith were born in the Livingstone community hospital in Dartford, Kent, twenty minutes along the A2 from my own home town. They landed in July and December 1943 respectively. They attended the same primary school, then went their separate ways. In 1960, while former choirboy and Boy Scout Keith was a student at Sidcup Art College, bookworm Mick was an undergraduate at the London School of Economics. They bumped into each other again on a Dartford station platform and discovered mutual interest in R&B and the blues. Inspired by blues pioneers – Howlin' Wolf, John Lee Hooker, Elmore James, Muddy Waters, Chuck Berry, Big Bill Broonzy and Robert Johnson – who influenced Keith's guitar licks and Mick's vocals, both proceeded to move in and out of the ever-changing line-ups that underpinned London's embryonic blues scene. The first incarnation of the Stones coagulated under the wing of Alexis Korner and his Blues Incorporated, pioneers with a regular gig at Ealing Blues Club. An occasional sitter-in with that band was Cheltenham-born guitarist Brian Jones. By early 1962, Jagger was a regular singer with Korner's men, while also rehearsing with Jones, Richard and other like-minded musicians such as pianist Ian Stewart. The aforementioned Marquee gig was billed as 'Brian Jones and Mick Jagger and the Rollin' Stones'. The classic line-up was not cemented until the following year, when Charlie left Blues Incorporated, and bassist Bill Wyman joined too.

The turning point was a residency at the Crawdaddy Club in Richmond. Their reputation spread quickly by word of mouth, drawing the band to the attention of teenage former Beatles PR assistant Andrew

Loog Oldham. He became their original manager and negotiated their first contract at Decca, the label infamous for having turned down the Beatles. Their debut release, in June 1963, was a cover of Chuck Berry's 'Come On'. While it was not a major hit, the public's appetite was whetted. As was the media's. Wily Oldham flogged his upstarts as a dangerous antidote to the lovable mop-top Beatles, and terrified the life out of parents of schoolgirl daughters all over this land. The Stones rapidly became the cult heroes of Britain's frustrated youth. Their first, eponymous album the following year, which consisted of R&B covers, topped the UK charts in April 1964. By June they were on their debut US tour and celebrating their first UK No. 1, their version of Bobby Womack's 'It's All Over Now'.

Thus did these white working-class and middle-class British kids, who set out to play the music of black African Americans, warm to their theme, gathering momentum. They developed an edgy, distinctive rock-pop style that maintained strong blues undertones while celebrating the diversions of women, sex and drugs. Did they address the issues of the day? Were politics and social awareness reflected in their lyrics? Not really. Most references of that nature were abstract. They cobbled shreds of ideas, smoking and distorting themes into motifs with memorable riffs. There was never a set formula. Going out on a limb, they struck gold. From 1965 onwards, all singles were officially Jagger/Richard compositions. 'The Last Time' made the American Top 10 and paved the way for their first No. 1 on both sides of the pond, '(I Can't Get No) Satisfaction'. By the end of the decade, the band had become an international attraction, second only to their Liverpudlian arch-rivals in popularity and cultural importance. They also achieved an impressive double whammy, giving America back its own music while reinventing themselves as the outlaws of rock'n'roll.

The Stones were surrounded by an almost permanent aura of publicity and notoriety. 'Let's Spend the Night Together' was censored by American television's *Ed Sullivan Show*. Jagger, Richard and Jones were all busted for drugs. Mick's relationship with aristocratic convent schoolgirl Marianne Faithfull stoked the gossip columns. Detractors from Bournemouth to Wagga Wagga denounced the group as corruptors of youth, destroyers of moral values and as messengers of the Devil. The end of the sixties delivered both the sacking and drowning of father-of-at-least-five Brian Jones, who gasped his last in the pool of his East Sussex home, Cotchford Farm. It was the first major death of the 1960s rock movement. Within two years, Jimi Hendrix, Jim Morrison and Janis Joplin had followed suit, their deaths all drug-related. All, including Jones, were the same age, giving rise to the conspiracy theory of 'The Twenty-Seven Club'. The Stones played at a free Hyde Park concert on 5 July 1969, dedicating the pre-planned performance to their tragic late bandmate.

Musically, apart from their 1967 flirtation with psychedelia in *Their Satanic Majesties Request* album and 'We Love You' single, the band were on a recognisable trajectory. *Beggars Banquet* and *Let It Bleed* were both classic rock albums, regarded by loftier critics as the Stones' finest hour. Their creative peak of 1968–72 saw the distillation of their blues, rock'n'roll, R&B and country influences into the dark, decadent, sexy noise that we came to know as the definitive, ironic Rolling Stones' sound. Mick's dynamic stage presence and Keith's fledgling pirate vibes made for an unrivalled double act. As irresistible rock gods they became an institution during the 1970s, living the profligate, self-indulgent high life of jet-setting tax exiles, setting new records for huge sell-out gigs, and perfecting the rock'n'roll cliché of their own invention.

In 1974, Mick Taylor quit and was replaced by the Faces' Ron Wood. There ensued a comprehensive toning-down of their earlier wild image, as befitting rebels slip-sliding into their thirties – which in those days was the onset of 'middle age' – when they bequeathed their 'two fingers to the world' stance to punk pretenders such as the Sex Pistols. But they didn't go resting on laurels. They continued to pump out worthwhile albums and a couple of classics. They maintained the standard they had set for themselves with the likes of 'Brown Sugar' and 'It's Only Rock 'n Roll'. Thousands of teenagers around the world started bands because of them. Although most never made it beyond the garage door, they shook up entire neighbourhoods and boosted the musical landscape. The Stones, as ever, were responsible for chaos, chance and change.

Most who cared assumed that the band would coast comfortably into the 1980s and start thinking about chucking in the towel. Most were wrong. 1981 was the year of the American tour that broke all box-office records, while their album *Tattoo You* reached No. 1 in the UK and also went all the way in the USA. *Still Life*, the live album of that tour, was almost equally successful the following year. For their twentieth anniversary, they transported that American show to Europe, and signed a new four-album record deal for $50 million with CBS Records, the then-biggest recording deal in history.

The mid-1980s was the era of the notorious Jagger-Richards rift. Mick had hitched his own deal to the Stones' CBS contract, and was keen to concentrate on solo work. Keith's nose was out of joint. Hence, the Stones did not perform as a band at Live Aid in 1985. Mick recorded a track and video with David Bowie instead, a cover of 'Dancing in the Street' that topped the UK chart and made No. 7 in the US. Keith and Ronnie backed Bob Dylan in Philadelphia. It was awful. Jack Nicholson must later have rued the moment he introduced the 'transcendent' Dylan to 1.9 billion people across the globe. Ronnie and Keith strolled on late armed with acoustic guitars, looking smacked up. Out of tune and out of time, they never really got into the received magic of 'Blowin' in the Wind'. It's the way it goes, sometimes. Maybe they should have rehearsed. Charlie suffered a massive mid-life crisis, became a heroin addict and almost lost everything, including his wife Shirley. He got a grip and got back on track. Bill threw away his credibility (and should perhaps have been relieved of his liberty) when he became sexually involved with a child. The band's twenty-fifth anniversary came and went with little more than a documentary to show for it.

Things took a turn for the better by the end of the decade. The *Steel Wheels* album resurrected the Stones of old. The Urban Jungle tour, their first outing for seven years, proved their biggest to date. It was also Wyman's last. He left the band before the serious money kicked in, wrote his long-threatened autobiography, and reinvented himself with his touring Rhythm Kings.

The Stones' next milestone was the *Voodoo Lounge* album of 1994, and the ensuing tour of the same name: again, the highest-grossing ever at that time. In November that year, they became the first mainstream act to broadcast a concert over the internet. They bowed out of the nineties with their *Bridges to Babylon* album. Their subsequent global excursion left them in no doubt that they were still an international attraction. Touring continued throughout the 2000s.

In 2002, they released their double greatest hits collection *Forty Licks* to commemorate their fortieth anniversary. It reached No. 2 in both the UK and US markets. Charlie battled throat cancer in 2004, and won. The *A Bigger Bang* album and tour accounted for 2005–06, and triumphed in Rio. Ronnie fell spectacularly off the wagon, dumped his wife Jo for Kazakhstani waitress Ekaterina Ivanova, and eventually went straight with theatre producer Sally Humphreys.

In 2012, the band marked their fiftieth anniversary. Album, tour, album, tour. The usual. Then the Stones came full circle. With their *Blue & Lonesome* album in December 2016, they returned to the songs that had originally inspired them. In April 2020, Mick, Keith, Charlie and Ronnie performed from their respective homes as one of the headline acts on the Global Citizens One World: Together at Home on-screen concert in support of the World Health Organization and front-line healthcare workers.

When Jagger was knighted for services to popular music in 2002, the dissident became Establishment. The owner of châteaux, riverside mansions, beach dwellings, brownstones and penthouses, Sir Mick has access to virtually anyone in the world he wants to reach. Silkscreened by Warhol and photographed naked by Cecil Beaton (his bum, at least), he goes unnamed by Don McLean on 'American Pie' but is writ large in its lyrics as 'Satan'. He was eulogised by Maroon 5 in 'Moves Like Jagger', and referenced in the Black Eyed Peas' 'The Time (Dirty Bit)' and Kesha's 'Tik Tok'. Rumours generate around him wherever he goes. Who cares if they're not true? A globally recognisable sex symbol, everyone over the age of fifty knows someone who knows someone who has slept with him: on a limo floor, in a Royal box, in the bathroom of a private jet. The Dionysian archetype of eternal youth has kept the legend of his virility alive. The father of eight, grandfather of five and great-grandfather of three is now swaggering towards his eightieth birthday. As is Keith, father of four, grandfather of five; while Ronnie, father of six including six-year-old twins by his third wife Sally, has just turned seventy-five. Makes you think.

Although ... technically speaking, Mick has never been a great singer; although his strutting, swaggering, finger-pointing on-stage antics, at once ludicrous and cool, have often veered hilariously towards self-parody; and although the ensemble instrumental work can sometimes seem irritatingly sloppy, the Stones can still lay credible claim to the title 'Greatest Rock'n'Roll Band in the World'. Their catalogue comprises some of the most thrilling music ever recorded. Not fade away, they blared defiantly, in the spirit of that song's creator Buddy Holly. They meant it more than he did.

Perhaps their relevance is questionable in the twenty-first century. Perhaps this is the irrelevant in the room. When irate and worthy objectors mobilise to cancel Stones compositions, they might be missing the point. 'Offensive', 'racist', 'sexist' or otherwise, the band have in fact survived the steady post-rock'n'roll decline that serves up more and more artists delivering less and less music – *real* music, of the beating-heart, gets-under-your-skin-and-into-your-blood variety. They contributed songs that moved us, thrilled us, angered us and turned us on, providing a soundtrack to dance to and by which to live. They gave our existence meaning. An exaggeration? Isn't that what music does? We listen, engage and respond collectively, to know that we are not alone. We circle back to the songs and stars of our adolescence, if only for a wistful swig of forgotten youth. We'll never be young again. But music, sweet music, reminds us of what that was like. We may, at times, feel uneasy about it. Did they really show us, at the height of their fame, a version of life as it might best be lived? Or was it all a con? Did they merely deflect us from the futility of being here, peddling distraction from inevitable, pending doom?

In order to contextualise the legacy of the Rolling Stones, it is to their own Greek chorus that we must turn. To their families and friends, their women and children, their colleagues and acquaintances, people who crossed paths with them while going about their daily lives, who are so often disregarded but who are significant. Many were casualties of the Stone Age, their names all but erased by time. Though we live in an age of cancellation, there can be no cancellation of them. No negation of negligence, degradation or disgrace. No restoration of virginity or dignity. No resurrection for the abused, the abandoned, the addicted, the miscarried, the murdered, the suicides. These people lived, they breathed, and they were part of the story. Rewind.

What a drag it is, getting old ... for others of their vintage, crabbing about like fossilised derelicts, inching ever closer towards the abyss. But not for these living, breathing reefs of ancient marvellousness, who defy gravity, fashion, political correctness and just about everything else. Elvis is dead. The Beatles are over. The Stones might be gathering moss, but on they roll.

Chapter Two

JONER

Truth lies. Time is not always final. History rewrites itself, for multiple reasons, not least to fit a narrative more convenient to those still here. The record informs us that Brian Jones was a blues enthusiast and naturally gifted musician whose fingers and mouth could find their way around any instrument, but who was mortified by the lack of a singing voice and adequate songwriting ability. That he was small, perfectly formed and irresistible to the opposite sex. That between the ages of seventeen and twenty-two, he fathered half a dozen children out of wedlock, all by different girls. That he founded and named the Rollin' Stones (the 'g' came later) as an R&B band. That the others envied his virtuosity, and even punished him for it. That fame, fortune and narcotics fuelled his fascination with the dark side. That he fell off the rails, was sacked by Mick and Keith, and sank to his death in his own swimming pool in July 1969, at the age of twenty-seven – 'so long ago that it no longer matters'. But it is not the whole story. It never is.

I went looking for Brian in the manors of the London dives he once frequented. In the Sussex Weald, the Ashdown Forest and in his home town, Cheltenham, Gloucestershire. A seemingly genteel place of charming architecture and a celebrated school, it boasts an internationally renowned horse racing festival that my late father returned to annually. I visited houses Brian had lived in, schools he had learned in, wandered the routes his own boots had once trod. In the realm of the living, beyond the odd blue plaque, there is little left of him. The Cheltenham Cemetery grave that contains his silver and bronze casket, buried deeply beyond the reach of the spades of desecrators, sits so close to a junction that the turf there is imprinted with tyre marks, from wheels that have strayed from the beaten track. Was this questionable positioning all that the family could get, or was it intentional?

Loath though many of us are to delve into devil worship and mysticism, we should at least pause to consider possibilities. In folklore, the points at which tracks and roads intersect are thought to be dangerous places of transition, where the living world and the underworld collide. Here may the polluted spirits of dead outlaws and witches, suicides and the executed be redeemed. Here, too, according to bygone belief, could Satan be summoned. Were those who buried Brian aware of this mythology? Brian himself, thanks to his obsession with the blues and bluesmen, must have come across the crossroads legend. He not only nursed a preoccupation with the occult, thanks to his involvement with spellbinding, ruthlessly spell-casting Anita Pallenberg, but also knew the fate of Robert Johnson: the Mississippi bluesman he discovered in his youth, came to idolise, and whose music he introduced to his fellow Stones.

Legend holds that the hard-times guitarist fell to his knees at a crossroads one night, pleading to meet his maker and to be blessed with the gift of musicianship. Out of the road, it is claimed, rose the Devil with a deal on his tongue. In return for the desperado's soul, he would bestow musical brilliance upon him. Robert rewound, back to the blues joints once dismissive of him, reinvented as a virtuoso prodigal son. He had the music in him, he was a one-man orchestra, but he would pay a terrible price. His brief life was tragic. Johnson's final recording, in 1937, was 'Me and the Devil Blues'. 'You want to know how good the blues can get?' said Keith Richards of the man who cut it. 'Well, this is it.'

Brian's headstone is plain and unyielding. No love went into its carving, not even the word. Across the way, beneath an arboreal canopy in an infinitely more tranquil setting, lie the remains of his little sister Pamela. She died from leukaemia[1] at the age of two, and was committed to her grave almost a quarter of a century before him. The inscription on her stone reads as plainly and as unemotionally as his: 'In Affectionate

Remembrance'. Why did his parents not bury their son beside her? Even now, there is room. Might they have feared that the innocence of their infant daughter would somehow be corrupted by his scandalous life and wretched death, to the point that they deliberately distanced him from her? Lewis and Louisa Jones are gone. They left no explanation.

Time dances. Leaping ahead and leaning backwards, it wafts and strays into faded forties photographs. Yellow-taped and torn-edged, they tell us more than words. Here is pudding blond cherub Lewis Brian Hopkin Jones, scratchy in his Dean Close prep school uniform, a cut above in a suburban middle-class house, at odds with his Welsh Methodist parents. Imperious Dada and disapproving Mam run a brisk household. He is an uncuddled child carrying a secret he cannot share, a mystery that is never referred to at home. He had a little sister but then she died. They got him another sister, Barbara, who arrived just as he was about to start school, and who could *be* him, staring back at himself in the mirror. But where is his other sister? Why didn't they tell him? Was her disappearance his fault? Emotionally unripe, he cannot grasp the concepts of death and mourning, though he worries that he should feel something. He hurts silently.

Not much is known, even today, about the development of children who suffer the death of a sibling. There was negligible knowledge and frankly more pressing things to worry about during the mid-1940s, a time when the country was emerging from war and the National Health Service had not yet been established.[2] Records and statistics from 1945, when Pamela died, are variable. Poverty, air raids, measles, whooping cough, scarlet fever, diphtheria and traffic accidents were the primary killers of children back then. Few families were immune to mortality.

Nowadays, a little boy like Brian would be given bereavement counselling. His mental health would be assessed, and he would likely remain under the watchful eye of psychologists for a long time. There is evidence that the damage can be even more devastating if the surviving child is older. Research has also shown that bereaved parents can lose the ability to support and nurture their other children. Marital breakdown, depression and other problems often ensue. The unique nature of the relationship suggests that a sibling's death can cause irreparable damage to the human capabilities of the survivor. The child becomes the 'forgotten griever', unaccounted for in the scheme. There is nowadays evidence of increased mental disorders in bereaved siblings. Such trauma has an impact on academic potential and attainment, causing many to look for escape. It also increases the likelihood of breakdown in the child's relationship with their parents.

The effects are greater when the lost brother or sister was close in age: Brian and Pamela were born only nineteen months apart. It is possible that Brian's asthma, which apparently plagued him for life, was triggered by Pamela's death. Epidemiologists have found that childhood bereavement leads directly to increased health risks, including extreme stress and higher rates of mortality in adulthood. Psychologists have established that bereaved children experience grief, sadness and depression that they cannot express. Many resort to pretend play with their deceased sibling, as though attempting to resurrect them. As adolescents, they can engage in increased levels of risk-taking: Brian did so at school, as one of 'the naughty ones'. He grew reckless beyond it, often life-threateningly. They may seek to 'replace' their lost loved one with children of their own: Brian fathered five acknowledged offspring. A sixth has been hinted at, and there may have been more. They can subconsciously select as romantic partners individuals who resemble themselves and/or their missing sibling: Brian favoured angelic, cupid-bow blondes, and fell hook and line for German-Italian model Anita Pallenberg, his spitting image, whom he met in Europe while on tour. When she later overthrew him for his bandmate Keith Richards, she shattered Brian's heart.

Bereaved children may also lack self-respect: Brian could be supercilious and contemptuous of others, but the person he loathed was himself. They may even harbour a death wish, possibly founded in survivor's guilt: while Brian's drowning under the influence of alcohol and hard drugs was recorded as misadventure, and while sensational claims based on death-bed confessions have suggested in recent years that he was murdered, it is entirely possible that, finding little to live for after being dumped by the band he co-founded and lived for, he simply allowed himself to go under and let go.[3]

'I am curious about Brian Jones' story and what we would call in psychotherapy his "presentation": the dysfunction around relating, the emotional release through drugs and alcohol, the disemboguement of precocious sexuality,' says respected British psychotherapist Richard Hughes. 'There is so much fury and anger in the adult Brian, lurking there just beneath the blond fringe. As Charlie Watts said, "He was not very nice … he upset people easily." I would say that this points to a catastrophic and sustained trauma during his childhood. There may have been sexual abuse. We will never know, of course. This is pure supposition, but the presentation fits with that from a clinical perspective. It is important to remind ourselves that, on a human level, there is always trauma behind psychopathology.'

The grief that Brian's family suffered at the loss of his two-year-old sister Pamela, asserts Hughes, constitutes complex trauma. 'There are few clinical studies about the loss of a sibling,' he notes. 'Albert and Barbara Cain's 1964 paper is still very much the primary source. It was written from a psychoanalytic and psychiatric perspective, and the focus is on the "replacement child": the sibling who is born subsequently.'

'We can only speculate on how his sister's death impacted three-year-old Brian. So much of this would have been experienced by him out of awareness. But it is interesting that a year later he had a croup infection severe enough to leave him with respiratory problems for the rest of his life. A psychosomatic response to the trauma? An unconscious communication to his parents that he needed caring for too, when their emotional availability was limited? In Chinese medicine and even psychoanalytic theory, conditions to do with the larynx and windpipe are associated with grief … the loss of a child can impact on the parents' ability to support and nurture their other children. It was not that they didn't want to, it's that they couldn't. They didn't have the emotional and physical capacity.'

How confused, the psychotherapist laments, this poor little boy must have been: 'As a three-year-old, all he must have wanted was to be picked up and reassured by his mother when there were so many unfamiliar feelings being expressed, or repressed, in the household. How did his mother respond? Did she hold him even closer, overcompensating for the loss of his sister, or was he too much for his parents to cope with as they tried to make sense of their own grief? In psychoanalytic theory, there is the idea of "the bound child", who is over-protected and held too closely in times of grief, usually by the mother. An outcome of this can be that the child experiences a sense of "engulfment". From a developmental perspective, the child is less able to manage feelings associated with separation and their emerging sense of self, which are important stages of child development.'

The 'bound child', Hughes further explains, may feel anger or hopelessness at their lack of autonomy; but this is complicated by feelings of guilt if they push away, and by the intensely pleasurable feelings of being mothered.

'From a Freudian perspective,' he adds, 'we are entering the territory of what may constitute an incestuous relationship. Whilst this might sound preposterous, it is the basis of the Oedipal complex, and is more common than you would imagine. Whilst the family was in the depths of their grief and Brian was being nursed though his croup infection, another child was conceived, this time a little girl, "the resurrected child". How did Brian feel about that? Whether he had tried hard to replace his sister, or had that role imposed upon him, he was now deposed and replaced. As a four-year-old, he was powerless to control this. All children feel a sense of displacement by a new sibling. We can only imagine how Brian experienced that.'

We can also try and find it by looking at close-up photographs, where we see clearly the untold story in Brian's adult eyes. 'What I detect in photographs of him are the eyes of a child who never cried,' says Hughes. 'He never cried because there was no point: no one came and comforted him. Again in psychoanalytic theory, there is an idea associated with sibling loss, about "the haunted child" who is overwhelmed by the unspoken grief and the guilt that they survived, but are unable to take the place of their dead sibling. There can be a deep sense of shame around this: that the wrong child died; that on some deep, dark level, their parents would have preferred it to have been them who died instead. The "haunted child" must be horrified that his parents' grief has somehow manifested their dead sibling via the birth of a new sibling, which only confirms to him his feelings of not being "enough", of being "replaceable". Once so close to his mother, he must now experience an overwhelming Oedipal fury that his father has won, that his mother has been taken away from him, and the outcome is another child. If Brian felt competitive towards his father, he certainly got his own back when he reached his own sexual maturity in his teenage years.'

Children who have been through the loss of a sibling and the associated developmental disruption may therefore grow up internalising unspoken beliefs that they are unlovable and not 'good enough'. They may struggle to connect at a deeper level. This in turn may lead them to be supercilious and contemptuous of others, as Brian was – which is a fear of connection whilst desperate for the simple affirmation that they are 'OK'. Sexual encounters may be easy to orchestrate and control, but the individual may end up finding this kind of connection emotionally overwhelming and even re-traumatising. We must remember that Brian grew up during an era when none of this kind of thing was spoken about, and therefore was not easily processed and come to terms with.

'A lack of self-respect? Clinically, I would call it the narcissistic wound,' says Richard Hughes. 'Brian wasn't born bad. Rather, as Mick Jagger says, 'He needed babying.' His development as a child was shaped by trauma. Nothing could compensate for the love, comfort and affirmation he needed. An outcome of this can be, according to John Bowlby, the father of attachment theory, "a disturbed personality development" which can lead to delinquency, anxiety states and depressive illness. The child becomes unresponsive and loses hope. Physically, he grows stiff and distant. Deep down, he feels as though he has no right to exist. Further on, there can be a sense of despair and detachment, where the child is prone to temper tantrums and violent, destructive behaviour. We can call it a 'mental disorder', but it is complex trauma. Trauma is a person's untold story.

'I believe that through his anti-social and dysfunctional behaviour, he was trying to communicate something about his pain. The "child" part of Brian was trying to say, "I'm hurting here", but no one heard him.'

Perhaps they *wouldn't* hear him?

'No. Brian himself made sure that no one could. Keith Richards called him a 'mimi'. Which is a strange description, as it refers to an elongated fairy-like being in Australian folklore that hides in rock crevices. Considered mischievous rather than malevolent, mimis would disappear into the wind whenever anyone got close. Which is exactly what Brian did.' [4]

*

Fulfilling lofty parental expectation by showing academic promise, Brian, known as 'Joner' by his classmates, passed his Eleven Plus exam, won a place at the somewhat pretentious grammar school where pupils still sported mortar boards, gained nine O levels and chose Physics, Chemistry and Biology to study to A level. He failed Biology, the easy one. He could have secured respectable employment with his science results, but already knew that he was not the steady-job type. His longing for an escape route from the tight-lipped misery of his childhood delivered him to the local music scene.

'(We) were keen music buffs and record collectors,' affirms Roger Gore, Brian's close friend at Cheltenham Grammar. 'We often visited a record shop off the High Street in the lunch hour to talk music, sample records and purchase LPs ... Brian liked trad jazz at this stage ... I specialised in collecting authentic blues records of such (American) artists as (blues and gospel singer and guitarist) Blind Lemon Jefferson, (boogie woogie pianist and singer) Cripple Clarence Lofton, (blues singer and harp player) James 'Boodle It' Wiggins, (hill country blues guitarist) Mississippi Fred McDowell, etc. – the more primitive and authentic the better. Brian once said to me jocularly, but also somewhat disparagingly, that my penchant was for "cigar-box guitars" as if I was a little naïve in my taste; and that of course is a source of great amusement to me, as he later became such an exponent of the slide guitar himself, emulating such (artists) as Fred McDowell or Elmore James.

'Brian became more and more blues orientated over time, and I remember us discussing the demise of Big Bill Broonzy, whose music we both liked, and the gloom we shared at his increasing poor prognosis and eventual death in 1958.'

When Brian, Roger and their friend Barry Smith were supposed to be doing cross-country runs, they would skive off and adjourn to Barry's house to listen to records, rejoining the race towards the finish line. 'Luckily,' recalls Roger, 'we were never caught out. I remember Brian being off school on the odd occasion with pleurisy caused by his asthma, but it was no big deal. He certainly wasn't disabled by it, and it didn't stop him playing clarinet, which was the main instrument he played when I knew him.'

Brian was so accomplished that he rose to first clarinet in the school orchestra. A rebel with too many causes, he grew skilled on his own saxophone. He got his first guitar for his seventeenth birthday, the year when he first became a dad. The misdemeanour shamed and angered his upstanding parents, stained his already compromised reputation and wrecked his chances of getting into Cheltenham Art College. He had applied hoping for a scholarship, perhaps to study Architecture. But he had blotted his copybook with teenage pregnancies. With oral contraceptives still a way off (June 1960) and no sign of the Abortion Act (not passed until 1967), his girlfriends had no choice but to go through with the births. Word got around, especially in a town like Cheltenham. The art college didn't want his type. Not that Brian's heart was in it in the first place. Nor was it in Applied Optics, another course that he was urged to consider, at Northampton Institute, Clerkenwell – soon to become part of City, University of London – with a view (actually, his father's) to becoming an optician.

This baby-faced blues purist with raging hormones and a covert disdain for and mistrust of females, perhaps linked to Louisa Jones's deficient mothering and to the loss of Pamela, had no intention of settling down. He took up his guitar, hit the road and crossed the Channel for a while, when his parents had arranged for their little blighter to lay low in Germany. He restyled himself 'Elmo Lewis', in honour of his idol Elmore James, the king of the slide guitar. How differently might he have done things, had he known at this point that he had only ten years left to live?

*

Time has withered the memory and diluted the significance of Brian so comprehensively that few millennial and Gen Z music lovers know he existed. Don't believe me? Ask around. My own kids, all three, had never heard of him. Older fans, particularly die-hard Stoners, protest that Brian deserves more recognition and respect, given that he founded the band, selected the team and dictated the music they started out playing. Bill Wyman is on that page. 'I do say,' he says, 'and do honestly believe that if there wasn't a Brian Jones there wouldn't have been a Rolling Stones. He named the band, and he enlisted the members one by one.' Many support the bassist's view. But in 2006, Bonhams the auctioneers offered a Lot, numbered 1451, that suggested otherwise. The neat nine-page letter, penned by Brian on 4 May 1963 to a young fan by the name of Doreen Pettifer, was presented at a guide price of £15,000–£22,000 and was later sold for an undisclosed sum. It explains the band's origins and sets out their ambitions. 'Personnel' are described as follows:

Keith Richards – Guitar. 19 years old. Went to Art school, then straight into Rhythm'nBlues.

Mick Jagger – Vocal, Harmonica. 19 years old. London School of Economics.

Charlie Watts – 21, worked in advertising for some years, now full-time musician. (Drummer)

Ian Stewart – Piano, 23, works with I.C.I. as a shipping clerk or something equally horrible. Only member of the band married – only one who'll ever be married. Proud father of a baby son (or daughter).

Myself, Brian Jones – Guitar and Harmonica, 21, was studying Architecture – more artistic satisfaction from R&B. (Mick, Keith and myself as I expect you noticed, wear our hair long, the others being more conventional.)

Elsewhere in the correspondence, Brian states, under the heading 'Formation & History', that 'the band is really an amalgamation of two bands. The one being an R&B band I formed about a year ago, and the other being a group run by Mick and Keith in S.E. London.' He was introduced to Keith, he explains, 'and we decided to pool our resources, so with Stu from my band and Mick from Keith's, we became the nucleus of the 'Stones'.

'What was comic about Brian was his illusions of grandeur, even before he got famous,' said Keith Richards in 2010.[5] 'He thought it was his band for some weird reason.'

Did he? There it is, from the horse's mouth, in his letter to Doreen Pettifer from Bagshot, Surrey. Brian acknowledging himself as a co-founder, and not as the sole founding father. Somewhere along the line, however, some wires got crossed. In a letter that Brian wrote to Mick and Keith dated 1 June 1962 – six weeks ahead of the band's first official gig, and almost a year before Brian wrote to Doreen, who had seen the Stones at the Ricky Tick Club in Windsor, and who became the first secretary of their fan club – he sets out what he describes as a 'sort of manifesto', with the thinly veiled insult 'Mick will explain that to you, Keith'. So …

Mick and Keith will be joining *his* (Brian's) 'beat combo'; that they will be known as 'Rollin' Stones' (no definite article and no 'g' … Howlin' Wolf hadn't considered himself in need of one, so neither should they); that the music they played would be nothing but 'authentic down-home rhythm and blues', because Brian was determined to 'spread the word of the blues to the world in the most legitimate way possible'; it needed, he insisted, to be 'pure'. Finally, he decreed, they would limit themselves to drums, guitar, keys and 'harp' (harmonica). As he pointed out, it worked for Muddy Waters, so it should work for them. No fancy additions, 'just for the sake of it. No choirs, no cowbells, no strings.' All of which would find their way into the Rolling Stones sound eventually. Examples? I give you the London Bach Choir's choral intro to 'You Can't Always Get What You Want'; the cowbell lead-in to 'Honky Tonk Women', tinked by producer Jimmy Miller; and the fiddle solo on 'Factory Girl', contributed by Ric Grech of Family.

A third letter leaves us in no doubt that Brian felt threatened, and that he was anxious to assert his authority. Writing to *Jazz* magazine on 2 July 1962, ten days ahead of that crucial first gig, he refers to a phone call made by Mick about the group to the publication … as if to say, 'That's *my* band you're talking about there, chaps.' He also alerts them to the forthcoming gig – sharing the bill with Long John Baldry's band – and explains the line-up, as follows:

Brian Jones – guitar, leader

Keith Richards – guitar

Dick Taylor – bass guitar

Ian Stewart – piano

Earl Phillips (yet another contender) – drums

with Mick Jagger – vocals

*

Not that Brian could be obliterated from the band's legacy, even if they wanted him to be. Without re-recording their early music with substitutes for Brian and Charlie, it would be impossible to eradicate him. He is easy to find, just reach for the records. They prove beyond doubt what an inventive, versatile and vital musician he was. He could breathe life into any song via any instrument.

'Brian would be able to walk into a studio and no matter what instrument was lying around, even though he'd never played it before, he would … be able to knock something out of it very, very quickly, y'know?' said Keith Richards. 'Hence, we used to have vibraphones (a percussion instrument similar to a xylophone) and stuff – mainly just because they were lying around the studio – and everybody thought, "what a wonderful bit of orchestration", but it was sheer accident and Brian's ability to be able to get something out of an instrument.'

So Jones was the Stones' secret weapon. Hear him on 'I Wanna Be Your Man', the first British hit to feature a slide. Brian infuses the track with echoes of Elmore James, played on his new 1963 Gretsch 6118 Anniversary guitar. It remained his favourite instrument until his death. That's his harmonica on 'I Just Wanna Make Love to You', Brian channelling Little Walter on the song Willie Dixon wrote for Muddy Waters. He's on slide guitar again on 'Little Red Rooster', using Keith's new Fender Telecaster. He also contributes the harmonica on that one. 'The Last Time', Mick and Keith's first original song, draws a line under Brian's disputed foundership and leadership, and sees the Dartford boys seizing the Stones as their own. Brian contributes the main riff, however, and may even have composed it. He's not done for yet, contributing syncopated marimba to 'Under My Thumb', sitar to 'Paint It, Black', dulcimer to 'Lady Jane' and recorder and some of the piano on 'Ruby Tuesday'.

*

'There were at least two sides to Brian's personality,' said Bill Wyman, who became his close friend. 'One Brian was introverted, shy, sensitive, deep-thinking. The other was a preening peacock, gregarious, artistic, desperately needing assurance from his peers.'

Snarling Keith was less sympathetic. He described Brian as a 'cold-hearted and vicious dwarf' who physically abused his girlfriends in his 2010 autobiography *Life*, thus spitting on Jones's memory. He more than made clear his loathing of the enigmatic blond whom others of his acquaintance described as 'down to earth and sweet'. We have no memoir from Brian's own pen to compare. But it seems unlikely that Brian would have lionised the rotter who took a sledgehammer to his most important relationship, his love affair with Anita Pallenberg. There can be no everlasting bliss between bitter-rival rockers when one pilfers a cherished girlfriend from the other. 'The idea of stealing a band member's woman was not on my agenda,' insisted Keith. Still, it happened. Good old Richards. Rock'n'roll.

All of that was to come during the green-grass days when Brian was watching, learning and playing around the flourishing clubs and jazz dives of Cheltenham; in and out of bands; forming his own, the Brian Jones Blues Band; honing his craft and working up the requisite sweat and drive. The town had its own equivalent of Liverpool's Casbah Coffee Club, where Mona Best, mother of soon-to-be-ditched drummer Pete, promoted the fledgling Beatles in her basement and became, effectively, the Fabs' first manager. For half a crown a year (two shillings and sixpence), some three hundred members were guaranteed entrance to the hallowed space where John Lennon's Quarry Men played on the opening night.

Cheltenham's variation on this theme was housed in a similar domestic basement at 38 Priory Street, run by sisters Ann and Jane Filby with the blessing and backing of their mum, whose house it was. Unlike the Casbah, it did not open to the public and never charged an entrance fee. Despite which, some of the leading musicians of the day – Lonnie Donegan, and also Chris Barber, the experimental electric bluesman and champion of Chicago blues who brought the likes of Muddy Waters and Sister Rosetta

Tharpe to the UK – would stop by and play there when they came to Cheltenham to perform at the Town Hall. Brian had been part of this set from the age of fifteen. He dipped a toe in the new rock'n'roll, the music of fifties teenagers. But his real obsession and one true love was electric blues. Listening to records and working out how to turn his acoustic guitar electric with makeshift bits and bobs, and to get it to slide, he effectively became Britain's first electric slide player.

A chance (is there such a thing?) meeting with exotic jazz and blues musician Alexis Korner proved to be the catalyst for Brian leaving for London. The 'father of British blues' would be taking the stage during a performance by Chris Barber's band at Cheltenham Town Hall on 10 October 1961. Nineteen-year-old Brian and his friends bagged tickets. After the show, Brian wormed his way backstage, made a beeline for Barber and introduced himself to Korner – part hairy Greek mystic, part Austrian kook, part lovable Jewish oddball – and insisting on taking them out to the Patio, one of the boys' favourite local haunts. Lemon squeezy. Thus did Brian inveigle his way into the lives of his two primary enablers. It was through Barber that Brian would meet Harold Pendleton, proprietor of the Marquee Jazz Club.

In Korner he found at last the devoted, encouraging father figure he had always lacked. It was a meeting of minds and spirits that would lure Brian to the smoke for regular meetings, and eventually to stay. Korner was launching his own electric blues band. No one cared about the blues. It was too niche, it wasn't commercial enough, it wouldn't turn on the kids. But these were exactly the reasons why these guys loved it. There prevails to this day a perverse elitism which decrees that the moment a sub-genre of music becomes mainstream, its original enthusiasts drop it and move on to something else as yet obscure. Brian was going to be part of it, come what may. He took up his blues harmonica, aligned himself with like-minded evangelists, and never looked back.

Notting Hill-based Korner opened his own venue in a grotty space opposite Ealing Underground station, the Ealing Jazz Club. It would gain an everlasting reputation as 'London's first dedicated R&B club'. The state of the place hasn't improved much since spring 1962. Think Liverpool's Cavern Club: same vibe, same danger, same legend.

Perspiration, condensation and desperation running down the walls. No more than a stinking drain of a dive, but with promise. Alexis Korner's Blues Incorporated seemed oblivious of its shortcomings. To Brian, aka Elmo Lewis, the special-guest guitarist on the poor excuse for a stage alongside another future legend, P.P. Pond (some claim that he was P.P. Jones at this point), it was Madison Square Garden.[6]

Nineteen-year-old Michael Jagger, a gauche, fat-lipped, front-room-band boy from Dartford on the verge of Mick, thought so too. There he stood in the sardine audience, hopping up and down, clutching a tape by his group the Blue Boys. What did he have to do to get a gig around here?

Chapter Three

MICK'N'KEEF

A hundred and forty miles south-east-ish of Cheltenham and eighteen miles east of central London, in the downbeat Thames estuary town of Dartford, two little boys from disparate families met at Wentworth County Primary School. Unbeknown to both, they had been born in the same local nursing home. The Livingstone Hospital is still there today, an NHS facility. There is nothing to mark its significance as the birthplace of fêted sons. Little did Eva Jagger and Doris Richards know that their babies, born nineteen weeks apart, were destined to spend their whole lives together; nor that, joined at the hip, lip and bank account, their Christian names would one day be slurred in a single, potent phrase as globally recognised as that of Her Majesty.

Michael Philip Jagger hailed from a house on Denver Road in 'Posh Town', as the other-side-of-the-tracks kids called that neighbourhood, kept spotless by his Australian-born mother. Having landed in England as a teenager, Eva assimilated rapidly. She also became an 'Avon lady', selling make-up, bath products, skincare and perfumes door to door.[1] His father Basil, known as 'Joe', was a respected PE teacher and physical education lecturer. Michael had a little brother, Christopher, four years his junior. These pretty, fine-skinned mummy's boys minded their Ps and Qs, said grace before tea, ate up their carrots and greens and liked to sing along to the radio. The brothers were put through their paces in the back garden, lifting weights, aiming arrows and bowling cricket balls under Joe's watchful eye. One parent fattening, the other fittening them. The result, in Michael, would be a lifelong obsession with leanness; an abhorrence of body fat; a preoccupation with stamina and appearance; and, thanks to his mother's cosmetics case, which he would plunder during his late teens when Eva was out and about and he was wooing potential girlfriends, a fascination with make-up and beauty. It was to Michael's blubber-lipped, beau-laid face that Mater's foundation cream, lipstick and mascara samples would be applied by female friends. He wanted them to show him how to do it. He also wanted (secretly?) to look like them. Their temporary refinement of Jagger's arresting ugly beauty rendered him an object of fascination among local fifth- and sixth-form girls, even if they found him too weird to be conventionally fanciable.

A couple of streets away, in a council flat above a greengrocer's on Chastilian Road lived a scrawny, cartoonishly jug-eared, nail-bitten classmate by the name of Keith Richards. That place is still there too, blue-plaqued. People still come out to look when you rock up to take photographs. The son of factory workers from Walthamstow who shifted east along the river to be near family, but unwittingly closer to the devastation of Hitler's bombs, little Richards could not have differed more dramatically from the Jagger kid. His high-spirited, music-loving mother, who had driven a van without a licence during the war, delivering bread and cakes, was delighted with her only child. Keith's father Bert, a stocky, pipe-smoking, one-or-two-beers-at-the-most man whose family were 'stern, rigid socialists', served as a dispatch rider in Normandy and was the sole survivor of a mortar attack, an experience that scarred him for life.

Bert returned to factory work post-war, travelling west to toil long hours. He was detached from his boy's upbringing, but spent time with him at weekends. They'd work the allotment together, or play a bit of football. Rationing was in place for years after the war ended. Keith would remember not being able to buy a bag of sweets until 1954. He recalls the looming, local lunatic asylums, where many unfortunates were housed, and where teenage Mike Jagger took part-time employment one summer, serving meals. Another of Mike's summer jobs was selling ice creams. Keith packed sugar for pocket money, acquiring a penchant for crystalline substances, and did a bread round. He liked swimming, a bit of cricket and playing tennis. He'd sooner not look back on the almost daily beatings and bullyings from the big boys that he endured on his way home from school. Though his father boxed, and urged him to stick up for himself, Keith took the pummellings without retaliation. It is interesting that both boys had such physical fathers, though both were kind and neither was given to corporal abuse. Joe Jagger, the gentlemanly sportsman with a working command of most disciplines, taking pride in corporeal excellence and instilling his values in his sons; brawny Bert Richards, rough and ready, 'a real athlete', 'an Irish boxer', a most unlikely tennis player; a man who grew food and took pride in potatoes and beans.

Mike and Keith knew each other because they were the same age and knocked around the same drab neighbourhood, rather than because they attended the same school, where they hardly overlapped. But then both families moved away: Mike's to the leafy village of Wilmington, all cricket teas, bright bunting and parish fairs; Keith's to a blank new-build council house at Temple Hill: a grey, edgy estate conjured from wasteland that became a hostile manor of hoods and goods off the back of lorries. Thus distanced, the boys grew in opposite directions. Mike was on course for grammar school. Keith couldn't be arsed with academia, felt detached and dispossessed, and sometimes fantasised about reinventing himself as a villain.

Mike had a brother, a home-grown ally, so Jagger family life had balance. Lonely Keith longed for siblings, forged brief, intense friendships with other kids during Devon family holidays, and would 'always be heartbroken when it was over, gone'. Mike's family ventured to more exotic climes, and favoured the suddenly fashionable Spanish Costas. By the age of ten he was toying with guitars. Keith had the edge on him there. He'd been around guitars all his life, thanks to his maternal grandparents. French-speaking, ladylike Emma and philandering Theodore Augustus Dupree had seven daughters, and were both eccentric and musical. His grandmother was an accomplished pianist. His pastry-cook grandfather played sax and violin. It was claimed that he was part of a musical double act during the First World War, entertaining the troops, and that injury impaired his ability to play. He later took up guitar, led a dance band during the 1930s and turned to factory work to pay the bills. By the 1950s he had his own square dance band, Gus Dupree and His Boys, performing on American air bases, at weddings and for the Freemasons. He kept a classical Spanish guitar on top of his upright piano; he'd get it out and put it up there, at least, when he knew that his grandson was coming round. When Keith was nine or ten and harmonising with his aunties, Gus reached for the guitar one day and offered him a strum. A chord and a lick later, Keith got the picture.

Mike Jagger lost his way at Dartford Grammar, working hard enough only to pass tests and exams. He saw through education early on. He soon grew bored with the inflexibility of the system, the redness of the uniform, the punitive stance of the place. His rejection of learning was a waste of his obvious intelligence and talent, but he couldn't care. The young rebel resisted the Establishment's public-school-like posturing and snobbery. He even lost interest in cricket, at which he had once considered himself to excel.[2] He grew disdainful of authority in general, and let slip his once respectable appearance, becoming stylishly slovenly in a manner reminiscent of the schoolboy John Lennon.

In 1955, the year when Mick and Keith turned twelve; when Britain experienced a treacherous freeze, an unbearable heatwave and crippling drought; when eighty-year-old Prime Minister Sir Winston Churchill resigned, and when Ruth Ellis became the last British woman to be hanged; when the *Guinness World Records* book was first published, the inventor of the world wide web Tim Berners-Lee was born and when Alexander Fleming, who discovered penicillin, breathed his last, the country found itself in the grip of the new rock'n'roll. Handed down from America where it had been conceived, it broke the banks of traditional music categories, shattered moulds and cracked open opportunities for musicians, singers and songwriters. Where adolescents had previously been little more than scaled-down versions of their parents, terrorised into toeing the line under the 'not under my roof' rule, there now surged a mutinous new demographic known as 'teenagers'. With their own culture, wild music, fashion and views, many of them clashed relentlessly with parents in their dictatorial domestic set-ups. Rock'n'roll's original golden age, soundtracked by Bo Diddley and Chuck Berry, Fats Domino, Little Richard and 'the King', Elvis Presley, seemed to many to have exploded the world. In 1958, when Mike and Keith were turning fifteen, Britain's answer to Elvis, Cliff Richard, was enjoying his first hit with 'Move It', and London's Marquee Jazz Club opened at 165 Oxford Street. Only four years later, on 12 July 1962, the Rollin' Stones would be performing their first gig there ... by which time the Beatles had hammered themselves into sensational shape on Hamburg's shit-stained, strip-club-and-brothel-infested Reeperbahn, and were coasting towards their first hit, 'Love Me Do'.[3]

What cataclysmic changes occurred in that brief interlude that led these ordinary, beloved, functioning boys from the relative safety of suburbia with their wistful dreams of the distant USA into the underworld dives and dankest dregs of London: a twilight realm of dodgy promoters, producers, managers, wheelers and drug-dealers, small-time crooks, cookers of books and floozies on the game? Perhaps the skiffle craze had a bit to do with it. Lonnie Donegan's cover of American folk song 'Rock Island Line' was the kick-off.[4] After watching him perform it on television, thousands of kids from St. Just-in-Penwith to Dunnet Head were electric-shocked into forming their own skiffle groups and having a go themselves. The traditional skiffle instruments – tea chest and broom handle bass, banjo and washboard – were mostly fashioned from bits and pieces around the home. John Lennon and fellow Quarry Bank boys were among them. Mike Jagger was not.

While the craze did hit Dartford Grammar School, and while some of his friends did get guitars and start jamming together annoyingly at break and after lunch, Mike kept his distance. Which was not for want of an instrument. He already had one. He didn't go a bundle on Elvis, and had been left cold by the Comets and their avuncular leader Bill Haley. Mike's first rock'n'roll obsession, if that's not too strong a word for such a laid-back boy, was 'the architect of rock'n'roll', Little Richard.[5] Which is interesting. This was rock'n'roll's first black purveyor, a hysterical hollerer and unhinged performer who whipped up a storm with his deranged act, overt sexuality and devil-may-care stance. There was both a bold masculinity and mincing femininity about Richard, which at first went over the heads of many onlookers. To be gay in the forties and early fifties, let alone to be black and gay, was to risk public lynching or a prison sentence. Richard, thumbing his nose, would take to the stage in drag, from the safety net of his alias, 'Princess LaVonne'. He fell into rhythm and blues in Atlanta, adopted the camp pompadour hairdo of jump blues singer Billy Wright, painted his face, got himself up in flashy gear and fashioned an ostentatious and highly provocative act. His were among the earliest shows at which black and white audiences would integrate, to dance with each other. Great swathes of America were alarmed by this fearsome racial mingling, holding rock'n'roll, the Devil's music, to blame.

Richard cocked his leg atop his piano, spilled his jewels into the audience and became more defiantly pansyish by the week, so that the white guys could tell for certain he wasn't after their chicks. Knickers were thrown. Urine was leaked. Collective loss of control went viral, all across the sexes. Richard played to both camps. He married, but batted and bowled. He came out, and went back in. He was openly homosexual again, then declared himself bisexual. He later experienced a Christian calling, denouncing sexualities other than straight as sinful. What was he on? His wife and a string of lovers protested his couldn't-be-more-masculine virility. Quelle hoot. The boy Jagger saw, read and listened. He was getting ideas.

Buddy Holly ('That'll Be the Day', 'Peggy Sue', 'True Love Ways') was Mike's other first musical love. Accompanied by his school mate Dick Taylor, Jagger saw him perform live during Holly's only UK tour, at the Woolwich Granada Cinema. He was entranced by the young American's gauche demeanour, by his hiccuppy vocals and sweet falsetto. Divine coincidence, then (is there such a thing?), that the Stones would have their first Top 10 single with a cover of Holly's Bo-Diddley-beat 'Not Fade Away', which saw its UK release on 21 February 1964.[6]

It was the secret musical tastes of Dick Taylor that awakened him. Mike Jagger's first visit to the humble Bexleyheath home of his school friend was a descent into Aladdin's cave. Plumber's son Dick had an unexpected record collection that almost caused his eyes to fall out. Forget Buddy and Little Richard, this was proper music: the gurglings, stirrings, whinings and twangings that comprised the sounds of Chicago and of the mythical Deep South. Here were Howlin' Wolf, Jimmy Reed, Muddy Waters and the rest. Mike was both thrilled and troubled by them. They got under his skin. They dragged him back, demanding his ears. Where could he get records like this? Nowhere local, that was for sure. Hunting them down required both effort and excursion. Mike and Dick took to jumping on trains to London on Saturdays, to scour the Soho record shops for imports. They spied Chuck Berry in a documentary.[7] Scales fell. The schoolboys were sold.

Thus enlightened, only now was Mike stirred to have a go himself, with a handful of classmates. Most of whom failed to hear things his way. Contrasting influences aforementioned drew a strange curdle from the raw Jagger throat. It did weird things to his already peculiar face, in particular his mouth, by which the lads in those here-today, gone-tomorrow schoolboy groups were put off. Embarrassed and unsettled by his cringey crooning, they gave him the 'Don't call us, we'll call you' brush-off. Was he bothered? Nah. He was already immune to criticism, even at sixteen. He had discovered and was harnessing his superpower, an astonishing out-of-nowhere gift for mimicry. His first group, Little Boy Blue and the Blue Boys, played no venue beyond Dick Taylor's front room, to no greater audience than a single gobsmacked fan, Dick Taylor's mother.

*

Where was Keith, at this point? Still out in the wasteland. Making his way to and from Dartford Tech, the runner-up school for boys who had failed the Eleven Plus but weren't quite hopeless enough for the Secondary Modern. Not bothered about most subjects. Turned on by English. Allergic to both homework and discipline. Playing truant when he could get away with it. Learning how to fight back. Getting the boot in. Getting minded, minding one or two himself, and getting his head round the hard life. Would you Adam'n'Eve it, Doris's littl'un in 'is short trarsers, havin' a good ol' ding-dong in front of 'Er Madge in Westminster Abbey. Come again? Keith Richards, rock's quintessential anarchistic reprobate, was once a wet-behind-the-ears chorister for the Queen? You heard.

'That's where I learned a lot about singing and music and working with musicians,' he asserts. 'I learned how to put a band together – it's basically the same job – and how to keep it together.' Then the voice breaks, farewell choir, end of cosy coach trips in and out of London on the way to competitions. Resit all the lessons from the year you mostly missed. Go down a year, even. What the fuck? Life's not fair. Take it on the chin or get bitter and take it out on other people, it's up to you. What did you expect? Richards has better reasons than Jagger to lose faith and kick back at authority. He becomes more than merely a rebel. Keith's an outlaw, now, a pirate. He dresses like one. He courts the reputation of the outcast. It starts small and builds. Like future bandmate Brian Jones, he takes cross-country in double P.E., but never runs it. He even wins prizes for it. He hunkers down elsewhere, taking the piss, having a fag and a laarf. He goes the distance to get himself expelled. In the end, he succeeds. If not for the art teacher who takes pity on him and paves his way into art school, he might have made Borstal.[8]

Keith's salvation, whaddya know, is music. Most of it emanates from the radio, songs that lighten his cheating mother's heart. He doesn't yet know that Ma Doris is carrying on with a toyboy taxi driver half her age behind husband Bert's back. Keith won't put two and two together for a few more years. When eventually he does, his childhood is rewritten. It'll all come out, and Doris will leave Bert once Keith leaves home. She'll even marry her toyboy, far down the line. He will oddly change his surname to her married name of Richards, not she hers to his. Life will have kicked off by then. Keith will be somewhat preoccupied, being a Stone, getting wasted, getting busted for drugs and guns. He will think, from time to time, about going in search of his long-lost father. But he is fearful. The only man whose approval he ever craved will surely be ashamed of him for all the law-breaking. He puts it off and off, leaving the longing on the top shelf of his mind. He won't see his father again for twenty years. When eventually Keith plucks up courage to track him down, through relatives, to pathetic digs in a Bexley public house, father and son are reunited. Does Keith see all this before it happens, as kids do sometimes? Does the ghost of his fall-out future steal in to torment? If it does, Keith's taking no notice. He is in denial. There are worse places.

Music is his compensation. He can't tell the difference between a black voice and a white one, but is lulled by the larynxes of Louis and Ella, of

Sarah Vaughan, Fats Domino and Big Bill Broonzy. Don't forget Grandad Gus's input, de lure of de jazz. The Django Reinhardts, the Stéphane Grappellis. There's even classical. The orchestras! The horns! The strings! Whatever it sounds like, it is Keith's first drug. He gets in and out of the Boy Scouts, emerging with a love of being in a boy band, another substitute for the lack of blood brothers. He also leaves with survival skills, deeply human instincts, an affinity with the natural world, and a knife. Thenceforth, for the rest of his life, he will rarely be without one. His love of weaponry will eventually prove fatal, though not to him. He gets his first guitar from his mother, a seven-quid job, at the age of fifteen. At around the same time that Jagger finds his voice.

*

The Dartford railway station Jagger-meets-Richards story is so old, so often told, its tread is more worn than the steps of St Paul's Cathedral. Along lopes Jagger, stripey-scarfed new student at the London School of Economics (motto: *Rerum cognoscere causus*[9]) and somewhat full of his old self. Dartford folk can smell cockiness a mile off. Who's this one going to be, then, Prime Minister? Better smarten hisself up a bit. He wears it well, his new-found confidence, and carries a clutch of records under one arm that might confuse the casual observer. Little Walter. *The Best of Muddy Waters*. Chuck Berry's *Rockin' at the Hops*. Not the kind of LP you see for sale down Woolworth's or reviewed in the rags. Who's this likely lad lolloping along the platform? Mind how you go, son, look at him, does he know which way is up? The boys do a double-take. Wait, isn't that wossname? Don't I know him from somewhere?

They board the same London-bound train, and get talking. Mick is heading for Charing Cross station and the LSE campus in Clare Market, Holborn, down the Strand and up Kingsway. Hapless Keith's on his way to his deadbeat, backstreet art school in Sidcup, where he has fallen in with a bunch of blues lovers including Dick Taylor, Mike Jagger's record-collector mate from the Grammar. The pale, drainpipe-legged one studies the cool-dude one. Something about him? Yeah, know what you mean. Didn't that kid sell the other kid an ice cream one summer? All the yob wants to know is where the cocky bloke buys his records. What do you mean, you send off to America for them? Where *to*? So distracted and kerfuffled is Keith that he almost forgets to get off. Yeah, it's me. You're singing a bit? I'm playing a bit. You know Dick Taylor? What you doing Saturday? It's 'Mick', now, is it? Gotcha.

But what's puzzling you is the nature of my game.

Chapter Four

DRUM'N'BASS

It wasn't a JFK moment. You'd be forgiven for thinking otherwise. Where was I when I heard? Taking a power-walk across Blackheath towards Greenwich Park, a daily constitutional. How did I hear? My son texted me. 24 August 2021, 17:49.

'Charlie Watts has died?!'

'WHAT? Where did you hear that?'

'Instagram. You heard it here first, Mumma. Piers Morgan posted it about seven minutes ago.'

'Shit.'

Everywhere you looked. The all-pervasive coverage of Charlie's demise was more fitting of a pontiff or a head of state than a rock star. Anyone with an inkling of Watts's significance in the pantheon was seized upon to expound, in the press, over the internet, on radio and on television. It was relentless. I did five radio broadcasts about Charlie in one morning the day after his death was announced, including BBC Radio 5 Live, BBC Scotland, and Robert Elms's show on BBC Radio London. And that was just me. We were all at it. There were obituaries in every newspaper. Retrospectives and think pieces graced the most serious of journals. Documentaries and tributes were broadcast back-to-back. His passing was universally acknowledged as the greatest loss to the music industry since the assassination of John Lennon, forty-one years ago. I couldn't help but think that Charlie would have been amazed.

What must Jagger's lips and tongue have made of all this? As I pondered Mick's possibly nose-out-of-joint reaction to 'his drummer's' coverage[1] – greater in death than it had ever been during his lifetime, on account of the fact that Charlie hated interviews; and of potentially finer, more affectionate quality than Mick himself might receive, come his own end – Diana, Princess of Wales sprang to mind. Her royal funeral procession on 6 September 1997 had been rehearsed on a regular basis for twenty-two years. Known as 'Operation Tay Bridge', it was activated in response to the necessity for an unexpected royal despatch. It had not actually been for Diana, but for HRH the Queen Mother. Who was said to have retorted, after the ceremony concluded, 'She's just had my funeral.' QM's own departure and broadcast thereof, when it came five years later, was modest. As the call, so the echo.

Why did Charlie matter? Because he was the backbone, the metronome of the Rolling Stones. What made him such a great drummer? He wasn't the best drummer in the world, but he was the best drummer for the Stones. He played with swing and swagger, crisply and cleanly. He was mild, but took no crap, and was a law unto himself. He never performed drum solos because he couldn't stand them. He didn't go in for flash-git-ness, he let the others do all that. He refrained from pontificating in the few interviews he granted, and never tried to blind his interrogators with batter heads and X-hats. Charlie was the dignified Stone, the antithesis of a rock star, and a joyous contradiction. It's why we loved him. He never made a song and dance about it. He just sat there, doing his job, 'watching Mick's bum'. Drummers often refer to their rear-centre upstage position as 'the best seat in the house'. Charlie was no exception.

What else did he have? The thing that all great drummers tell you great drummers have to have: he had *feel*. What is *feel*? It's challenging to understand if you're not a drummer. A drummer with feel doesn't just play the song. He wears the song. He breathes it. It gets under his skin and into his heart. It plays *him*. He goes at his kit with his whole being, with his gut and his grit and his nerves. He plays with his *face*, not just his hands. It was all there, in Charlie's expressions: the jaw clenched, the cheeks sucked, the lips rolled inwards and fixed in a thin horizontal line. What's that thing of him playing a tad too slowly, behind the beat a bit?

It's complicated. Always is. But yeah, it's a thing that Charlie did. He played behind the backbeat.[2] How so? Charlie's bass drum tended to be a little ahead of the beat, actually, with his snare drum backbeats behind. There was drag in the feel and volume in the whole. He had technique, a groove, innate ability. It had to do with the way he heard a song, how he processed it, and how he converted its energy into rhythm. He made it look effortless. That was Charlie.

DJ Andy Kershaw pays social media tribute, addressing our man directly. 'I'll never forget, when I worked on the Rolling Stones' Roundhay Park concert, in Leeds, in 1982, how you brought the whole preposterous caper back down to earth,' he says.

'Amid all the ridiculous extravagance and corporate self-importance, there was, on the morning of the gig, set up on a stage the size of an aircraft carrier, a tiny little drum kit of a bass drum, a snare, a tom-tom, a hi-hat and a couple of other cymbals. Not for Charlie Watts the willie-waving rock drummer's conventional gear of the time: double bass drums, and a forest of cymbals. It was the drum kit of a 1940s dance band drummer. For that's what, at heart, Charlie was.

'When I once talked to Keith Richards we agreed on many things. But uppermost was that all bands know how to rock, but few know how to roll. Charlie Watts had that roll. Thanks Charlie. And so long, brother.'

Brian Bennett calls me. The legendary Shadows drummer is upset. 'I loved Charlie, though I never really spent any time with him,' he reflects.

'You loved a man you never really got to know?'

'That was Charlie.'

'What was his secret?'

'I loved the Stones mainly because of Charlie,' says Brian. 'He is the epitome of cool. He looks as if he's doing nothing, but he is doing everything. Working for the song. A pure minimalist. His drums are all rare, retro Gretsch kits. Very cool. Manny's in New York had the best collection of drums old and new. It's closed now, but Charlie would have gone there. It was his kind of place.[3] I think his secret is that he seems to do nothing but in fact he does everything. He is Mick's solid ground.'

'What about Keith?'

'Ah, well … he was the one who said that the Stones didn't even exist until they played their first gig with Charlie. He also said, "Charlie Watts is the musical bed that I lay myself down on."'

'Exactly.'

*

We had an inkling that things were not right when Charlie pulled out, at the beginning of August 2021, of the band's resuming thirteen-plus-date No Filter US tour. 'For once, my timing has been a little off,' deadpanned the octogenarian thumper as he confirmed his withdrawal for rest and recuperation. A statement bare-boned that he had just emerged from a 'successful procedure' at a London clinic, following a routine pre-tour medical that had flagged up an issue. This would be the first Stones tour Charlie had missed since 1963. 'No one saw this coming,' they said, and we wondered. His stand-in would be an acclaimed session drummer, Stones collaborator and friend of many years, sixty-four-year-old New Yorker Steve Jordan.

'It is an absolute honour and a privilege to be Charlie's understudy and I am looking forward to rehearsing with Mick, Keith and Ronnie,' enthused Steve. 'No one will be happier than me to give up my seat on the drum-riser as soon as Charlie tells me he is good to go.'

Charlie himself had chosen Steve, so no arguments. The *Sun* reported that Watts would rejoin his bandmates for their sixtieth anniversary bonanza across Europe in July 2022, when they planned to release their first album of all-original material for seventeen years. It was not to be. Within three weeks, Charlie had left the Stones forever. No cause of death was officially given. Speculation was relentless that the throat cancer for which he had been treated in June 2004 had returned. The once excessive smoker who had quit his lifelong habit had found a lump on the left-hand side of his neck. A biopsy was performed at London's Royal Marsden cancer hospital.

'It was benign, but [the doctor] said we should take it out,' Charlie told *Ultimate Classic Rock* in 2011. 'On the slide, it had tiny cancer cells on it. He said, "You have cancer of the whatever." And that night, I thought I was going to die. I thought that's what you did. You get cancer and waste away and die.'

There was a follow-up operation to remove the lymph nodes.

'The muscles go,' Watts explained to *Rolling Stone*. 'Then you sit around for eight weeks in treatment. You can't lift your arm. It's like being minor-ly paralysed. It was a worry, because of what I do for a living. We've got a tour, and I don't know if I could get through a song. You can't stop once you get going, if you're a drummer ... I didn't know if I could make it ... but it's amazing how quickly your body heals.'

His funeral was a private, family affair, no details or images leaked. The media had no part to play in this one. We expected his bereaved bandmates to ditch the tour. But the show must go on, and it did. Bad call? Many thought so, lambasting the remaining Stones for their 'heartlessness' and 'lack of respect'. Damned if you do ... Again, I thought about Mick, who had relinquished heavy drinking and drug-taking years earlier. He had also reinvented himself as an extreme fitness fanatic, and had only recently survived heart valve replacement surgery. I thought of Keith, who had overcome levels of alcohol and drug addiction that might have killed the rest of us, and who had fractured his skull in 2006 after falling from the low-hanging branch of a tree on an island off Fiji. Suffering acute subdural haematoma, he was flown to New Zealand for surgery, and survived, because he is Keith. I remembered that Ronnie, another lifelong smoker, had beaten cancer twice, if 'beating' that disease is what humans do. Their former bassist Bill Wyman popped into my head, as I recalled that the thirty-fags-a-day man who had started smoking at seventeen had held his own against prostate cancer. Old rockers richer than they could ever in a lifetime spend, but who can't buy time because not even they can; who are nose to pane with their own mortality; who couldn't give a sod what anyone thinks of them; and who have always knuckled down and got on with it against all odds: guys like these don't go cancelling the tour that might turn out to be their last. Not for any reason. As Keith has so often insisted, they'll rock 'til they croak.

So on they rolled, *qué será*, *será*. Missing Charlie so hard, it hurt, but whaddya gonna do about it? They did so with the blessing of one of the greatest drummers of his generation. It was what he would have wanted. That was Charlie.

*

He was in so many ways the most unlikely Stone. Mick called him 'the

Wembley Whammer', because that was where young Charlie lived. Born in London's University College Hospital to former factory girl Lillian and named after his lorry driver father, he spent his earliest years in a damp, cramped and basic West London prefab.[4] He had a sister, Linda, to whom he remained close throughout his life. His best mate from junior school, Dave Green, likewise. When Charlie was eleven, his close-knit family relocated to Kingsbury in Brent, north-west London, where he enrolled at Tylers Croft Secondary Modern School.[5] Academic lessons he could take or leave, but he was artistic, musical and sporty. He loved football and cricket; collected jazz records, in particular old 78s, of Charlie 'Bird' Parker, Duke Ellington, Thelonious Monk, Miles Davis and Jelly Roll Morton.

Inspired by American drummer Chico Hamilton, he took tentative steps on bits of improvised kit. He got a proper drum kit from his parents for his fourteenth Christmas. Ah, the never-look-back moment. Charlie taught himself to play by drumming along to his collection of jazz records. He left school at fifteen, found his way to Harrow Art School[6] and took a job as a graphic designer with the Charlie Daniels Studios advertising agency. All the while, he tinkered away with local bands in down-the-road clubs, pubs and coffee shops. It was a stint with jazz band Jo Jones All Stars that lured him into rhythm and blues.

All of which led Charlie to his maker, the enabler of all the original Stones. They met in 1961, when Alexis Korner asked Charlie to join his new band, Blues Incorporated. Becoming part of that line-up in February 1962, he still didn't give up his day job: by this time, as a designer with another ad agency, Charles Hobson and Grey Ltd. Within months, Charlie had met, on the R&B circuit, Brian Jones as Elmo Lewis, pianist Ian Stewart, and the Dartford boys, Jagger and Richards. In January 1963, he became a Rolling Stone. His first performance with the band as their drummer for life was at the Ealing Jazz Club on 2 February 1963.

But, if there is such a thing, Charlie was never 'just a drummer'. He was arguably the most enigmatic and most interesting Stone. He doubled up from the earliest days as a designer for the band's record sleeves. He would later co-curate and design their stand-out stage sets. He never renounced jazz for rock'n'roll, but invested in his first love, continuing to record and perform it throughout his other career, with Mick and the boys. We could go so far as to say that Charlie was never a rock star, not in the truest sense. He was a one-woman man for a start, keeping himself only unto the bride he took in 1964, sculptress Shirley, until the day he died. Immune to the sex-drugs-rock'n'roll lifestyle (apart from a blip, which we will come to), he ignored the come-ons from whores and groupies, spent his free time sketching every hotel room he ever slept in, and collected rare records, first-edition books and classic and vintage cars he couldn't drive because he never learned. His fleet included the lemon-yellow Citroën 2CV driven by Roger Moore as 007 in *For Your Eyes Only*, and a 1937 Lagonda Rapide Cabriolet, one of only twenty-five ever made. The Wattses would later breed Arabian horses and care for rescue greyhounds on their peaceful Devonshire farm. The rural life grew on him.

The most fascinating thing about Charlie, for me, was his image transformation: from dirt-poor prefab sprout to impeccable linen-, silk- and flannel-draped style icon and latter-day Great Gatsby, flaunting magnificence and presence via his clothes. Small, square-shouldered and five feet eight inches tall, Charlie was a Savile Row man, frequenting the ateliers of tailors the likes of Huntsman, Chittleborough & Morgan, Tommy Nutter and Henry Poole. He owned several hundred suits; as many pairs of shoes, most of them handmade at George Cleverley of London's Royal Arcade; and hundreds of bespoke shirts and handmade silk ties. His finely woven socks always echoed his shirt. He favoured old clothes over new. He collected, cherished and rarely disposed of them, confessing that he still wore garments he'd owned for thirty or forty years, and rarely settled for off-the-peg. When he did so, the item tended to come with a Prada or Ralph Lauren label. He even purchased, and stepped out in, suits once worn by an abdicated king, Edward VIII, which he acquired from an auction of the Duke of Windsor's effects at Sotheby's in Paris.

The image that Charlie projected was suggestive of a lifestyle that did not exist. Not for him, anyway. He looked sophisticated, highly educated, cultured and to the manner born,[7] but was none of those things. It was an act. He had only to open his mouth and spill a few glottal syllables to reveal so. The contradiction defined him. He never signed up for elocution lessons. The only thing Charlie had in common with those born to privilege was enormous wealth. For which one had to admire him. He already had, in Shirley, his Daisy Buchanan.[8] It was not as though he felt the need to project a desirable alter ego in order to win his perfect woman, the ultimate prize. The look was a guise rather than a disguise. There was no disappearing of the original. He wasn't kidding anybody, least of all Charlie. He dressed and projected the way he did to please nobody but himself.

What prompted his sartorial obsession? His lorry-driving father had his own tailor. You heard. 'A little Jewish guy in the East End of London,' said Charlie, as if it were the most normal thing in the world for a trucker to retain a bespoke outfitter. He 'stitched him things.' Little Charlie used to accompany his dad to the tiny Dickensian off-Brick Lane tailor's shop. In that setting from a bygone, 'proper' age, he would bed down among the fabric swatches, smoothing thick tweeds and glossy worsteds between fingers and thumb, inhaling their mustiness, their peaty fragrance, and imagining. The idea of having clothes made to measure enchanted him. He later fell for the style and substance of Hollywood icons, and of 1950s and '60s jazzmen, in particular Dexter Goodman.

'He made a record called *Our Man in Paris*, and he had one of these pins through his collar, which I now have hundreds of,' Charlie told *GQ* magazine. 'The lovely thing about all of them, though, was that their clothes were worn. They weren't just put on, to the office and back. They sat all night in the things. They played in those suits. How they played in those suits, I don't know.'

This all called to mind my encounters during the 1990s with another sartorial obsessive, the tempestuous footballing legend Stanley Bowles. His heyday was at Queens Park Rangers during the 1970s. He was later voted their all-time greatest player. The gambling addict and ladies' man routinely spent his last five hundred quid on a greyhound and yet another bespoke three-piece. 'It's as my old man used to say to me, "It's not a crime to be poor,"' he told me. 'But it's a crime to *look* poor. I never will.'

Charlie Watts performed in short-sleeved shirts and slacks or plain T-shirts and shorts, as I witnessed on numerous occasions. Never in trainers, always in shoes. Brown leather loafers, more often than not.

'But I still imagine that I'm playing in a club in New York,' he said. 'The Apollo, or somewhere in Chicago.' In other words, he was dressing the part in his head.

*

As for Bill Wyman. The so-called 'Quiet One' had never seemed that interesting. Not until I met him. Bassists are not as peculiar as they are sometimes painted. Those inclined to dismiss them as 'failed guitarists' forget Paul McCartney, Jack Bruce, John Paul Jones, John McVie, Flea of the Red Hot Chili Peppers, Suzi Quatro and the rest. Queen's John Deacon never had much to say. Frank Allen of the Searchers more than holds his own. The Who's John Entwistle was a livewire, I hung with him often. He and Wyman had for years been bosom pals.

Bill was the first member of the Stones I'd ever encountered face to face. He was out there, in a way that Mick, Keith and Charlie were not. His was a familiar face in London's places to be and on the celebrity circuit. You'd run into him at Tramp, Langan's Brasserie, the Caprice and in Joe Allen. He would soon open his own Kensington restaurant, Sticky Fingers, named for that Stones album, and serving the bland American fare that his own gut could stand. It was more of a mini-museum showcasing Stones and Wyman memorabilia than a restaurant. He was the accessible Stone, the one who accepted invitations to gallery openings, album launches, opening nights and after-shows. He liked to say he wasn't into all that. I wasn't aware of any doppelgänger.

A friend of a friend worked as his personal assistant, in the office of his flat at 344 Kings Road. This was the apartment to which coiffeur to the stars John Frieda rocked up once a month to dye and style his strange aubergine-mahogany hair. The flat topped the building that stood opposite a women's boutique, Joanna's Tent, where Bill was in the habit of buying quite feminine garments, and next door to a French restaurant, Thierry's, where he often hosted lunches and suppers. I was co-presenting a rock magazine show on Channel 4 at the time – *1984* – and making the most of the fifteen minutes of 'fame'. Bill saw me on television and asked his PA to contact me, not realising that she knew me. Her oldest friend and I had been colleagues at Chrysalis Records, where I had until recently worked for artist John Pasche, designer of the original Stones' lip-and-tongue logo. Round and round we go.

We went out for dinner a couple of times, to Thierry's and to the iconic original Ivy on London's West Street. He would apologise for his painfully plain tastes as he plumped for a burger or a bit of bland chicken over anything 'with sauce on'. He spoke of his childhood in the manner of John Cleese, Eric Idle, Michael Palin and Terry Jones in the 'Good Old Days'/'Four Yorkshiremen' sketch, in which Cleese et al send up the classic prosperous old men trying to outdo each other with the most deprived childhood, exaggerating the depths of their poverty. Only Bill wasn't exaggerating. I laughed out loud when he told me he had consumed both whale meat and horse as a child. I assumed that he was joking. No, he insisted, he really had. But those were 'luxuries', apparently. Most of the time it was bread and dripping: leftover fat from the roasting of meat.

He later wrote about all this convincingly, or at least his ghostwriter Ray Coleman did, in his memoir, *Stone Alone*. This time I believed him. He also said that the only food he still liked from his childhood was bread pudding.[9] It amused him no end to see primped-up versions of the working-class 'afters', made with brioche, panettone, gourmet chocolate drops and Fortnum & Mason candied fruit, on the menus of gilded restaurants. He almost always had a cigarette on the go. That or chewing gum. He didn't believe in health foods, supplements, gyms or even sleeping very much. He was too busy for all that lying around, he said. He never went to work on an egg, preferring to swallow a couple of cups of builder's tea washed down with a few more fags.

There was nothing weird about hanging with him. The London music scene was a cosy world back then. Artists, record-company people and media folk overlapped and socialised together routinely. We discussed the possibility of Bill appearing on our show, and he agreed to do it. I was also working on a book for Sony, alongside radio producer Phil Swern and pop journalist Robin Eggar, for which Bill offered to write the foreword.

He seemed to relish his reputation as rock's most prolific shagger. Three or four women a night when the Stones were on the road, he was wont to boast. Three or four at a time, sometimes. He wasn't shy about it. Women threw themselves at him. You'd be sitting there having a quiet meal and random females would sidle over and practically force themselves on him.

I could never fathom it. He'd shrug it off with a smile, making a joke of his 'irresistible sex appeal'. I searched for it incessantly, but it never revealed itself to me. He would throw in the odd stat, such as that he'd been with more women than Willie Nelson and Julio Iglesias put together. Which sounds like an eye-boggling lot. He was animated on the subject of artist Marc Chagall, his neighbour in St Paul de Vence in the south of France where Bill had built a house. He was 'doing a book about him'. He was also championing the cause of various young musicians and doing his bit for the ARMS charity, Action Research for Multiple Sclerosis, the disease that had cut short the career of Small Faces and Faces bassist, his close friend Ronnie Lane.

Bill had left a lot behind to be who he had become. I was fascinated by all that he had to say about his roots and his childhood. He was at times reluctant to divulge. You could tell there was pain there.

He was born William George to bricklayer William Perks and mother Kathleen May, known as Molly, in Lewisham Hospital, South London in October 1936 – which made him the oldest Stone, and the only one to have vivid memories of the Second World War. He, his mother and two siblings (there would be three more) were evacuated to Pembrokeshire, south-west Wales, and later to Nottingham in the north, while his father was in the army. His childhood was bleak, his education minimal. His maternal grandmother Florrie, with whom he lived at one point, taught him times tables by rote and how to read and write. His family inhabited an unheated, infested, bathroomless terraced house with a backyard privy on a brutal Penge backstreet.

While gang warfare raged around him, he claimed to have taken piano lessons from the age of ten. God knows how his parents could have afforded it, there was barely the money to put basic food on the table. Family hygiene was a once-a-week, in-out, one-after-the-other shared bath in a zinc tub on the kitchen floor; a single toothbrush between them and salt instead of toothpaste. There were fleas, scabies and terrible tooth decay. Clothes were hand-me-downs, infrequently washed. Despite which, Bill went to Sunday school, was a Wolf Cub and had a milk round, enabling him to contribute to the family purse. Even as a child, he was cataloguing the few books the family owned, showing early signs of the collector, archivist and historian he would become.

Bright enough to pass the Eleven Plus exam, he attended Beckenham and Penge County Grammar School[10] from the age of eleven, which in Bill's day was situated on dingy Penge High Street. He was small, and was bullied. He was good at maths and art, learned the clarinet, loved football and cricket, fishing and 'building things'. He also joined a church choir. At thirteen, he had his appendix out. Me too: we had some mileage out of that one. He frequented a local church youth club, and couldn't keep his eyes off the girls. Just before he was due to sit his GCE exams, which could have led him on to A levels and even to university, his bitter, often-unemployed and physically abusive father hoicked him out of school and shoved him into work, to help support the family. So damaged was Bill by this unforeseen injustice that he kept the letter the headmaster wrote to his father, begging him to change his mind. Clinging to the proof of what William the elder had deprived him of, in terms of a full education and a promising future, prevented Bill from getting over it. He nursed his anger. Resentment gnawed at him for years, he said. That loss of confidence, the fall-out nervousness, must have fuelled his nicotine addiction.

'I think he did it out of spite,' Bill would reflect of his father, later. 'There was that resentment about me going to a posh school, trying to talk posh, and wearing a uniform that he had to pay for. He was very working class, and a very cold person.'

He went to work for a London bookmaker. He sold his precious stamp collection to purchase a second-hand record player, took to hanging around the local coffee bars, and booked himself dance lessons at the Beckenham Ballroom. An early girlfriend had a brother with a great record collection, exposing Bill to his first recorded jazz. During his stint of National Service in Germany during the fifties, he saw the Stan Kenton Band in Bremen, got into Elvis Presley, bought a cheap guitar and started a skiffle group. Post-demob, he worked for a firm of meat importers, became a regular at Royston Ballroom in Penge run by dance stars Frank and Peggy Spencer, became a champion jiver no less.

In 1959, when he was twenty-three, he married his dancing partner, eighteen-year-old bank clerk Diane Cory. He landed a job with a company of diesel engineers and settled down to making-ends-meet married life.

Threadbare and poorly accommodated, he moved jobs yet again to work at a department store, where he befriended a colleague who played guitar. It prompted Bill to hire-purchase one of his own, his first electric. A little Beckenham group came together, fell apart, and other musicians crept in. Bill HP'd himself an amp. They performed at weddings, parties and youth clubs, taking what they could get. A line-up gelled as the Cliftons, with drummer Tony Chapman. A chance dance on a visit to his sister's in Aylesbury brought Bill face to face with the group the Barron Knights. He was so impressed by their bass guitarist that he realised, aged twenty-four, what he wanted to be. He bought a second-hand bass and customised it, leaving the frets out, thus creating what he believed to have been the first fretless bass guitar in the country.

Tony Chapman was the first among their little gang to come across the embryonic Rollin' Stones. Having rehearsed with them in Soho, he told Bill in December 1962 that they were looking for a bass player. The pair trolled along together to see the band at the Red Lion pub in Sutton, Surrey. Through heavy snowdrifts a couple of days later, Bill and Tony traipsed to the Wetherby Arms in Chelsea for a Stones rehearsal.[11] They were a right bunch of scruffs at point-blank range. Neatly-coiffed and turned-out Bill couldn't imagine for the life of him what he might have in common with this lot. And Mike Jagger, Keith and Brian were equally dismissive of Bill. Until, that is, he lugged in his impressive Vox AC30 amp from the car. They got into his kit; Bill got into their twelve-bar blues vibe. It wasn't until he changed his surname legally by deed poll in 1964 – to that of his best friend in the forces, Lee Whyman, dropping the 'h' – that he located his confidence, let go of his hang-ups and began to hope that he might be deserving of a future in music. Already a dad and unhappy at home, he almost instantly became the Stones' resident shagger.

But was he any good (at *the music*)? He must have had something. He would not have lasted for thirty-odd years with the Rolling Stones otherwise. He was noticeably older than and different from his bandmates. He lacked formal training. He projected as somewhat pedestrian and conformist, compared with these dynamic, insolent, out-there upstarts … Mick, Brian and Keith, at least. The fact that he had already 'settled down' set him apart from them. It made him the 'grown-up', for which they sneered at him and tended to put him down. As a bassist he was a basic plodder. Isn't that the idea?

Most of the musicians I asked rate him as average, while conceding that he and Charlie made a fantastic rhythm section. It is true that Wyman was quite often missing from recording sessions, when Keith, Mick Taylor or Ronnie Wood would stand in for him. Bill's contributions to 'Miss You' and 'Bitch' lend weight to the argument in his favour. But that's Keith, solid and insistent, all over the bass on 'Jumpin' Jack Flash', despite the persistent rumour that Bill coined the song's main riff. 'Sympathy for the Devil'? It's Richards on the bass again, flamboyant and daring, while Bill is relegated to shakers. Keith created the original groove on this track, and no one else has ever matched it live. 'Street Fighting Man'? That's Keith yet again, echoing 'Jumpin' Jack Flash' on electric bass. Wyman wasn't there for the recording, they say. Wasn't he? He says that's him on the Hammond organ. If it is true that Bill stepped up more reliably during the *Let It Bleed* era, his heart was by then no longer in the Stones. That was 1969, leaving him only a quarter of a century to go. 'Tumbling Dice', my favourite Stones track? It's not even Wyman on that one, disappointingly. Ladies and gentlemen, on bass, Mr Mick Taylor.

Chapter Five

HUSTLERS

Brian Jones rented a flat for fifteen pounds a week at 102 Edith Grove, World's End, during the late summer of 1962. The neighbourhood took its name from a famous Grade II Listed pub on the main drag, the Kings Road. 'World's End' was the size of it, the place being practically unfit for human habitation. The damp, fetid fleapit with its redundant bathtub in the kitchen and a disgusting communal lavatory on the floor above became even more squalid after Mick and Keith moved in. It was as if they took pride in the filthy environment so at odds with the clean, warm homes from which the three of them hailed. The virtually destitute trio pilfered food from the fridges of other tenants in the building, returned empty beer bottles gathered at parties to local off-licences to claim refunds, and hurled cutlery and crockery into the backyard from the kitchen window instead of washing it up. The floor was a moving, mouldering feast of grimy garments, stinking underpants, discarded food and fag ends. Keith's mother Doris wasn't having it. She started visiting once a week to tackle the slum and take home laundry. But she was fighting a losing battle, and soon gave up.

The band, which at this point still included pianist Ian Stewart, supported Blues Incorporated for the next few months. Mick and Brian also sat in with the main act. Harold Pendleton was persuaded, by Chris Barber and enthusiast Giorgio Gomelsky, to launch a blues night at his

Marquee Jazz Club every Thursday. When Blues Incorporated were booked by the BBC for 12 July 1962, they were invited to leave their 'long-haired effeminate singer' Jagger behind. Alexis talked Pendleton into allowing Brian's and Mick's group to perform at the Marquee instead. The audience was underwhelmed by these lanky louts, and made clear their displeasure. Pendleton was livid. But Korner, still convinced that these boys 'had something', continued to champion their cause. Pendleton relented, and booked them again to appear at the Marquee. They carried on performing at the Ealing Club.

Promoter, ducker, diver and all-round lovable character John Mansfield had launched his own successful Ricky Tick Jazz Club at the old Star and Garter Hotel in Windsor, Berkshire, about twenty-five miles west of central London. Alexis Korner's Blues Incorporated had gone down such a storm on the opening night, 7 December 1962, that he was now champing at the bit to book these curious Stones for the follow-up, a week later. He phoned Ian Stewart, the only day-job-employed band member who had become by default their booker. As 'Stu' was the only one with a car, a pre-war Rover, he had also become their roadie. While Stu delivered the drum kit, speakers and amps, the group travelled to Windsor by train.

'By the time they were nearly ready to start their first set, the room had already filled to capacity,' recalled John in his memoir, which he self-published shortly before his death in 2019. Because he printed only a handful of copies, few Stones fans are aware of his importance in the band's development. Margaret Kirby, former manager of both Arts and Heritage and the local museum in Windsor, shared with me her personal copy of John's book, one of few in existence.

'It's fair to say, most of the crowd had no idea what they were about to experience,' John wrote. 'The physical appearance of the Stones was quite shocking to many of the teenagers who had crammed into the club that night. They looked more like caged wild animals. Their stage presence was unlike anything they had witnessed before. At the front of the stage, two microphones were set out in pole positions. Behind these, the band were busy getting the final things ready for their first set. An eerie sense of anticipation hung over the audience, many of whom were looking on, wide-eyed and open-mouthed.'

Their opener that night was 'Bo Diddley', the great man's own number from 1955.

'It was electrifying,' said Mansfield. 'Forget the reception they'd received at the Marquee, back in July. Here in Windsor, the reaction to the band could not have been more different ... Other numbers followed, like Muddy Waters's 'I Want to be Loved', Bo Diddley's 'Road Runner' and Chuck Berry's 'Come On'. The clapping and stamping was becoming frightening.

'This phenomenal debut by the Stones had been a triumph. What a night! ... [It was] probably the most amazing reception the Stones had ever had, and the most amazing response to a group I'd ever witnessed. I tried to book them straight away for the following Friday, but they already had a gig booked for then. They were eager to play again, so we booked them on 11 and 25 January. Bill Wyman mentioned the Paramounts from Southend as a possible alternative, and gave me Gary Brooker's telephone number. The two had met when Bill's group, the Cliftons, played on the same bill as the Paramounts earlier in the year.'

Despite the fact that the Ricky Tick was the Stones' first-ever provincial booking and their biggest success to date, as well as being Bill Wyman's own debut with the band, none of the band ever referred to it. Not even Wyman, the meticulous diarist and collector of Stones memorabilia and ephemera, who assumed the role of Rolling Stones' unofficial historian, and who might have been expected to record the fact for posterity.

'[Not] in any book, magazine or radio interview that I know of,' said Mansfield, clearly baffled. 'Bill did subsequently acknowledge it in a later book, but only after I had pointed out the oversight to him. In contrast to the Windsor gig, just six days later on 20 December, the Stones appeared at the Scene Club in London, and attracted six people!'

*

The winter of 1962–63 in the UK was the coldest since 1740. Heavy snow obliterated England over Christmas and the New Year, rendering roads impassable and paralysing communities. Businesses closed, and coal, food and other necessities were in short supply. Back at the Edith Grove hellhole, life was getting desperate. Not only were the water pipes frozen and the toilet too iced to flush, but Brian had been sacked from his job for stealing and there was very little money coming in. Brian, Mick and Keith took to a shared bed and stayed there, just to keep each other warm. Brian did somehow manage to wash and dry his baby-blond locks every day. The others could barely believe that this was his priority. Bill rocked up every couple of days with food, cigarettes and coins for the electricity meter. Brian hustled even harder to get the group gigs. He spent cash they couldn't afford on having fly posters printed, which he and Stu went plastering across west and south-west London. It was the only way they could keep their burgeoning barmy army informed where they would be appearing next.

Drummer Tony Chapman pulled out, and was replaced by Charlie Watts. John Mansfield insisted that Charlie played his first gig with the band at the Flamingo Club on Wardour Street on 14 January 1963. It is indeed on record that the band made an appearance at that club on that specific date. The Stones and others have stated that Charlie's debut happened at the Ealing Club two days earlier. Wherever, whatever: the classic line-up was now set in Stones. On Friday 11 January, ahead of either of the aforementioned, John and his business partner Philip Hayward, a firm friend since their army days, welcomed the Stones back to the Ricky Tick for their second gig at that venue. Guess what, another roaring success. John and Philip took the band to the local Drury House restaurant afterwards to celebrate.

'We sat at a large table by the front window, and treated them to a three-course meal with wine,' said John. 'They devoured it like it was their first meal for a week. Philip and I were to do this a further six times. You would think that the Stones would remember our generosity. You'd be wrong.'

As well as the good time had by all, a new marketing ploy was first thought of. 'Sat just behind us,' recalled John, 'was Henry the [local] bookmaker with his wife and twin daughters. Across the tables, Mick and Keith were having a chat with the two girls. Henry looked at them disapprovingly; they looked as though they might have just survived a blizzard [they probably had]. As we were leaving, Keith said something flirtatious to the girls. Henry stood up, and with hands stretched out in front of his daughters, declared, "I wouldn't let a daughter of mine go out with a Rolling Stone!'"[1]

John Mansfield's wry aside about the Stones' ingratitude was justified. This was a man whose investment, perseverance, enthusiasm and flair had helped the band to turn a corner and begin their assault. He had staged the Stones to great acclaim eight times in as many weeks, and had turned hundreds, perhaps thousands of fans on to their music. But he was never accorded so much as a footnote in the fairy tale, except as a prompted afterthought by Bill Wyman in a book published after he had left the band. The corporate line has always been that the Crawdaddy Club at the old Station Hotel in Richmond was where it all began, having been the setting in which the line-up that would push on into fame and glory was consolidated. But Mansfield deserves a formal place in Stones history as a principal enabler.

There is no question that his vision, commitment and support were vital to the band's progress. That he and partner Phil Hayward found themselves wiped from the narrative suggests an extraordinary level of control in the rewriting of Stones history from its earliest stages, before there was ever such a thing as 'the Stones machine'.

We are well aware that deletions, omissions, embroidery and blatant fiction were the name of the PR game back then. Massively so. A good example of this is the way in which Freddie Mercury's academic qualifications, should I say lack of them, were 'fixed' by Queen's original publicist Tony Brainsby in order to match his intelligence to that of his three impressive bandmates, all of whom were educated to the Nth. Brian May, Roger Taylor and John Deacon could have gone on to pursue careers in astrophysics, dentistry and engineering respectively. Their singer, who had shown early academic promise but lost his heart to rock'n'roll and was kicked out of his expensive boarding school in India, had no choice but to become a superstar.

Either the Stones, their playmakers or both plotted a trajectory that required streamlining. Less being more, their dramatic, rags-to-riches tale needed as few passengers and hangers-on as possible. In order to concentrate and focus their brilliance, superfluous middle men were deleted. They would make stars of the most headline-worthy individuals, whose personal flamboyance would reflect back favourably on the band

and in turn become part of their legend. The same tactic was employed in the dismissal of pianist Ian Stewart, whose jaw, indeed his whole face, didn't fit. A musician too many in the line-up, he was deemed surplus to requirements on stage. By whom? We are getting there.

*

Septuagenarian Scottish singer-songwriter Rab Noakes swore allegiance to the Stones right from the start. The musician and producer who has enjoyed a fifty-year career both as a solo artist and with the likes of Lindisfarne, Stealers Wheel, Gerry Rafferty and Barbara Dickson recalls intoxicating days when he and his brother Alan purchased the Stones' first single, 'Come On', and saw the band on *Ready Steady Go!*, their first major television exposure. 'They wore,' Rab recalls, 'matching waistcoats.

'In September 1963, I travelled from my home town in Fife to Glasgow [sixty-five miles away] to work there. On my first night in the city, I went out to explore. As I walked up Renfield Street, I saw a poster at the glorious Odeon Cinema – a fabulous art deco building formerly known as the Paramount, opened in 1934 – advertising a forthcoming package tour. Topping the bill were the Everly Brothers, who had always been a big deal to me. Also performing were Bo Diddley, Little Richard, and way down in the small letters, the Rolling Stones. Being there was a must, so I was back the following night with enough money to purchase my ticket for the early show on 17 October. I treated myself to a good ticket: I was in Row D.

'The Stones were thrilling,' Rab remembers. 'Their set was probably no more than about twelve minutes long. They were dressed in "the band-suit": short houndstooth-checked jackets and black trousers. Even then, that was looking a little incongruous. It didn't survive beyond that tour.'

Jagger the watchful student observed Little Richard intently from the wings, making mental note of the seasoned entertainer's sexually charged stage presence and outrageous antics. Everything about Mick's future stage personality was ignited that night.

'Little Richard's stage show was terrific,' affirms Rab. 'At one point, he left the stage and went up the right aisle. He somehow traversed a row of seats and came back down the left aisle. It was really exciting. Next, he removed his jacket and draped it on his piano stool before taking his shirt off. He tossed it into the crowd, and it landed right in front of me. How could I resist? I leaned forward and grabbed a sleeve. For years afterwards, the cuff of Little Richard's shirt lurked in a drawer in my childhood bedroom. One day, after I wasn't really returning to stay there any more, my mum did some tidying. Without realising its significance, she threw the rag into the refuse. It was gone.

'It doesn't detract, though, from the excitement of the evening. The Everly Brothers, who were on the wane by then, frankly weren't that thrilling. They strolled through the hits without much enthusiasm. It was the stately Bo Diddley, the astounding Little Richard, and of course the newly exciting Rolling Stones, who brought the night alive.'

His next encounter came not long after that.

'On reading the *Sunday Mail* on Sunday 12 January,' he says, 'I spotted an ad for the Rolling Stones at The Barrowland Ballroom the following day. I went there and, like many others, paid at the door. What a difference a few months had made! The band was tight, and fully on top of what they were doing. The Barrowland's layout was very different back then. There wasn't a stage as such, only a bandstand. The Stones were pretty close to the audience down at the front. The over-capacity crowd in those pre-health and safety days was tightly packed. Dangerously so. There was much screaming and yelling, and a constant stream of people, mostly lassies, who had fainted and were being moved aloft to the exits.

'This show was great. There had been more releases such as the second single, 'I Wanna Be Your Man' and the 'You Better Move On' EP. All those songs and other raw blues numbers were the repertoire. Their first LP was an essential acquisition. The Stones, along with being great in themselves, took their place among the essential gatekeepers. Long before algorithm connections began their often hilariously misguided "If you liked that, you'll love this" routine, we had to follow the leads given by the artists we admired. The Beatles, for example, opened a window on Tamla Motown. Bob Dylan later led us to folk songs, including even the riches available from my own Scottish territory. The Stones' huge revelation was an astonishing list of blues stalwarts. Their single releases were a must, over the years.

'I remember reading a quote from Keith along the lines of, "You've got to hit it hard with your first record and keep on doing it". And so they did. Their manager Andrew Loog Oldham famously locked Keith & Mick in a room and made them write songs. This action bore fruit soon enough with the early 1965 release of "The Last Time", followed soon after by "Satisfaction". They've kept them coming. It's worth recalling that in those days, an old record was a dead record. It was gone. As soon as a hit tumbled down the charts and was replaced on the jukeboxes, it was finished. That was one of the reasons why you had to keep releasing new stuff. A gap could be fatal.'

Rab waited nineteen years for his next live experience of the Stones, at St James' Park, Newcastle, the home of Newcastle United Football Club. At the first major rock show ever staged at that stadium, on 23 June 1982, they played for 38,000 fans in support of their *Tattoo You* album.

'It was exciting to see them, but I've never been much of a fan of the big outdoor event,' Rab admits. 'Especially if you have to stand. I like to stand to perform, but to sit when I'm in an audience. So I have no significant memory of this one.' Maybe the rain dulled his memory, as it drizzled all night. The twenty-five-song show kicked off with 'Under My Thumb' and blasted through hits including 'Tumbling Dice', 'Miss You', 'Honky Tonk Women', 'Brown Sugar', 'Start Me Up' and 'Jumpin' Jack Flash'. It finished with 'Satisfaction', the best bit of Tchaikovsky's '1812 Overture' and a pyrotechnic spurt. Phil Collins and Sting were hanging out backstage. You can't always get what you want. The Stones would not return to St James' Park for the next eight years.

'The time after that,' says Rab, recalling his next Stones adventure seventeen more years down the line, 'was the Bridges to Babylon tour. My late wife Stephy and I went to Murrayfield[2] to see that one, in June 1999. I really liked this outing. We were seated, and the stage set was astonishing. The bridge to the small stage was ingenious, as was the set they played, including blues interpretations.

'Mick Jagger's stagecraft is a remarkable thing. I thought it the first time I saw them, and I think it to this day. Even now, at this great age, you can hardly take your eyes off him.'

*

Rewind. Giorgio Gomelsky, a Georgian immigrant and dashing film industry entrepreneur with fingers in pies from shepherd's to fish via steak and kidney, wrote about his passion for blues and jazz, and dreamed up the term 'British Rhythm and Blues'.[3] He established his own blues venue in the Station Hotel opposite Richmond railway station, in south-west London, after his boat wafted in on waves of realisation that the blues couldn't explode as a popular mainstream genre until the teens were lured on board. Its loyal flock of nodding male beatnik aficionados was never going to take it stratospheric. So he went looking for teenagers, and chose the Station Hotel strategically: being situated only a hop and a skip from Wimbledon Art College up the road, it was likely to attract its droves of students. The Stones made their debut appearance at what was originally called the BRRB, later the Crawdaddy Club (after Bo Diddley's song 'Crawdad', with which they would always end their set) on 24 February 1963. They performed to an audience of just three. There were double that number on stage.[4] Undeterred, Gomelsky invited the faithful three back the following week, promising them free entry if they would each bring two friends. Previous books and biographies tell clashing stories.

'One puts the figure at thirty people there on the opening night, and the Stones were paid seven pounds,' recalled John Mansfield. 'Another says that there were sixty-six people, and that they were paid twenty-four pounds. As Giorgio Gomelsky was the promoter, and was actually there, I assume that the version he told me is the most accurate.'

Word got out, putting the Crawdaddy on the map. Entrance queues began snaking around the block in the early afternoon ahead of each gig. Future Stone Ronnie Wood and other as yet unknowns – Ray Davies, Eric Clapton – waited patiently in line, as keen as anyone who pitched up to see the band billed as 'inimitable', 'incomparable' and 'exhilarating'. As did the Beatles, by this time big stars, who attended on 14 April. They then went back with the Stones to the Edith Grove hellhole. God knows what they made of that. Perhaps they were by then too tanked to notice the squalor. New to the music scene in the capital, the Liverpudlians were keen to immerse themselves on every level.

'When we started hanging around London, the Stones were up and coming in the clubs, and we knew Giorgio through [Brian] Epstein [the Beatles' manager],' said John Lennon. 'We went down and saw them and became good friends. I remember Brian Jones came up and said, "Are you playing a harmonica or a harp on 'Love Me Do'?" Because he knew I'd got this bottom note. I said, "A harmonica with a button," which wasn't really funky-blues enough; but you couldn't get "Hey! Baby" licks on a blues harp, and we were also doing "Hey! Baby" by Bruce Channel.'[5]

Said Jagger, in a somewhat roundabout way, 'They were both rivals and they were also, I mean, they were also showing the way, 'cause they were the first at this kind of ... They were kind of trailblazers in a lot of ways, and they went to the United States first, y'know, they showed the way, they were big international stars – because in England, most people have never really been stars outside of England. You had your little patch, and that was it. And the Beatles kind of showed you could be big internationally.'

Illustrious visitors notwithstanding, nothing happened for the Stones immediately. Most of those early clubbers were in two minds, as well as unsure as to how they ought to react to the music. Up flashed another Gomelsky brainwave. He coerced his assistant, future rock photographer Hamish Grimes, into clambering on to a table and flinging his arms about, as if on drugs. Maybe he was. Cue audience primed to let rip in unfettered exuberance. The press roared in and wrote outraged pieces, comparing the club's uninhibited atmosphere to frenzied religious revivalism. What? The Station Hotel's owners threw wobblies. Afraid that such adverse publicity would bring them into disrepute, they gave Giorgio notice of heave-ho. Undeterred, the promoter simply shifted his club to a huge room under the grandstand at nearby Richmond Athletic Ground, and gifted the Stones a residency that would keep them in rent, electricity and beer for the next eight months. He also booked them to appear at the 1963 Richmond jazz festival. Take that, losers.

Re-enter John Mansfield, as though pursued by a bear,[6] with whom Gomelsky was in talks about combining forces and launching their own management agency. Their intention was to sign the Stones. But the Georgian had the ball and he ran with it. He poured every drop of spunk into the band. Bill Wyman later described him as 'a catalyst, giving the

Stones the confidence when the odds were against them'. The gleeful Georgian bounced around whipping up passion for 'his' boys, charming press contacts, splashing publicity, yanking in favours to get them a promo film. He even managed to pull off a free demo recording, negotiated on the understanding that the studio, IBC in London's Portland Place, would receive first refusal on the band's first five songs. He encouraged his carefully cultivated hack friends down to see them, making clear that he expected favourable write-ups. One such journalist, Peter Jones of the *Record Mirror*, arrived at work the next morning raving his socks off about the band he had seen in Richmond the night before. And look, come on, you were expecting him. Another man of wealth-to-be and taste. Hope you guess his name. This blond, exigent hustler is Andrew Loog Oldham. He minces and shimmers on down to Richmond with a glint in his shark-like and the smell of lucre in his nose. He is nineteen years old. What kept him?

*

I found him on Twitter. He found me back. We introduced ourselves over email, and got chatting. It seemed strange, me in my urban eyrie in south London, he in his wilderness hideaway beyond Bogotà. Some 5,250 miles' worth of North Atlantic saline separated us. That, and a whole other lifetime. I had at that stage read two of his three memoirs (I later caught up with 2011's *Rolling Stoned*). He didn't need to answer questions, he said, 'because it is all in there'. It wasn't quite. Contradictions prevailed, suggesting a man in the habit of revising his life as he went along. I wanted to know which Andrew I was about to get.

'I will come,' I said.

'To the jungle?'

'I'd love to meet you. I always prefer to interrogate face to face.'

'I'll get back to you.'

He did so. Many times. He couldn't take the responsibility, he regretted to say. He described Colombia as 'fifth world', implying a backwater of terror and derangement from which I might not return. Why the hell was he living there, then? In the end, it couldn't happen ahead of deadline. Not only was Colombia Covid red-listed, with all non-essential arrivals prohibited, but their government was refusing entry at El Dorado

International to passengers landing directly from the UK. I explored other routes, preferably via the US. But Bogotà was on fire with Covid protests and mass disruptions. To reach Andrew, I would be looking at precarious rides from the capital along notorious terrorist and hostage routes. Forget insurance. I would run a high risk of being shot. Phone reception and internet access there are unreliable. He doesn't bother with Skype or Zoom because connections disintegrate, and he has no IT help. It's just him, his wife and five dogs.

The image is deliberate, echoing Oldham's first impressions of Jagger as he stood watching him perform in the Station Hotel that first night he dragged himself down there, utterly mesmerised. He would later describe Mick as 'an adolescent Tarzan, plucked from the jungle, not comfortable in his clothes'. Perhaps he couldn't make up his mind whether to scarper or ejaculate.

He had never seen anything like it, he said. 'They came on to me. All my preparations, ambitions and desires had just met their purpose ... the music was authentic and sexually driven ... It reached out and went inside me – totally. It satisfied me. I was in love ... I heard what I always wanted to hear. I wanted it; it already belonged to me. Everything I'd done up until now was a preparation for this moment. I saw and heard what my life, thus far, had been for.'

*

Conceived during a wartime liaison between his Australian-born mother Cecelia Oldham and United States Army Air Corps lieutenant Andrew Loog, an American of Dutch heritage, he was born on 29 January 1944. He would never know his father, on account of the fact that tall, handsome airman Loog was shot down and killed over the English Channel seven months before his youngest child's birth, and was buried in Belgium. His legitimate child and widow were back home in Texas. Andrew said that he was given his father's surname despite the fact that it was not recorded on his birth certificate.

From the off, he was the upstart. Almost two years younger than Brian Jones, six months younger than Mick and a few weeks younger than Keith, what this privately educated lad lacked in maturity and experience he more than made up for in determination and cheek. A schoolboy songwriter, he was determined to make it as something, anything in the music business. He chased and chased the Stones until they caught him. Dasvidaniya, Gomelsky.

History paints Loog Oldham as the Stones' first manager. Stealing them from under Giorgio's nose while their trusting enabler was back in Switzerland burying his father, Oldham took his lead from the Beatles' mastermind Brian Epstein, for whose NEMS management organisation he had briefly worked. Those goody-two-shoes mop tops deserved an antithesis, and he was going to be the one to give it to them. He would turn the Stones into the anti-Beatles. He would even get them signed to the very record label, Decca, that had famously sent the Beatles packing. As journalist Don Nicholl of weekly music paper *Disc* wrote, 'The Beatles, who recommended the Stones to Decca, may well live to rue the day. This group could be challenging them for top places in the immediate future.'

Calculated to the point of cynical, ALO's job was to fake it while the boys kept trying to make it. The ploy worked, and didn't take long. Because he was too young to negotiate legal contracts, he went in with agent Eric Easton to create Impact Sound, through which they would manage, market and exploit the group. He nabbed Paul McCartney and John Lennon outside Leicester Square underground station, so the story goes, and hustled them into the Studio 51 jazz club on Great Newport Street (or was it De Lane Lea Studios? Both have been claimed) where Mick and the lads were rehearsing. There's a nice yarn about John and Paul polishing off a song they'd been writing, right in front of the Stones. They had not only finished it, in fact, but had recorded it. With no plans to release it as a Beatles single, they handed it over to the Stones to do their worst with it as a cover. Their second single, 'I Wanna Be Your Man' produced by Oldham and Easton, was released in September 1963. It zapped to No. 12.

Years later, John Lennon admitted that the Beatles' gift of a song to the Stones had been less than altruistic.

'It was only really a lick,' he said, 'so Paul and I went off in the corner of the room and finished the song off while they were all sitting there, talking. We came back and Mick and Keith said, "Jesus, look at that. They just went over there and wrote it." You know, right in front of their eyes. We gave it to them. It was a throwaway. Ringo sang it for us, and the Stones did their version. It shows how much importance we put on them. We weren't going to give them anything great, right? That was the Stones' first record.'

Lennon was mistaken. It wasn't. He had missed their cover of Chuck Berry's 'Come On', released on 7 June 1963.

'Anyway,' concluded John, 'Mick and Keith said, "If they can write a song so easily, we should try it."'

Within four years, under Oldham's assured tutelage, the Stones had become global superstars. By the end of that same forty-eight-month-long madness, he was off the case and out on his ear. But they owed him, this they knew. He had not only created their identity but had also produced their earliest hits, at a time when few understood what record production was. He launched the UK's first independent production label and got away with it. But he was sucked in by the lifestyle even more comprehensively than they were. He descended to such drug-addicted depths that he came close to losing his life three times. He then vanished. He got himself back some time during the nineties. He fell in love again, married a Colombian model and actress, Esther Farfan, and moved home with her. 'I not only fell in love with her, but I fell in love with the country,' he said. 'I couldn't stand the idea of staying in England and becoming a relic.'

Now seventy-eight, he re-emerged a dozen years ago, having relaunched himself as a band manager in South America. Flaunting the wares of a rock band from Buenos Aires called the Ratones Paranoicos, whose favourite group and primary influence were the Rolling Stones, he was going at it again with all guns blazing. 'I fell in love with them immediately,' he said, that phrase again – well aware, because he had been there before, that that's what it takes. He also worked with multi-instrumental Colombian artist Juan Galeano,[7] who appeared to have seen the future. But Andrew's main preoccupation was his daily satellite radio show, which connected him with Stones fans around the world and garnered him a whole new audience.

Andrew's memoirs are whole books of cryptic throwaways. Packed with euphemisms and double entendres, they are too clever for their own good. Do we ever get a glimpse of the real him? I am still in three minds. His recollections have the awful ring of truth, but often smell as though they are straying into fantasy. Much of his prose seems to be written in code, with obscure references, suggesting that he is afraid to confront reality. Perhaps reality, for all of us, is in the habit of coming and going. Or perhaps he has forgotten what that is. His memory appears to work in movie frames and celluloid sequences. He speaks of the ambitions of his mind and groin. He alludes to homosexual encounters, to gay boy toys in the marital bed, to orgies with Brian Jones and bunches of birds in New York, even to Afghan hounds between the sheets. Did these things happen? He is mischievous about the lifts in Mick's shoes, and about Jagger being allegedly under-endowed, a revelation that Keith also shared with the world; and about the miracle that is the Jagger hair. Did he really have sex with him? He is not going to tell me in so many words. Others reckon so. By which, we wouldn't be surprised. The idea of the omnisexual hustler in the bed of the defiantly bisexual rocker is not exactly a stretch.

'People say I made the Stones,' Andrew muses in an email. 'I didn't. They were there already. They only wanted exploiting. They were all bad boys when I found them. I had to find a home for the songs that Mick and Keith were writing. So what if they were soppy and imitative to begin with – they had to come to the process of songwriting, through trial and error. That takes a lot of balls and front, as you find out what you really want to say and develop the confidence to believe that others will want to hear it.'

'You must remember that I did dreams, not money,' he tells me during our exchanges. 'Therefore, I was inevitably expendable. This was all instinctual to me, and all that went on around my departure was, of course, horrendous and painful to a twenty-three-year-old ego (suaged by ECT, thankfully),[8] [and] was par for the course for somebody who would eventually realise that this may be the last of his many lives. For me it was always about the fun of getting it done, the actuality of work. Downfalls are for the masses, the tabloids and those masquerading as above it.

'I hired Leslie Perrin (the publicist) in 1966 in an attempt to head off the inevitable. It was too late, and the big lessons of life started to be doled out to us, or over us.

'I do not know the Rolling Stones,' he insists, when I ask what he thinks about them today. 'I knew them for four short years as kids who played on the same block. And I did manage to get them into the sweet shop. It all worked very well until it didn't, and wasn't that a blessing. I always subscribed whatever war drum Mick and Keith beat to be a result of Allen Krime,[9] with blame attached to me as it would be convenient, and you cannot expect them to have the thinking capacity beyond that of being an act.

'He (Klein) stole our songs. That is like stealing your family and your dreams. I would not expect them to see it that simply. They have to get up every day, dust themselves off and get back into the ring. Choice, admittedly, but did Mother Teresa do anything fundamentally different?

'They were perfect until they were not. The songs, they remain the key to life. That is why they are still there. The rest is happenstance and a work ethic. And having Joe Jagger for a father and Keith as your forever friend.

'They were seamless. 45rpms, albums, image and stage. Always on the same level. You cannot say the same for the competition, who begrudgingly served up the hits and then retreated back to the blues.

'I recently saw an Australian TV interview given by Roger Savage, the engineer of our first recording session at the original Marble Arch-based Olympic Studios. He emigrated shortly thereafter to Melbourne. He was in love with Carol, the receptionist, and has a very successful business there. As you'll know, I am credited with having removed the sixth band member Ian Stewart. Obviously it's not quite as simple as that. Anyway, Roger describes mixing the music with me and me telling him to take the piano out, not turn it down, but to take it out. He does so, reasonably astounded. The band and Stu, who is a member, come up to listen to the result. None of them says a word about what has just passed . . .

'A few years later the gods of balance and free fall gave me a life, a wife and a country. I really do not speak the language [Spanish] because I have never had to work here to put food on the table, but I do speak the dream. Obviously your job is to break that down into just desserts.

'The Stones played Bogotà a few years ago,' he finishes. 'I missed it. I was bringing a broken femur back into the game in Montreal, and catching up with Ozzy Osbourne. I saw them last in Seattle in 2005 with my youngest son. That band with the Pamela Anderson husband [he means Tommy Lee of Mötley Crüe, to whom Anderson is no longer married] were the support playing on their allotted stage, size the width of a handkerchief. That was a Tuesday. The very next day, the same venue was hosting Paul McCartney. The difference is time equals zeros and multitudes. Only the strong survive. And the songs are the weapon.'

This is Oldham's redeeming shot. It may well prove, in time, to be his epitaph. It was the thing he had perceived instinctively, the secret he had always known. It always was, and always will be, about the songs.

Chapter Six

HEYDAY

Little did Andrew Oldham know what he had started when he pitched the Stones against the Beatles, dividing the country and by default the world in a war of cultural rivalry that would rage, simmer and boil again in the twenty-first century. Even though the fans who engaged originally in this petty clash of allegiances have grown up, faded away, shuffled off this mortal coil[1] or could give no further toss, the feud persists, thanks to the artists themselves.

I'm having you on? Let's see. Witness restrained but widely reported rantings by Sir Paul McCartney during the resumed Rolling Stones tour of America, autumn and winter 2021. While it may never have mushroomed to Liverpool v Manchester United or Spurs v Arsenal proportions, passion provoked by the discussion continues to rile the head rockers to an almost Premier League degree. Why do they care? Might it be time to get a life? Why on earth would something so trivial still bother them after all these years? Excellent questions. When Macca dismissed his former group's arch-rivals as 'a blues covers band', explaining that the Beatles' net was 'cast a bit wider than theirs', was he goading Jagger deliberately, and asking for trouble? Whether he was or not, he got some. Mick lashed back, during the Stones' Los Angeles outing, with the tongue-in-cheek announcement that Paul was waiting patiently backstage, and was about to be 'joining us in a blues cover'. Many a true word spoken in jest.[2]

I have a soft spot for the rivalry, ironic or otherwise. It affords us an inkling of the searing energy and fierce competitiveness that drove these groups in their angry young days, forcing fans to follow one or the other but never in a million to dare to like both. Playground battles were fought over it. Tanksful of saliva were spat. Miles of hair were torn. Swear allegiance and fall on your sword, was the size of it. Whether or not all this conflict was inspired by the friction between gangs of mods and rockers, the rival British subcultures that reigned from the early 1960s into the first half of the following decade and later experienced a brief revival, it rapidly gained momentum. It's not hard to see why. The Stones were suggestive of the rockers: greasy, long-haired, black-leathered menaces on motorbikes, styled in the image of Hollywood heart-throb Marlon Brando in his 1953 hit film *The Wild One*, the original outlaw-biker movie. Their soundtrack was rock'n'roll, the music of American artists such as Bo Diddley, Elvis Presley, Eddie Cochran and Gene Vincent. The Beatles evoked some of the spirit of the mods, who had defined hairstyles, sharp suits and parkas, and who rode about on motor scooters. These were the soul boys, the aficionados of R&B, following British blues-inspired bands like the Who, the Yardbirds and the Small Faces.[3]

There was obviously musical overlap, as well as scope for interpretation. But neither the Beatles nor the Stones were oblivious of the significance of gang culture at a time of disaffected youth, rising drug abuse and a collective urge, at certain levels, to both destroy and self-destruct. We have all watched footage of both bands in their sixties incarnations, hounded and screamed at by hoards of hysterical girls leaking from every orifice. Bill Wyman recalled the stench of urine at shows not yet known as 'gigs' as 'unbearable'. But the thrust of their popularity did not depend exclusively on frenzied females. The Beatles' Hamburg residences saw them playing to shiploads of drunken, violent male sailors, their performances descending more often than not into furniture-and-skull-smashing brawls; while the Stones' appearances incited angry gangs of ferocious male youths to attempt to wreck stages, venues and vehicles, attacking security guards, riot police and each other. Not that the fans were mad at the band. It was the energy generated on stage that provoked their collective loss of self-control. As Mick Jagger remarked, the Stones were not the cause, they were the catalyst.

In those early days, where the Beatles went, the Stones followed. Anything they could do ... The latter clearly held the former in high esteem. After all, Ringo, George, John and Paul had reached the summit ahead of them, and had route maps to share, ropes to hand down, hard-won wisdom and experience to impart. But when the Beatles performed their last live concert at Candlestick Park, San Francisco, on 29 August 1966,[4] the Stones were just getting going ... and have hardly stopped since. The Beatles matured outwards, and away from each other. In order to grow and evolve creatively, they needed to go their separate ways. All four achieved success as solo artists. Had John Lennon not been assassinated in December 1980, a decade after the Beatles' official dissolution, it is perfectly reasonable to imagine that they would have found their way back to the mothership, their collective identity, and that the band would have ridden again. No chance? I like to think otherwise.

The Stones endured long periods of separation, particularly when Mick and Keith were feuding, during which every member of the band developed solo interests. Jagger and Richards may have given Lennon and McCartney a run for their money as one of the greatest songwriting duos in music history. But they couldn't light a candle to John, Paul or George in terms of solo achievement. Paul recorded twenty-six studio albums, four compilation albums, nine live albums, seven classical and five electronica, both solo and with Wings. John, working solo, with Plastic Ono Band and with his wife Yoko Ono, achieved eleven solo albums. George scored twelve solo albums, two live and four compilations. Mick managed four solo albums; Keith three; Bill six of his own and half a dozen with his post-Stones band, Bill Wyman's Rhythm Kings. Charlie was the most prolific solo Stone, releasing ten albums with the Charlie Watts Orchestra, his Quintet and his 'Tentet'. Pause to compare these busy drummers. Ringo enjoyed a string of hit singles during the early seventies, became a session musician for Tom Petty, Bob Dylan and more, forged new careers as a voice actor and author, and recorded twenty studio albums. It wasn't all about Mick'n'Keef and John'n'Paul.

So there remain valid reasons for the rivalries. While we can no longer compare 'Beatles' with 'Stones' – given that the former as a viable entity have not existed for more than fifty years, while the latter, to borrow back my own quote, still roam the world like rusty tanks without a war to go to,[5] sixty years after they were conceived – we can take vicarious pleasure from the all-too-evident fact that Jagger and Macca still ruffle each other's feathers. Who knew what was to come when the two bands paid tribute to one another on their respective album covers? Seen that? Check out the sleeve of 1967's *Sgt. Pepper's Lonely Hearts Club Band*, to find a doll wearing a striped sweater bearing the slogan 'WELCOME THE ROLLING STONES'. The Stones returned the favour on *Their Satanic Majesties Request*, working the faces of all four Beatles into the flower heads. That same year, John and Paul provided guest vocals on the tracks 'Sing This All Together' and 'We Love You' on the *Satanic Majesties* album, while Mick and Keith joined the Beatles for their historic telecast performance of 'All You Need Is Love'.

But animosity is insidious. Undischarged, it accrues. John had clearly harboured resentment against Mick and Keith for some considerable time, for having plagiarised the Beatles on *Satanic Majesties*. In his interview for Jann Wenner, editor of *Rolling Stone* magazine, he finally erupted.

'I would like to just list what we did and what the Stones did two months after, on every fuckin' album,' he raged. 'Every fuckin' thing we did, Mick does exactly the same. He imitates us. And I would like one of you fuckin' underground people to point it out, you know, *Satanic Majesties* is *Pepper*. "We Love You" (on which Paul and John sang backing vocals) – it's the most fuckin' bullshit. That's "All You Need Is Love".'

Had he been as mad as all that with them, however, would he and Yoko have pitched up to take part in the Stones' *Rock and Roll Circus* TV special? You may well ask. Then again, there's that line in 'Dig a Pony' from 1970's *Let It Be*, featuring John singing, 'I roll a stoney/Well, you can imitate everyone you know.' Incidentally, that's Brian Jones on sax on 'You Know My Name (Look Up the Number)', the B-side of the 'Let It Be' single. Jones was already dead by the time it was released. What was the message here?

Lennon's rambling, all-encompassing interview with Wenner, later published as a book, features John calling Mick 'a joke', and accusing him of 'fag dancing'.

'I was always very respectful about Mick and the Stones,' he points out, 'but he said a lot of sort of tarty things about the Beatles, which I am hurt by, because you know, *I* can knock the Beatles but don't let Mick Jagger knock them. I resent the implication that the Stones are like revolutionaries and that the Beatles weren't. If the Stones were or are, the Beatles really were too. But they are not in the same class, music-wise or power-wise. Never were.'

Cut to 1988, when the Beatles were inducted into America's prestigious Rock and Roll Hall of Fame. Who should be the inductor but Mick Jagger? Imagine Lennon revolving in his grave at Mick's speech.

'We went through some pretty strange times. We had a sort of … a lot of rivalry in those early years, and a little bit of friction, but we always ended up friends,' said Jagger. 'And I like to think we still are, cos they were some of the greatest times of our lives, and I'm really proud to be the one that leads them into the Rock and Roll Hall of Fame.'

The Stones themselves would be inducted the following year, by Pete Townshend. Ironic, then, that his bandmate Roger Daltrey should follow McCartney into the public Stones-pummelling in November 2021, dismissing them in less than flattering terms.

Asked during an interview about the Who's contemporaries, the veteran frontman responded, 'You've got to take your hat off to [Jagger]. He's the number one rock'n'roll performer. But as a band, if you were outside a pub and you heard that music coming out … some night, you'd think, "Well, that's a mediocre pub band!"'

McCartney, incidentally, was inducted into the Rock and Roll Hall of Fame a second time in 1999, as a solo artist. Ringo Starr was recognised too, in 2015. No such honour, to date, for any Stone man.

The guitarist should have taken heed of Mick's words, and kept his gob shut. We're talking Keith Richards, though, right? He has never been one to hold back when an opportunity arises to let rip and cause offence; which to his mind falls under the category of 'telling it like it is'. It was no holds barred during his interview with *Esquire* magazine, when he dissed *Sgt. Pepper* as 'rubbish'. He couldn't help himself.

'The Beatles sounded great when they were the Beatles,' he sneered. 'But there's not a lot of roots in that music. I think they got carried away. Why not? If you're the Beatles in the sixties, you just get carried away. You forget what it is you wanted to do. You're starting to do *Sgt. Pepper*. Some people think it's a genius album, but I think it's a mish-mash of rubbish. Kinda like *Satanic Majesties*. If you can make a load of shit, so can we.' What were the millions of Beatles fans in every corner of the globe who have long prayed to *Sgt. Pepper's Lonely Hearts Club Band* as the greatest album ever made, supposed to make of that?

Paul McCartney may have seethed, but he kept his counsel. We now know that he was biding his time. An opportunity to redress the balance leapt out at him in 2020, when, during an interview with American shock-jock broadcaster Howard Stern, Macca was invited to comment on Stern's personal assessment that the Beatles really were the greatest of the two rival bands.

'You know you're going to persuade me to agree with that one,' responded Paul, God love him. 'They are rooted in the blues. When they are writing stuff, it has to do with the blues. We had a little more influences [sic]. There's a lot of differences, and I love the Stones, but I'm with you: the Beatles were better.' Then he got provocative, hinting strongly that the Stones were blatant copyists.

'We started to notice that whatever we did, the Stones sort of did it shortly thereafter. We went to America and we had huge success. Then the Stones went to America. We did *Sgt. Pepper*. The Stones did a psychedelic album. There's a lot of that. We were great friends. Still are. Kind of. We admire each other. The Stones are a fantastic group. I go see them every time they're out. They're a great, great band.'

A bit too great, in the end, for McCartney's liking? And did Jagger have the last laugh on that occasion?

'That's so funny. He's a sweetheart,' said Mick of Macca on Zane Lowe's Apple Music show. 'There's obviously no competition.' The big difference between the two groups, he explained painstakingly, 'is that the Rolling Stones have been a big concert band in other decades and other eras when the Beatles never even did an arena tour ... with a decent sound system. They broke up before that business had started' – the touring business, he means. 'That started in 1969, and the Beatles never experienced that. Yet they played and did a great gig. I was there: at Shea Stadium. But the Stones went on. We started doing stadium gigs in the seventies, and are still doing them now. That's the really big difference between the two bands. One band is unbelievably, luckily still playing in stadiums, and then the other band doesn't exist.'

Mick must have missed every Wings tour between 1972 and 1979, including Wings Over the World (a phenomenal sixty-six shows) as well as everything solo that Macca has done since: a modest sixteen solo concert tours, nine of them global. Not 'Beatles' tours as such, granted, but major sell-out tours nonetheless, by the man who represents one half of the most successful songwriting duo in history. In a nutshell? Shall we? Over a career lasting sixty years, the Rolling Stones have scored eight UK No. 1 singles and twelve No. 1 albums, and have shifted 200 million albums worldwide; while over a period of only eight years, counting from 1962 when Ringo joined the band to 1970 when Paul officially left (even though John had declared he was quitting the previous September), the Beatles notched up seventeen UK No. 1 singles and fifteen No. 1 albums. They have sold, to date, around the world, in excess of 600 million albums. They spent 176 weeks at No. 1, longer than any other artist, ever. The figures tell it. Perspective is all. In the words of Henry David Thoreau, 'It's not what you look at that matters, it's what you see.'[6] Mick might be kidding himself a little. He knows.

*

Following the Oldham-Easton takeover, recalled John Mansfield, 'we were no longer allowed to pay the Stones in person. In future, all cheques or postal orders were to be sent directly to Eric Easton's office. We later received a letter from their accountants, requesting confirmation of any monies that we had paid to the band.' Which was not the least of the changes wrought by the new Stones' management. The apostrophe had to be dropped from 'Rollin'', decreed Andrew, and its 'g' restored. Stu, too, was dropped. Brian Jones was the designated executioner. He found this particularly galling, given that Ian Stewart had been both his friend and pianist long before they met Mick and Keith. Bill Wyman began to quake in his Chelsea boots at this point, fearing that he would be the next to be axed – for being too old, too square, a boring married father, because his feminine hands were not really big enough for the bass. Not even Keith, who had to be one of the least dispensable, measured up to Loog Oldham's vision. The 's' would have to go from the end of his surname, for a start. 'Oldham felt it was somehow better for their profile!' said Mansfield. ¿Qué?

'He (Andrew) wasn't interested in the music,' claimed Mansfield. 'Such issues were of no consequence to him, it was all about maximising exposure and making the most money he could. He also wanted Jagger and Richards to start writing their own material, to avoid paying royalties.'

Was it that? I wonder. Mansfield had his reasons for feeling embittered. Andrew may well have had crazy ideas about world domination. He had met Phil Spector, and was desperate to reinvent himself in the wizard American producer's image, despite the fact that he had not an hour of production experience to his name. But so many were doing it and getting away with it back then. He wasn't the only one. He clearly has a genuine feel for and love of music, and is ignited to this day by brilliant songs. I could tell that simply from chatting to him over email. Isn't it that he had found the key to the Stones' success and longevity? That it had occurred to him that they would have to follow the glaring example set by John Lennon and Paul McCartney and roll their own, if they were to have a hope in hell of getting anywhere? Sure, he probably did have pound signs revolving before his eyes at the same time. Shame on him? Get real. He could hardly have called himself a music biz manager otherwise.

'It was all about the rough edges,' declares legendary publicist Keith Altham, who would soon find himself working with the band. 'The Beatles were taken by Brian Epstein and had their rough edges knocked off. Andrew Oldham thought that this was the way to go. The Beatles were four Elvises. Oldham wanted his own five Elvises. Not six, that was too many, so bye bye Stu, who I was very fond of. It then dawned on him that, instead of merely copying the Beatles, he'd make more impact by having them do the exact opposite. The main lesson he had learned from Epstein was attention to detail. Make it leaner, shorter, better. Knock the odd letter off a name – especially an 's', which dilutes its impact by making it sound plural – and the man who goes by it becomes singularly harder.

By the time Keith added his 's' back on, he didn't need it any more. But the most significant change of all was Andrew locking Mick and Keith in the kitchen and making them write songs. It was the best thing he ever did for them. Maybe they haven't realised it yet. Maybe, given their penchant for rewriting history – not uncommon among artists, by the way – they just thought it was their own idea.'

It has been said that the animosity that flared between Brian and Andrew after he was forced to offload Stu continued to build until it began to deprive poor Brian of reason. As early as the band's first showcase on TV's *Ready Steady Go!*, Brian feared that the rug was being pulled from under him. Jagger, supported and egged on by Oldham, was already stealing Jones's thunder and assuming the role of Stones leader and mouthpiece. Jones didn't have a leg to collapse on. How could he be a frontman if he couldn't even sing? It was a fact of which he was reminded at regular intervals. But it had been angel-faced Brian with his golden hair, perfect pout and undulating body who had, from the outset, been the band's principal showman. It was he who had whipped up audience participation by getting down among the guys and gals, shaking tambourines and maracas in their pretty faces (he avoided the ugly ones), playing instruments while he was flat on his back, jumping around like a lad insane. Stagecraft came naturally to Brian. He was born with it, more fool him. Mick had to learn, which made him the lucky one. Once Jagger had mastered the dark arts and had embraced his power, he was lethal and there was no stopping him.

Perhaps Brian knew even at that stage that his days with the Stones were numbered. But there were Stones thrills and spills galore to come before the Jones boy succumbed. There was America. It was not on Brian's casual virtuoso musicality that this new band would voyage into the Promised Land of all their musical dreams since they had been wet behind the ears and everywhere else. It was Jagger's reptilian ruthlessness that drove them onwards into the terrifying oblivion of superstardom.

Unlike most other artists of their era, they do not resort to the cloak, the smoke, the masks, the wigs and the rig-outs to render themselves oven-ready. They are who they will become. Their stage personas are not inflated versions of their usual selves. There are no 'usual selves' to be had, here. What you see is what you will never get. Authentic in their forsakenness, they are doomed to succeed.

Mists rise in shrouds over the vast and distant past, playing tricks with dates and times and woebegoneness. Do the Stones in their dotage chortle as they look back, or don't they dare, and just keep squinting ahead? Is the big-break thing ever a blessing, or always damnation? Though most would have exchanged, in a heartbeat, their own life for those of the Stones, few could have guessed at the volume of blood that would be spilled. It is coming.

Chapter Seven

REACTION

Blink and they might have missed it, it happened so fast. At least, it appeared to. On Friday 10 May 1963, the Stones checked into Olympic Sound Studios near London's Marble Arch[1] to record what would turn out to be their debut single: a cover of Chuck Berry's rich, catchy 'Come On'. The man who once said, 'I wanted to play the blues, but I wasn't blue enough; we always had food on the table' had forged a reputation as the definitive reeler and rocker, but he failed to score a hit with this one. The decision to cover it was probably Keith's: 'Chuck had the swing,' swooned Richards, one of his biggest fans. 'There's rock, but it's the roll that counts.'

If there had ever been a more clear-cut case of the blind leading the blind, it might not be on record. 'I'm the producer, and this is the first session that I've ever handled,' declared a defiant Andrew Oldham. 'I don't know a damned thing about recording, or music for that matter.' His disingenuity was disarming. 'A bunch of bloody amateurs going to make a hit single,' was Mick's recollection. He didn't care for the band's take or Oldham's skittish production. Nor did the others. But listening to it now, almost sixty years down the line, the recording has an innocent, moreish charm. The Stones' cover may be shriller and less stately than Chuck's. Its raw twang, clipped vocal and urgent harmonica, wailed by Brian Jones at the top of his game, do nicely. Mick's comically stretched vowels – 'Cum-OUNN!' – linger in the ear long after the conclusive drum flourish. Some expected the Stones to be a flash in the pan and for it to have been all downhill from there. Some ate their words. Released on 7 June, 'Come On' managed a respectable No. 21. Their follow-up, John and Paul's 'I Wanna Be Your Man', released on 1 November, was the first song ever performed on BBC's *Top of the Pops*, presented by the now-disgraced late DJ Jimmy Savile on New Year's Day 1964. The Stones' new record was at No. 13. Their appearance on the show took it up a notch, where it peaked, at No. 12. Getting warmer. At No. 1 that week were the Beatles, with 'I Want to Hold Your Hand'.

The following month, they were back with 'Not Fade Away', their cover of Buddy Holly's and Norman Petty's composition for the Crickets, released as the B-side of 'Oh, Boy!' in 1957. The Stones' version made it to No. 3 in the UK, and was also their first US release, where it achieved a modest No. 48. 'It's All Over Now', written by Bobby Womack and his sister-in-law Shirley Womack and released by the Womack brothers as the Valentinos, scored them their first British No. 1 in July 1964.

'We cut that in Chess Studios the first time in Chicago,' recalled Keith. 'The year before, we were playing bars in England, you know. And then we're walking into Chess Studios, which was where all of these records had been made that were so important to us. Now and again in life you get this feeling that you've died and gone to heaven. Luckily, neither was true. American studios at that time were so much more together than in England. I mean, they had some good stuff in England, but they didn't have knowledge of how to record it. We were lucky. There were a couple of guys like Glyn Johns in England who had a rough idea of recording. But the way you'd get a sound in an American studio in those days was the difference between day and night, compared to working in England or Europe. I mean, these cats, in America, they'd done it already. So to work in Chess was our first taste of American record[ing].'

The first of five consecutive chart-toppers, it would be followed by 'Little Red Rooster' (November 1964), the song recorded for Chess by Howlin' Wolf as 'The Red Rooster' three years earlier. The Stones' second single to conquer the UK chart, it spent a single week at the top that December. 'The Last Time' (March 1965), co-produced by Phil Spector and recorded at RCA Studios in Hollywood that January, was their first 'original' song to be released as a British A-side. Except that it wasn't entirely original. Do yourself a favour and pull up the Staple Singers' 1954 recording 'This May Be the Last Time' a traditional gospel song. Its eerie, haunting holler will never leave you. Keith Richards later confessed that the Stones had ripped it off. Ah down' knouw.[2] '(I Can't Get No) Satisfaction' ensued (September 1965), as did 'Get Off of My Cloud' (November 1965). There would be three further No. 1s, making eight in total. In May 1966, 'Paint It, Black'; in June 1968, 'Jumpin' Jack Flash'; and in July 1969, 'Honky Tonk Women'. Pause to reflect on the startling fact that the Stones enjoyed their last No. 1 record fifty-three years ago.

Back we go, to the song that changed everything: not only in the field of musical endeavour, but in terms of moving on from the past, grabbing the present by the short'n'curlies, and embracing a brave new future. To the chroniclers of music history, this sharp encapsulation of the status quo, this incisive slice of social commentary, was a watershed.

'(I Can't Get No) Satisfaction' remains one of the world's most popular songs. 'It was the song that really made the Rolling Stones,' Jagger told *Rolling Stone* magazine's Jann Wenner in 1995. '[It] changed us from just another band into a huge, monster band. You always need one song. We weren't American, and America was a big thing and we always wanted to make it [t]here. It was very impressive, the way that song and the popularity of the band became a worldwide thing. It's a signature tune, really … a kind of signature that everyone knows. It has a very catchy title. It has a very catchy guitar riff. It has a great guitar sound, which was original at that time. And it captures a spirit of the times, which is very important in those kinds of songs. Which was alienation. Or it's a bit more than that, maybe, but a kind of sexual alienation. Alienation's not quite the right word, but it's one word that would do.' Gotcha.

There was no shortage of sixties artists establishing names and reputations as capturers of the zeitgeist. But it wasn't only about harnessing prevailing moods, breaking beliefs and challenging values. The times were a-changin' across the board. Music seemed almost to rise to a new self-imposed remit to deliver on multiple levels, reflecting social progress and enlightenment as never before. Many artists sought to achieve popularity not only as entertainers but also as provocateurs of thought.

They hunkered down to write songs that projected alternative viewpoints, expressed objection or took a stand. The Greenwich Village folk revival scene that flourished in the neighbourhood's coffee houses is credited as the genesis of the sixties. It delivered the likes of Pete Seeger, Judy Collins, Woody Guthrie, and Peter, Paul and Mary. It offered up Joan Baez and Bob Dylan: musicians who set themselves the mighty task of changing the world with songs. The soundtrack of '64 featured Dylan's 'Only a Pawn in their Game', Buffy Sainte-Marie's 'Universal Soldier' and Sam Cooke's 'A Change is Gonna Come'. Within four years, Godfather of soul James Brown was funking his way through 'Say It Loud: I'm Black and Proud': a new national anthem. The 1960s came to be regarded as the golden age of the protest song, inspired by causes from civil rights to Vietnam. Protest marches and sit-ins needed a soundtrack. The counterculture and hippy movement preached peace, love and wretched longing for a utopian world.

Bob Dylan, a key figure in the protest movement, influenced both the Beatles and the Stones. His songs were less about specific events, more theme-focused and intent on raising awareness. He would later distance himself from the movement, but not before he had tentacled into the cerebral lobes and creative muscles of those who followed him. Artists like the Stones, Pete Townshend and especially the Beatles. They discovered him via his second studio album, 1963's *The Freewheelin' Bob Dylan*, and met him in person in August 1964 at New York's Delmonico Hotel. He introduced them to marijuana. Their drug use soared, as did their courage. They began to experiment beyond the accepted boundaries of popular songwriting. 'I started being *me* about the songs, not writing them objectively but subjectively,' commented John Lennon. 'I'd started thinking about my own emotions ... instead of projecting myself into a situation, I would try to express what I felt about myself ... it was Dylan who helped me realise that.' He wasn't the only one. McCartney had hitched to the same paddle. Check out John's 'I'm a Loser', 'In My Life', 'You've Got to Hide Your Love Away', and Paul's 'I'll Follow the Sun' and 'Yesterday'.

It was no longer enough to get up, look pretty and strum and hum some ditty of the boy-meets-girl, happy-ever-after, babe-you-broke-my-heart variety. The shifting socio-political landscape and changing sensibilities demanded much more. Jagger was well aware of this. He had identified Dylan as a major exponent of the new songwriting long before he flew the family nest.

'I was playing Bob Dylan records at my parents' home when he was still an acoustic folk singer,' Mick said. 'But he was already very important and his lyrics were on point. The delivery isn't just the words, it's the accentuation and the moods and twists he puts on them. His greatness lies in the body of work.'

Mick later picked out his all-time favourite Dylan song: 'Desolation Row', recorded in August 1965 and released on the *Highway 61 Revisited* album. One of Zimmerman's greatest songs, it wraps sinister imagery and worrying scenarios in fine layers of sublime melody, deft guitar work and a compelling, unforgettable vocal. What is that if not a direct influence on the songwriting of the Rolling Stones? Dylan rated the Stones in return. '[They] are truly the greatest rock'n'roll band in the world, and always will be,' he said. 'The *last*, too. Everything that came after them, metal, rap, punk, new wave, pop-rock, you name it … you can trace it all back to the Rolling Stones. They were the first and last, and no one's ever done it better.'

'Satisfaction', a classic from the moment it was born, demonstrated beyond doubt that the Stones were more than they were cracked down to be. Much more than rock'n'roll, this song was rock and pop's answer to the Greenwich Village folk theme. Its hard-drive sound provided the perfect vehicle for unexpected lyrics expressing dissatisfaction in the status quo. Its tight, sneery lyrics projected anger and exasperation in superficial obsessions such as materialism and consumerism. It confronted sexual frustration. It raged against the confining, contradictory, controlling attitude of the older generation towards the sex lives of the young. It connected and chimed perfectly with its target audience. It was their breakthrough.

The story of the song's conception is legendary. Keith Richards created its immortal riff without knowing he had done so. Just ahead of the band's 1965 North American tour, he popped awake one night in bed in his London flat – 'I slept with a guitar in those days' – and committed a three-note riff, some basic chords, the elementary refrain and forty minutes' worth of snoring to the Philips cassette recorder that was lying beside his bed, there on standby to capture flashes of inspiration. He then dropped back into a deep sleep. He later awoke to find a recording on his machine that he had no recollection of having put there.

Jagger suspected that Keith's subconscious had dredged a memory of Chuck Berry's 1955 song '30 Days', featuring the line 'I don't get no satisfaction from the judge'. Not that a little thing like possible plagiarism was going to stop them. Mick started to work up the song, attacking the advertising and media industries in graphic terms. He and Keith began to hone it together once they hit American soil and started their trek across the states. In Chicago, they had a go at recording it at Chess Records. They weren't satisfied. They razored it down at RCA's studios in Los Angeles with the help of the infamous Gibson Fuzz Box, which Keith had intended as a placeholder until they could get a horn section in. But the buzzy, urgent energy imparted by the fuzz box gave the song something unique and addictive. A vote was taken, and the horns were off the case. Mick and Keith, going on twenty-two and on the threshold of a career they could never have dared to dream of, had just created their greatest ever hit.

'The fuzz tone had never been heard before anywhere, and that's the sound that caught everybody's imagination,' said Keith in *Life*. 'As far as I was concerned, that was just the dub. [But] ten days on the road and it's No. 1 nationally. The record of the summer of '65 ... I learned that lesson – sometimes you can overwork things. Not everything's designed for your taste and your taste alone.'

Perhaps the most extraordinary thing about 'Satisfaction' was that it emerged at a time when it could have been sunk by a barrage of greatest hits by other artists; records by acts so powerful that they ought to have seen it off. As the British Invasion marched on, embracing new groups all the time including Freddie and the Dreamers and Herman's Hermits; as the Beach Boys kept building their surf-around sound with 'Help Me Rhonda' and 'California Girls'; as Dylan went electric at the Newport Jazz Festival, Rhode Island, and performed his first rock'n'roll set to the dismay of his fans, and the Beatles played New York's Shea Stadium; as Motown's Supremes triumphed with 'Stop in the Name of Love' and the Four Tops with 'I Can't Help Myself (Sugar Pie, Honey Bunch)', the Byrds with 'Mr

Tambourine Man', the Yardbirds with 'For Your Love' and Sonny and Cher with 'I Got You Babe' ... up swaggered these cheeky-boy Stones with the cut to eclipse them all.

But 'Satisfaction' was more than a record. It was more than a song. We could stick our necks out and say that it was nothing less than a clarion call to sixties youth, an exhortation to quit the flock, recognise an emperor in the altogether when they saw one, and to say it loud and proud. If not exactly a 'protest', it was a song with the requisite anti-Establishment message. Key to its phenomenal success was that its young, impressionable listeners were dissatisfied too. They felt as the Stones felt. It was as though the songwriters had tapped into their brains and had been jump-started by their own emotions. Relatively tame by modern standards, the song was raw and controversial for its time. The older generation, the so-called Establishment, perceived it as a nuclear threat. Not only were its lyrics aggressive, but its sound, its attitude and the bile with which they performed it constituted an all-out attack.

Crucial to its success was the fact that the band, who were in the middle of their third outing to the States, performed the song on American television before the single appeared. Just over a fortnight ahead of its release on 6 June 1965, they debuted 'Satisfaction' on the Los Angeles ABC show *Shindig!* (when the line 'trying to make some girl', interpreted as a boy attempting to coerce a girl into sexual intercourse, was censored. This would happen again on *The Ed Sullivan Show* the following year. Both must have missed the obscure, in those days offensive references to menstruation).[3] The turnout to the university and small-stadium shows had hitherto been modest. After their latest television exposure, the single climbed the Billboard Hot 100, felled the Four Tops and snatched the No. 1 slot as easy as pie. It shifted half a million copies over the first eight weeks, lingered on the chart for a further six, and earned the band their first gold record from the Recording Industry Association of America. The song that marked the true beginning of their matchless career would never go away.

'Satisfaction' made it to the runner-up position on *Rolling Stone* magazine's '500 Greatest Songs of All Time' list in 2004, behind Bob Dylan's 'Like a Rolling Stone'. Seventeen years later, when the list was at long last updated, it had dropped. The 2021 reckoning featured Aretha Franklin in the top slot with her version of Otis Redding's 'Respect'. Second was Public Enemy's 'Fight the Power'. The Beatles came in at No. 7 with 'Strawberry Fields Forever', and at No. 15 with 'I Want to Hold Your Hand'. John Lennon made No. 19 with 'Imagine'. The 1970s turned out to be the best-represented era in the whole update, cited by the publication as the decade that resonates most with younger audiences. The times, they a-change yet again. Dylan's previous chart-topper had slipped to No. 4. The Stones bagged the No. 13 slot with 'Gimme Shelter'. 'Satisfaction', now languishing at No. 31, had been displaced. What the hell, it's not going anywhere.

Chapter Eight

MARIANNE

The Edith Grove hellhole having at last been abandoned during the summer of 1963, Mick and Keith relocated to a Kilburn flatshare with Andrew Oldham. Brian moved in with yet another new girlfriend's family in Windsor. Charlie was desperate to marry his fiancée Shirley, but Mick and Andrew denied him permission. Who did they think they were?! They must have taken their lead from Brian Epstein, who forced John Lennon to conceal both his marriage to pregnant girlfriend Cynthia Powell and the birth of their baby Julian, because news of both would 'damage the reputation' of the Beatles. Likewise, a married Stone was an oxymoron, and something that could only be disastrous for their image. There wasn't much that they could do about Bill, already a husband when he came on board. But he was only an auxiliary member, so blind eyes were turned.

Keith seemed to be take-it-or-leave-it about women most of the time, except when they were on the road with irresistible females such as Phil Spector's Ronettes. Mick, on the other hand, was shameless, having his cake and eating it wherever he could. While projecting as footloose and fancy-free to the band's hoards of hopeful, hysterical fans, and getting his end away with as many of them as possible, he had for some time been embroiled in a semi-covert, tempestuous affair with his first love. She may only have been a trainee secretary, but his pretty wannabe model and actress Chrissie came with an impressive pedigree. Her sister was Jean Shrimpton, 'the Shrimp', famous model and partner of celebrity photographer David

Bailey. Mick had met his posh-totty builder's daughter at John Mansfield's Windsor Ricky Tick club, on 11 January 1963.

'Chrissie had been a fan of Mick's for several months, having seen them play at Ealing,' said John. 'Not happy to be at the back (the venue being packed by the time she made it there, through arctic conditions), she climbed on to a table and clambered into the fish nets dangling from the ceiling. Over the heads of the fans, she proceeded to crawl towards the band, helped onwards by those underneath paddling her towards the stage with their hands. This was "crowd surfing" before it had been invented. As she reached her goal, the net finally gave way and Brian had to catch her. She had literally fallen for Mick!'

The couple moved in together. But home life was not harmonious, thanks to Mick's relentless womanising. She'd find out about the latest, he'd weep and wail at her feet, she would take him back and he would do it again. He wrote 'Under My Thumb' about her. What drove him to be unfaithful? We know what: biology, novelty, ego, immaturity, commitment phobia, curiosity, opportunity, you name it. Because he was who he was, and therefore could.[1] If girls just wanna have fun, dirty dogs just wanna have sex, willy-nilly, with as many partners as possible. Because fame and fortune are nothing if not aphrodisiacs. Because what kind of man could Mick call himself if he didn't rise to the occasion and take advantage of all who were dropping in his lap and falling at his feet? Don't go there. Poor Chrissie, who only wanted happily-ever-after. With a rock star. I mean. But she was young, innocent and starry-eyed. She couldn't have known better. They got engaged, Mick's proposal undoubtedly prompted by yet another humiliating infidelity.

Chrissie got a job at the Stones' label Decca, going on to work for Andrew in the band's own management office. So that she could keep an eye on her wayward fiancé? As their popularity increased, and as female fans continued to invade their privacy and even their apartment, the relationship started to crumble. It would be destroyed, ultimately, by a girl Mick had first set eyes on at a party, when she was still a Reading convent schoolgirl on the verge of sitting her A levels. Brian, Keith and Andrew Oldham were all at the same party. Andrew waded in, visions of self-reinvention as the new Phil Spector with his own impressive stable of artists dancing in his head, and declared that he was going to make a star of the innocent seventeen-year-old. 'I saw an angel with big tits,' he famously said, 'and signed her.'

Marianne Faithfull was taken at the time, by Cambridge undergraduate John Dunbar. She had a post-exam plan to follow Dunbar to university, to read English Literature, Philosophy and Comparative Religion, and then to pursue a career in the theatre. Floored by her fragile beauty, her eye-popping architecture, her raspy voice and insouciant elegance, daringly eye-shadowed Oldham proffered his calling card, which bore the words 'Andrew Loog Oldham, darling'. He enquired, 'Can she sing?', didn't bother to wait for an answer and offered her a recording contract.

Marianne's debut was one of Mick's and Keith's first toddles into songwriting, the Elizabethan-flavoured ballad 'As Tears Go By'. It was inspired by 'As Time Goes By', the famous song from the 1942 Humphrey Bogart and Ingrid Bergman picture *Casablanca*. Andrew changed 'time' to 'tears', of course he did. The twelve-string acoustic guitar on her rendition was played by future Led Zeppelin star Jimmy Page. Recorded at Olympic Studios under the watchful eyes of Mick and Keith, and released on 24 August 1964, it shot to No. 9 and proved several of Oldham's points. Marianne would later claim that Mick and Keith wrote the song for her. She would eventually admit that they probably didn't. The Stones recorded it themselves a year later. Marianne re-recorded it when she was forty, twenty-three years after her first attempt: '... and at that moment I was exactly the right age and in the right frame of mind to sing it,' she wrote in her memoir *Faithfull.* 'It was then that I truly experienced the lyrical melancholy of the song for the first time.' The newly minted pop singer quit school, deserted her mother, and abandoned herself to relentless, gruelling, sexually abusive pop tours masquerading as stardom.

Two things about Marianne, apart from the obvious, made her irresistible to Mick. One, she had exotic and aristocratic roots, which impressed him, as he was already hobnobbing with gentry and royalty, and hoicking himself up in the world. Two, she was somebody else's, therefore a prize to be pilfered and won.

She was descended on her mother's side from Leopold Baron von Sacher-Masoch, author of *Venus in Furs* who lent his name to the syndrome masochism.[2] Her mother Eva, whose name matched that of Mick's mother, was Austro-Hungarian Baroness Erisso. Eva had danced in Berlin during the 1920s Weimar Republic era, returned to Vienna during Adolf Hitler's climb to power, was active during the resistance, and like her Jewish mother had been raped by occupying Russian Red Army troops. She met and married British army major Glynn Faithfull, a closet eccentric of Welsh descent, and returned with him to live in England, where they welcomed their only child. But Marian Evelyn's mismatched parents separated when she was six. Her father joined a commune, leaving mother and child to fend for themselves. A bitter divorce and greatly reduced circumstances led to her mother, who maintained delusions of grandeur, becoming a boarding school dance teacher, and subsequently scraping a living as a shoe shop assistant, a bus conductress and a café waitress.

When Marian was seven, she was enrolled as a 'charity boarder' at St Joseph's convent school in Reading. She converted to Catholicism. When she was seventeen, she was taken to a Cambridge university ball, and fell in love at first sight with almost twenty-one-year-old student Dunbar. One of John's great friends was Peter Asher, the brother of Paul McCartney's girlfriend, actress Jane Asher.[3] Peter had enjoyed pop chart success as half of Peter and Gordon. He invested generously in John's new business venture, the Indica art gallery and bookshop in London where John Lennon first met Yoko Ono. Along the way, she extended her name by two more letters, and glamourised herself with elongated pronunciation.

Her first face-to-face with Mick occurred at a *Ready Steady Go!* party, when the inebriated rocker approached her and emptied his champagne flute down her low-cut dress. If that was all he could think of to gain her attention, he failed to impress. Marianne was on the road with Roy Orbison when Dunbar travelled to see her, and proposed to her 'on Wigan Pier'.[4] Weighed down with guilt as a result of tour affairs with Gene Pitney, Allan Clarke of the Hollies and others, Marianne seized the opportunity to redeem herself. She was desperate to draw a line under her promiscuous lifestyle. 'The sixties and the to-hell-with-what-they-think attitude hadn't happened yet,' she reflected. 'Feminism wouldn't affect me for another fifteen years. There was John who I loved and wanted to marry

... He knew me very well, and he knew that if he asked me to marry him I would just say yes ... I had a child with the right man, and it was the best thing I ever did.' Does she still think that now?

Having aborted Gene Pitney's child, at a time when abortion was still illegal, Marianne was desperate for a baby to cleanse herself of both the sin and the crime.[5] Her wish was granted in April 1965, when she discovered that she was pregnant again. But while Dunbar was back at Cambridge sitting his finals, Bob Dylan landed in London. 'I wasn't simply a fan,' she admitted. 'I worshipped him ... I was quite aware that the tribute traditionally laid at the feet of pop stars by their female fans was sex. I was incredibly ambivalent. I was pregnant, I was about to be married ... and what [John] didn't know might not hurt him ...' The fantasy lingered for a bit. Bob was writing a poem about her, he told her. That old chestnut. She informed him she was with child and immediately regretted it. He threw her out, perhaps fearful that she might be planning to pin the deed on him. She married John in Cambridge the following month. His best man was Peter Asher. They honeymooned, predictably, in Paris. Just before the bride's nineteenth birthday, she gave birth to their baby Nicholas. How fucked up was all this, how drugged, how detached, how dismally sixties?

And, wait, this is where it gets complicated. Brian Jones is by now with Anita Pallenberg, a consuming, exotic, alien creature who lures Marianne under her wing. Marianne, bored and trapped by young motherhood, who is still recording and performing though her heart is hardly in it, who resents having to be the family breadwinner, who is fed up with tripping over the bodies of John's junkie pals all over the floors of their flat, spends less and less time at home with her husband and baby, and more and more time with Brian and Anita at their place. Keith Richards comes too. Anita is away one time, they are doing a ton of drugs, and Brian finds his way into Marianne. He is so high on Mandrax that he cannot perform. Marianne crushes on 'beautiful, gorgeous' Keith, with whom she is falling in love, if she's not there already. Poor baby Nicholas is forgotten at home with his nanny, surrounded by drug addicts. Then Mick, who is still co-habiting with Chrissie, starts finding his way round to Brian's.

'There were lots of things I could have done at the age of nineteen that would have been more healthy than becoming Mick Jagger's inamorata,' wrote Marianne. 'In the end it doesn't matter that hearts got broken and that we sweated blood. Maybe the most you can expect from a relationship that goes bad is to come out of it with a few good songs.'

The last two standing in Mick's hotel room in Bristol one night after a Stones gig and an impromptu after-show, they wondered about getting it together and went for a walk to decide. Inevitably, they made love. She returned to London, then took off with Nicholas and nanny to a rented villa in Positano, Italy. She arrived to find a pile of messages from Jagger. When she decided to wend her way home, motherhood was clearly not her priority. She left the nanny to drive Nicholas back. That's a long drive for a young girl, from Positano to London. More than a thousand miles. With a baby in the back. In an unreliable car, which broke down, no one could get parts, there were no mobile phones, they didn't speak English, the child's wellbeing was endangered and all. But, hey.

On 15 December, when Chrissie and Mick were due to depart on holiday, she discovered that her boyfriend had disappeared. Chrissie phoned the Stones office, only to be told that their flights had been cancelled. Not even then did she twig that he must be with Marianne. But all alone in their palatial Harley House, Regent's Park apartment with her menagerie of pets – half a dozen cats, a dog and a cageful of birds – the devastated twenty-one year-old knew that he had deserted her. She gulped back a bottle of sleeping pills, not as a cry for help, she would later protest. Without Mick, her life was over, she said. She really wanted to die. This was the first attempt at suicide that would dog Mick's footsteps. It was by no means the last. When Mick wrote '19th Nervous Breakdown', was he oblivious?

Chrissie would never get to the bottom of what happened next. Maybe it was Mick who found her, and saved her life by getting her to St George's Hospital. She came to, only to find nursing sisters addressing her by a pseudonym. Whoever got her to hospital had taken the precaution of furnishing her with an alias, to throw the press off the scent. Perhaps the realisation that Mick's public image was more prized than her life was Chrissie's first step on the road to recovery.

She had little say in the way things unravelled. Wheelchaired into a truck, she was conveyed to a private clinic in North London, drugged to the false eyelashes and subjected to sleep therapy. She eventually managed to contact her parents, who came to the rescue and carried her home. Only then did she read in the papers about Marianne Faithfull. When she composed herself sufficiently to return to Harley House to collect her things, she found that the locks had been changed.

But what was the old slut Mick on? Nothing more potent or more disastrous than testosterone. It controlled him, that much is obvious. Behind Marianne's back, he tracked Chrissie down to her new address and started turning up at all hours, demanding sex. Perhaps convincing herself that he loved her after all, and not recognising that she was being used – women crave romance, men just want breasts – she put up no fight. But whenever their paths crossed at parties, he simply ignored her. Drained of pride and confidence, she said nothing. When he stopped coming round after a year or so, the blessing was mixed.

Did Chrissie find her happily-ever-after? Kinda sorta. After falling for another rocker, Steve Marriott of the Small Faces – once bitten, forever smitten, if only by the lifestyle – she withdrew from the swinging London scene that was growing a bit threadbare and boring anyway. She married a normal guy, and had a couple of normal kids. She studied sociology, perhaps in an attempt to make sense of the everywhere and nowhere years. Did she follow Mick's phenomenal career down the decades, watch the fantasy unravel and lament to herself, 'All that and more could have been mine'? Or did she thank her lucky stars that she'd had a lucky escape? I want to say the latter.

Marianne, too, would be discarded. Not just yet. When someone told her that Mick had actually wanted to get with the actress Julie Christie, and set his cap at Miss Faithfull only when he found out he couldn't have Julie, she was neither surprised nor miffed. She put it down to his 'Dolly Fixation'. It suggests the strong possibility, more or less proven since, that ordinary-mortal females would never satisfy him. Only the most exaggerated specimens of beauty and femininity were good enough for Jagger. It speaks volumes about his personal insecurity. He would thenceforth wear his women the way a woman flaunts a designer handbag: rare, gorgeous, impossibly stylish, outrageously expensive, the best that money can buy.

Only a real man loves a woman for qualities other than her reflection. Only a confident, carefree woman settles for (and admits to) the thirty-quid fake.

*

Life with Mick had its compensations. He was a 'genuine haven', Marianne said. He was 'affectionate, interesting, funny and very attentive. He called me constantly. He wasn't fucked up like Brian, and he didn't do drugs (those came later). You could actually lead a life with Mick.' She acknowledged that his money helped: she no longer had to work, not for the dosh, anyway. She dared to reconsider her theatrical aspirations. In quiet, contemplative moments, she had her misgivings. Certain things she had found disturbing about Andrew, she was beginning to recognise in Mick.

'[They] were birds of a feather. [Mick] was camp and he wore make-up, at a time when this was still very unusual. I had an inkling that there was a sexual undercurrent between them. I think I knew in some part of my mind that Mick was bisexual ... but what I somehow thought that meant was that he would be nicer to me. "Real men" scared me, but Andrew didn't, and Mick felt safe and easy to be around.'

You see where she was going with this. She actually wanted a 'real man'. The one that she wanted was Keith. She turned to the Stones' new business manager Allen Klein for advice, inexplicably, and confessed that her heart lay elsewhere. Rottweiler Klein warned her that Mick would be destroyed by such betrayal. Klein was unlikely to have been prioritising Mick's personal wellbeing as he articulated those words. If she dumped Mick for his boyhood pal, bandmate and crucially his songwriting partner, she would kill the Rolling Stones. Persuading Marianne to stick with Mick and leave Keith well alone was in Klein's best interests, not hers.

Marianne, oblivious of financial implications, heeded Klein's words. Still, one for the road, baby, shall we? Why not? She wound up at Brian and Anita's. The cat was away. She dropped acid with Brian, Keith and Tara Browne, their friend the Guinness heir, fully aware that they all wanted to have sex with her. She fumbled with Brian, but something made her get the hell out. She found her way back to the marital abode. And then the phone rang. It was Keith. He picked her up in a cab, and they went back to the May Fair Hotel, where Marianne had been staying prior to the acid trip.

And that, she said, 'was the night I ended up with Keith. It was a wonderful night of sex. As a matter of fact, that night with Keith was the best night I've ever had in my life … It was sublime. I was in heaven. I had always been in love with Keith, but very shyly. Now I was totally bowled over.'

But the over-endowed cherub's ecstasy was short-lived. As he was dressing to leave the next morning, the guitarist uttered unforgettably crushing words: 'You know who really has it bad for you, don't you? … Go on, love, give him a jingle, he'll fall off his chair. He's not that bad when you get to know him, you know.'

And she simply accepted it. Passed like a box of Turkish Delight from Brian to Mick to Keith, then back to Mick, Marianne became the first unofficial Stones broad. Had she been a little older, a lot wiser, she would have told Keith in no uncertain terms that she loved him. Perhaps she was wiser than she knew. Something stopped her. She must have known already that Keith was in love with Brian's girlfriend Anita. He would screw whoever he liked, but he had eyes only for her.

*

Marianne and Mick moved from Harley House into a place on Chester Square, and eventually into an impressive mansion on Cheyne Walk, beside the River Thames. She furnished it lavishly, on money her parsimonious partner was loath to spend. They did a lot of drugs – she worked her way from cannabis to cocaine before she got to heroin – had a lot of sex, and did a lot of talking – though not so much about meaningful, personal things; and only when Mick was not otherwise engaged with his endless stream of sycophantic visitors. She told him almost everything. Her lesbian affairs she mostly kept to herself. Mick's homoerotic fantasies about Keith, he shared with her openly, to her astonishment. It disturbed her because she was still in love with the guitarist. In 1968, when Mick decided to become a movie star and got involved with directors Donald Cammell and Nicolas Roeg on the notorious film *Performance*, Marianne's gut told her that she needed to distance herself from the 'seething cauldron' that the production rapidly became. She relocated to Ireland with her mother and three-year-old Nicholas. Now pregnant with Mick's baby, a daughter they named Corrina, she was determined that the child would have the best start possible, away from the madness that was consuming her partner in London. But she failed to carry the baby to term, and miscarried at seven months. Both she and Mick were devastated.

Any miscarriage is a terrible experience. But to lose a baby at such a late stage is a trauma from which it can be impossible to recover. Marianne would have been approximately twenty-eight weeks along, if she had calculated her dates correctly. Given that a full-term pregnancy lasts around forty weeks, and that a loss can only be termed a miscarriage up to twenty-four completed weeks of pregnancy, she technically suffered a stillbirth. When a baby dies before she is born, it is usual today for an obstetrician or midwife to induce labour. Marianne did not say whether she gave birth to Corrina naturally. Nor did she describe what happened afterwards. Was Mick with her? Did they get to see, even hold, their dead baby? Did they take photographs, keep the blanket that she was wrapped in, register her birth and give her a funeral (all of which are recognised aids to recovery)? Did her parents receive bereavement support? It seems unlikely. Marianne has indicated that she and Mick never discussed it. His way of dealing with it was to immerse himself in work, and in his affair with American actress Marsha Hunt. To add insult to injury, it was Marsha who would bear Mick his first child, in November 1970, their daughter Karis.

Mick and Marianne stayed together for four years. She knew that it was only a matter of time before her life, emotions and habits would become fodder for Stones' songs, just as Chrissie's had. Not only for songs, but for newspaper column inches and full-scale media speculation. Where Chrissie had seemed to lap up the attention, Marianne hated it. But she acknowledged that Mick's affairs inspired some classic hits.

They were the most beautiful couple of the 1960s. Marianne was Mick's muse. She beefed up his basic knowledge of dance, classical music and literature. She sophisticated him, and raised his game. It was she who gifted him a copy of Russian author Mikhail Bulgakov's *The Master and Margarita*: a controversial work of philosophy that dissects the concepts of good and evil and their impact on human life, concluding that the two are inter-dependent. It inspired the song that many regard as the Stones' finest and most defining hour, 'Sympathy for the Devil'. She stood by Mick throughout his 1967 drugs trial and brief imprisonment. But she was deeply disturbed by a double betrayal, by both her partner and her best friend Anita Pallenberg ... who had left Brian and was by then Keith's girlfriend. What happened? Anita, Mick's co-star in *Performance*, had slept with Mick for real (as opposed to 'just acting'). With three Stones notched on her bedpost, she had by default superseded Marianne as the band's unofficial broad. More of which, coming.

Marianne's depression was compounded by the mental frailty of Brian Jones, who never got over the betrayal by his bandmate. Brian's death by drowning in July 1969 seemed to tip Marianne over the edge. Like Anita and Keith, she and Mick stayed away from his funeral. Guilt? Fear? Couldn't be bothered? All three? The Jaggers set off for Sydney, Australia, where Mick was about to begin filming the doomed biopic *Ned Kelly*.[6] A hallucination of Brian drove Marianne to attempt suicide. She would have hurled herself from the window of their fourteenth-floor suite, but couldn't get it open because the wooden frame was sealed with paint. So she swallowed 150 Tuinal barbiturates, a highly addictive depressant, washed down with hot chocolate. Mick found her just in time, and rushed her to hospital. He had been here before, hadn't he. Marianne's mother flew down to assist. The last rites were administered at Marianne's bedside by a Roman Catholic priest. Mick wasn't there for that bit. He was back on set, going on with the show. He was also writing passionate letters to Marsha Hunt, while his suicidal girlfriend was recuperating.

*

Back in London, against steep odds, Marianne won the role of Ophelia in a Roundhouse production of *Hamlet*, opposite Anthony Hopkins as Claudius. Her understudy was Anjelica Huston. The leading lady took smack before she went on. She couldn't stand that Mick was still seeing Marsha, and was tormented by the gossip about him and Anita. So she started an affair of her own, with Italian artist Mario Schifano. Jagger was incensed. He turned up at the Berkshire cottage he had purchased for Marianne's mother Eva to find the lovers ensconced. A scrap ensued, which Jagger won. It was Mick who slept in the bed with Maid Marianne that night. Mario left at dawn. Era finito.

She left Mick in 1970. Helplessly addicted to heroin, she lost custody of Nicholas. She slept rough for two years in St Anne's Court, Soho, in those days the location of one of the world's most famous recording studios.[7] The Chinese restaurant in that cut-through, which we journalists used to frequent, served lethal cocktails in plastic washing-up bowls with a straw for each person. They kindly allowed her to wash her clothes on their premises. A stallholder nearby used to bring her cups of tea. She was on an NHS drugs programme at the time, and had to present in person daily at a local chemist's to get her twenty-five jacks of heroin. According to Catherine James, the American model whom Mick moved into Cheyne Walk soon after Marianne moved out, she tried desperately to get Mick to take her back. What baffles me is his callousness and meanness. How was he able to wash his hands of her and walk away?

Whatever. Their love affair was over. The woman who had inspired 'Wild Horses', 'Dear Doctor' and 'You Can't Always Get What You Want' was left penniless.

*

Marianne married punk rocker Ben Brierly in 1979, but they divorced seven years later. She submitted to treatment for her drug addiction in 1985, at Minnesota's Hazelden Clinic, where Eric Clapton had been a patient, and fell into a relationship with fellow inmate Howard Tose. When she told him it was over, he jumped to his death from the window of their Boston apartment. Her three-year third marriage, to American writer Giorgio Della Terza, also ended in divorce. In 2009, she separated from her lover of fifteen years, French record and film producer François Ravard, who had helped nurse her through her 2005 bout of breast cancer. He continued to act as her manager. She would recall a night when she lay recovering from cancer surgery in a Paris hospital room, when the phone rang at around two in the morning. 'This voice came on,' she said. '"Hello, Marian, how are you?" I'd know that voice anywhere, he's the only one who ever called me "Marian". We had a chat. It was lovely.' It was the first time in thirty-five years that Jagger had called her.

*

Cut to a plummy, rounded matron poking around Putney, nipping in for a loaf and out for a latte, and lurking in florists', choosing blooms. Nothing about her appearance at seventy-five spoke of the hell she had lived through. She had beaten heroin addiction, homelessness, bulimia, cancer, suicide attempts, a broken hip, post-operative sepsis, hepatitis C and emphysema, the result of her lifelong nicotine addiction. She had done endless therapy and had become a huge gay icon. Really? Maybe the bee-stung lips, cascading blonde locks and foppish fringe gave a clue. But noo, that can't be Marianne Faithfull, can it? Well, I'll be. Will you look at the thickened waist, her drooping jowls! She was a goddess! Why did she let herself go like that? Get over yourselves, carpers. The antediluvian rock star with the plugged-in barnet can still go leaping around a stage like a good'un to cries of 'He's incredible! Look at him go!' But his former lover, who is in fact three and a half years younger than him, is expected to recede modestly into the shadows, to conceal her ageing and to live out her twilight years under the counter. Her collapsing appearance is considered shameful, while his is endlessly celebrated. What? Human race, help me out here.

Covid-19 has taken its toll. Marianne fell victim to the virus in April 2020 and was hospitalised, during the recording of her twenty-first solo album, *She Walks in Beauty*. She emerged with memory loss, extreme exhaustion and lung damage, which meant that she could no longer sing. She was talking about the biopic, announced in February 2020, based on her memoir, *Faithfull*, that she wrote nearly thirty years ago. Lucy Boynton, she who played Freddie Mercury's girlfriend Mary Austin opposite Rami Malek in Queen's *Bohemian Rhapsody*, was set to play her in Ian Bonhôte's picture, as well as to exec-produce.

It is extraordinary to think that Marianne's pop career collapsed in 1967. Pouf, just like that. Her final pop recording, released in February that year, was 'Is This What I Get for Loving You?' Where were those who had benefited from her ticket sales and her recording royalties? Weren't we asking the same questions after the demise of Phil Lynott, Amy Winehouse, Prince, George Michael, Tom Petty and the rest? Why weren't they supported in their hours of need? But Marianne was world-famous for having been Mick's girlfriend, and for an allegedly misplaced

Mars bar. Not for her music. Even now, they still refer to her as a Rolling Stones muse.

'That's a shit thing to be,' she told the *Guardian* in 2021. It's a terrible job. You don't get any male muses, do you? Can you think of one? No.' But it wasn't the worst thing that ever happened to her. That was when she lost Nicholas. In many ways, she had only herself (and Jagger) to blame. She was only properly reunited with her son when he had children of his own. She returned from Paris to London to be close to him and her grandchildren. That blameless little boy whom she neglected so much, who was once abandoned by a thieving nanny in a strange house in Ireland and was found two days later, eating wallpaper off the walls, had made a success of his life. After having trained as a physicist at Manchester, Cambridge and Harvard universities during the late 1980s, he became a financial journalist, analyst and consultant, and has authored several books.[8]

There was always more to her. What became of her was too high a price to pay for her fleeting moment in pop's spotlight and a few so-what years on the arm of a rock star. Knowing full well that she had much more to offer, and envious of what Mick and Keith had made of themselves – as she explained, 'what pop music could become' – she went deeply into herself and emerged with 'Sister Morphine': 'an attempt to make art out of a pop song'. It was, she insisted, not about herself, nor based on her own experiences. She conceived it well before she became a junkie.

'By 1972 [she means 1971] when it came out on [the album] *Sticky Fingers* [as a new version recorded by the Stones], I was the character in the song,' she said. 'You have to be very careful what you write because a song is a gateway, and whatever it is you've summoned up may come through. It happened to Mick and Keith with that whole satanic business.'

Mick and Keith set Marianne's song to music, and her original recording of it became the B-side of her 1969 single 'Something Better'. You see, she was still trying. But she was not credited as co-writer of the song on the Stones' album. She had to resort to the law to achieve recognition. Where were Mick'n'Keef's manners? Why did they force the poor girl, who had been important to both of them, to suffer this indignity? It would not be until the 1994 Virgin Records re-issue of the Stones album back catalogue from *Sticky Fingers* to *Steel Wheels* that the record, as it were, would be set straight.

Feast your ears on Marianne's 1979 comeback, *Broken English*, featuring her eerie cover of Dr. Hook and the Medicine Show's 'The Ballad of Lucy Jordan'. It depicts a housewife's middle-aged disappointment and descent into mental breakdown. When she recorded it, Marianne was only thirty-three. Although she didn't write the song, it could have been autobiographical. The wistful desperation in that once sweet voice, shattered by heartbreak and substance abuse, is rendered terrifying by the undercurrent of Steve Winwood's insistent synth. It reached only No. 48 in the UK, but was a Top 20 hit across Europe. The album remains a masterpiece. *A Secret Life*, released in 1995, is also notable. I met her during her promotion of that one. We lunched. I liked her. I admired the small tattoo of a swallow on her left hand, between her thumb and her index finger, which she said she got in Italy in 1967. She was still with Jagger at that point. Bird tattoos are said to represent freedom and spirituality. They are also symbolic of peace, happiness and optimism.

'Perhaps I chose it because I wanted to fly away,' she laughed throatily. 'We all fantasise about having wings, and about taking to the skies to escape. I got right out of my comfort zone to have it, I can tell you. I was terrified of the tattooist. I think it was supposed to go higher up my arm, but I kept snatching it away. He only got as far as my hand, which had to do.

'But birds, yes. They are incredibly spiritual creatures. It's about going higher, about becoming more than you are. Sailors used to have swallow tattoos, didn't they. That must have been about hoping for a safe journey home. Perhaps that was what I was hoping for too.'

The album received 'mixed reviews'. Mine was favourable. My editor briefed me to pan it. I praised it anyway, and my interview with her was spiked. She was forty-nine. She needed us to like her poetic offering. No one but her got to read my feature. She was glad that I 'got it', she said. It was a commercial failure for Island Records. But honestly, it was and is good.

Her most recent work might be at best an acquired taste. 2021's 'poem album', *She Walks in Beauty*, features Marianne reciting eleven Romantic poems, including Thomas Hood's 'The Bridge of Sighs', John Keats's 'La Belle Dame Sans Merci', 'Ode to a Nightingale' and 'Ode to Autumn', Percy Bysshe Shelley's 'Ozymandias', a few by William Wordsworth including 'To the Moon', and Lord Byron's 'So We'll Go No More A Roving'. Perhaps she could have stopped short of Alfred, Lord Tennyson's 'The Lady of Shalott', which does go on a bit, mirrors cracking from side to side – hands up if you did it at school. What it is, this album, is the soundtrack of survival. Because, as Marianne has always known, there is a pared-down purity in poetry. There is a return to lost innocence. There is renewal.

All of her husk is still there. All of her fight remains. It's worth a listen between the lines, to savour her spirit. Three Rolling Stones fucked her, figuratively and actually. There's another side to that story. She is still living it.

Chapter Nine

ANITA

The stories of Stones' women are relevant because of what they reveal about their men. Hearing that Mick treated Chrissie and Marianne heartlessly, that he was serially unfaithful, had moths in his wallet and failed to support them after things fell apart – which he should have done, given that he was a rich celebrity and that the attention he attracted impinged upon both their privacy and their ability to recover – we recognise a pattern of behaviour from which Mick would never veer. He professed to welcome the baby he conceived with Marsha Hunt, until Karis was actually born. He then denied paternity, and left Marsha with no alternative but to launch a humiliating battle to force him to contribute to the cost of educating and raising her. Only years down the line would he forge a close relationship with his firstborn.

When his first wife Bianca filed for divorce after seven years of marriage, on grounds of his adultery, he lawyered her down to a fraction of her due. As for Jerry Hall: after fifteen years together, she discovered that he cheated on her with a future First Lady of France, actress Carla Bruni, only a day after Jerry had given birth to their third child, Georgia May. When she learned that Mick had conceived a son, Lucas, with yet another woman, Luciana Gimenez Morad, Jerry threw in the towel, before being deprived of the satisfaction of divorcing him, since their ceremony in Bali was not a legal marriage in the first place. As a result of which, Jerry bit the dust with a shameful settlement. If only in recognition of the fact that she had given him four children, he should have left her both dignified and comfortably off. Mick's victory, though, was hollow. That single act of gross disrespect diminished him. It turned factions of the public against him. Like he cared. All that mattered was the dosh in the bank. What he cared about was that it stayed there.

It must comfort Chrissie and Marianne a little to know they were not the only ones; that Mick behaved just as selfishly with the women who came next. A victim of his own rapaciousness, he was driven to pursue what he couldn't have – a monarch's sibling, a Madame Head of State, the spouse of a pal, a fellow musician's daughter, his best friend's girl – until he got her. Once his desire was satiated, he craved her no longer and went sniffing for someone else. This was not the kind of man to make a life with. Mick was never marriage material, a safe bet, someone who would keep himself only unto you so long as you both lived. They must have known. Yet still they fell at his feet, as predictably as autumn leaves.

Flattered by his initial rapt attention, they basked in his reflected glory and were bewitched by his wealth and fame. Not just the groupies and the party girls. Not just the models, the actresses, the television personalities and the porn stars he favoured. Not only the Americans and South Americans for whom he must have a soft spot (there having been many). Mick pulled women of every nationality, profession and walk of life. He seduced socialites, aristocrats, political wives. He bedded publishers, editors, photographers and journalists, perhaps to pay the media back. What about the workers, the nannies, cooks and housekeepers? Was that just a *droit de seigneur* thing? Did any of them truly believe they would be gifted the Jagger heart? Or were they well aware that they were being used and would soon be discarded, but dropped their drawers for the hell of it, perhaps thinking it might be something to tell the grandkids? Were they simply curious to know what it would be like, a rock around the cock of the world's most exaggerated sex symbol? Have many not wondered?

Even when Mick did commit himself to long-term relationships, it was only half-heartedly. His philandering broke the women who loved him. He seemed fascinated by females who gave the impression of not needing 'a man', yet who were in fact utterly dependent on them. He appeared to be enchanted by that beguiling combination of innocence, worldliness and dysfunction such as he found in Marianne – who was a doll, a perfect physical specimen, with a wide-eyed child's face and the body of a whore, with daddy issues and boarding-school hang-ups, bereft of siblings, the product of a broken home. Marianne, sex on legs, daring, damaged and frail, was the ultimate rock'n'roll woman. Mick would keep searching for and finding her throughout his life, for she came with all kinds of names. The young, silly, pretty, careless, impressionable girls he gobbled for breakfast. They made him look good. They must have made him feel like a stud. Which suggests that he lacked confidence in his masculinity. Because of his bisexuality? There's a question.

He was clearly attracted to men. His long-rumoured dalliances with Brian Jones's replacement Mick Taylor, screen actor Helmut Berger, *Rolling Stone* magazine publisher Jann Wenner and even with his old mucker Keith have never been denied. His decades-long obsession with David Bowie erupted into the public domain in 1985, when the pair recorded a cover of Martha Reeves and the Vandellas' 'Dancing in the Street' for Live Aid. The sexual tension between them in the David Mallet-directed video ignited the screen. The record shot to No. 1 in the UK and No. 7 in the US, and all the old rumours resurfaced.

The two A-listers had always hung together and hero-worshipped each other. They often ravished each other in print. They are known to have indulged in frequent threesomes. Backing vocalist Ava Cherry was once the meat in that sandwich: 'Even though I was in bed with them many times,' she revealed, 'I ended up just watching them have sex.' Playboy Playmate Bebe Buell had similar experiences with David and Mick. 'I used to get some pretty strange phone calls from [them] at three in the morning,' she told American author Christopher Andersen for his biography of Jagger, 'inviting me to join them in bed with four gorgeous black women ... or four gorgeous black men.' Bowie would tease the press with ambiguity, never confirming or denying anything. Jagger evaded questions with a 'stick to your knitting' expression. Besides, rock'n'roll has always flirted with androgyny. It's about performance, the spectacle, entertainment. What else is sex to an entertainer, if not performance art?

Could it be that he harboured a deeply rooted aversion to that aspect of himself, and pursued endless females in order to suppress the homosexual urge? Just asking. Different times, back then. Upbringing, social prejudice, traditional values and views on decency and acceptability all played their part. Only a theory, of course. He's not telling us, is he. But it fits. For a man like Jagger, the dissonance between who he really is and the character he projects is something he has always managed brilliantly. Reticence about accepting a bisexual identity may have been the very thing that led him to womanise so relentlessly. It could equally have been the thing that allowed him to continue indulging in homosexual encounters. Because we didn't expect it of him, we didn't see it. Picture Jagger the shagger as a bisexual icon: pretty powerful in our enlightened age. Rock'n'roll really would have come full circle.

*

For all that they had in common, Anita Pallenberg was the antithesis of Marianne. Tigrine and confrontational, with a bite as bad as her bark and a right hook to dodge if you saw it coming, she came with her own baggage and complications. It was she, not Marianne, who embodied the spirit of the Rolling Stones. More than merely a muse, she was intrinsically a part of them. 'Anita is a Rolling Stone,' was the view of Jo Bergman, a PA and later manager to the band between 1967 and 1973. 'She, Mick, Keith and Brian were the Rolling Stones. Her influence has been profound. She keeps things crazy.' Keith won her, loved her, became addicted and was devoted to her. He procreated with her and could barely tear himself away from her, not even when their newborn died on her watch, though he did draw the line after her teenage lover shot himself in the marital bed. Although he fell in love with and married someone else, he never got over her. It must have been to his great relief that his only wife Patti Hansen – the American model and (briefly) actress whom he married on his fortieth birthday in December 1983 in Cabo San Lucas, Mexico, and who gave him daughters Theodora and Alexandra – was big-hearted enough to respect his previous relationship, and embraced Anita as part of their family. 'I like a high-spirited woman,' Keith admitted in his memoir. 'And with Anita, you knew you were taking on a Valkyrie: she who decides who dies in battle.' He also once observed that she 'knew everything and she could say it in five languages. She scared the pants off me.' Not for Richards the shy, retiring wallflower. Patti has always been a force to be reckoned with too.

Anita lied about everything, starting with her age, which the writers of her obituaries misreported. The error was understandable. Born in Rome during the Second World War, her birth certificate was not accessible. After her death in 2017, her survivors confirmed that she had arrived on 6 April 1942, and had therefore been seventy-five. She has been described as Italian, German, Swiss and Swedish. A cross-breed of all four, and more. She kept her origins ambiguous and was a snarl of self-constructs and contradictions, with the result that her identity was more a matter of who she set out to be than of who she was. Although she projected as being vaguely blue-blooded and a descendant of old European money, her family were not well-off. She seemed to me to personify Peter Sarstedt's evocative 1969 hit 'Where Do You Go To (My Lovely)?' about a Neapolitan street urchin who faked her way into high society, swanning from Juan-les-Pins to St. Moritz, designer-dressed and hanging with Picasso. With looks and charm enough to carry her into the most rarefied circles, Anita conned everybody.

Her German parents Arnoldo and Paula were both working in Rome at the turn of the forties: her amateur-musician father for a travel agency, her mother at the German embassy. Anita's elder sister Gabriella had been born pre-war. By the time their second daughter was on the way, the country was under Nazi occupation and her father was in the north, cooking for Italian troops. She didn't meet him until she was three years old. Like her future soulmate Marianne Faithfull, she had daddy issues.

Anita's earliest ambition was to become a Catholic priest. 'It had great allure and mystery,' she said. 'I like what's forbidden.' Verboten could have been her middle name. It was certainly her modus operandi. Her default was to go against the grain. She attended the Swiss School in Rome, and was later despatched to her parents' homeland to board at Bavaria's Landheim Schondorf school, where she was expected to acquire the native language and culture. One of only twenty girls at the establishment housing two hundred pupils, in a foreign country a thousand kilometres from home, Anita swallowed her separation anxiety and stood up to the offspring of Nazi officers. She held her own, excelled academically, sailed, skied, smoked, drank, partied herself sick and was expelled, damn it, which precluded her acceptance into university. She decamped to Munich, got into art school, thwarted an attempted rape, developed an abhorrence of men as a result and reinvented herself as a lesbian. She would later declare that she had always been bisexual.

Back in Italy in 1959, she signed up at the Accademia di Belle Arti di Roma to study restoration and graphic design. She grew bored and dropped out. She fell in with Federico Fellini's crowd, who were in town to shoot *La Dolce Vita*.[1] She was seventeen, blonde, beautiful and up for anything. She watched the Wall go up in Berlin, and discovered rock'n'roll on Hamburg's Große Freiheit, witnessing the embryonic Beatles hitting their stride. She hung with Andy Warhol's Factory studio gang in New York, and absconded to Paris on a modelling assignment. Not because she was enamoured with the fashion industry. The opposite. Like so much in her life, the pursuit was a means to an end. She slid into screen acting during her sojourn in the French capital. She got to know and shacked up with bohemian artist and film-maker Mario Schifano, eight years her senior ... the same Schifano with whom Marianne Faithfull would later elope, the one whom Mick sent packing from the cottage he had bought for Marianne's mother.

She was trolling about in 1965 when she was invited by a friend to a Rolling Stones gig in Munich. They wound up backstage before the show, where the fledgling groupie offered around her hash. The boys declined, explaining that they couldn't do drugs before going on stage. It wouldn't be long before they reversed that habit, to the point that pre-gig indulgence virtually became mandatory. It was Brian Jones who nabbed her. She was like gazing into a mirror, his own exquisite hair and visage reflected back at him. She slipped into his hotel bed that night, and that was that. They were joined at the hipness for the next two years, garbed identically. These Beautiful People shared everything, including their clothes. She styled and beguiled the Stones, transforming the raw, raucous tykes into rock stars.

It couldn't have been all bad, or it would not have lasted that long. But Brian's grip on reality and on the Stones was sliding. Ostracised by Mick and Keith, egged on by Andrew Oldham, Brian lost control. Drink and drugs made him paranoid. He took his insecurities out on his girlfriend.

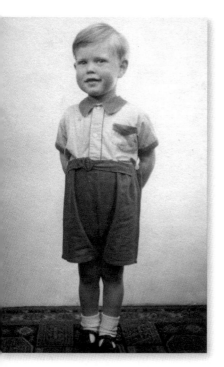

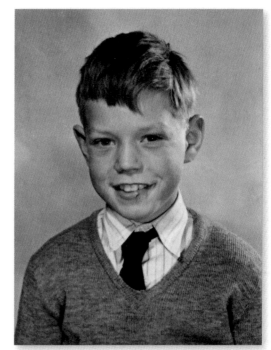

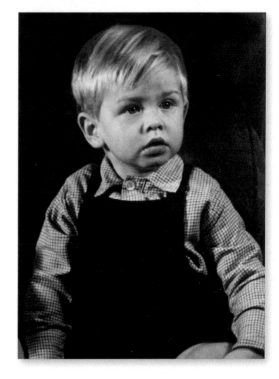

bove: A young, and schoolboy-aged, Mick Jagger. No sympathy for the devil there. © *Getty / Stones rchive*. *Below left*: Charlie Watts looking as smart as ever, as he feeds the pigeons with his parents. *Getty / Popperfoto*. *Below right*: Brian Jones. © *Getty / Linda Roots*.

Left: Brian's innate musicianship let him come up with a tune on any instrument, as demonstrated here as he plays a sitar during a television appearance in 1966. © *Getty / David Redfern*

Right: Taken in the 1960s. Note Brian's baleful glance at Mick's back, as he fronts the band. © *Getty / Avalon*

Left: Rock journalist and future Stones publicist Keith Altham interviews Brian Jones.

Above: Large crowds – very decidedly female – gather outside the stage door of the Royal Albert Hall. The [St]ones and the Beatles are on the bill. 1963. *Below*: Rocking the Albert (r-l Bill Wyman, Brian Jones, Mick [Ja]gger, Charlie Watts and Keith Richards). © *Getty / Mirrorpix*

Above left: The rare sight of Keith Richards making merry. Backstage, an early tour, 1963. © *Getty / Chris Ware*. *Above right*: Mick's flair as a harp player is all too often overlooked. Seen here playing in Great Newport Street, London. © *Getty / Mark and Colleen Hayward*. *Below*: The originals. © *Getty / Avalon*.

Right: Mick and Brian's relationship told in pictures defies easy categorisation. Here, Mick gazes coolly while Brian leans affectionately toward him. © *Getty / Mondadori Portfolio*

Left: Yet here the two, unusually bearded, share a genuine laugh at a party on the Kings Road. 1968. © *Getty / Mark and Colleen Hayward*

Right: The two enjoy the mania of a food fight at the Kensington Gore Hotel, where the band staged a mock-medieval feast for the launch of their new album 'Beggars Banquet'. © *Getty / Hulton Archive*

Left: Brian pictured with Yoko Ono, John and Sean Lennon. In the UK, December 1968. © *Getty / Evening Standard*

Above: Mick and Keith pictured outside Keith's long-time home, Redlands, in West Wittering, Sussex – the scene of the infamous drugs bust in 1967. © *Getty / Icon And Image. Below*: Out on bail for their drug charges. Mick was sentenced to three months in jail for possession of pep pills. Richards got a year for permitting his home to be used for the smoking of marijuana. Even The Times suggested the sentence wa overly harsh. © *Getty / Bettmann.*

The Stones Women: Keith and Anita
Pallenberg at his home in Cheyne Walk,
Chelsea (*above*), Mick and Marianne
Faithfull (*middle*) and Mick with the
alluring Bianca on their wedding day in
St Tropez (*below*). © *Getty / McCarthy /
Bettmann / Lichfield*

Above: Five years after his death, a mourner kneels at Brian Jones's unassuming grave. © *Getty / Mirrorpix*. *Inset*: Brian died here, in the swimming pool of his home at Cotchford Farm, Sussex. © *Getty / Jim Gray*. *Below*: Suffice to say that, given the turnout, his funeral at Cheltenham Parish Church was standing room only. 1969. © *Getty / Mirrorpix*.

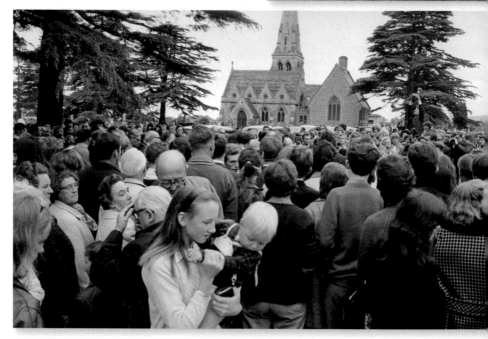

On a jaunt to Morocco in 1967, Keith witnessed a particularly vicious attack. In love with Brian's woman for as long as he could remember, he took his chance, hurled her over his shoulder and carted her back to Blighty. They were together for the next twelve years. Once he got with Anita, Keith shaped up. He started wearing make-up and getting his hair cut in designer salons. He began to fashion an idiosyncratic look that would soon become the template of 'quintessential rock star', and which would eventually go whole-hog pirate. Brian couldn't stand it. Wherever Keith went, Anita followed, a reminder of what they'd once had. He couldn't overcome the ignominy and move on because Anita was always there, right under his nose.

'Anita seduced everybody,' said rock journalist Robert Greenfield, who lived with her and Keith while he was writing his book *Exile on Main St. A Season in Hell with the Rolling Stones*. 'She was so powerful that very few people were immune. There was her extraordinary physical beauty and the sharpness of her mind. She was crazy and beautiful, and crazy beautiful.'

She was also astute. She perceived immediately that there was only one person on earth for Mick, and that no woman could compete. 'From when I first met them, I saw Mick was in love with Keith,' she explained. 'It's like they're married, and they'll probably be that way for the rest of their lives.'

*

Life as Keith's lady was lush in those salad days. But then the thrill began to wear thin. The mega-wealth alone would have satisfied most rock wives, but Anita always wanted more. Boredom was the killer.

'At that time no girls were allowed in the studio when they were recording,' she said. 'You weren't allowed even to ring. I did other things, I didn't sit at home.' She reignited her movie career, to Keith's dismay. He reportedly offered her £20,000, enough to buy a house back then, to refuse a part in *Barbarella* with Jane Fonda.[2] Yeah, right. She co-starred as Nurse Bullock in the sex romp *Candy*,[3] and she did a lot of drugs. She said that she started using heroin while filming *Performance* with Jagger, aborting a pregnancy to secure the part of Pherber, the dangerous other half of Mick's imagination. She probably did screw Jagger during the shoot, but would always deny it. Keith was consumed by jealousy. He and

Anita were already parents by then, their son Marlon having been born in the Dulwich maternity unit of Kings College Hospital, London, in August 1969. Anita had convinced herself that Brian Jones's spirit would be reincarnated in their baby, whose given name was a perverse dig at Anita's *Candy* co-star Brando. The star of *The Wild One* had kidnapped Anita, and had tried to seduce her with poetry. '... when that failed, he tried to seduce Anita and me together,' Keith scoffed. Nice try, joker. She had already been seduced psychologically by Kenneth Anger, an American occultist and film-maker who had wormed his way into the rock scene during 1968. He befriended Mick, with whom he also worked, as well as Keith and Anita. Anger had the name 'Lucifer' tattooed across his chest. He promoted Satanism, witchcraft, sadomasochistic sex and the use of hallucinogens such as LSD. It was from him that Anita learned her spells, with which she loved to terrorise people. Their reaction to them gave her a sense of power.

When the band quit England for the South of France and recorded *Exile on Main St.* at Keith's rented villa, the couple were often busted for drugs. Anita lived up to her position as lady of the house, running the staff, the visitors, the suppliers and the dealers and seeing off the local constabulary. Keith could handle his habit, most of the time. Although his girlfriend was joining him for a hit now and then, they said, it was mostly recreational. She could stop any time she wanted, she would say. And then she couldn't.

'It wasn't like that,' insists former journalist and newspaper editor John Blake, who knew them personally. 'I got so involved with the Stones over the years, and it was fascinating to watch what happened to them. Anita was indeed in thrall to Kenneth Anger, a very nasty piece of work, and there were all the implications of black magic and sinister goings-on. She was very sophisticated and worldly. She got hooked on heroin first, and she wanted to get everyone else shooting up. She dragged Keith in. He was young and innocent when she got hold of him. He and Mick were just working-class kids who didn't have a clue. They fell in with women who showed them a different side of life and made them aspirational. Marianne got Mick hooked on fifty-grand chandeliers. Anita got Keith hooked on heroin.'

Her second baby was conceived while Keith was by his own admission 'hooked big-time'. She couldn't say for sure who the father was. This desperate period is one that Keith neglects to confront in his memoir, perhaps for fear of hurting his eldest daughter, or quite possibly because he doesn't remember ... even though, as he says, 'I haven't forgotten anything.' Fearing that the child was Mick's, Anita begged Keith's PA to help her get an abortion. She made arrangements several times to have the pregnancy terminated, but never made it. In the end, it was accepted that Keith was the dad.

Anita used heroin during her second pregnancy, perhaps as an antidote to her desperation regarding paternity. She was terrified that her baby would be born an addict. She gave birth in a Swiss rehab clinic in April 1972, to a baby with a cleft lip and palate. Keith wasn't present for the birth, but he wasn't far away: he was 'being cleaned up' by a doctor up the road in Vevey. Which was, he said, 'fucking awful ... you wonder why you're doing this to yourself when you could be living a perfectly normal fucking rich rock star life. And there you are puking and climbing the walls.' He was still in the clinic when she delivered. He picked up his guitar and started singing out of nowhere 'Angie', not knowing that he had a daughter, nor that the word coming out of his mouth would have anything to do with her name. It was Anita who called her Dandelion Angela Bellstar.

*

Four years later, beyond the Stones' legendary Touring Party of America, beyond the searing success of *Exile on Main St.*, across Europe, the Pacific and out the other side, through *It's Only Rock 'n Roll* and on to the Tour of the Americas, more suicides, deaths and destruction and with the Richardses back on the smack, Anita managed to give Keith a third child. They named their second son Tara Jo Jo Gunne, after their friend the Irish Guinness heir who had blown his mind out in a car a decade earlier. Soon afterwards, Keith hit the road with seven-year-old Marlon. The feral child who should have been at school became his father's minder, on the 1976 Stones' Tour of Europe. Hiding the smack, cleaning up his cack and tucking the gun back under Dad's pillow, he was growing up way too fast. Anita, hopelessly out of it, should never have been left at home alone with a newborn and a four-year-old. But she was, and the consequences were tragic.

The caller reaches him in Paris, just as the band are about to stroll out on stage. Anita has found Tara lifeless in his cot. He was a little over two months old. Does Keith abandon the gig, burn rubber through the night back to Geneva to support his distraught partner, pick up pieces and hold his loved ones tight – which is what anyone else would have done? Does he fuck. The show must go on and it does, his glassy-eyed, sleep-deprived son gazing at him from the wings through infant eyes that have seen too much. Keith hasn't had the heart to tell that him his baby brother has died. Denial most desperate. Keith knows.

'Only Anita knows,' he wrote. 'As for me, I should never have left him. I don't think it's her fault; it was just a crib death. But leaving a newborn is something I can't forgive myself for. It's as if I deserted my post.' They never talked about it, and never got over it. Keith didn't even know, when he came to confront it during the writing of his memoir almost thirty-five years later, where his son was buried ... 'if he's buried at all.'

He was right when he said that a dead child never leaves you. He lives inside you forever, a nagging reminder of where you went wrong. But *was* it 'just a crib death' or 'cot death' (as we used to call SIDS – Sudden Infant Death Syndrome[4])? Anita was a smack addict. Heroin use by a mother during pregnancy often results in neonatal abstinence syndrome (NAS). An unborn baby who becomes dependent when heroin passes through the placenta into their system, suffers withdrawal when the drug is no longer forthcoming. Symptoms include excessive crying, fever, irritability, seizures, inability to feed, slow weight gain, tremors, diarrhoea and vomiting. It is not uncommon for such babies to die. 'I am sure that the drugs had something to do with it,' Anita admitted. 'And I always felt very, very bad about the whole thing.'

As for Keith, he had never discussed the tragedy. Not publicly, at least. He cut himself slack thirty-nine years after it happened when he revisited, during his appearance on BBC Radio 4's *Desert Island Discs*, his decision to go out and play instead of rushing home to confront the unthinkable. 'Maybe it was a sense of self-preservation ... it was a rough, rough thing,' he told presenter Kirsty Young in October 2015. 'And I had a feeling ... I must go on stage now and I'll worry and grieve and think about all this after the show. Because if I didn't go on the stage, I'd probably have shot myself.'

He had given up heroin for good in 1978. He continued to use cocaine until 2006, when he jacked it in after he fell from that branch while on that holiday, and was rushed into theatre for emergency brain surgery. Until then, he had continued to take risks because he had always got away with it. 'The man who death forgot' had made a habit of dodging the reaper. He was almost electrocuted during a soundcheck in 1965; nearly burned to death six years later when his bed caught fire; survived a blaze at his country home Redlands in 1973, and another there in 1982; walked unscathed from a Laurel Canyon, Los Angeles house that burned down around him in 1978, escaping naked with a blonde who wasn't Anita. One of his favourite guitars was destroyed in that fire, his five-string Zemaitis Macabre with custom pirate artwork;[5] and he suffered severe concussion in 1998 when he fell in his library as he reached for a book. Few cats have had more lives than Keith. How many to go?

After Tara died, Keith continued to take care of Marlon. Where he went, so did his boy. Anita being in no fit state to look after Angela, their little girl was lodged with Keith's mother Doris in Dartford while they tried to sort themselves out. Which never happened. The child lived with her grandmother for the next twenty years. Keith stood by Anita, but things were never the same. When he was arrested in Toronto in February 1977 with so much heroin on him that he was accused of importing in order to deal it, he found himself facing a possible life sentence. At which point he blinked, stepped backwards and saw the light. The Stones, their music, had to come first. Had Keith gone down, the band would have been over. Oh yes, better stay alive and out of prison for the sake of the kids. He had no choice but to get clean. So did Anita. He succeeded.

In 1979 – the Toronto court having stunned the world by letting him off drug charges with no more than a year's probation, and having submitted to electro-therapy treatment in the US – Keith was recording with the band and with his new best friend Jack Daniel's in Paris when Anita really did hit rock bottom. Still paralysed with guilt over the death of her child, she was confused and disoriented. The family were by then based at Frog Hollow, a glorious nineteenth-century clapboard manse with all the trimmings –

wooden shutters, dormer windows, acres of land – in South Salem, New York State, a quick commute north-east of the Big Apple.[6] The house had all the familiarity and charm of the kind featured in American Christmas movies,[7] give or take the beefy bodyguards.

Set in a desirable hamlet with rich, respectable neighbours and access to excellent schools, it was not Anita's speed. She was a city chick. A life of isolation in the bucolic reaches did not suit her. All too aware that Keith was out there cavorting with other women – specifically one other, Swedish model Lil Wergilis – while she was stuck at home orchestrating Marlon's school runs and homework, depression got the better of her. Because she was drinking and taking methadone, a medicine used to treat heroin dependence, and after having fallen and broken her hip, she gained so much weight that her beauty deserted her, never to return. Her once glowing skin was saggy and bruised. She nursed an almost permanent cold. She was only thirty-seven but looked hunched and spent, on the brink of old-womanhood. Her little boy bore the brunt of her mood swings and angry outbursts. She would later express deep sorrow at the way she treated him. 'Marlon was fine until he had to go to school,' she told me years later in London. 'He was better off on the road with Keith. That might sound crazy, given how Keith was, all those years. But I'm telling you, he was a much better parent than me.' She was seeing ghosts, of her younger, more hopeful, spirited self, and of indigenous Americans. They were sometimes the same thing. She drowned her sorrows and took a teenager to bed. The seventeen-year-old, Scott Cantrell, was one of four kids from a broken home. He was also a high school dropout on a road to nowhere. Like Anita, he was needy and dysfunctional.

Cantrell was on the Richards household payroll, employed as a groundsman. He commuted to work from his father's home in Norwalk, Connecticut, on the north shore of Long Island Sound, half an hour each way. Knowing that his boss's common-law wife was attracted to him, the chancer took advantage of his position. In a blink, they were sleeping together. From that point on, the kid was unpleasant to the child, taunting Marlon that he was closer to his mother than he was, and promising to shoot his now estranged father if he dared come around.

Things came to a head during the evening of Friday 20 July, when Anita and Scott were up in the marital bedroom and Marlon was in the living room, watching the tenth-anniversary retrospective of the Apollo 11 moon landings on television. His tormentor was lying in his mother's bed above his head, toying with one of Keith's guns, a .38-calibre Smith & Wesson revolver. Then he shot himself, at point-blank range. Anita tore screaming down the stairs to her child, drenched in Scott's blood. Marlon rushed up to his mother's bedroom, and saw a sight he would never unsee. How did Scott find the gun? Did Anita give it to him? Did she shoot him? Were the wild ones playing some sick, sordid game, or was it, as later reported, Russian roulette?[8]

Somebody came for Marlon, the Lewisboro PD came for Anita, and the story (naturally) leaked to the press. It hit London via the wire and reached John Blake, who was at the time a rising star music writer on the *Evening News*.

'We heard this guy with Anita Pallenberg had shot himself dead,' recalls John, and we knew that the Stones were recording in France at the time. The news editor said to me, "Get yourself out to Paris, see what you can get." I had no idea where they even were, and no clue as to where to start looking.

'I got lucky. I found myself sitting next to this guy on the plane who was a music business executive. We got chatting, and I told him what I was up to. "That's no problem," he said, "the Stones always work at Pathé Marconi Studios [in Boulogne-Billancourt, about five miles to the west of central Paris; the studios are no longer there]. They start recording at about eleven o'clock at night and they work through to the next morning. If you want to see them, go down there really early and you should catch them."

'Off I trot at about five o'clock the next morning. I find the studio and walk straight in, no trouble. And there's Mick, standing in the middle of the room with a great long beard. He looked round at me and stared. I could tell he recognised me from somewhere, but he couldn't quite place me. He paused, as if trying to remember, and then he said, "Ah, have you got the stuff, man?" He thought I was the bloody dealer! There was this hideous, pregnant pause, and then I said, "No, Mick. I think you've mixed me up with someone else. I'm here to see Keith, to find out what he has to say about this awful tragedy with Anita."

'It was at that point that I noticed Keith standing there, staring at me from across the room. And he started wailing. "Oh, man," he went, "oh no, this is terrible, it's horrible!" And then he ran off and hid behind Charlie's drum kit. I'm in the middle of the room surrounded by Rolling Stones, feeling rather threatened and thinking, "What do I do now?" And all the while, Keith is going, "Oh shit, oh shit, oh no, I don't wanna talk about it!" It was really awkward. "Fuck," I thought. I had no idea what to do. Then Ian Stewart, their lovely keyboard player who was always such a gentleman, wandered over and said to me, "Can you go away now? Would you mind?" "I'm so sorry," I said to him, "I have to ask. I'm only doing my job." And I left the studio with a single quote to my name. We got the splash.'

Former Stones' publicist Keith Altham remembers it well. "John Blake did indeed get himself into the recording studio in Paris," he affirms. 'Bloody good journalist. Everyone was out of it. John must have looked the part, and he walked right in. Imagine that, now. He had also tipped me off that he was going, because he didn't want to do the story. A kid had died, and it seemed inappropriate. I tried to get hold of Mick in the studio, but he wouldn't take my calls for some reason. I had to laugh when I heard that Mick thought John was the drug dealer. Then John turning to speak to Keith, and him keeling over on the studio floor like a dead dog, behind Charlie's kit. At which point, as Stu reported back later, Mick had the last laugh.

"'As you can see, John,' he drawled, "Keith wants to talk to you *real bad*."'

*

But neither Stones nor their women wind up in jail. Money talks. So do lawyers. It was rumoured that Keith's millions marched Anita out of trouble. Not that this deprived the media of their exposé-fest. Tales of satanic rituals and drug-fuelled orgies in 'that evil house' ran for weeks. Anita was part of a witches' coven, and the sisters at a local convent were helping hacks with their enquiries, the whole nine. But Homicide got nowhere. A verdict of suicide was ruled. Anita paid no higher price than a thousand of Keith's dollars, a fine for unlawful possession of firearms.

What has never been explained is how the gun got from the bed to the top of a chest of drawers across the bedroom. Who moved it? Why? How come it bore no identifiable fingerprints?

Scott Cantrell's family attempted to sue Anita and Keith, for corruption of a minor and all that ensued. The case went nowhere, but maybe should have done. 'People fail to understand that this was a thirty-seven-year-old woman and a seventeen-year-old child,' said Cantrell's sibling Jim in a statement. 'Even if Scottie pulled the trigger, I hold her responsible for my brother's death.'

*

The lawmen may have saved Anita, but it was nail-in-the-coffin time for their relationship. She and Keith partook of a farewell fling in a New York hotel. She was so ashamed of her bloated body that she couldn't fathom what he still saw in her. 'I was really overweight,' she said, 'and I really didn't think he liked me, but I guess he loved me because he wanted to make love to me. But I didn't feel worth it for him. I said, "You brought out the worst in me."

'Anita Pallenberg was the image of every man and every woman's worst fear of what they would become,' snarled American journalist Greil Marcus in *Rolling Stone* magazine. 'Fat, bloated and ruined – not simply to excess but beyond recognition, not simply beyond sex but beyond gender. She seems likely to be remembered, if she's remembered at all, as just one more cast-off.'

Anita is certainly remembered. She is even, in certain circles, almost revered. The shocking fall-out of her extreme drug abuse – the death of her baby; the blown-out brains of a teenager spattered across her walls; the trauma suffered by her ten-year-old son – are referenced openly, and even glamorised. It has been said for years that there should be a film about her. There likely will be, if the Faithfull flick works out.

Her detractors hasten to damn. Not so fast, suckers. Because Anita turned herself around; she went back to college in 1994, investing four years in a degree in fashion and textiles at Central Saint Martins in London. Having despised the fashion industry for most of her life, it was a curious career choice. She appeared in a few more flicks before whisking herself off to work in 'the Pink City of India', Jaipur.[9] One could see why:

the place is a wonderland of culture, heritage and architecture, and famous for its traditional fabrics, jewellery and handicrafts. Anita found her way back to beauty. 'I would have stayed in Jaipur forever,' she said. 'We were doing organic textiles and spending most of the time out in the desert.' But a mercy dash to tend to her dying mother detained her in Europe for the next five years. By the time she was free to return to India, she felt too old and creaky, and had lost her nerve. In 2001, she popped up in Jennifer Saunders' and Joanna Lumley's *Absolutely Fabulous* on television, playing the Devil opposite Marianne Faithfull's God.

Into her sixties and with less than a decade to live (had she known that, what might she have done differently?), Anita was living alone in London. Did or didn't she marry one Gabriel Roux in 1982? No one seems sure. She spent her time whizzing around SW3 on her bike, growing her own food on her Chiswick allotment, and drawing and painting at art class. Old lady pursuits. She developed diabetes but resisted insulin treatment, probably horrified by the thought of having to self-inject again after the line-drawn-under low years of shooting up. A host of ailments and illnesses afflicted her. She had both hips replaced, became sick with hepatitis C, took to the bottle again after surgery in 2004, and signed up for AA meetings.

When I met her at a supper party at the Chelsea home of mutual friends, she looked riven and almost mummified, but was still full of herself. She was bitching about model Kate Moss, whom Anita's old friend Marianne had recently called a 'style-stealing vampire' in *The Times*. 'She is, too,' snapped Anita. 'We invented our style from scratch, and these gyps of girls just copied us, passing our look off as their own. Makes me want to shoot them!' She was brilliantly self-deprecating, recounting the time when singer Courtney Love had asked her if she'd consider plastic surgery. 'As I said, I told her straight. "Darling," I said, "I was the most beautiful woman in seventeen or eighteen countries. I *love* being ugly!"'

Keith supported her financially from the moment he split until the day she died. He even paid for her new teeth, she said. What a gent. It was complications from hepatitis C that finished her.

'I don't want who she really was to be forgotten,' commented Marianne in the *Guardian* in 2017, shortly after Anita's death. 'People think of her in one way – a '60s muse, all that shit – but she was so much more than that. A really talented artist, a great actor, intelligent, funny, thoughtful, fearless. She truly didn't give a fuck what anybody thought of her. I was desolate when she died. Until she got very ill, we spoke on the phone most days. I don't want to sound sentimental or sappy, she's worth more than that. She was so important to me.'

A Rolling Stone Anita Pallenberg surely was. Not only did she appear in Jean-Luc Godard's film about them, *Sympathy for the Devil*, she also sang backing vocals on the track itself; summoning her obsession with the occult and giving rise to hysterical rumours that the Stones were agents of Satan. Right. If anyone was, it was her! What a laugh she and Keith must have had about that. She was the one casting spells, holding séances, flaunting a ouija board and dragging the others out at night on the hunt for UFOs. It's said she 'believed in all that', ho hum, but she certainly used it to control others, by making them fearful and insecure. Keith wrote 'Gimme Shelter' about her alleged affair with Jagger while they were filming *Performance*, tormenting himself that their love scenes were not pretend.

'Beast of Burden' and 'All About You' are blatantly about her, even though Keith would sometimes argue otherwise. But it is the song 'You Got the Silver' from the December 1969 album *Let It Bleed* that really showcases his love for this strange, erotic, erratic woman from the Eternal City who in so many ways was more than him. Who made him what he became. It was the first Stones song on which Keith sang solo lead vocal. It was that special to him.[10]

'Can I touch a feeling here?' he mused on the Ask Keith YouTube channel, when somebody enquired about it. '… I always try and capture feelings rather than explain things or make a point about anything … cos you're usually wrong if you try and do that, at least I am.' Which actually reveals the very thing we need to know, if you read between lines: that Keith is because Anita was. He couldn't articulate it in so many words, but it's there.

Keith came from New York to spend time at her bedside in St Richard's Hospital, Chichester. She let go only after he left. 'A most remarkable woman,' he wrote on Twitter. 'Always in my heart.' He, Patti and their daughters Theodora and Alexandra returned for her humanist funeral. Ronnie Wood's daughter Leah and her husband Jack, and friends including 'gyp' Kate Moss and designer Bella Freud attended too.

'I saw her four days before she died,' said her friend Jo Wood, ex-wife of guitarist Ronnie. 'It was natural. She was not very well. She had a fall last year.' As my mother says, it's always a fall. 'Keith is devastated,' Jo added. 'Everyone is.'

Anita had found her way home. On her deathbed, she was only a wander from Redlands.

Chapter Ten

REDLANDS

I had a friend, long gone, who used to drive down from London to Redlands a couple of times a month to 'do Keith's accounts'. This had nothing to do with band business, nor with his own personal taxation or living expenses. The 'accounts' that she was paid to manage were those of the considerable number of individuals on his payroll. Not session musicians or personal staff such as drivers, gofers and cleaners, but former girlfriends, his children, their children, extended family members and a handful of other individuals for whom he had, over the years, assumed responsibility.

According to my friend, the sums he shelled out monthly were gargantuan. Some of these fortunate folk lived in grace-and-favour properties owned by Keith, or in dwellings he had purchased for them. Their monthly living allowances, utilities, medical bills and school fees ran into hundreds of thousands. Not to mention their travel expenses: airline tickets, hotel bills, et cetera. For some, he also ran cars and covered legal costs. Small beer, you might think, for a man with an estimated net worth of $500 million – around £377 million. He can't take it with him.

Keith has been making the most of his good fortune ever since serious songwriting royalties first started flowing in for him and Mick, leaving the rest of the group awestruck while by no means boracic. First things first: boys' toys. Mick treated himself to an Aston Martin DB6 and a

Mini Cooper S. Bill got an MBG and Brian a Rolls-Royce Silver Cloud. Keith's first four-wheeled luxury acquisition was a 1965 Bentley S3 Continental Flying Spur sports saloon, which he affectionately dubbed 'Blue Lena' after American artist Lena Horne.[1] He posted her a picture of his new car, which he'd had modified with a sunroof, darkened rear windows, a Philips record player and a secret compartment in which to hide his illegal stash. Next up, a pad fit for a rock star. He forked out £13,000 (some say £15,000, others report £17,500) for his first 'proper home', the Redlands estate near West Wittering, Sussex in April 1966. By the time of the raid the following year, it was being described by journalists as 'Richards's £20,000 farmhouse'.

The tumbledown Tudor manor complete with wide, muddy moat required extensive renovation. A lesser mortal might have shrunk from the surgery required, but Keith had fallen hook and line for her charms. The house had his name on it. Its worth, today, is reckoned at around £5 million. He maintains and uses it as a UK residence, but his main home these days is a colonial mansion in Weston, Fairfield County, Connecticut, in the eastern region of New England.[2] He and his wife Patti built it on eight acres of land with a river running through it, breathtaking lake views and the Devil's Den Preserve nature reserve on their doorstep. Weston, said to be named after the North Somerset seaside town Weston-super-Mare, lies off the beaten track forty-five miles north-east of New York City. Its first English settlers arrived during the seventeenth century. Artists, writers, actors and musicians were drawn to live there from the 1930s. Bette Davis, Marilyn Monroe and Robert Redford all had homes there.

Keith's eight thousand square-foot pad boasts his proudest possession: a vast library of rare volumes and first editions which he loves to read and wallow in by himself. He and the Mrs are seen regularly in nearby Ridgefield, a quaint colonial town a twenty-minute drive away where they frequent low-key hang-outs such as Luc's French bistro and Hoodoo Brown BBQ. Ten minutes out of Ridgefield and he's back in South Salem. Although one doubts that Keith heads that way too often these days. He's better off swerving the house always there to remind him of the time when his lover's teen lover pulled the trigger.

Working regularly in downtown New York studios, Keith paid $10.5 million for a four-bedroom, four-bathroom Fifth Avenue New York apartment in 2014. It must have proved surplus to requirements, as he and Patti put it up for sale two years later, by which time it had gone up by a couple of million. They also own a hideaway on the private resort island Parrot Cay in the Turks and Caicos Islands, the British Overseas Territory south-east of the Bahamas. But those in the know insist that Redlands, only Redlands, is where his heart lies; that it will be his final resting place, come the time.

The name Redlands is synonymous with the 1967 drug raid that unintentionally made Marianne Faithfull a household name. Naked but for a large orange fur throw hastily yanked off the bed and tucked around her to protect her modesty, she was allegedly found by police giving birth to a piece of confectionery that Mick lay devouring as it emerged. This unlikely Cronusesque[3] tableau has been exaggerated beyond imagining down the years. You only have to google 'Did anyone see Mick eating the Mars bar?' Marianne insisted that it never happened. In her memoir, she called it 'a dirty old man's fantasy – some old fart who goes to a dominatrix every Thursday afternoon to get spanked. A cop's idea of what people do on acid.' But the chocolate bar stuck. It still has her name on it. Mars, Incorporated should be paying her a dividend.

It struck me as curious that, while Keith has been tried on drug-related charges five times – in 1967, twice in 1973, and again in 1977 and 1978 – it is the Redlands raid that remains the most notorious. Neither the narcotics nor the amounts involved were especially mind-blowing, as was pointed out. Redlands is remembered as a monumental blunder on the part of the Establishment, which served as the first nail in its own coffin and which had the opposite effect of the raid's intention. Falling over themselves to frame and cage these disgusting specimens of indecency, these vile scourges of society, these, these … Your Honour, I am stunned into inarticulacy by the outrage … the police and the *News of the World* exposed their own corruption and shot themselves in the foot. In seeking to eradicate them, their opponents made the Stones even more popular and desirable. No greater exposure for degenerate lowlife could any publicist worth his sodium chloride have conjured. They found themselves cast as the outlaw folk heroes of a generation sick of being controlled by strict parents, teachers and other dictatorial superiors with heads buried in their backsides and minds lost in the pelmetted past of their re-imagining; a forgotten dimension in which there would always be an England and where they would keep the home fires burning, come what may. Patriotic to the point of pathological, the world war-surviving elders force-fed their stale ideas and morals to their kids like French farmers inflicting gavage on ducks and geese. Free thinking and progress on the part of the young was to be quelled at any cost.

Then out of the mists on metaphorical steeds bolt a daring band who break rules and make up their own. Cue dropped jaws: what is this but a catalyst for change? The Beatles, them again, adored by grans and tots, seemed wholesome and unthreatening. Everybody thought that *Revolver*'s 'Got to Get You Into My Life' was a typically Fab lovestruck ode to some elusive female. McCartney himself revealed years later that it was a song about weed. Wool was often pulled by the Beatles. Their arch-rivals never bothered with such subterfuge. They flew the colours of their cohort in the face of a rear-view world. That which Pete Townshend had distilled into the anthem of a generation,[4] the Stones grabbed and adopted as a lifestyle.

There is a huge so-what factor to the story of the Redlands raid. If you were born too late and are not obsessive about Stones history, chances are you may never have heard of it. The 'biggest rock and pop drugs scandal of all time' would most likely have been here today, gone tomorrow were it not for the fact that it came to be seen as a significant watershed. A squad of twenty policemen tipped off by the *News of the World*, who were out to get Jagger because he was suing them for libel after a case of mistaken identity (a reporter in a nightclub having mistaken Brian for Mick, and having written about his drug use as if it were the lead singer), turned up out of the blue at Keith's home, knocked nicely, then took the place apart. A tiny amount of prescription drugs was found, for which Mick and Keith were later jailed to huge public outcry.

Compare and contrast: Detective Sergeant Norman Pilcher of Scotland Yard's raid on John Lennon's rented Marylebone flat in October 1968. The officer who made a name for himself targeting rock stars including

Donovan, Brian Jones and Eric Clapton as well as Mick and Keith was on a mission. The late-night raid turned up negligible traces of illegal substances because John and Yoko had been forewarned, and had scrubbed the place clean. That the press rocked up a few minutes after the squad said it all. Lennon was charged and fined. The crime would blight his life for years. He had to fight US Immigration for the right to continue residing in the United States, where he and Yoko had gone to look for her abducted daughter Kyoko.

The following March, Beatle George and his wife Pattie were arrested for possession at their Esher home on the day of Paul McCartney's and Linda Eastman's wedding. A platoon of policemen, a policewoman and a detective hound rocked up at the Surrey bungalow to take it to bits. Pilcher's squad arrived with a chunk of hashish, which an officer planted in one of George's shoes. Obsessively tidy Harrison realised that he had been set up the moment it was 'found' there. It caused him endless problems with his US visa. Norman Pilcher's corruption would eventually be exposed. Jailed for four years for perjury by an Old Bailey judge, he was told that he had 'poisoned the wells of British justice'. That may be him, ridiculed for posterity as 'Semolina Pilchard' by John Lennon in the nonsense song with a rhythm like a police siren, 'I Am the Walrus'.

Consider David Bowie's massive drug intake down the decades. If you are interested in the effects of extreme cocaine addiction, check out Alan Yentob's 1975 BBC documentary *Cracked Actor*. David was busted for marijuana possession in 1976. Two hundred and fifty grams could have landed him in jail for fifteen years. Thank you, lawyers.

Paul McCartney flew to Japan for a Wings tour in 1980, having at last been granted permission to enter a country that had previously banned him due to earlier drugs offences. But common sense deserted him on the day he packed 250 grams of marijuana into his luggage. The drugs were found on arrival by customs officials. Macca was banged up for nine days, the longest that he and his late wife Linda had ever been apart. One minute he was facing a lengthy jail term, the next they decided to deport him. It's a wondrous thing, the regularity of reprieve in the realm of rock'n'roll? Suitcases stuffed with readies changing hands at dead of night, you mean? It's your dirty mind.

Another famous bassist, U2's Adam Clayton, was arrested for marijuana possession in Dublin in 1989. A generous donation to charity later, the charges were dropped. You see.

The experiences of some have had tragic consequences. Janis Joplin succumbed to a heroin overdose in 1970. So did the Doors' Jim Morrison in 1971; he died on Brian Jones's second anniversary. Jimi Hendrix was asphyxiated after an accidental overdose of barbiturates in September 1970. All four were the same age, giving rise to the myth of the 'Twenty-Seven Club'. The Who's thirty-two-year-old drummer Keith Moon was trying to wean himself off alcohol when he fatally over-ingested the sedative clomethiazole in September 1978. Boozed-up, smacked-out Thin Lizzy frontman Phil Lynott died of pneumonia and heart failure caused by septicaemia in January 1986. He was thirty-six. Michael Jackson, fifty, suffered cardiac arrest in June 2009, following an administered propofol overdose. Amy Winehouse was busted for marijuana possession in Norway in 2007 and was denied a US visa. She was done many times for pill and powder possession, her lawyers pleading mental illness to keep her out of jail. The bulimic singer died four years later, aged twenty-seven, with five times the legal drink-drive limit of alcohol in her blood. Fifty-seven-year-old, opioid-addicted Prince was killed by an accidental overdose of the pain medication fentanyl in April 2016. Troubled George Michael was done for marijuana possession after crashing his car into a branch of the Snappy Snaps photo-processing chain in 2010, on his way home from London's Gay Pride march. Though his substance abuse was well documented – he had been busted before, in 2006 – cause of death was given as dilated cardiomyopathy, myocarditis and a fatty liver.

No musician sets out to become a drug addict. No rock star ego nurses a death wish, that's a contradiction in terms. It happens by stealth, and starts small: from the 'prellies'[5] sold to the Beatles by a lavatory attendant to keep them upright during their Hamburg residences when they were banging out five or more shows every hard day's night, to the speed bought by the Stones under the counter in diners and gas stations across America's tumbleweed states. They didn't invent the habit – mod-friendly amphetamines such as Purple Hearts, French Blues and Black Bombers had long been seeing the youthful masses through weekend-long partying

– but they soon developed a taste for medication obtainable legally only on prescription.

No way are we getting addicted, boys, right? We can give it up any time we want. Except that you can't. Soon comes the day when too much is not enough. Then it's weed, it gets acidic, people are tripping all over the place on LSD and the Beatles release *Sgt. Pepper's* brimming with thinly disguised drug references and girls with kaleidoscope eyes. The Stones' 'Mother's Little Helper' issues a stern, two-faced warning on the dangers of valium. I mean, steady. Could they get more blatant than the coke and sympathy of 'Let It Bleed', the cocaine eyes and speed-freak drive of 'Can't You Hear Me Knocking', the gas gas *GASS* of 'Jumpin' Jack Flash', the heroin undertones of 'Brown Sugar', the needle and spoon of 'Dead Flowers', the can't-feel-the-pain-no-more of 'Rocks Off', the obvious in 'Sister Morphine', written by Marianne, who sued them for a songwriting credit and *won*; and the lyrically sparse 'stoned … out of my mind' of 'Stoned', the B-side of 'I Wanna Be Your Man'.

Granted, they weren't the only ones. Nor did they invent it. Recorded drug use among musicians dates all the way back to the Jazz Age. When Bob Dylan protested that *Blonde on Blonde*'s 'Rainy Day Women #12 & 35' referred to a biblical, not a herbal, stoning, vociferous was the disbelief. Many of Bob Marley's songs, not least 'Kaya', promoted ganja openly, claiming that it inspired his songwriting and conveyed him closer to Jah. Check out Black Sabbath's 'Sweet Leaf', Peter Tosh's 'Legalize It', Neil Young's 'Roll Another Number (For the Road)'; and, more recently, Tom Petty's 'You Don't Know How It Feels', Snoop Dogg's 'Gin and Juice', Amy Winehouse's 'Addicted' and Miley Cyrus's 'Dooo It'.

Booming beats, urgent rhythms and confrontational lyrics ring out a warning: that hip hop culture and rap music have more to answer for than the Stones ever did. While rap tends to be made by artists who emerged from low-income neighbourhoods where drug abuse was prevalent, not all rap songs about drug use are celebratory. 'Rappers' Delight' by the Sugar Hill Gang was hip hop's breakthrough. The first mainstream single of the genre and the one featuring Chic's 'Good Times', for which Nile Rodgers sued (Say *what?*) is all for; while 'The Message' by Grandmaster Flash and the Furious Five details drug use in frightening ways. Cypress Hill and

Dr. Dre laud marijuana. Snoop Dogg jokes about it. Schoolly D bigs up the criminal lifestyle in general, the scoring of drugs and the prostitution of women in particular. Acid rapper Esham pays homage to hallucinogens and other evils. Public Enemy, the so-called 'Rolling Stones of rap', blare on the state of black America and take a stand against narcotics. 'Night of the Living Baseheads' is their rage against dealing brothers. N.W.A. rant similarly, notably on 'Dopeman'. Afroman's 'Because I Got High', Eminem's 'Drug Ballad' and Lil Wayne's 'I Feel Like Dying' tell it straight.

Speed, hash, acid, speedballs – a blend of cocaine and heroin taken together, sniffed or injected – then coke straight up, smack smoked or intravenous, it's all the same down the line. All a stumble up the same hazy staircase, rotten treads giving way under your feet. Or maybe not up, but down, to where *he* lurks, titfer tipped, spine flattened against a stony pillar in the swirling smoke, eyes glinting and ventricles flaring at every retch. Whipping them on like nags in a steeplechase, booze *more*, neck *more*, smoke yourself cancerous, snort your way to eternal damnation, see if I care and I do, I *do*, I promise you, just a little scratch. And the winner is … And they wonder why drugs became the focal point of growing conflict between the generations. Had to happen, somebody planned it. The Stones are no longer symbols of sympathy for the Devil. They personify him.

*

As I write, the UK government announces a record £780 million for drug treatments in England, on top of the £300 million pledged to crack down on supply chains and drug gangs. This, they declare, is part of a new ten-year strategy to tackle drug abuse in England and Wales. Every local authority in England is promised additional funding to improve access to treatment and increase the capacity of services over the next three years. The fifty local authorities that need it most will receive the money first. By getting more people into treatment, authorities hope to break the cycle of crime driven by addiction and to reduce drug-related violence. The investment, thought to be the largest ever boost in funding, will bring the total spend on drug enforcement and treatment to more than £3 billion during the time frame. Special attention will be paid to the estimated two thousand so-called 'county lines' drug gangs, with extra police deployed to crack down on the supply of class A drugs by city-based crime rings into rural areas and small towns. Some three hundred thousand 'problem drug users' driving both drugs crime and approximately half of all drugs-related murders in the UK have been identified. The emphasis, declares the Prime Minister, will be on rehabilitation rather than prosecution and imprisonment.

'Drugs are a scourge on our society, fuelling violence on our streets which communities across the country are forced to endure,' adds Boris Johnson. 'That's why, to cut crime and truly level up across the country, we must step up efforts to wipe out the vile county lines gangs who are blighting our neighbourhoods, exploiting children and ruining lives. Backed by record investment, the strategy we're setting out today will attack supply and break the county lines model which sees criminals profit from people's misery. Those who break the law will have nowhere to hide.'

According to the Home Office and the Department of Health and Social Care, there are three hundred thousand heroin and crack addicts in England who are responsible for nearly half of all acquisitive crime, including burglary and robbery, while drugs drive nearly half of all homicides. The cost to society is reckoned to be almost £20 billion a year. Measures to be ramped up include drug testing on arrest, and guidance by police of positive-testing individuals towards treatment and other forms of help including drugs-awareness courses. There will be criminal sanctions for offenders who continue to use, such as depriving them of their passports and driving licences. And when dealers are arrested, police will be able to seize their mobile phones and use them to send messages to their clients discouraging drug use and directing them towards support. There is a world of difference between recreational users and damaged people who have experienced traumatic life events, or who are so stressed and under pressure that they can no longer cope without drugs. The criminal justice approach has failed all whose problems ought to be treated as health issues.

And Mick and Keith think what, exactly, when confronted with all this? For read and watch it they must, these intellectual, socially conscious, family-focused fathers, grandfathers and great-grandfathers. This respected knight of the realm and pillar of the Establishment, in Sir Mick's case. Do they secretly thank a few twinklers for their lucky escapes? Is it a 'do as I say, not as I do' scenario, back home on the gilded range? Have they ever and do they still warn their own children and grandchildren about the horrors of a drug-addicted lifestyle? Do they stand up to be counted as examples, conceding that there but for the grace of God would they have gone too? Or do they have a good side-split about it among themselves, musing that that was then, when 'times were different', while this is the get-real now?

Were times really different? they might ask themselves. The relevant Stones must feel *some* responsibility for the cataclysmic drug crisis of today, mustn't they? A generation of rock fans, possibly two or even three generations, were undoubtedly influenced by their habits and behaviour. Many of those fans will have been driven to dabble according to their own example, which is all over their music. The musty male music writers of yore with their pull-out bedroom-wall posters and their homoerotic fantasies didn't tell you *that*, did they. And so the scofflaw ways of rock's drug-abusing days are flagrantly celebrated. Still! Don't believe me?

The Stones are still singing and playing the same songs, aren't they? Fans in their millions around the world turn out to be thrilled by the geriatric spectacle whenever they get the opportunity. There is approval by default in every extortionate ticket purchased, in every T-shirt sported, in every physical record, CD and download forked out for. 'The Stones are the coolest creatures on earth', is the sixty-year-old message. Long may they live, reign and crash around the globe like etiolated teenagers, getting away with it, the greatest rock'n'roll band on earth. The greatest confidence tricksters who ever lived? There's a question. It's all right for them: they had the money to buy 'good drugs'. They had access to the best lawyers dosh could lure. They had marionette friends in elevated places, with strings ripe for the pulling. They had the wherewithal to pay for five-star treatment, and as much lucre as it took to pave their way out of clink. They have specialists at their beck and call to preserve them in their dotage. Lesser mortals who became hooked on illegal substances because they bought the defiant message that the Stones and their ilk purveyed were often rather less fortunate. Jagger ditched heroin for Jerry Hall.[6]

Keith was the hopeless junkie who got clean and lived. They could give it up any time they liked. They did so.

*

It seems ironic, in light of all that we know about the two essentially disparate women, that Marianne, not Anita, should have become the poster girl for the drugs bust that both exposed the 'lowlife' Stones and consolidated their fame and influence in a single swoop. Anita was still with Brian at the time of the raid. They were in Munich, where Anita was filming *Mord Und Totschlag*,[7] for which Brian had composed the soundtrack. Fascinatingly, Keith was there too. He returned to London that February to discover that the Stones' new best friend, drug dealer and so-called 'Acid King' David Sniderman (some write 'Schneiderman') was in town. The Redlands party was swiftly arranged to initiate Mick in his first acid trip. Only later, once she had swapped sides, would Anita get her hands on Keith's beloved Redlands and become the chatelaine of his country retreat. By the time she did, the place was known throughout the world as a den of iniquity, following the raid that nearly destroyed the Stones for good.

David Sniderman was not only a guest at this party. He supplied the drugs. But he disappeared soon after the bust, and they never saw him or heard from him again. Having long suspected that the raid was contrived by the Establishment to frame the band and kill its hold over Britain's youth, Keith speculated in his 2010 memoir *Life* that it was Sniderman who grassed them to the police. This led to Mick's and Keith's arrest and imprisonment for possession of amphetamines and cannabis. They would be acquitted on appeal. There was touching support from fellow rock stars, notably the Who. There ensued a huge surge in the Stones' popularity. Even the press (with the exception of the *News of the World*) did a volte-face and came out on their side, most surprisingly *The Times*, whose editor William Rees-Mogg published a piece entitled 'Who Breaks a Butterfly on a Wheel?'[8] The editorial, now legendary, highlighted the fact that Mick's and Keith's punishment was out of all proportion to the crime: 'It should be the particular quality of British justice to ensure that Mr Jagger is treated exactly the same as anyone else, no better and no worse,' he wrote. 'There must remain a suspicion in this case that Mr Jagger received a more severe sentence than would have been thought proper of any purely anonymous young man.' Thus exonerated, they still wanted their pound of flesh. Support was engaged to help track down the culprit. They would get whoever was responsible, no matter how long it took.

But they did not know the whole story. They were unaware of David Sniderman's true identity and desperation for wealth. Far from being the affluent New Yorker he posed as when he wormed his way into their circle, he was a penniless Canadian actor who had resorted to drug-dealing to make ends meet. Following the Redlands raid, he fled the UK for Los Angeles. Reinventing himself in Hollywood as 'David Jove', he became an independent film-maker and producer. Sniderman/Jove would later tell relatives and friends that he was recruited by British and American intelligence as part of a plot to discredit and finish the Rolling Stones. His identity was confirmed by James Weinstock, a member of a notable family of American philanthropists. Two years after the Redlands bust and a fortnight after meeting her, 'Dave Jove' married Weinstock's sister Marlene 'Lotus' Weinstock, a stand-up comedian and former fiancée of renowned comic Lenny Bruce.

'I first met David when I returned to California from Bali, where I had gone searching for God,' said James Weinstock. 'One New Year's Eve, he showed me a gun and said he'd just killed a man who was messing with his car.' To warn Weinstock not to mess with him? On Christmas Day 1969, Lotus presented Jove with a baby girl whom they called Lili. Although their marriage lasted some eighteen years, they never co-habited. When the child was three, she moved with her mother to a commune from which Jove later had to rescue them. The couple divorced during the late 1980s, after which Lotus embarked on a relationship with British actor Steven Berkoff. She died in 1997 of a brain tumour.

Maggie Abbott, a talent agent during the 1960s, met Jove in Los Angeles in 1983 and began a relationship with him. He regaled her with tales of how he had befriended the Stones, and confessed that he was now 'on the run'.

'David was a heavy drug user but had a quick wit,' she told my friend and former colleague Peter Sheridan, who investigated Jove's story with fellow journalist Sharon Churcher. 'He was the perfect choice to infiltrate the Stones. He never showed any remorse for what he did. It was all about how he had been "the victim". He was a totally selfish person. Mick [Jagger] had been my friend as well as a client, and I thought about trying to persuade David to come clean publicly. But he was always armed with a handgun, and I feared that if I gave him away, he'd shoot me.

'They'd come up with some new way to make acid, and decided to go to the UK and sell it,' she reported. But customs officials detained him after finding cannabis in his luggage. '[He said that] some other guys turned up – he implied they were MI5 or MI6 – and they gave him an ultimatum: he'd get out of prison time if he set up the Stones.'

The British agents were allegedly working with America's secret Counterintelligence Program, Cointelpro, a subdivision of the FBI that operated from 1956 until 1971. Their remit was to discredit and neutralise organisations and individuals considered to be a threat to national security. Their smear tactics and covert activity were mostly illegal. They even carried out political assassinations. One of their known targets under FBI Director J. Edgar Hoover was 'the subversive' John Lennon, who was murdered in New York in December 1980. Deranged fan Mark Chapman confessed to the crime, was sentenced to life, has several times been denied parole and is still inside. Conspiracy theories have swirled for years as to whether Chapman acted alone or was a 'Manchurian candidate', programmed by sinister government forces to exterminate the musician. We will never know.

It was later rumoured that Jove, described as 'dangerous', 'a loose cannon' and 'a violent cocaine addict', had killed singer-songwriter, harmonica player and television host Peter Ivers, presenter of a show that Jove produced. 'There was talk that Peter had decided to leave the show and David was angry,' said Maggie Abbott. Thirty-six-year-old Ivers was found in a downtown loft in 1983. His head had been smashed in. No arrest was ever made, and the murder remains a mystery. Maggie only discovered that 'Jove' was not her lover's real name when he accidentally shot himself in the foot, literally, with his own handgun. She rushed him to the emergency room, and was with him when he gave a fake name. She later learned that he was actually called Sniderman.

Sniderman/Jove told his brother-in-law that he had been close to the Stones, but that there had been a falling-out. 'He was arrested for some serious offence, but managed to extricate himself, and he said it all looked very suspicious when the police busted the Rolling Stones,' said James Weinstock. 'They froze him out after that.' His cover would not be blown until 1985, when Maggie Abbott met an old friend for dinner one night in Los Angeles. That friend was Marianne Faithfull, whom Maggie introduced to her boyfriend David. Horrified Faithfull made her excuses and left. Abbott went after her. As they sat talking in Maggie's car, Marianne revealed Jove's true identity. 'It's him!' she cried, 'the Acid King. He set up the Redlands bust. Don't ever see him again.'

'Two months after the evening with Marianne, I finally had it out with him,' said Maggie. 'To my amazement, he told me everything. He said, "It's a relief to be able to talk about it."' Following which, they went their separate ways. Jove's drug abuse escalated. Dropped by his rich and influential friends, he died a recluse in 2004.

Jove made a deathbed confession to his daughter, Lili Haydn, now a fifty-three-year-old rock fiddler known as 'the Jimi Hendrix of the violin' who has worked with Robert Plant and Jimmy Page, Josh Groban, Sting and Herbie Hancock. 'Shortly before his death, he said he was the Acid King,' said Haydn. 'He told me he wasn't a drug dealer. He felt he was expanding the consciousness of some of the greatest minds of his day.'

The band played on.

Chapter Eleven

MOUCHE

I once spent a weekend with director Ken Russell in the Lake District, in Borrowdale.[1] It was 1986, the year his 'tortured bit of cinematic epilepsy' *Gothic* was released.[2] We were filming a documentary for Channel 4 television, in a rowing boat on Derwentwater. On the edge of that vast and tranquil lake stood his home, which he shared with his second wife Vivian. Ken had raced from the kitchen clutching a bottle of champagne and a head of raw broccoli for us to snack on. The camera crew were in a second boat, bringing up the rear.

The celebrated director's shock-horror flick starring Gabriel Byrne as Lord Byron and Julian Sands as Percy Bysshe Shelley sparked a conversation about David Bowie and Marc Bolan as the Byron and Shelley of rock. Were those Romantic poets the original rock stars, I wondered? No, Ken begged to differ. That honour went to Hungarian composer and pianist Franz Liszt, he said. The term 'Lisztomania' had been coined a hundred and twenty years before 'Beatlemania' in reference to the terrifying hysteria that gripped women during Liszt's recitals. This was no mere social phenomenon, but a recognised medical condition. It was also the title of the film that Ken had made about him. Fifty-nine at the time of our interview and as avid a rock fan as ever, Ken had cast the Who's frontman Roger Daltrey as Liszt, and had enlisted keyboard wizard Rick Wakeman to compose the soundtrack.

Since he rated Bowie and Bolan so highly, I suggested, he should make a film about them as the reincarnations of Shelley and Byron. 'I'll have to wait until David dies,' mused Ken. 'I know too much. Besides,' added the creator of Oscar-winning *Women in Love* and *The Devils*, of videos for Elton John, Bryan Adams and Cliff Richard, and of the film adaptation of the Who's 1969 rock opera *Tommy*,[3] 'there is only one rock star I long to work with now. I've lost interest in all the others. I was denied the opportunity to direct Mick Jagger on *A Clockwork Orange*, and I've never got over it. It would have made superstars of us both.'

Wasn't Mick already a superstar by then? 'Well yes he was, of course, and that's *precisely* why he would have been brilliant,' enthused Ken. 'His detractors love to douse him in excrement and scoff that he can't act. Poppycock. If a director can't tease a perfect performance out of someone like Mick, he is in the wrong profession. What do they think he does up there on stage if it isn't acting? Do they think he's that extreme all the time? Of course he's not! The character he portrays is an alter ego, an extension of himself, something he summons from within and puts away again at the end, for next time. The best kind of film actor is one who has never had a minute's training and who knows absolutely nothing about what the luvvies call *technique*. There's no such thing!' he screamed, gesticulating wildly. Over the side went his champagne flute. He snatched mine from my hand and glugged lavishly.

'Look at Daltrey, who played Tommy in my film. He hadn't a clue, bless him, but he trusted me. He said, "Tell me what to do, Ken, and I'll do it. Anything." He took direction very well, I have to say, and the result was exactly as I'd envisaged. He was mesmerising. A god. I got him back to do Liszt, and yet again he was sensational. All I wanted, I told him, was for him to play Franz Liszt as a nineteenth century Mick Jagger. He wasn't offended by that, *no*. Not at all! He was as great an artist as Jagger, though not quite as busy a shagger, I think I'm right in saying. He had to shag himself stupid with as much posh totty as he could cope with, in that one, without doing himself a mischief. All pretend, of course.'

Couldn't Ken have hired Mick himself, to do it for real? Carnality being his forte. 'Mick wasn't box office,' sighed Ken. 'Roger had already proved himself. He was also stunningly beautiful and exceedingly fanciable. Even *I* fancied him, and you know what I'm like with women.

I could have achieved the same result with Mick, of course. I can make a silk purse out of a sow's ear better than the best of them. I mean, he might be a sex god but he's no Adonis. Why do you think he tortures and denies himself to maintain the figure of a teenage boy? Because he's got to look in the mirror every day. It would upset anyone. But the decision was out of my hands. The same thing happened with *A Clockwork Orange*. In which Mick Jagger directed by the *enfant terrible*, as they call me, would have acquitted himself brilliantly. I would have made sure that he did. And he wouldn't have the reputation for being a failed film actor that he has today.'

*

Mick was always desperate to make it in movies. He had grown up on the singer-turned-actor phenomenon: Frank Sinatra in *Anchors Aweigh* and *From Here to Eternity*, Bing Crosby in *High Society* and *White Christmas*, Frank and Bing together with fellow crooners Dean Martin and Sammy Davis Jr. in *Robin and the 7 Hoods*; not forgetting Elvis Presley in *Jailhouse Rock*, *Blue Hawaii*, *Viva Las Vegas* and the rest. Backed by labels only too eager to take advantage of their charges' cinematic success and convert it into multi-million record sales, they started a trend that would in future embrace artists from across the genres: from Kris Kristofferson, Barbra Streisand and Dolly Parton to Madonna, Beyoncé and Lady Gaga; from Mark Wahlberg, Justin Timberlake and LL Cool J to Tom Waits, Snoop Dogg and Lenny Kravitz; from Bette Midler, Bowie and Cher to Iggy Pop, Jennifer Hudson, Courtney Love and Harry Styles.

Above all, possibly because they were his band's most obvious rivals, Mick envied the Beatles their motion picture success and crossover appeal.[4] The Stones having matched their popularity, he didn't see why they couldn't achieve similar. He overlooked the fact that while the Beatles oozed charm in films full of harmless fun, he and his boys would never get away with such schmaltz. Their reputation was menacing. The Stones could never in a million have made a Beatles kind of movie, as Jagger well knew. He also knew what kind of film he *did* want to make. A fan of Anthony Burgess's depraved 1962 novel *A Clockwork Orange*, Mick leapt to challenge obvious choice Oliver Reed for the role of psychopath Alex DeLarge, the main character, in the screen adaptation.

The rest of the Stones would have supporting roles, as Alex's droogs (gang members), even if they didn't want them. Screenwriter and film-maker *du jour* Ken Russell would direct. But the screenplay's horrific content prevented the producers, who had snapped up Burgess's rights for a song, from getting the project past the British Board of Film Certification. They gave up, and Russell was offloaded. By 1968, the picture still didn't have a director. Mick remained as keen as ever to play the lead. When it was suggested that David Hemmings would be cast, the Beatles petitioned in writing that their friend Mick should get the role instead.

Another document came to light in 2008, a letter which showed that the film's executive producer had tried to talk John Schlesinger[5] into directing it, and had also suggested that the Beatles should compose the soundtrack. In the end, Stanley Kubrick, director of 1968's *2001: A Space Odyssey* was appointed, and Malcolm McDowell was cast in the leading role. Mick's disappointment must have made him all the more determined to land a part he could make his own and establish a major screen presence. He jumped at *Ned Kelly* but needn't have bothered.

Then along came *Performance*. It seemed an infinitely better fit, given that the script required him to portray nothing more demanding than a version of himself. Anita Pallenberg and James Fox would co-star. *Peyton Place*[6] ingenue Mia Farrow, who was at the time Frank Sinatra's third wife, had been engaged to play Lucy, the supporting female character. But she was forced to withdraw after suffering a bad fall in New York, which left her with a fractured ankle. An unknown French waif by the name of Michèle Breton was brought in to replace Mia. She went by the nickname 'Mouche', the French for 'fly'. Because she dwelled among degenerates and fed on shit? Exploited by the producers and director and corrupted by the experience, she was abandoned beyond to a life of destitution and obscurity, discarded like a broken toy. She casts a long shadow over the Rolling Stones legend. She may be their most tragic victim.

Where did Mouche come from? Accounts conflict. Some claim that she was born in Brittany, a picturesque peninsular of north-western France jutting into the English Channel. Her peasant parents are said to have thrown her out when she was sixteen, palming her off with a one-way train ticket to Paris and a hundred francs to be going on with. Their parting shot was a bit harsh: they never wanted to see her again. Why? Does that sound likely? Perhaps her surname is a clue. 'Breton' is both French for Brittany and the name of the regional language spoken there. Could she have thrown off her original family name and have adopted that as a pseudonym?

Her official movie bio stated that she came into the world in Déville-lès-Rouen in Normandy, north-western France. It also placed her, at the age of fifteen, in Alpine Grenoble, south-eastern France, her 'university-teacher' parents having moved there for work. She is said to have made her way unaccompanied to Saint-Tropez, to live with her grandmother. There, she became a beach bum and fell in with the trendy movie crowd, much as Anita Pallenberg had done in Rome. Another version, the most plausible in my opinion, claims that pretty, scrawny, uneducated Michèle, who was dark-haired and strong-featured with a flat chest and a prominent nose, was from a family of peasants living in the hills above the French Riviera, where her father was a garagiste: a small-scale, what we might call 'cottage', wine-maker.

What is the truth? Were different versions of her story concocted and disseminated to disguise her origins, throw authorities off the scent and prevent a search for her family and birth certificate? Or did she change her story on a whim whenever she felt like it, rewriting her past to fit in with the scenario of the moment, to render herself more interesting and to maximise her chances at a future? Could she have been coerced into doing this? If so, *Performance* director Donald Cammell is the most likely culprit. The Scottish society portraitist and bohemian bon viveur with his own Chelsea studio and a fascination for real-life gangsters including the Kray twins had plenty to hide. Having reinvented himself as a screenwriter, the wildly ambitious social climber was keen to establish a reputation as a director. This would be his first official film, which he would co-direct with Nicolas Roeg.[7] Thirty-four-year-old Cammell did not want the industry to know that he and Deborah Dixon, a stunning, blonde, internationally successful model who was bankrolling her boyfriend, had scooped the allegedly fourteen-year-old Michèle from the beach at Saint-Tropez and had enticed her to reside with them in a ménage-à-trois in

Paris. Pubescent flesh and girl-on-girl action were Cammell's weaknesses. This set-up lasted for about a year, during which Michèle, encouraged by Deborah, did a little modelling in the French capital.

Although it has been written that *Performance* was her only film, she can clearly be seen, albeit fleetingly, in the Jean-Luc Godard 1967 black comedy *Weekend* starring Mireille Darc and Jean Yanne. Michèle was not credited. IMDb also lists her as having played Greek goddess Athena in three episodes of Italian state television's 1968 mini-series *L'Odissea*, based on Homer's *Odyssey*. Was that really her? She was not known for linguistic prowess. She spoke negligible English when she was brought to London to film *Performance*.

When journalist Mick Brown found her years later in Berlin, Breton told him about her life after *Performance* wrapped. She said that Cammell drove her back to the Paris apartment, let her stay for a couple of nights, then kicked her out. Once again homeless, with little money and few possessions to her name, it seems likely that she was remunerated inadequately if at all for her work on the film. She drifted aimlessly around France, turning up in Villefranche in 1971 and finding her way to Nellcôte, the villa that Keith rented during the recording of *Exile on Main St.* She was probably dealing drugs. She ambled on down to Spain and was arrested for possession on Formentera, a small island off Ibiza. She reportedly gave the *policia* the slip, legged it back to Paris and then hit the hippie trail, washing up in Kabul, Afghanistan, during the mid-1970s. She lay low for a year, shooting morphine. When she hit rock bottom, she sold everything she had left including her passport. She was destitute, starving, tripping on LSD and in a frail mental state when it occurred to her that she had to stop and change her life or she would die.

She spent the following few months in hospital in India – we have no clue as to who might have supported her financially – before making her way back to Kabul and thence to Europe, sans ID. She quit the road when she reached Berlin. If it sounds like a script, much of it may be. But her recollections about the filming of *Performance*, during which she was stoned out of her brains most of the time, ring true. 'I was very young and very disturbed,' she said. 'I didn't know what I was doing, and they used me. Everybody was sleeping with everybody,' she later shrugged. 'It was those times.'

Keith did not mince words in the comprehensive damnation of Donald Cammell in his memoir *Life*. 'The most destructive little turd I've ever met,' he called him. 'Also a Svengali, utterly predatory, a very successful manipulator of women ... putting people down was almost an addiction for him ... when I first heard of him, he was in a ménage-à-trois with Deborah Dixon and Anita, long before Anita and I were together, and they were all jolly jolly. He was a procurer, an arranger of orgies and threesomes – in a pimpish way, though I don't think Anita saw it like that.'

Performance may well have been warped Cammell's way of getting back at Keith, because he'd had Anita first, and was jealous of the guitarist's wealth, success and hold over her. Casting Keith's girlfriend as Pherber, the fierce lover of faded rocker Turner (Jagger), and throwing in an androgynous, out-of-it French teen for hot threesomes in a shockingly decadent and violent piece was always going to have incendiary consequences. Add monstrous, mind-addling drug consumption to the daily shoot and stand well back. Cammell messed with everyone's heads in the name of performance art (he called it), especially co-star James Fox, who gave his best murderous gangster. A year after the film, Fox joined a religious sect and turned his back on acting to become an evangelist. Rumours persisted for years that he went off his rocker during the shoot. He later denied this, insisting that he had been heading in a more spiritual and cerebral direction anyway.

Anita, always up for anything, admitted that initially the sex scenes had happened for real but that she put it down to 'method acting'. Which suggests penetrative sex, doesn't it? She later denied it, but was not believed. She had, after all, aborted Keith's child in order to keep the role. The price she paid for her callousness was full-blown heroin addiction: her own and possibly even Keith's. Who sat tormenting himself in his car outside the location house while his 'old lady' was inside, getting it on with Mick. Keith denounced the finished film as 'third-rate porn'. He also recalled Anita having told him that Michèle needed shots of Valium before every take, so distressed was she by the acts she was made to perform.

How was this allowed? Why didn't anybody question it? Assurances were made that qualified doctors were on set every day, administering the anxiolytic. Had they been General Medical Council-registered physicians, they would have required proof of Michèle's age before they could sedate her. Given her extremely youthful appearance and vulnerable demeanour, why was her wellbeing not safeguarded? How had she obtained a work permit in the first place? Did somebody falsify her application? Insiders intimated that Cammell did. It has long been rumoured that Jagger engaged in sexual activity with Michèle. There was certainly nudity. Photographs from the shoot depict them lying naked on a bed together, side by side. An equivalent film production company today might find itself staring down the barrel of a statutory rape investigation because she may have been underage during the shoot. Nobody knew, and no one was bothered. The film's American producer Sanford 'Sandy' Lieberson described her as 'someone who didn't care who she slept with. A strange little creature, totally androgynous-looking – the way Donald liked them.'

The operative word is 'little'. It implies a childlike state. Who was looking out for this drugged and misguided kid? Clearly, no one. 'I was taking everything that was going,' she said in 1995. 'I was in a very bad shape, all fucked up.' What might Mick have to say about that now? What he *did* say, when interviewed for film writer Jay Glennie's study of *Performance*, was this: 'All the stories around the filming of those scenes were so good, I'm not going to deny any of them.'

Nor did Mick deny actress Rae Dawn Chong's February 2020 allegations that she had slept with him when she was only fifteen. While talking to the *Hollywood Reporter* about her starring role in Jagger's promo film for his 1985 solo single 'Just Another Night', an aggressively sexual piece in which he appears heavily made-up and bouffant-coiffed in a hot and sweaty club, Chong let slip that they'd had sex together twice in 1977: once after a Rolling Stones recording session and a second time after Mick took her to a Fleetwood Mac concert. Immediately regretting the revelation, she gave further interviews to insist that she had not been a 'victim of unwanted advances' and that Jagger had not known her age. 'He never asked how old I was, and I never told him,' stated the self-confessed 'Lolita'. 'It never came up. He did nothing wrong. He didn't make me do anything I didn't want to do.'

The actress, who starred in 1981's *Quest for Fire*, *The Color Purple* and

Commando in 1985, and in the 1990s American soap opera *Melrose Place*, explained that 'it was the 1970s, a different era. I wasn't a victim. I don't want him to get into trouble about this. It wasn't traumatising. I knew what I was doing. I wasn't an innocent schoolgirl. I always acted a lot older than I was. I was a grown-up at fifteen ... he wasn't that much older than me in my brain. He was thirty-three and young and gorgeous, with a nice body. It wasn't a bad thing, it was fabulous. Totally rock'n'roll.'

But whether she wanted it or not, Rae Dawn could not have consented. She was under the age of unrestricted consent.[8]

Co-director Nicolas Roeg admitted that some scenes in *Performance* were so explicit, they caused problems when he went to collect the rushes. He turned up at the lab to find technicians destroying the film with hammers and chisels, so fearful were they that they'd be charged by police with holding pornographic material.

Disgusted by its depravity, Warner Bros shelved the film indefinitely. A radically re-edited version was eventually released in August 1970, only to be butchered by the critics who damned it for its graphic sex scenes and denounced it as the most loathsome and pretentious picture of all time. 'The film that horrified Hollywood,' screamed the headlines. 'You do not have to be a drug addict, pederast, sadomasochist or nitwit to enjoy *Performance*,' said the *New York Times*, 'but being one or more of these things would help.' It has since become a cult classic via video and DVD sales. I suspect that more Stones and Jagger fans may have read or heard about it than have seen it. In any case, is this not yet another example of 'the Emperor's New Clothes'? People claiming to like something because they have been led to believe that it will make them look hip and cool to say that they like it? Doesn't anyone worry that a minor may have been manipulated and abused in the making of it? It is called, today, 'one of the most influential and innovating films of the 1970s', and 'one of the greatest films in the history of British cinema'. It was even voted, in 1999, the forty-eighth greatest British film of all time by the British Film Institute. How bad were the others?

It was 'Donald's vision,' Pallenberg said. 'He was notoriously into threesomes, rock stars and criminal violence. He injected all of his deviant sexual fantasies into the movie ... [which] seems to me to be about the end of an era of hippie innocence, free love and sexual experimentation.' His 'vision' just happened to capture a turning point in the sixties, when exuberance was giving way to degradation.

As for Cammell, who made only three films over a quarter of a century, perhaps his guilty conscience caught up with him. Having stated unambiguously that the sex in the film was real, he committed suicide in 1996, when he was sixty-two. Keith had advised him to take the gentleman's way out three years earlier. The rocker later dismissed *Performance* as 'the best work Cammell ever did, except for shooting himself.'

No one knows what happened to Michèle Breton. Various authors and commentators have written her off, perhaps prematurely. She accidentally overdosed; she killed herself; she died a natural death. All assumption. The used and abused little French girl evaporated into the fog and has never re-emerged. If she is still alive, she would be in her late sixties. She didn't simply lose her way. She never found it.

*

Nor did Mick ever triumph in Hollywood. 'I would like to have done a lot more,' he told *USA Today*, 'but it's a funny world, film. You don't get that many interesting things. You get a lot of rubbish offered to you that you might do if that was the only job. But I have other things to do.'

Having expressed a fervent wish to play androgynous, stockinged and suspendered Dr. Frank N. Furter in the screen adaptation of Richard O'Brien's 1975 global hit theatrical extravaganza *The Rocky Horror Picture Show*, Mick was disappointed to lose out to the role's originator, Tim Curry. Beyond which, no major roles came his way for years. He was about to celebrate his fiftieth birthday when he appeared in 1992's *Freejack*, playing bodysnatcher Victor Vacendak to tepid acclaim in the dystopian cyberpunk sci-fi flick. Despite the film's hefty names – Anthony Hopkins, Rene Russo, Emilio Estevez – it bombed. Mick slunk away yet again with his tail between his legs. He launched his own production company Jagged Films in 1995, and gave the world his autobiographical television documentary *Being Mick* six years later. For this, he had followed himself around for a year, shooting much of his own footage on a small handheld camera. In 1997, ridding himself of his *Rocky Horror* demons, he played transvestite singer Greta in a piece called *Bent* about the persecution of homosexuals in Nazi Germany. It wasn't bad. In 2001, he portrayed craggy Luther Fox, a high-class pimp of male hookers in *The Man From Elysian Fields*. His co-star was Andy Garcia. And eighteen years later, in the 2019 thriller *The Burnt Orange Heresy*, here's seventy-six-year-old Mick the wily art dealer trying to nab a painting by reclusive artist Jerome Debney, played by Donald Sutherland.

'Jagger, though never quite an actor as such, puts in a very good-humoured and game performance that takes this beyond stunt casting, playing the manipulative art dealer, spring-heeled with athletic malice, grinning like a relief map of the Lake District and with a distinct whiff of sulphur about him,' wrote film critic Peter Bradshaw in the *Guardian*. 'It would be great to have Keith Richards play the aged, cantankerous, whiskery painter Debney,' he added. 'But you can't have everything.'

Some people can. How Mick must have fumed when screen fame and acclaim fell into Keith Richards's leathery lap without him having to twitch a muscle, after Johnny Depp confessed that he had based the look, speech, expressions and mannerisms of his *Pirates of the Caribbean* character on his guitar hero. It was only a matter of time before the rock god himself would be invited to step inside the fantasy. In 2007, Keith surpassed himself as Captain Teague, father of Depp's Captain Jack Sparrow in *At World's End*. He also played guitar and sang the self-penned song 'Only Found Out Yesterday'. He got the best line in the picture, too: when Sparrow asks him, 'That's the trick, isn't it? To survive?' Keith as Teague responds, *a basso profundo*, 'It's not just about living forever, Jackie. The trick is living with yourself forever.' Could that perchance have been a pop at Mick? Keith bagged the Best Celebrity Cameo gong at that year's Spike Horror Awards, and returned to the franchise four years later in *On Stranger Tides*. He is as compelling in his role as Depp is in his. And that's saying something.

As for Jagger. Charisma on stage. Charisn'tma on screen. You get what you need.

Chapter Twelve

CHRISTOPHER ROBIN

Keith and Anita were not the only ones whose drug use had spiralled out of control. Brian Jones, who had taken up with fringy blonde nineteen-year-old Anitalike Melanie 'Suki' Potier, the girlfriend who survived the car smash that killed Guinness heir Tara Browne, was skating thin. Aware that the Stones were making plans to tour America without him, because he would not be permitted re-entry by US Immigration with drugs convictions to his name, he started to panic. Friends who tried to help him, including Paul McCartney, had their hospitality and kindness flung back at them. Brian was looking like a lost cause. As his supporters shrank away, it must have dawned on him that only the man in the mirror could help him. He pulled himself together enough to submit for treatment at the Priory Hospital in Roehampton, West London, long before it gained its reputation as rock'n'roll rehab. Down the line, any number of sapped stars would follow him there.

The psychedelic compounds he had first sampled at San Francisco's Monterey festival in June the previous year were playing havoc with his health and making him more susceptible to asthma attacks.[1] His dependence on the sedative Mandrax, he realised, was an addiction he had to conquer. While the downers did help him sleep, something that had eluded him for months, they were robbing him of the versatility, precision and co-ordination that hallmarked his musicianship. Pressure had been mounting for a while, and there was plenty to blame: the busts, brief imprisonment, humiliating publicity, band bickerings, the scornful spectre of Anita, his vain, deluded quest to win her back and the spiteful behaviour of a vindictive double act who should have known better. While many people down the years, including Brian's own father Lewis, have blamed Anita for his downfall, others have gone so far as to say that Mick and Keith killed him – with passive aggression, intimidation and mockery.

'I watched them do it,' said an industry professional on a promise of anonymity: 'I would stand up to be counted, but I can do without them coming after me. They could be vile gits, the pair of them, if you want to know. They wore Brian down. They took pleasure from it, and sniggered quite viciously about it. You could almost see them rubbing their hands with glee. The times I wanted to take Brian outside and shake him, tell him to stand up to their nonsense, the stupid couple of kids, and not let them get away with it. But the band was the most important thing to him. He wouldn't give it up for anything – not until it was too late, and had convinced himself that he was better off out of it.'

'All cruelty springs from weakness,' wrote the Roman philosopher and playwright Seneca.[2] Who had a point. We are well aware, today, of the causes and implications of bullying, and of why it is now regarded as a form of abuse, against which there are laws. Persecution, harassment, discrimination and prejudice are all forms of it. It is understood to be about gaining power, and is usually perpetrated by individuals with low self-esteem. They may resent their target, for all kinds of reasons. This causes them to project their own feelings of inadequacy on to them. The thing that all bullies have in common is their use of power to counterbalance their own psychological shortcomings and inferiority. Every time they attack someone weaker, they feel better about themselves. But only for a moment. Because that feeling of power is fleeting, so the bully has to bully over and over again. They know what they are doing, and that it is wrong. But they choose to ignore the ethical and moral implications, and they keep on doing it. If confronted, they invariably blame their victim.[3]

Brian simply didn't know how to stand up to Mick and Keith, or how to confront their behaviour rationally and make them back down. He had no idea how to defend himself. He took more and more drugs to block out his torment, numb the pain and blur the circumstances. He didn't know how to 'kill them with kindness', which is recognised now as a way of deflating bullies.

'The problem with Mick is that he has no real allegiance to people,' said publicist Keith Altham. 'For example, when I came in, they had Les Perrin as their PR. Les was very well respected and much loved by clients and press alike. Then one day, Jagger summoned me to the Savoy Hotel to talk about getting rid of Les and me replacing him. "But Mick," I said, "if you sack Les, that would be very bad public relations. People won't like it. He hasn't done anything wrong. Why not take me on as the foot soldier, and keep him on in a supervisory capacity?" "We don't need two press agents," growled Mick. He shows no loyalty towards people who work for him when their usefulness is used up. He always has to slam a door in your face. This is exactly what he did to Brian Jones. It's that very ruthlessness, of course, that keeps him at the top.

'When I eventually went to work as the Rolling Stones' PR, someone said to me, "Congratulations on getting the job as Mick's butler." What did that mean, I asked. "Oh, you'll find out." And I did. I knew what I was dealing with the day I asked Mick for the phone numbers of the other Stones. "You won't need those," said Jagger. "They do as I tell them. Keith's out of it all the time. Bill's boring, and Charlie doesn't do interviews. Everything goes through me." And that was my experience of him.'

The first time Keith ever met the Stones, he recalls, was at the Great Pop Prom at London's Royal Albert Hall on 15 September 1963. 'It was the first time the Beatles and the Stones had ever performed together on the same bill,' he says. 'The Stones opened the show and the Beatles closed it. It was part of an annual fundraising event for the Printers' Pension Corporation, and was compèred by DJ Alan Freeman. Can you imagine the Albert Hall back then, sedate venue that it was, besieged by thousands of screaming teenagers? The Beatles performed on the main stage, and the Stones on a small dais in the round. I was standing in the [Sir] Henry Cole Room on the Grand Tier when these roughs came in. I'd seen the photos, so I wasn't too taken aback. I got talking to Brian Jones, and found him really nice and intelligent, not at all like one of those oafs they were portrayed as in the papers. Then there was Keith Richards, who was picking his nose and flicking it at the flocked wallpaper. "You're lucky they weren't green ones," Brian observed. "He eats those."

'I could see clearly from the start that this was Brian's band. He had depth in his thinking. He was clean, well-mannered, kind and generous. He understood the value of press and publicity, and he was invariably accommodating and helpful to me when I was trying to do my job. There were some unpleasant traits with women, and all that stuff about girls being passed around members of the band: Marianne, Anita, and so on. But until the booze and the drugs kicked in, Brian was by and large a gentleman, exceedingly musical, and very much in control. They have tried to insinuate since that they got rid of him because of the booze and drugs. My feeling is that it was the other way round, and that he took to substance abuse in a big way after he realised they had it in for him. I always felt that, had they appreciated and included him, they would have been a much better band. They could have been making inventive and thrilling new music all these years, instead of resting on their laurels and going on endless tours to rehash the ancient hits, which is all anybody has wanted from them for about half their career. Brian was the truly musical Stone. A jack of all trades. He could pick up more or less any instrument and get a tune out of it. That gave them an edge that they lacked, after he died.

'Stu used to say that the Rolling Stones would be over when Mick found his own identity.'

'So he still hasn't found it?'

'What do you think?'

'Would Keith still turn out to see the Stones today?'

'I saw them at Shepherd's Bush Empire on 8 June 1999, when they were halfway through the No Security tour and were doing a warm-up for the British dates. Tickets were changing hands for a grand each, and thousands of people turned up that night who hadn't even got tickets. Just to be there, outside on the pavement. I was invited, so I went along. They were fantastic. They hadn't made a decent record for about twenty-five years by then, but they were so good that I knew I didn't want to see them ever again. Jagger, as ever, was amazing on stage. So charismatic.

But I decided to leave it there. They're a tourist attraction now, like the Eiffel Tower. People go because it's there. Less Rolling Stones, more Stonehenge. Megalithic monuments. The music hasn't evolved further. Perhaps, had Brian still been around, it would have done.'

*

Music should have helped Brian. Music was where he came in. It had aided his escape before: from the tragedy of his little sister's death, from his cold, unaffectionate parents and from his fear that he was unworthy of love, because no one had ever loved him. Was that true? Could it have been paranoia talking? Either way, Brian was getting desperate.

It is always fascinating to talk to musicians about the dawning of music in their lives. What they have to share on the subject can sometimes sound fey or far-fetched, but only because describing it in words defeats them. Their eyes tend to glaze over at such questions, or they roll them in mock irritation. They tilt their necks and lift their faces skywards, as though in deference to some deity, or thanking stars. They have no idea where it comes from, they insist. George Michael and David Bowie could impart no more wisdom about it than Joe Bloggs on an open-mic night down the Railway Tavern. Nor do they know why they were 'touched' or 'blessed'. They are grateful to God, Apollo, the Universe and whoever else for it, but they can never in a million explain it. I have been interviewing artists all my adult life. I always ask, and have never received a definitive explanation ... because there isn't one. But sometimes they will come out with some gem that distils the phenomenon of music in a whole new way.

I didn't get the chance to ask Brian Jones. Born too late. I wouldn't mind betting, however, that he would have said the same sort of thing: that the art of music had randomly favoured him. That it had reached out to him, enveloping and embracing him, awakening and coaxing emotions from him as nothing else could. That he willingly played host to the ghost that rippled through his senses, played on his lips and danced in his heart. They really do eulogise in this way. He'd say that he was thrilled by the feeling of it filtering into his fingers, igniting him. That he loved how it compensated for what he lacked. That it let him in on its complex language, and welcomed him into its secret world. That it gave him confidence. That it drew him back and back, on a voyage of discovery that both broadened his tastes and made a purist of him. Brian, we know, responded to the blues because he felt the blues. He knew pain and learned to translate adversity into notes that resonated with others. His virtuosity should have been his salvation. Powerful and vital though music was to him, it could not save him.

If only he could have found something to make his own. He did try, on his various excursions to northern Africa, where the rhythms and sounds of local music enchanted him. Gripped by palinacousis,[4] he had been toying with the idea of returning yet again to spend time exploring Gnawa, the ancient folk music of Morocco. Its name derives from that of Guinea, the predominantly Islamic West African country on the Atlantic coast. Notorious for its slave trade during the eleventh century, that land's musical tradition arose out of the howlings of the enslaved. The deeply spiritual music that evolved over centuries comprises healing chants, strange rhythms and hypnotic dance. Its principal instruments are solid iron castanets known as qraqeb, a three-stringed lute called a hajhuj, hejhouj or sentir, and large tbel drums. This music, hugely popular today, has been celebrated annually since 1998 at the Gnaoua World Music Festival of Essaouira, Morocco, drawing massive audiences. Jimmy Page and Robert Plant are aficionados. They call it 'world music' now.

Brian rocked the casbah[5] ahead of all of them in his ambition to harness Gnawa and combine it with other disciplines to create a thrilling new hybrid. He planned to capture voices, drums and other instruments on tape, transport the recordings to a New York studio and embellish them with layers of rhythm and blues, funk and jazz. He and producer Glyn Johns went to stay at the Marrakesh mansion of oil heir Paul Getty Jr, which was to be their base while they worked. But Brian hit the hashish as soon as they landed. He never emerged from the haze. Left to his own devices, Johns tried to glean what he could from local bands. The project disintegrated. Another Brian brainwave bit the dust.

Back in London, on 12 May 1968, he performed with the Stones as part of the *NME*'s Poll Winners' concert at Wembley's Empire Pool alongside Lulu, Cliff Richard and the Shadows, Dusty Springfield, the Bee Gees, Status Quo and the rest, and managed to rise to the occasion. That brief flare of focus and control would not last. Few could have guessed that 'this would be the last time he would play live with the Rolling Stones'. Was it? We can't count *The Rolling Stones Rock and Roll Circus*[6] concert show in December 1968, 'they' say, because that was filmed before a private audience, various members of whom took part in the show. But it should be counted, as Brian's unofficial swansong. Although conflicting excuses circulated, it must have been because he died mere months after filming it that the Stones and their management cancelled its release.

*

Brian's romance with Suki staggered along. The more she adored him and lavished him with love and devotion, the worse he treated her, lashing out as though punishing her for the manner in which Mick and Keith were treating him. Rumours about their contemptible behaviour towards him in the studio, unplugging his amp, switching off his microphone and ridiculing him 'behind his back' but effectively to his face turned out to be true. Ostracised and unable to stand the persecution, he would drug to the nines to drag himself there, but was ineffective when he arrived. He started missing rehearsals. When he managed to get to the studio at all, he contributed less and less. What made them stoop to such cruelty? It is hard to fathom.

It would have felt, to Brian, like a concerted campaign to grind him down and drive him out. Long in the habit of penning copious handwritten notes, he wrote begging letters to Mick, said Marianne Faithfull and others, pleading to be given another chance. Did those pleas fall on deaf ears? We can assume so, given that John Mayall's Bluesbreakers guitarist Mick Taylor had already been approved as Brian's replacement. Baby-faced 'Little Mick' was only twenty at the time. He would light up the Stones' next six albums – *Let It Bleed*, *Get Yer Ya-Ya's Out!*, *Sticky Fingers*, *Exile on Main St.*, *Goats Head Soup* and *It's Only Rock 'n Roll*, regarded by many as their definitive run – before quitting abruptly in 1974. We know why, too. We will get there.

Hurt has to go somewhere. Brian was taking his out on Suki, who in his blurred mind's eye morphed into Anita every time he looked at her. His beautiful, feisty, relentless Anita, the one true love (he convinced himself) who haunted him. After a particularly vicious row in Tangier, poor Suki could take no more. She attempted suicide, smashing a mirror and ripping through the veins in her wrists with its jagged edge. When the ambulance arrived, Brian made no move to accompany her to hospital. He was said to have shown negligible concern, and seemed to brush the incident off as an inconvenience. Was he stoned, or were there shards in his heart?

Back in England and spending more and more time languishing at Redlands while lord of the manor Keith was in London, impotent in his flashy motor outside the house where Mick and Anita were shooting *Performance*, Brian was seized by the idea of getting a country retreat of his own. The haven he found, near Hartfield, East Sussex, ninety minutes inland from Redlands, was perfect. Here at last was the hideout in which to take stock, come to terms with his divorce from the Stones and work out what to do next. He had no way of knowing that Cotchford Farm, where Alan Alexander Milne had created charming, eternal stories about a teddy bear called Winnie the Pooh, had itself been the setting of much misery.

I could barely believe my eyes when I switched on the television on Saturday 13 November 2021. I selected from the movie menu the 2017 film *Goodbye Christopher Robin* starring Domhnall Gleeson as A.A. Milne, Margot Robbie as his wife and Kelly Macdonald as Olive the nanny. It was none of these actors who caught my attention, however. It was Will Tilston, the child playing eight-year-old Christopher Robin Milne. Staring out at me from the screen was Brian Jones as a little boy. The resemblance was remarkable.

Billed as offering 'valuable insight into the darkness shadowing the creation of a classic children's tale', the film seemed to reflect Brian's own sad boyhood. It occurred to me that his purchase of Cotchford Farm was not symbolic of going forward, it was about looking back. Less investment in a post-Stones future, more the purchase of a childhood he'd never had.

Brian was enchanted by the rambling, timber-framed sixteenth-century house that sat at the end of a private lane on the edge of the Ashdown Forest. Milne had bought it in 1925 as a country home for himself and his family. Beloved places in the *Winnie the Pooh* stories that he wrote there – places such as Poohsticks Bridge, Pooh Corner, Galleon's Lap and the Hundred Acre Wood – were all based on actual locations. There were statues in the garden of Christopher Robin and of his friend Owl, and a sundial with its stone stand featuring carvings of Piglet, Eeyore, Tigger, Kanga and Roo, characters dear to generations of children including Brian. The estate also boasted nearly ten acres of land, its own woods, fields and a paddock, landscaped gardens, a summer house and a fish pond. The previous owners, an American couple by the name of Taylor, had also installed a large, heated swimming pool.

Christopher Robin Milne wrote in his autobiography, *The Enchanted Places: A Childhood Memoir*: 'Cotchford was different. Cotchford was ours, and on an autumn morning we drove down to take possession. No. I have got it wrong. It was Cotchford that took possession of us.' It had the same effect on Brian, who couldn't say no to it. He snapped it up in November 1968. Eight months later, like A.A. Milne, he would breathe his last there.[7]

I struggled to concentrate on the film, preoccupied as I was with the actor's likeness to little boy Brian. The Christopher Robin character seemed uncannily imbued with Brian's own melancholy. The uncomfortable truth was that Milne regenerated his son into something that did not exist. He conjured stories that turned private father-son moments and childish fantasies into public property. Christopher Robin was already desperately unhappy when he was sent away to boarding school, where he was bullied and ridiculed for his winsome appearance, stuffed companions and disagreeable fame. He would reject the Pooh fortune in adulthood. All that he wanted was to be a real person, not a shadow of someone else's interpretation.

Brian would not have known any of this. He had bought not only a country house, but a whole new lifestyle. Suki moved there with him, but her tenure was over within months. When she left during the spring of 1969, Brian wasted no time in moving in her replacement: a twenty-two-year-old dancer, yet another beautiful blonde Anita clone, by the name of Anna Wohlin. The couple had first met five years earlier, when Anna had travelled to the UK from her native Sweden as an exchange student. She had lodged in Wales, but subsequently moved to London. She got to know Brian when she danced at the Speakeasy, or was it at the Revolution? All clubs taste the same after a few wines. Now here she was, living with him as the lady of the house, conversing over the marmalade about livestock. The dark horse! He intended to get some for his paddock, he told her. He already had a family of cats breeding enthusiastically, as well as a cocker spaniel and an Afghan hound. He loved walking them through the woods and along the country lanes to the Hay Waggon, his local on Hartfield High Street. He'd have a pint, play pool and chew the cud with neighbours there. He also befriended folk who lived in cottages on the Cotchford Farm estate, including his gardener. He was particularly close to his housekeeper Mary Hallet (or Hallett), who had been born on the estate.

The pollen count was high that hot summer, but Brian was taking care of his health. He had respirators installed in each room, and made sure he didn't run out of inhalers. Apart from a modest amount of alcohol and his sleeping pills, Anna insisted, Brian was not taking anything. He was more than happy in his new environment, she said, and was focused on the future. The subject of marriage was broached, as were children. So soon? Who needed the Stones when one had all this. Brian wasn't happy about the direction in which the band were taking their music. He was ready to go his own way. While, in common with his bandmates, he had experienced problems obtaining his money when he needed it, he must have been unaware of the truly precarious state of their finances. The band was in fact going steadily broke. As a result of the deal they had done with their business manager Allen Klein, royalties from the sales of all their albums released in the US were funnelled through Klein's company ABKCO in New York City. It had now dawned on Mick that all the money flowing into ABKCO wasn't coming back out.

There was only one thing for it, as far as their new financial advisor Prince Rupert Loewenstein was concerned: they were going to have to go back on tour. Not the hop-and-a-skip trailing around the European capitals and nipping over the pond to do the modest-venue short-haul flings through a few American cities that they were used to. They were going to have to up the stakes, get big-time and hit the US concert circuit full-on. They couldn't, however, do this with Brian. With a drug conviction hanging over his head, US Immigration were never going to allow him in. Thus were the Stones presented with the perfect excuse to fire him.

When Mick, Keith and Charlie came to Cotchford on 8 June 1969, Brian was ready for them. They informed him that they wanted him to leave the band, and were surprised when he agreed to it so serenely. He also accepted their offer of a £100,000 pay-off. He was dignified about it, and did not haggle for more. There was to be an annual allowance on top of that, they promised, at an amount to be agreed. While no one knows for sure, this is sometimes quoted as £20,000. Because of the band's multiple issues with Klein and the problems they experienced getting their hands on what was rightfully theirs, we don't know whether Brian, or his estate, was ever paid.

*

What the world remembers is that Brian Jones drowned in his swimming pool on 3 July 1969 at the age of twenty-seven. Which is curious in itself. Given that Brian was dead well before midnight, the date of his death should have been recorded as the day before. A comparable anomaly would occur eleven years later, when John Lennon was gunned down outside the Dakota building, his Manhattan apartment block, on a date preserved to eternity as 8 December 1980. But John was killed at around 22:50 Eastern Standard Time. In Liverpool, his place of birth, it was ten to four the next morning. Given that John was British, fans felt it would have made more sense to record his death as having occurred on the following day; especially as he had been born on 9 October and was obsessed with that number, which recurred throughout his life.[8]

What many still question is the verdict, recorded at East Sussex coroner's court, of 'death by misadventure'. The coroner's report concluded that Brian died as a result of 'drowning by immersion in fresh water associated with severe liver dysfunction caused by fatty degeneration and ingestion of alcohol and drugs'. The post-mortem had revealed that Brian's liver was double the normal weight for a man of his size and build. And that was that. The case was closed, and Home Office records were sealed by the court for a period of seventy-five years. Why? What of their content was so explosive and potentially damaging? Who stood to be harmed by publication of them? Allen Klein, who had no faith in the police investigation, was said to have ordered his own. But that was the last that anyone heard of it. Did it happen? If so, what was the outcome?

In the absence of evidence, conspiracy theories flourish. Of those proven to have been present on the night of the drowning – builder Frank Thorogood, who was staying at the property; Stones fixer, lackey and driver Tom Keylock, a man of questionable morality who had been fired by Keith and then fobbed off on Brian; Thorogood's girlfriend Janet Lawson and Brian's partner Anna Wohlin – only Anna remains alive. Was Brian killed by thuggish Thorogood after a scuffle over unpaid wages? Had the disgruntled builder meant only to scare him, ducking him under a few times until he 'gave in'? Or had Keylock been contracted to kill Brian because he had become a liability and an embarrassment? Keylock claimed, ahead of his own death in 1994, that Thorogood made a deathbed confession to him personally. 'It was me that done Brian,' Tom reported that Frank had said to him. Could that have been a cover-up? Could Brian's death even have had some sacrificial connotation? Believe it or not, this was mooted. Get a grip.

Fifty-three years on, the hangdog house is less inclined than ever to yield its awful secret. And there he lurks to this day, just to be sure. Rustling among the leaves, swirling like lung-choke mist, whispering into the brittle night, lips stiffer than the wings of frozen wrens. Don't ask, he'll never tell you. He's jangling voodoo bones in his pockets, just like the ones Anita keeps in her drawers back home. Does she still wear the garlic? He wonders. What kind of person would live here, in this sanctuary of peril and death? Had you been the next to move in, wouldn't you have filled in the pool with earth? Who could knowingly swim in a hole another human had drowned in? Anita could. Hmm. He sees them coming, whoever they are. That's his gasp beneath the water, shimmering cold. Those are his fingertips, trippling up your spine. Keeping Brian's memory alive. Never letting it drift away. May the others forever be tormented by him. It is all that he asks.

*

If it is true that a few individuals would have liked to see Brian conveniently dead, plenty more would have preferred their meal ticket to go on living.

He was also rumoured to be in talks with John Lennon and Jimi Hendrix about forming a new rock supergroup. Although the notion has been ridiculed by serious music writers, is it that far-fetched? Even if it did not involve those specific fellow rock stars, wouldn't this suggest that Brian had plans and plenty to live for, thus dispelling the notion that he could have committed suicide?

In 1994, an episode of BBC's *Crimewatch* revisited the unsolved mystery. Interviewed for the programme, Home Office pathologist Dr Chris Milroy stated that Brian's 140-milligram blood alcohol level – no more than the equivalent of about three and a half pints of beer – was 'not that high'. The negligible trace of amphetamines in his urine did not prove that the drug was in Brian's body, he said. Huh? Anyway, there was no evidence that Brian was intoxicated by drugs. The pathologist concluded that it was 'quite likely' that Brian had been drowned deliberately. Asked about the absence of bruising or other injury, Milroy responded that, had Brian's head or shoulders been pushed down forcefully below the water level, such action would have caused no visible damage.

Fifteen years later, after new evidence and witness statements collected by investigative journalist and BBC producer Scott Jones over a period of four years were presented to police, it was announced that the case would be reopened. The following year, however, in October 2010, the police released this statement: 'This has been thoroughly reviewed by Sussex Police's Crime Policy and Review Branch, but there is no new evidence to suggest that the corner's original verdict of 'death by misadventure' was incorrect. As such, the case will not be reopened.' Nine years on, in July 2019 – the fiftieth anniversary of Brian's death – a new Netflix documentary revisiting the conspiracy theories was announced, inspired by author Terry Rawlings's 1994 book *Who Killed Christopher Robin?* And Sky News interviewed a woman called Barbara Marion, who had discovered only seventeen years earlier that Brian Jones was her biological father. Not that she had a shred of a memory of him. Yet she had this to say: 'I don't think his death was investigated as it should have been.'

*

Anna Wohlin suffered nightmares for years after Brian's death. She was adamant that he was still alive when he left the water. By the time a doctor arrived on the scene, she said, he was dead. Could a slip of a girl like her have pulled the heavy body of a grown man from the depths of a swimming pool? Although there was a trained nurse in the house, a local woman called Janet Lawson, she was unable to assist. Why, was she out of it? Fresh hash cakes were kicking around, apparently. Anna wrote a book about her involvement thirty years after Brian died, and maintains that the truth was hushed up to protect the Stones' image.[9]

'Brian is still portrayed as a bitter, worn-out and depressed man who was fired because of his drug habit ... and who died because he was drunk or high,' she said in 2013. 'But my Brian was a wonderful, charismatic man who was happier than ever, had given up drugs and was looking forward to pursuing the musical career he wanted.'

After his death, she wrote a letter to Mick Jagger. She is still waiting for a response. She remarks that it 'felt so unfair he was alive and thriving ... a reminder he and the other Stones were continuing as if nothing had happened, while Brian was gone forever.'

The Stones' management ushered Anna off the crime scene and insisted that she return to Sweden just days after the tragedy. Bill Wyman told me that they had to hide her in a wardrobe at one point. She was thus prevented from attending his funeral. Suki Potier was there, however, her previously blonde hair darkened and covered with a headscarf. Soon after she got home, Anna claimed, she discovered that she was pregnant with Brian's baby. She miscarried and fell into depression, deprived of both father and child. She then pulled herself together and decided to return to London, to bid a formal farewell to Cotchford and collect her things. She arrived to find that the place had been stripped bare. She was never reunited with her possessions.

*

The death of Brian Jones continues to fascinate and enthral more than half a century later not only because accounts of those who were present conflict, but because it begs questions that can never be answered. He cannot rest in peace. Obsessive fans won't let him. The more macabre among them call for his body to be exhumed, in order to establish once and for all that he was murdered. What would be the point? There is no one left to hold accountable, other than the remaining Rolling Stones.

What are we to make of the revelation of Jan Bell, the daughter of Frank Thorogood, the man who made that killer 'deathbed confession'? She said that Mick and Keith had turned up to Cotchford to force Brian to relinquish his claim to the name 'the Rolling Stones'. Having coined it himself, he had made it known to the others that he intended to continue to use it. The encounter, Bell declared, got 'heated', and Keith threatened Brian with a knife. Did she witness this? Did her dad tell her about it? Might not her motive have been to clear her late father's name?

Then there was the housekeeper, a Mary Haddock, who was named in the BBC's 7 July 1969 report as having raised the alarm. It was she, the Corporation stated, who found the musician's body at the bottom of his pool. But nurse Janet Lawson said that *she* found him, while Anna Wohlin insisted that *she* had been the one who dived in, pulled Brian out and gave him the kiss of life. Mary Haddock's name appeared in several reports, when in fact she had not been present that night. She probably didn't exist, however. The Cotchford housekeeper to whom Brian had grown close was called Mary Hallet(t). The two Marys namechecked must have been one and the same. This was probably no more than a case of sloppy reporting.

It has been written ad nauseam that the only individuals present that fateful night were Brian, Anna, Frank Thorogood, Tom Keylock and Janet Lawson. Mick Jagger contradicted this, insisting that there had been 'a party going on'. But Jagger wasn't there. 'Lots of famous people were present,' 'they' said. If so, why has none of them ever piped up? Even a police constable admitted that there were more guests in attendance at Cotchford that night than had officially been accounted for. Another PC made reference to another 'six or so other associates' on the premises, none of whom has ever been publicly identified. Did they scarper? What were they afraid of, if so?

Yet another piece of the puzzle has Suki Potier's name on it. A few accounts confirm that Suki was at Cotchford that night, but that she left 'about half an hour before Brian died'. Who observed her arrival and departure? Who timed it? What was she doing there, and how come she left? Why didn't East Grinstead police ever interview her? Still weirder, she apparently returned to the house not long after the drowning, and remained there for several days. What was that about? She and Brian were history ... or were they? We can't ask her. She and her husband were killed in a car crash in Portugal in 1981, when Suki was thirty-three. Having survived one car smash, she was taken by another. Horrific symmetry.

On the night of Brian's death, Frank, Tom, Anna and Janet gave witness statements to the police. They all said that Brian had been drinking. Lawson added that he was taking medication to help him sleep. They all said, too, that they had got out of the pool and had returned to the house, leaving Brian in the water alone. But Thorogood was in there with him when the women went back to the house. Another discrepancy.

In 2008, Scott Jones tracked Janet Lawson down and persuaded her to talk. The former nurse, who was twenty-six at the time of the tragedy, had not discussed it with anyone for forty years. She told the journalist and producer that her original statement, taken at East Grinstead police station, had been 'a pack of lies': 'The policeman suggested most of what I said,' she said. 'It was a load of rubbish.

'Frank was not doing the building work properly,' she went on. 'Brian had sacked him that day. There was something in the air. Frank was acting strangely, throwing his weight around a bit. In the early evening, Frank, Anna, Brian and myself had dinner – steak and kidney pie.' Wait: Brian sat and partook of an amiable meal with a fuming individual whom he had only just fired?

After supper, Janet said, they went out to the garden for a swim. Brian asked Janet to bring him his asthma inhaler, and she returned to the house to look for it. While she was gone, Brian drowned. Could he therefore have died of an asthma attack in the pool, brought on by the high pollen count, which must have caused him to become breathless and go under?

Janet's conclusion, forty years on, was that Frank Thorogood had killed Brian, though unintentionally. She came to believe that it was horseplay that got out of hand. Where had she been all those years? She had quit nursing, she said, and had left the NHS. Other, sinister but probably unrelated goings-on had prompted her to go into hiding. She later changed her surname to Tallyn. She died of cancer in 2008.

*

When Mick Jagger was asked in 1995 whether he felt guilty about Brian Jones's death, his response was defiant. 'No, not really,' he said. 'I do feel that I behaved in a very childish way, but we were very young, and in some ways we picked on him. But unfortunately, he made himself a target for it. He was very, very jealous, very difficult, very manipulative, and if you do that in this kind of a group of people, you get back as good as you give, to be honest.'

Keith was more philosophical. 'There are some people who you know aren't going to get old,' he said. 'Brian and I agreed that he, Brian, wouldn't live very long ... I remember saying, You'll never make thirty, man," and he said, "I know."'

Rock manager supreme Simon Napier-Bell once said that the best thing a rock star can do for his back catalogue is die young. Once the possibility of further releases has been extinguished, his fans will value him even more highly and his – the band's – stock will soar. Look at Queen. Leaving aside John Deacon – who retired not long after Freddie Mercury's death, insisting that there could be no more Queen without their frontman – Brian May and Roger Taylor have had a thirty-year career as Freddie's tribute act, hashing out the hits of yore. No, Brian Jones was neither the frontman nor the vocalist. But what he was, to purists, was the genesis, backbone and essence of the Stones.

*

'My first ever out-of-town job was for the *London Evening News*, when I went to Cheltenham to cover Brian Jones's funeral on 10 July 1969,' Stuart White tells me. The esteemed Fleet Street journalist who rose to become the California-based West Coast Editor of the *News of the World* had never previously attended any funeral, let alone the farewell of a celebrity. 'The photographer was David Stephens,' Stuart recalls. 'We went down to Cheltenham together in his open-top MGB. But when we got there, David and I were somehow separated.'

A 'scrum' is remembered with disgust by bassist Bill Wyman:

'The press was so bad at the funeral,' he said. 'I mean, everybody's around the grave, you know, and they're putting the coffin in and all that, and the preacher's reading out and all his family and relatives are all like tranquilised and everything. Everybody's crying, upset. There's thousands of fans everywhere. There's kids running up to you asking for autographs, and there's press guys with cameras everywhere, like all leaning over you and getting snaps in the grave ... there was no respect at all.'

Blame it on the press. Stuart White recalls infinitely more civilised behaviour on the part of fans and journalists alike: 'I followed the fourteen-car cortège, and was close to the family in the graveyard. I recall a quite unbecoming decorum by the usually wolverine British press pack. I mean, they'll monster someone at a court hearing, but a funeral? And the funeral of a star, at that? Nope, it was calm and respectful. What's this, a Rolling Stone railing against alleged unseemly behaviour? The Stones personified unseemly behaviour! There were also flocks of ten, fifteen, nice, upset girls in their early, mid- and late teens. I chatted to a few of them. Then I saw Brian's huge, very American-looking coffin covered in floral tributes.'

The Stones' wreath was a tall floral arch representing the gates of heaven – what were they thinking? – with a life-sized guitar made of roses. The card read simply, 'From the Stones'. It was reported that the casket was of silver and bronze (it must have been plated, otherwise surely it would have been too heavy to lift), and had been a gift from 'Brian's friend Bob Dylan' (was it really?). Come the moment of no return, it was lowered into a twelve-feet-deep hole.

'A few words were said at the graveside before the interment,' said Stuart. 'There were no stand-out guests as far as I could tell. Not even the other Stones. No Mick or Keith, anyway. Bill Wyman and Charlie Watts were hovering, but they were very low-key.'

Mick had taken off for Australia with Marianne to shoot *Ned Kelly*. 'I wasn't understanding enough about his drug addiction,' he confessed to *Rolling Stone* magazine twenty-six years later, in 1995. 'No one seemed to know much about drug addiction. Things like LSD were all new. No one knew the harm. People thought cocaine was good for you.'

Where was Keith? It is reckoned that he remained in the recording studio. Anita was heavily pregnant, with only four weeks to go until the 10 August birth of their son Marlon Richards. It was the reason, 'they' said, that she stayed away.

Stuart identified ashen-faced Lewis and Louise Jones, Brian's parents, and his sister Barbara arm in arm with Suki Potier.

Chapter Thirteen

ALTAMONT

They should have cancelled. It's what any other group would have done, as a mark of respect to a bandmate who had died so suddenly only forty-eight hours earlier. It was not as though they stood to lose a fortune if they pulled out. The festival was free. There were plenty of other artists performing. They would have got by without a little help from these friends. So why didn't they just abandon it, lie low for a while, pause and reflect, put their other plans on hold, show solidarity at Brian's funeral, washed and brushed, then re-emerge after a respectable mourning period and release a tribute song or even an album in their co-founder's memory?

Perhaps Jagger perceived that any such deference on their part might be interpreted as weakness. Having never knowingly been the kind to kowtow, they were not going to start now. They had planned to make this, their first public gig for more than two years, the official unveiling of Brian's replacement. With his blessing, too, because Brian had accepted an invitation to attend. But tragedy overtook. Realising that they would have been castigated otherwise, they hastily reconfigured their performance as a memorial to their late founder, pooling guilt, bewilderment and sorrow in homage to him. The Stones ceased rolling for no man, dead or alive. Not even for one of their own. If nothing else, this show would be the ideal warm-up for the forthcoming US tour.

Two days after Brian died – which seems shocking now – they turned up at Hyde Park to rock London alongside King Crimson, Family, Roy Harper, Alexis Korner's New Church and more at the free festival. Two hundred and fifty thousand fans? Half a million? Reports varied, but vast numbers, anyway. Introduced for the first time as 'the greatest rock'n'roll band in the world', the performance itself fell agonisingly short of what the epithet promised. The band knew they were out of groove and out of tune. The audience didn't. All these years later, original fans still insist that they were brilliant, that it was a great day and how lucky they were to be there. Others remember a set that hung in the air like crystallised phlegm. How could a garishly maquillaged Mick poncing about in a white frock and studded leather collar reciting highbrow poetry to impress not one but two actress girlfriends present, each of whom was blissfully unaware that she was competing for his affection, have contributed to the solemnity of the occasion?[1]

Old school friends David Stark and Paul Levett, now a musician and publisher and a lawyer respectively, were in Hyde Park for the Stones gig that day. The then seventeen-year-old rock fans were in their element. 'People say their playing was terrible,' says David. 'It was a very raw sound, I admit, which we never got from them again. But it was an amazing experience. It was a really hot day, the weather was brilliant, the crowd was on their side and they rose to it. All you could think about was Brian Jones, but in a good way. The film of the gig captures its essence very well, particularly the "Sympathy for the Devil" sequence with the African drummers.'

'After Hyde Park,' recalls Paul, 'we went over the back to the Royal Albert Hall to see the Who supported by Chuck Berry in the Pop Proms. Equally astonishing. All the Stones were in the box right behind us. At one point, Jagger got up and went outside. My friend and I jumped up and ran out after him. He walked the circumference of the Albert Hall, kissing girls, then came back inside the venue to Marianne.'

Stuart White was also at the Hyde Park concert. 'I was in the press pen with the Hells Angels, who had been brought in as stewards,' said the former *News of the World* West Coast editor. 'What sticks in my mind is Mick Jagger waiting to do his poetry reading for Brian Jones and goading the crowd. "Are ya gonna be quiet?" he was yelling at them. And I remember thinking, you sod. They've been sitting here since eight o'clock this morning, some of them. You're late coming on, and you're telling *them* what to do. It was my first glimpse of rock star arrogance, and it really annoyed me. They played atrociously that day, too.

'I saw them again in August 1976 during their European tour, at Knebworth Park in Hertfordshire. "The Glyndebourne of Rock", they called it,' said Stuart. 'There were upwards of two hundred thousand people there. Topless girls all over the place, drugs freely for sale, and a host of celebrities backstage: Paul and Linda McCartney, Jack Nicholson, Ian McLagan from the Faces, Van Morrison, Jim Capaldi, Dave Gilmour and more, all off their bonces on free champagne. Lynyrd Skynyrd, Todd Rundgren and 10cc performed too. The event of the decade, you might have thought. But there must have been "technical hitches". The Stones went on really late, about half past eleven, and played thirty or so songs into the early hours. Badly. Were they blind drunk? I thought so, and I wasn't the only one. They were literally staggering about up there. Keith was missing notes and Mick was slurring his lyrics. I saw again the arrogance of Jagger. I was cast right back to that day in Hyde Park, and to that utterly unfathomable poetry reading.'

Written in 1821, Percy Bysshe Shelley's celebrated pastoral elegy *Adonais*, dedicated to the Greek god of fertility though actually about the death of John Keats, cut closer to the bone than Mick may have known. 'I am aware indeed,' said Shelley of Keats, having invited his ailing fellow poet to stay with him in Pisa, 'that I am nourishing a rival who will surpass me, and this is an additional motive and will be an added pleasure.'

So Mick cast himself unwittingly as Shelley and Brian as Keats, did he? Read the whole poem, not just the bits that Mick recited. Mourners are urged to weep no longer, because Keats lives. He is at last free of his attackers. He is not dead: it is the living who are deceased! Brian, likewise, has 'outsoared the shadow of our night; Envy and calumny and hate and pain, And that unrest which men miscall delight, Can touch him not and torture not again.'[2]

Even if the wider implications went over his head, the reading of some of that poem was a curious volte-face on Mick's part, given his reaction when he heard that Brian had died. He and the rest of the band were down at Olympic Studios in Barnes at the time, pushing on with their next album *Let It Bleed* when Ian Stewart imparted the shocking news. Their publicist Keith Altham was with them.

'And it was as if Brian had gone and died on purpose, just to spite them and put a spanner in the works,' said Keith. 'Where the others were genuinely shocked, I mean really upset and actually weeping – especially Marianne, who was totally overcome, poor kid – Mick was fuming. I couldn't tell you his words exactly, but he was spitting blood. It was as if poor Brian had committed this act of sabotage to deliberately steal the thunder from Mick's big moment, a poxy gig in Hyde Park. I thought at the time and I still think now: how can anyone be so deluded, so immune to reality and priority? Mick's insistence all these years that he and Keith treating Brian so shamefully was only what he deserved, because he was selfish, jealous and lazy – which I never saw, and which wasn't my perception of him – has got guilt written all over it.'

And yet. Brian got to escape his torturous existence, leaving Mick, Keith and the boys to a lifetime's unrest. Will they ever be free of him? Are they not condemned in perpetuity for his demise, 'their hearts grown cold, their heads grown grey in vain'? Have they ever found, or will they ever find, the courage to look themselves in the eye over it?

Meanwhile, bivouacs of asphyxiated cabbage white butterflies, 3,500 of them (who counted?) were freed to flutter over the vast Hyde Park audience, an evocation of Brian's spirit rising to the blue. Instead, the doomed creatures sucked their last, and their corpses were crunched underfoot. It was, muttered the drummer, 'like the Battle of the Somme'.[3]

There was more self-delusion and death to come. As if one free concert were not enough, the Stones had to go bigger and better. Hubris gone mad. Thus did Lucifer lollop on down to Altamont in December '69. West Coast winter's answer to East Coast summer's Woodstock was to prove not only the killer culmination of a controversial US tour. It would slaughter the fantasy. According to the mythology, it pulled down the curtain on the sixties and called time on the hippie dream. There is always more to it.

*

History's first mythic rock'n'roll tour in the winter of 1969 had 'firsts' written all over it. Held back by drugs busts and other controversies, this was their first advance across America since the summer of 1966; their first tour without Brian; their first with Mick Taylor playing in his place. Hurled in at the deep end with little idea of what to expect, Taylor's first outing with them since the Hyde Park free festival raised their game, fetching a mournful, melodic and searing edge that the Stones had never benefited from before.

'I just couldn't believe how bad they sounded,' Taylor would later remark. 'Their timing was awful. They sounded like a typical bunch of guys in a garage – playing out of tune, and too loudly. I thought, how is it possible that this band can make hit records?'

This would also be their first tour comprising America's largest basketball arena and early stadium concerts. A massive step up. Kicking off with a 7 November warm-up at Colorado State University, the Stones opened at the Los Angeles Forum with Ike and Tina Turner, B.B. King/ Chuck Berry and Terry Reid in support, and rolled their way east through the arenas to climax at New York's Madison Square Garden and the Boston Garden at the end of the month. The pace was full-on, with the first five dates consecutive, a single day off followed by another seven shows in a row, then a six-day break before landing in New York City to perform on *The Ed Sullivan Show*. They then circled west to Detroit, east to Philadelphia, down to Baltimore, back up to New York, on to Boston and about-turn down to Florida for the West Palm Beach International Music and Arts Festival. Twenty-four live shows and a televised performance in under a month. They proceeded to Muscle Shoals Sound Studio in Sheffield, Alabama, to record 'Brown Sugar' and other tracks, sending their representatives ahead to San Francisco to set everything up for that trip's final performance. Six days after the last show on 30 November came the horror of Altamont.

The Free Festival at the remote Altamont Speedway motor racing track in Tracy, northern California, on 6 December 1969 is rock's nadir. Bad publicity over extortionate ticket prices on the tour having seen them denounced as mercenaries, the Stones were in need of damage limitation. A free concert to acknowledge the support of the fans was a good idea.

Demonstrating an embarrassing lack of awareness, Mick announced his hope that this congregation would 'create a microcosmic society that would set an example for how the rest of America can behave at large gatherings'. In other words, he tried to hijack the counterculture, and to hitch the Stones' wagon to the hippie ideal. Rarely has a rock band been less altruistic. Jagger's primary motivation for agreeing to the free concert was the opportunity to film it for the documentary they were making. The result would be seen in the now notorious *Gimme Shelter*.

There was a scramble to secure a suitable location. The festival could have taken place at San Francisco's Golden Gate Park, but the city put its foot down. Sonoma Raceway at Sears Point was a possible, but the site owners demanded $100,000 when they heard that the event was to be filmed. *Next*. Altamont was by no means ideal, but was the last resort. An agreement was hastily struck with its owner, and Santana, Crosby, Stills, Nash & Young, Jefferson Airplane, the Flying Burrito Brothers and the rest were lined up to perform there. It was risky from the outset. The facility had negligible facilities. Nowhere near enough toilets or medical tents were provided to service the hundred thousand fans expected to turn up, never mind the three times that number who did. In place of security barriers to separate artists from audience and keep both sections safe, somebody ran a ball of string from pillar to post at breast height. That was it. And nobody had any idea who was in charge. None of which bothered Mick. He had astutely avoided adding ink to any release form or contract that might render the band legally liable for either the concert or anything that might occur during or after it. Whatever the outcome, the Stones would not be responsible. It was almost as if they'd had a premonition.

A posse of beefy, unbriefed, simmering-for-action Hells Angels who had been hired in place of professional security guards were positioned at strategic points, and were paid in beer. Whose outrageous idea was that? Worst of all, the hastily constructed stage that the Angels were there to defend was too low, only about four feet off the ground. The musicians effectively found themselves performing among the crowd, most of whom were out of it on booze and drugs. Not just your basic hippie hash, either. LSD laced with speed was the dangerous cocktail doing the rounds in huge quantities, leaving the hillside heaving with tripping fans. Too few paramedics were on hand to administer Thorazine, the antidote. Who cared, they soon ran out of it. Paranoia set in and violence broke out, which quickly escalated. Many of the casualties limping into the med tents had fractured skulls. A pregnant singer was bottled, and a girl was torn across the stage by her scalp. As darkness descended, the cloying air, which seemed to have solidified according to some of those present, was carved by the blades of the chopper carrying the Stones.

The Grateful Dead had signed up to play bridesmaid to the headliners. But hell was unleashed during Jefferson Airplane's set by the accidental knocking over of one of the Angels' motorbikes. The leathered henchmen went berserk, and started attacking people with pool cues and bike chains. Fans retaliated with whatever they could find, empty glass bottles, mostly. Singer Marty Balin jumped off the stage to try and intervene, and was knocked clean out by an Angel. The Dead saw all, and were sore afraid. They packed up their gear and got the hell out. 'The vibes were bad,' said the Airplane's co-vocalist Grace Slick. 'Something was very peculiar. Not particularly bad, just real peculiar. It was that kind of hazy, abrasive day.'

Nobody mourned the Dead. Meredith Hunter didn't, anyway. The Stones were the act this clean-cut teenager had come to see. He must have picked up on the bad vibes and realised that he and his date were risking their lives just by being there, because he barged back through the crowd to his borrowed car to pick up the handgun he had brought with him as a protection measure. This act alone suggests how precarious the scene had got by then, and how frightened this harmless-looking couple must have felt. They must also have known that their very presence was inflammatory: a good-looking, lime-suited, Afro'd black guy and his pretty, white, long-blonde girlfriend in her pew-worthy crocheted tunic. What was he, that guy, her pimp? Believe it or not, this was written. We're talking 1969, an era when racism was still rife in the backward Californian provinces. Basic folks back then didn't care for that kind of behaviour, and made their displeasure felt. But who cared what folks thought? Hunter probably didn't, or couldn't, given that he was higher than a kite on methamphetamine: the stimulant otherwise known as 'yaba', 'crank' or crystal meth, with an effect similar to, but much longer-lasting than, crack cocaine. He was fearless and excited, this was the *Rolling Stones*!

Leaving little Patti on the ground, he clambered on top of a speaker cabinet beside the stage, most likely to get a better view. An Angel reached up, wrenched him from his perch and flung him to the ground. The boy floundered and kneejerked, pulling at his pistol as he went down. Then came the flash of the knife brandished by big bikerman Alan Passaro, who stabbed him, apparently five times. All of this was captured on tape, preserved and used, horrifyingly, in the 1970 Stones doc *Gimme Shelter*. The frame of the pack of Angels closing in for the kill is blood-chilling. Hunter was pronounced dead at twenty past six that evening. Terrified, bewildered, heartbroken Patti is seen sobbing in the footage as his lifeless body was whirlybirded into the sky.

*

Hunter's schizophrenic mother never recovered from her loss. His sister Dixie avoided the trial, unable to bring herself to witness the inevitable: another white man walking free from the killing of Just Another Black Man. Which is what happened. Passaro, the knife-wielding Angel, was charged with murder. The jury viewed the footage and concluded that he had acted in self-defence. He was acquitted, but he wouldn't live long. Sixteen years later he was found drowned in a California reservoir, wearing $10,000 in cash. Revenge, the dish best eaten cold? Or an accident?

*

As far as the Hells Angels were concerned, the Stones, the track owner and the promoters were to blame for the tragedy of and fallout from Altamont. They resented that the media had tried to pin it on them, and made their feelings known. Forewarned is forearmed: Keith would be carrying a gun on the road from then on. Though Jagger had no idea at the time, the Angels resolved to seek revenge by assassinating him. Tracking him down to his home on Long Island, their hit squad hired a boat and attempted to sail across to do the deed. But on the appointed day they were scuppered by a violent storm. Forced to turn back, they survived. They must have gone cold on the idea after that. News of the plan was leaked to the FBI in 1985, and was only made public in 2008.

All those years, Mick had been oblivious of how close he came to being the Angels' second Altamont victim.

It was in 1995, twenty-six years after the event, that Jann Wenner of *Rolling Stone* magazine questioned Mick as to how he felt about the Altamont tragedy.

'Well, awful,' Jagger said. 'I mean, just awful. You feel a responsibility. How could it all have been so silly and wrong? But I didn't think of these things that you guys thought of, you in the press: this great loss of innocence, this cathartic end of the era … I didn't think any of that. That particular burden didn't weigh on my mind. It was more how awful it was to have had this experience, and how awful it was for someone to get killed.' His words seemed cold enough to freeze eyeballs.

*

Some still blame the Rolling Stones for Meredith Hunter's death. What did they expect, others reason, of a rock gig, especially a vast open-air festival, which after all is all about crowds and surging masses? Collective loss of control often leads to tragedy. Were the Who to blame for the deaths of eleven fans and the serious injury of twenty-six others in Cincinnati, Ohio, December 1979, when 18,000 fans stormed the venue and only twenty-five policemen fought in vain to control them? Were Queen responsible for the fatal stabbing of twenty-one-year-old Scottish fan Thomas McGuigan at Knebworth in August 1986, the last gig with his band that Freddie Mercury ever played? What about the terrorist attacks at the Manchester Arena Ariana Grande gig, and at the Las Vegas Route 91 Harvest musicfest, both in 2017? Or the nine killed at Roskilde in Denmark – Pearl Jam's concert in June 2000, when the crowd rushed the stage? And did the buck stop at the feet of rapper Travis Scott after nine lost their lives at his Astroworld Festival in Houston, Texas, in November 2021?

There is no question that the Stones should have called a halt at Altamont, and have quit the stage the moment the scuffle broke out. According to them, they had no idea until afterwards that anyone had been killed. But we know they smelled danger, that they sensed a satanic panic. What else would have spooked them back into the chopper that had conveyed them there, cramming in more bodies than it was designed to lift so that they were lucky it didn't go down?

And still the myth persists. Still they bang on about Altamont closing the door on the sixties and extinguishing the hippie dream. The assumption that this was its outcome obnubilates shudderingly sinister reality. The Stones never cared about the flowery-powery counterculture. Their passing interest in what the masses were into extended only so far as what was in it for them. Posing as believers in peace and love and a better world would make the punters more inclined to buy their records. The latest of which had just been released. Only yesterday, folks, come and get it! *Let It Bleed*, their eighth studio album in the UK (their tenth in the US) bore the hallmarks of a band which had come of age and grown into their reputation. No. 1 in the UK and a No. 3 in America, it was thin on singles chart hits but was a crucible of live-performance classics. 'Gimme Shelter', 'Midnight Rambler', 'You Got the Silver' and 'You Can't Always Get What You Want', specifically. Which may have been intentional. They were finally free from comparison to the disintegrating Beatles, as well as of a defeated key component who had been dragging them down. Cynical? You are right, reader, I wasn't there. But friends who were, who ran for cover once they had seen that particular emperor in the altogether, are under no illusions. They saw right through Jagger that day, and they've been seeing ever since. There was, it was said, evil in the hillside that night.

'They did Altamont for the money,' remarks a retired industry executive who declines to be named.

But they didn't get paid …

'They got paid. Ya think they'd do it for nothing? Hell, they earned it, too. Played like their lives depended on it. We knew at the time it was probably the greatest set we'd ever see. All that tension vibing in off the audience that stretched farther than the eye could see, it went all the way to hell, and it sent them. Like putting rocket fuel in a pair of skis. Watch the film. It doesn't capture their brilliance that night, and this is the thing about their genius: it *can't* be captured. You gotta experience it live. The records don't even come close, and it's what the Rolling Stones are about. The secret? Don't ask me. You can't see it, you can't hear it, there are not words to describe, you just gotta get in their faces, open up your pores and hope that the Devil himself doesn't jump in there before they do.'

Then what?

'Then they got the hell out of America. Mick was paranoid that someone was coming for him. Had a feeling, he said. Keith and the guys went to London, but Mick flew directly from San Francisco to Geneva to drop a coupla rocks in a Swiss bank.[4] *He's* the one doing this. Which tells you a lot. A *lot*. The next year they're raking in box office from *Gimme Shelter*, which, get this, is a snuff movie.'[5]

He would refer to it as that?

'How can we *not* refer to it as that? It features the black kid Meredith Hunter's murder. Not an actor. Nobody's pretending. This guy gets killed in cold blood *and they leave it in.* You see it twice. They replay it, it's horrific. The stabbing is captured, you see both the murder weapon and the gun belonging to the deceased, and the Stones keep the footage to redeploy as entertainment. *As entertainment.* Without ever approaching Hunter's family for permission or offering them a share of the profits or even some basic financial support, nothing. Because to do so, I guess, would have been taken as an admission of guilt. And the Stones want us to believe that *they* were the victims at Altamont. Why is that film still out there? Why has Black America never torn its hair out and taken them to task over this, with everything else that's going on? It is beyond me. All the Black Lives Matter protesters, where are those guys? Like I said, there was evil in the hillside that night. Pure evil. If he hadn't gotten to them before, Satan sure got to the Stones that day. He's been riding the bastards bareback ever since.'

Never again would they leave logistics to chance, perform in an inadequate setting or hire Hells Angels to belch about, pretending to be security. That was then. And just as they had clicked into a superior gear on stage at Altamont that night, a chemical reaction was stirring. In time, it would change not only their perception of themselves and what they were capable of; it would also change the world, in terms of its reaction to them. Shrugging off the conventions of the music business and their status as a band, they would break moulds and take things stratospheric. Leviathans from the soup would soon roam the earth, and would dominate.

*

The next time that David Stark and Paul Levett saw the Stones together was in London on 21 December 1969, at the Lyceum Ballroom on the Strand. This show followed the band's two performances a week earlier at the Saville Theatre.

'They'd just got back from Altamont,' remembers David, 'and they were absolutely brilliant. I'd go so far as to say exuberant. They were promoting the *Let It Bleed* album, and they opened with "Under My Thumb". We were blown away. Jagger wore a white puffed-sleeve shirt, and looked like a Greek god. Nobody mentioned what had just happened. There was no indication at all of what had gone on. They must have been very relieved, I reckon, to get out of America and back to London in one piece.'

Did David feel they were somehow responsible for the death of Meredith Hunter? 'I did not. I don't believe anybody else did either. It was shocking of course, but not surprising, when you look back. It does feel in some ways as though tragedy has always followed them around.'

The Stones were at the top of their game at that point, the lifelong friends agree. 'The songs from *Let It Bleed* were outstanding,' says Paul. 'I still pinch myself when I think about it. It was one of those nights you think, *God*, I'm glad I was there. It was so great to see them back then, when we were so young and naïve and so thrilled by it all. David and I have seen them on every single tour, during the seventies, eighties, nineties and the two thousands. The best? The Steel Wheels tour, 1989–90, promoting their brilliant comeback album. "Love is Strong" was the first single, and they really pulled it off. They were stronger than ever. And the 1994 Voodoo Lounge tour too, of course, which was exceptional.

'They still put on a great show. But it's different now. Perhaps it's because we are older, because we no longer get comps from the PR, and because we find their ticket prices ridiculous! It's all so vast, so corporate, so distant, so geared to the masses now. It feels as though it's not so much about the music but more about the spectacle – the miracle, almost, that these old crocs are still standing, still doing it. A lot of people must feel compelled to part with a fortune to experience them live because it might be their last chance. It's not a band, now.

It's an institution, banging out predictable numbers we've all heard a thousand times. Which is a shame, because they've got such a huge back catalogue of great songs that they never do. 'I don't want to hear them play "Satisfaction" ever again. I want to hear "Who's Driving Your Plane" and "Cocksucker Blues".'

Chapter Fourteen

EXILE

The most surprising release of 1970 was *The Madcap Laughs*. The first solo album by ultimate pop recluse Syd Barrett had been several years in the making, not least because the erratic former Pink Floyd frontman had submitted to psychiatric care. He performed his one and only solo gig that June, but dropped his guitar and stomped off stage after only four numbers. His departure two years earlier from the band beloved of all rock stars was, commented the *Guardian*, 'on a par with, say, Mick Jagger leaving the Rolling Stones in 1964 to live quietly with his parents.' The frontman had now become a yardstick by which other rock stars were judged.

Also that year, Led Zeppelin performed, incongruously, at London's Royal Albert Hall. Diana Ross dumped her Supremes. Black Sabbath presented both their first and second albums in the same year, the latter the indelible *Paranoid*. Simon and Garfunkel released *Bridge Over Troubled Water*, the multi-Grammy Award-winning album that would become Britain's biggest seller of the decade. The Who recorded their outstanding *Live at Leeds* album and performed *Tommy* at the New York Met. David Bowie married his Angie, Mike Nesmith quit his Monkees, and the Isle of Wight Festival drew Jimi Hendrix, the Who, Leonard Cohen, Joan Baez, Jethro Tull, ELP and close to 700,000 fans, the largest rockfest of all. Within weeks, Hendrix was dead, and so was Janis Joplin. Neither tragedy came close to the cataclysm caused by the Stones' oldest rivals calling it a day. Paul McCartney threw the world into meltdown with his dissolution of the Beatles via a Q&A press release on 10 April. Lennon fumed at the snatching of his thunder, having informed the others months earlier that he was quitting. Paul presented his eponymous first solo album, the one with the cherries on the sleeve that he had recorded at home in secret. The former Beatles offered their going-away gift, *Let It Be*.[1] 'The Long and Winding Road' became their last US No. 1 hit. The single was not released in Blighty.

Mick and the boys rolled on frantically as if terrified to stop, in case the same fate befell them. Not that life within the band was exactly harmonious. Bill Wyman was no longer talking to Keith. Theirs was a frost that would not thaw for the next ten years. Keith's desperate heroin addiction had come between them. Dropping pennies caused fury and grief so deep in Bill that he simply could not bring himself to get over it. His good friend Brian had been ousted not only for spurious 'visa issues' but also for a 'drug problem' that Bill considered mild compared to Keith's mounting excesses. Those things had been excuses, it occurred to Wyman now. Having been somewhat in denial about the fact that Mick and Keith had hounded Brian out of his own band, he reached a point at which he could no longer ignore the unpalatable truth. Had they treated him with more kindness and compassion, and had matters been resolved in a more civilised way, Bill realised, Brian might well still be alive.

By the time the Lennons were on their way to spend the rest of John's life in New York, chasing the abductor of the daughter they would never get back, the Stones were in tax exile. Despite vast sums having swelled coffers during their biggest and best tour to date, catastrophic miscalculations had left them wanting. Their outgoings had exceeded their income. I mean, imagine a rock band doing that. The upshot being that they were unable to cover their colossal tax bill. Interest on their liability to H.M. Revenue had been accruing steadily over the past eight years. When he discovered this, Mick was stumped. He had believed that their affairs were in order and that their returns were up to date. The highest rate of income tax at that point was 83 per cent.[2] The band had no choice but to get out sharpish. Leaving the rest of the band to weigh up the implications and practicalities of this, Mick started genning up on tax havens. They wound up with a business address on Sark, a tiny isle in the Channel Islands off the coast of Normandy.

Their European outing during the summer and autumn of 1970 was give or take a continuation of the previous year. Beset by riots, notably in Hamburg, West Berlin and Milan, it proceeded from Malmö, Sweden to Amsterdam in the Netherlands via Finland, Denmark, West Germany, France, Austria and Italy. Europe and the world now regarded them as rich-as-fuck, do-as-they-please rock superstars, unaware that they were facing financial ruin. The band wrapped the tour and relocated to the South of France. Not the most affordable destination, you might think, especially during a period when that country's cost of living had gone Tour Eiffel. Still, it was comfortably close to home. Off they went. Oh, and by the way, goodbye Decca. Their leader was on the lookout for a brand-new record company to distribute the output of their brand-new label, Rolling Stones Records.

At twenty-seven, Jagger was no contender for the grim 'club' then claiming the lives of fellow high-profile rockers. He was happy in the land of the living, thanks. A highly controlled as well as controlling individual, he dabbled in his share of drugs and booze but would never have let addiction get the better of him. He was a man in charge of his destiny, accustomed to the good life, to calling the shots, and to a band and entourage who deferred to him and did as they were told. When he said he could not imagine himself as a rock star past the age of thirty, he meant it. Not that he hoped he'd die before he got old. Mick was in the business of preparing for rock retirement. He invested his money astutely and stayed in front of the game. To add to his property portfolio ahead of the Stones' relocation – he would not offload for a few more years his 48 Cheyne Walk, Chelsea residence, acquired in 1968 for fifty grand – he paid another £55,000 for Stargroves: a Victorian Gothic stately home with a landscaped park in East Woodhay, Hampshire.[3] Before long, the Stones' mobile recording studio had trundled into the vast park and plugged in. There, they recorded tracks that would feature on *Sticky Fingers, Exile on Main St.* and *It's Only Rock 'n Roll*, before they departed for France. Other artists took advantage of the facility too, including the Who, Led Zeppelin, Status Quo, Deep Purple, Iron Maiden and Bob Marley.

When he first landed in France, Mick established himself in a Paris hotel while he went on the hunt for a suitable château. The one he rented eventually, in Saint-Tropez, would not be welcoming Marianne as its mistress any time soon. Now that she was living in Italy with Mick's replacement, Jagger had dismissed her and moved on. Or had he? He had last seen her in December 1969, when they were both obliged to attend court for their cannabis possession hearing. Marianne was acquitted while Mick was found guilty of possession and handed a £200 fine. He was also banned from travelling to the United States for eighteen months, which both clipped his wings and put him in a hypocritical position. Hadn't the band fired Brian for his 'visa issues' the previous year? Was the band going to fire Mick for the same offence? Hardly.

Marianne, her four-year-old son Nicholas and her new partner Mario Schifano travelled to Berkshire after the hearing, to spend Christmas at the cottage Mick had bought for her mother. Here we are again. On Christmas night came the inevitable knock at the door. Marianne answered it to find Mick standing there with her present, an engraved solid silver box containing cocaine. Just what the desperate drug addict had always wanted. Still, it appears that she was gratitude personified. She welcomed Mick into her bed that night, while poor old Mario was relegated to the sofa with a blanket, and sloped off back to Italy the next day. But it did not turn out to be the happily-ever-after Christmas that Marianne might have craved. Mick left too, to spend what was left of Yuletide with Keith and Anita. He didn't really want Marianne. He just couldn't stand the idea of anybody else having her. The classic, exasperating, territorial male, Mick enjoyed Marianne's obvious devotion for the simple reason that it boosted his ego. Having seen her again, albeit in court, he'd found that he hadn't yet broken the habit. But he had other habits too, namely the one called keeping his options open. This is where it gets all musical beds.

Marsha Hunt, who had been staying at 48 Cheyne Walk, perceived that Mick was still in love, if only a bit, with Marianne. Marsha moved out of Cheyne Walk and into her own St John's Wood flat. Marianne moved back into Cheyne Walk. Mick spent half his time at Marsha's. He took her to dinner one night, told her he loved her and that he wanted to have a child with her. What on earth was scrambling his mind when he said those things? Were they mere romantic nothings, sipped from the second bottle and cooed into the candlelight, which he never in a million expected her to take him up on? How could he sit there muttering about big, adult, responsible things when he was happily footloose, relishing his way through the pick of the pick'n'mix chicks? But Marsha took him at his word. It was what led her to abandon her contraception, while Mick was doing a Judas on Marianne.

Marianne overheard Mick's conversation with Ahmet Ertegun in the house one day, during which the boss of Atlantic Records agreed to slap $30 million on the table, provided that Mick agreed to offload Marianne. The drug-addled creature had become a liability, Ahmet pointed out, and was likely to bring his label into disrepute. It was too risky.

What Mick should have done, out of respect for all that they had meant to each other, was refuse to barter and tell Ertegun straight that his private life was not subject to any Stones contract. He should then have set about getting Marianne the medical help she needed, and have helped her on the road to recovery. Hearing her lover accept money in return for dumping her was a slap in the face with a whale. No, she would not allow treacherous Mick this final humiliation of her. She packed and fled. Leaving Mick not exactly heartbroken.

He was soon out jaunting with Patti D'Arbanville, getting it on with Pamela Miller,[4] dilly-dallying on the way with Carly Simon.[5] With whom the world was in love, at that point, and what a beautiful couple they made. Rumours about her signature song, written in 1971 and released the following year, persist to this day. Was 'You're So Vain' really about Mick? In 1983, Carly flatly denied it. She did not deny, however, that Jagger had recorded its backing vocal. She hardly could, I suppose, as that's obviously Mick. Even though he went uncredited for his contribution.

While Marsha was preparing to give birth to Mick's firstborn, Karis, in St Mary's Hospital Paddington – not in the private, exclusive Lindo Wing but on a standard NHS ward – Mick was obsessing over an exotic young woman he had met at the band's after-show party at the Georges Cinq Hotel on 22 September, following their gig at the Paris Olympia. The curious thing was, he recognised her. Wouldn't that be because he had seen her staring back at him from the mirror for the past twenty-eight years? Her sulky eyes, sculpted philtrum and pendulous underlip could have been his own. Which is what Marianne meant when she remarked that Mick had fallen in love with himself. He would do more than that. He would take her as his lawfully wedded wife. As an acknowledgement of his own narcissism, subconscious or not, it was priceless.

By the time Mick tied the knot with Bianca Pérez-Mora Macías on 12 May 1971, the Stones had completed a spring 'Farewell Tour' of England and Scotland, he had told Marsha he'd never loved her, had threatened to sue her for custody of Karis, had been threatened in return that she would 'blow his brains out if he dared' and was expecting another child with his new bride. The former actress had changed the L in her name to an I, incidentally, when she was sixteen. She told Mick that she was twenty-one, though she was actually five years older. How desperate does that seem, lying about one's age in one's twenties? Bianca must have been aware of Mick's penchant for tender youth, and feared that he might go off the boil if he knew the truth: that she was only twenty-one months younger than him. Perhaps she was even aware of 'Stray Cat Blues', the prurient celebration of under-age sex that Mick co-wrote for *Beggars Banquet*, featuring the line 'It's no hanging matter, it's no capital crime'.

She hailed from a broken home in Nicaragua, a country under rigid dictatorship, where she had witnessed a student massacre and mass discrimination. Pledging to spend her life making a difference, she sought a scholarship to further her ambitions and was accepted at the Paris Institute of Political Studies. Earlier boyfriends during her years there included screen actor Michael Caine and French musician, producer and record label boss Eddie Barclay. She was still involved with the latter, who was almost a quarter of a century her senior, when she locked eyes with Mick across a crowded and noisy but vacant and silent room. The throng parted like the waters of the Red Sea. Having perceived in a heartbeat that this was no one-night stand and that he had better be on his best behaviour and put the work in with this one, Jagger was hooked.

Mick thought he was the one doing the running. In fact, Bianca was reeling him in. He whisked her away to the Bahamas, locked a weighty diamond bracelet around her hummingbird wrist and denied to everyone who asked that they were an item. Game on. Their civil and Roman Catholic nuptials on the French Riviera, at Saint-Tropez Town Hall and the tiny seventeenth-century church La Chapelle Sainte-Anne in Ramatuelle, and at the Brasserie des Arts for afters, were drooled over in thousands of column inches as 'the wedding of the year'. In reality, it was a bun fight. Having been invited only the day before, the family-and-friends package tour who rocked up to witness it and partake of the knees-up – which included Beatles, Brigitte Bardot, Julie Christie, Keith Moon and the Queen's cousin Patrick, Lord Lichfield, but no Stones other than Mick's best man Keith (what was that about?) – put their best shoes forward. Not only did the world's media rush in for the scrum, but most of the locals too. French law decreed that the public could not be excluded from proceedings. Aprons and braces all round. The bride wore Yves Saint Laurent: tuxedo jacket with nothing underneath, a bias-cut skirt and a veiled, wide-brimmed hat. Rewriting the rules of bridal chic, her look has never been outclassed.

A good time was had by some, if not by Bianca. But you have to ask. What did this fine, worthy woman with altruistic ambitions that she would one day achieve see in the multimillionaire rock superstar, who was out of his hemispheres on cocaine on his wedding day? What kind of life did he imagine, in turn, with her? Had he convinced himself that her beauty, dignity and gravitas would take him up a notch? While Mick rather fancied himself as Renaissance Man and could play the culture vulture with the best of them, it was impossible to picture Bianca getting down and dirty in the studio after midnight with Keith and his cohorts, loosening her girdle, passing the spliffs and knocking back the moonshine straight from the bottle. These were impossibly colliding worlds and inclinations. Bianca was as unlikely to nip out on the totter with smacked-up, capsizing Anita as Mick was to join his wife's professors for a lecture on political oppression. Imagine his *soignée* missis out on the road with the Stones: goldfish out of bowl doesn't begin.

Don't tell me she hadn't intuited this. Rock stars are not that hard to read. They are for the most part unreconstructed, especially those who like to kid us earnestly otherwise. Spend enough time around them and their primary motives become clear. They crave a mother they can have sex with;

a soulmate to praise and approve of them; an indulgent partner willing to turn a blind eye to their peccadilloes, bandage their bloody knees, pick up after them and be waiting whenever they call – not necessarily attired in designer silk lingerie and hot to trot, with a casserole under one arm and a rosy-cheeked child under the other, but you get it. Jerry Hall's mother set back the cause by centuries when she taught her exquisite daughter the secret of keeping a man: by being 'a maid in the living room, a cook in the kitchen and a whore in the bedroom'. Right. And the intransigent rocker is the last type of male to grow out of such nonsense. Ain't gonna happen. Because rock stars treat their women the way they treat their cars. It's just a crate, right? Goes rusty. Bits drop off. There'll be a new model out next year. More gears, more gadgets, whole lotta tread in her tyres, know what I'm sayin'? Simplest thing in the world to trade her in.

'Mick married Bianca because he needed his Wendy,' comments consultant psychotherapist Richard Hughes, 'and he gave himself a wife he thought reflected the man he now was. Because who is Mick other than Peter Pan, with Keith, Charlie and Bill as his tribe, his Lost Boys? He's on this endless quest for a Wendy – in other words, his mum. All those bimbos were the Tinkerbells. He'd had all the groupies and he'd had the most beautiful women in the world, but had found fulfilment with none of them. He sensed that he had to couple, in order to survive – not that he would have had any intention of staying faithful. So he winds up marrying himself: Bianca. He then proceeds to disown all the aspects of her that he cannot tolerate or accept about himself.

'From her point of view, it was a good move. She really came into her own during that marriage, and succeeded in making a worthwhile life beyond it. But the public never warmed to her. They perceived her as frosty and tricky. Looking back, Mick did nothing to ease her passage into public life, did he. Partly because he both envied her and was jealous of her. Partly because once he had what he wanted, he lost interest. She gave birth to their baby Jade, who became his jewel and usurped her mother, and that was that. He was back out there on the prowl, she knew what he was up to, her contempt for him grew and grew. Not only was Bianca never right for him, but he was never right for Bianca. Only Jerry Hall was perfect for Mick. She was the one who got away. He will probably regret losing her, though of course he would never admit it, until his dying day. No way back there.'

But it's still about him. The woman who won't get down to his level stands no chance. The most perfect rock star women, incidentally, were Linda McCartney and Yoko Ono. Having identified the gap in the market, sized up the weaknesses of their intended and worked out what he was short of, they focused on fulfilling his every need and making themselves indispensable, knowing that it's via giving that we receive. Bianca Jagger was never that kind of woman. She expected equality. She had her own agenda, her own objectives to fulfil. While she may or may not have uttered the immortal words attributed to her, 'My marriage ended on my wedding day,' they encapsulate why their union was doomed. They gave it seven years. Nice try.

*

We have only to compare the refined lifestyle that Mick was now living with the underworld Keith had conjured for himself to comprehend the gulf between the Dartford boys at this juncture.

Here we are in Villefranche-sur-Mer on the glistening Côte d'Azur. Just west of the border with Italy and only ten minutes in a Maserati from Monaco, this little paradise basks in its reputation as one of the five most beautiful bays in the world. Shouldered by Cap de Nice and Cap Ferrat, its mediaeval Old Town spills off the hill into a perfect horseshoe cove. The views over pastel buildings looking out to sea are like paintings. Hollywood location scouts seeking 'traditional French fishing villages' would miss a trick if they failed to find this one. Perched at a table on the market square sipping a glass of Jas d'Esclans Côtes de Provence while watching the fishermen flog their catch, who could wish to be anywhere else? Whiling away the day, inhaling potent aromas of garlic, orange and freshly baked loaves, seeking refuge in quaint covered streets, lingering out of the noonday sun in the sixteenth-century Chapelle Saint-Pierre, once used by the locals to store fishing nets and restored during the fifties with murals by poet and artist Jean Cocteau, it is a place of dreams. Kick along the Plage des Marinières after lunch and down to La Darse for an aperitif before dinner. It doesn't get better.

It's not hard to imagine what they made of him, the rank mainlining rocker gurning through sunburnt lips, flashing his mouldering incisors and his narcotised cronies, who crowed like roosters as they tore around town in Keith's red convertible Jag; terrorising widows out of their black support hose each time they took the boat out for a spin; cutting through the waves like boy racers, reckless fifth-form bullies flipping the kids over the side for laughs. He was a fish out of water in this place. He hadn't wanted to come here. He loved it.

'Keith's place' housed the infamous dungeon of debauchery and disgrace that has become synonymous with the album that was recorded there. You can't see it from the road, and you couldn't get into it if you tried. Snapped up by a Russian oligarch for €100 million in 2005, the Villa Nellcôte, a sixteen-room Belle Epoque mansion on the Avenue Louise Bordes, is these days strictly out of bounds. From April 1971 until October 1973, Keith rented this gaff with its own private beach for a grand a week. He made space for the Stones' £65,000 mobile recording studio on the drive, installed himself, producer Jimmy Miller and assorted musicians in its dank, multi-roomed basement and set about recording their most fabled, some say most overrated work, *Exile on Main St.*

Reports imply that he and his family – Anita and Marlon – were there for much longer than they were. Which is all part of the mythology. An untimely gendarme intrusion caused them to beat a hasty retreat at the end of August, only months after they had arrived. The French government ordered Keith to honour his rental agreement, so he had to keep coughing up long after he moved out. But he could never go back there. On 15 October he was found guilty by the court in Nice of trafficking cannabis. He earned a one-year suspended prison sentence, a 5,000 franc fine and was banned from entering France for the next two years. Despite which, Villa Nellcôte inhabits rock history as a legendary Stones location. It has drawn fans from all corners to catch a glimpse of it from the sea, and to wallow in their imaginations in all that went on there. Some even quiz the locals as to what became of Keith's speedboat, *Mandrax.* Like everything else that happened half a century ago, that little craft is now less than a memory.

Mischievous Keith, evidently brimming with *joie de vivre* and whatever else he was ingesting, gave oxygen to a rumour that the house had been the headquarters of the Gestapo during the Nazi occupation of France in World War II. The floor vents in the basement were covered in gold swastikas. Honest, guv. It wasn't true. No Germans resided in the vicinity for long enough. Nazi occupation commenced only after Benito Mussolini's forces withdrew, meaning that the tenure of the Germans in the South of France was fleeting. The Gestapo HQ was established in Nice, not in Villefranche. Maybe the rumour began because the villa came with its own German housekeeper, ironically named Elizabeth. As you were.

As for the album. Said guitarist Mick Taylor of *Exile on Main St.* 'It's got a raw sound quality, and the reason for that is that the basement was very dingy and very damp. The roof leaked, and there were power failures. We had to deal with all that, and go with the flow.'

Quelle flow. Of drug dealers, itinerant musos, exotic acquaintances, family members and hangers-on by the limo-load; Joe Cocker, John and Yoko (who floated around naked), Eric Clapton, Alain Delon, Catherine Deneuve, folk from the record industry, their kids, their mistresses, anybody's dogs, and a steady zipping in and out of journalists and groupies. Upwards of twenty round the table most days, most nights, most mornings. Who knew what time it was? Follow the sun. Most of those present were on liquor diets, too. Losing days.

But recording was no pique-nique. Marshall Chess, boss of Rolling Stones Records, remembered that Jagger was vexed. *Exile* was regarded as 'Keith's album', because it was being made in his domain. Keith was now a junkie. Mick was not. If there was still common ground between them, neither of them could put their finger on it. Mick was also irked that his old mucker was getting far too close to his guest Gram Parsons,[6] the American singer-songwriter and friend of the band who arrived with his new wife Gretchen Burrell[7] at Keith's invitation, and instantly became his fellow guitarist's abettor. Because Parsons was out of it all the time and fighting constantly with his bird, who was also throwing her weight around, pissing off Anita, who ejected them. Keith later blamed Jagger for Gram's departure, adding weight to Chess's theory that Mick was jealous of all the time he and Gram spent plucking together. Fans have speculated since its release that Parsons features on *Exile*. Keith concedes that he is probably one of the singers on the track 'Sweet Virginia', although there is no proof. Others insist that his influence can clearly be discerned throughout. Maybe. Anyway, things got arctic after that, and goodbye kisses were blown. Gram's efforts to re-befriend the band during their 1972 US tour were rejected. He fell into a deep depression from which he never recovered. The coffin that went up in flames at the ghostly Joshua Tree National Park in southern California the following year had Gram in it.

*

Nellcôte was not, despite the chandeliers, gilded chaises and polished-to-perfection parquet, what you could call an elegant environment. Mrs Jagger, always perfectly dressed, coiffed and made-up, and who was also with child, visited only when she had to and kept her distance while she was there. Tiptoeing through toddler excrement to get to the bathroom, the Richardses having neglected to potty-train little Marlon and letting him doo wherever he would, must have sent her gagging. These were not Bianca's people. They were in Paris. She sat it out among friends, awaiting her baby's October birth.

And bad stuff happened. Not only busts but outlaws, shady Corsicans, chancers, fly-by-nights, burglaries. Keith was relieved of a dozen guitars, some of which were irreplaceable. He never got them back. A chef was rumoured to have gone berserk when he discovered that Anita had apparently injected his daughter with heroin. But American journalist Robert Greenfield, who stayed briefly at Nellcôte and wrote a book about his experiences named after the album recorded there and sub-titled 'A Season in Hell with the Rolling Stones', discounts the rumour. He states that the employee was trying to blackmail Anita, and that he did not even have a daughter. The chef was replaced by a twenty-three-year-old cook, Gérard Mosiniak, whom I interviewed in 1983 for society and celebrity magazine *Ritz*.

'It was sex, drugs and rock'n'roll all the way at Nellcôte,' Mosiniak told me. 'Everything they say is true. I wondered at first whether it was Hades I had walked into. Anita interviewed me, I went to see Keith, he asked me if I wanted the job and they hired me. I had no experience of this kind of work, and no idea what to expect. They would go down into the caves (cellars) at about eleven at night and stay down in the sweaty hellhole until five in the morning. They wanted food during the night, and I never knew until they called for it how many I was cooking for. Mostly they slept through the mornings. Some of them went to the beach. But the days were slow. I had to go to the market to get food to prepare. I couldn't drive in those days, so Keith's chauffeur would take me in his Bentley or in the Jaguar.

'The food Keith wanted wasn't challenging. It was home cooking. Wholesome food, as made by Maman. He liked roast dinners, pies, barbecues. Mostly meat, nothing "too foreign". There would be a big evening meal, around the time the little children needed to eat; there were always several running around. Those dinners could sometimes go on and on. There was a lot of drugs, and strange types turning up to deliver them, who sometimes stayed on to join in. Keith and Anita and a number of those who came and went were on heroin. I never tried it myself, although I was offered. There was no sense that they were risking their lives, or that it was anything all that bad.'

Rosie Bell was also at Nellcôte, with her then partner Mick Taylor and their child. 'I was twenty-four. I moved to the South of France with a six-week-old baby, our daughter Chloe, which was not a happy thing to do,' she said in 2017. The former Rose Millar Taylor was once a drop-dead gorgeous wild child who had been expelled from her smart London school, St Paul's, and who had previously been the girlfriend of Muddy Waters and Peter Green of Fleetwood Mac.

'I missed my mother and the sort of support I was getting. I had a succession of nannies, English ones, who just wanted to sleep with the Rolling Stones. They were always a problem. And then we had a wonderful French girl. She just walked around everywhere in a bikini with a Gitanes, the baby under her arm, a beer, a fantastic French book in her hand, and she wasn't the least bit impressed with anyone. Anne-Marie. She was great. We kept her for years.'

But there was 'too much hanging around', Rosie said. She and Taylor would turn up for a recording session but either Jagger or Richards or both would not be there: 'Mick would have gone to Paris, and Keith was not available because the train hadn't arrived from Marseille. Mick

(Taylor) was unhappy and depressed having to wait around all the time in order to play. I thought they were crazy, basically. I still think they are. But I loved the music.' Just not the other stuff. Were the epic drug-taking and orgies for real?

'Yes, they certainly were. There were guys who were procuring women from here, there and everywhere and bringing them along. Yes, it was dealers and groupies and hangers-on as well as some lovely people. Gram Parsons was there, a lovely musician, and some other famous people like John Lennon, falling down the stairs, and it was mad.

'We were there for the sessions in the basement, which was a very strange and a very odd environment. There was no air conditioning. You'd have Bobby Keys, the saxophonist, in the toilet, and Mick in some other funny little room, all in the basement which was simply, acoustically not the place. An absolute nightmare in the summer in the South of France. Everyone was really uncomfortable down there. It was amazing anyone got any music done at all, really. I think it was very creative. I think Mick played very well, but I am hopelessly biased, though a lot of people say he added a lot to the music. With him it became more than just thrash rock, and I think he is quite proud of his contribution, although he'd like a few more credits.'

An encounter that Rose would forever wince to recall involved one Mick too many. It may have been the real reason behind her Mick quitting the Stones abruptly in December 1974.

'Years ago, I went to a party given by Robin Millar, who was producing the singer Sade,' recalled lawyer Paul Levett. Millar, a CBE and one of the most successful record producers in the world, was born with a condition that led to him losing his sight when he was thirty-five. In addition to Sade, he produced the Style Council, Randy Crawford, the Christians and Fine Young Cannibals. He was seventeen when his elder sister Rose married Mick Taylor, and spent his teens hanging out with the Stones.

'Apart from Robin, I didn't know many people at the party,' said Levett, 'and I spent the evening sitting quietly talking to Rose, who was lovely. She told me that she found her husband Mick Taylor in bed with Mick Jagger. This got out years ago, and has been gossiped about ever since. It tends to be dismissed as a vicious rumour. But why would she say such a thing to me if she hadn't seen it with her own eyes, and if it were not true?'

Some insist that Taylor quit the Stones after Jagger allegedly seduced him. He was addicted to heroin at the time; an easy target, young and vulnerable. We know that Jagger was predatory, and of his omnisexuality, at least in his younger days. It is said that Taylor was so shocked by what he'd done, he turned around and married Rose in 1975 when their relationship was already on the slide. The marriage failed, predictably. He fathered another daughter by an American woman who had sung backing vocals for his own band. He tried marriage a second time, but failed again. He went off the rails, became virtually destitute, and sadly lost contact with his daughters.

'People are always asking me whether I regret leaving the Stones,' he said in September 2009. He was living in near squalor in a Suffolk semi, and working on and off as a pub musician. 'I make no bones about it – had I remained with the band, I would probably be dead. I was having difficulties with drug addiction, and couldn't have lasted. But I'm clean now, and have been for years.'

In 1982, taking advantage of a loophole in his contract, Taylor revealed, the Stones suddenly cut off his royalties for the six of their albums to which he had contributed.

'I should have got a lawyer. Instead, I called them rude words and asked how they could just stop paying me. They all know it's not right. In fact, it is outrageous. I've tried to talk to Mick a couple of times, but I realise that hiring a lawyer is probably the only way they'll take me seriously. But they figure I'm not going to do anything about it.'

Chapter Fifteen

CRISIS

In December 1971, the Stones were back in LA, recording at Sunset Sound and planning the following year's tour. But while Mick and Bianca were living in domestic semi-bliss with their baby, Keith and Anita were disintegrating. Addicted to alcohol and cocaine as well as heroin, they needed urgent professional help or would not survive. At Mick's insistence, they were flown out of California and deposited in Montreux, Switzerland, where Keith would submit to stringent detoxification while strung-out Anita gave birth to their second child.

Once the tax-exile year was over, the entire band shifted to Switzerland to rehearse. *Exile* was released on 12 May, Mick's first wedding anniversary. The album was an instant hit, and remains a classic. Mick's marriage, on the other hand, had only seven more years to run. The following month they were in Vancouver, embarking on their seventh North American tour to promote the new album. They faced with trepidation their first US performances since Altamont two and a half years earlier, not knowing what reaction they would get in the flesh from their fans.

The Stones Touring Party, the 'STP' as it became known, was the most hedonistic of their career. Orgies at the Playboy mansion, free-for-all crew screws on the private jet, drug smuggling, gun-toting, the works. They have striven to play it down since, but there were witnesses, some of whom wielded cameras. The raffish scofflaws were well on their way to going down in history as black-hearted outlaws. Their fans, most of whom appeared content to live law-abiding lives, seemed to adore them for it. The harder the Stones played, the greater the fans worshipped them. Wasn't it simply about the music, or were the songs merely the soundtrack of an Excess-All-Areas lifestyle that their followers could hardly imagine, let alone experience? If so, perhaps we should question the concept of the vicarious thrill. Why were the world's most outrageous rockers revered for the kind of extreme behaviour most ordinary mortals would rather die than risk ... if you take my meaning? Is it because most would do exactly as they did, given half the chance, if they knew they could get away with it? Some would. But surely most would be content simply to sit back and enjoy the view. In which case, is it fair to call the Stones a bad influence? Isn't that akin to suggesting that watching a Bond film incites moviegoers to hurl themselves from tall buildings or go around gunning people down? To say that the Stones were only rock's equivalent of cinematic escapism is to forget a fundamental difference: that the action heroes in thrillers are acting. Their antics depend on the magic of special effects. The Stones were living it up and getting down and dirty for real. There would be consequences.

'They were just living the dream,' deadpans David 'Kid' Jensen, the popular Canadian-born former BBC Radio 1 and *Top of the Pops* presenter who first met the Stones during his tenure at Radio Luxembourg. Eighteen-year-old David relocated almost five thousand miles from home to the Grand Duchy in 1968 to host his own show, and championed the band from his first day at the station. They invited the baby-faced DJ, whom David Bowie once tried to pull in the back of a cab, to join them at various points around the world. I joined him and his Icelandic wife Gudrun at their home for tea, to reminisce.

'I might have been the first to call them "the greatest rock'n'roll band in the world" on air,' David suggests. 'I went to the Bahamas to talk to them; they flew me down there. They also asked me over to stay with them at the Georges Cinq hotel in Paris. I remember I ended up with an ear infection, couldn't fly, and had to stay an extra two days. They were, as always, generously accommodating. I later caught up with them in Philadelphia.'

When Mick Jagger asks you to join him on the tour plane as the

Stones dashed around the United States, you don't argue, reasons the now seventy-two-year-old Parkinson's sufferer.[1] 'This was the band's private plane, with (graphic designer) John Pasche's iconic red tongue and lips logo emblazoned on the tail fin. My presence was not wholly popular, with American record producer (and Rolling Stones label boss) Marshall Chess making clear that I wasn't welcome. I know this because the seating arrangements on the small aircraft meant I witnessed every heated word. Chess and Jagger had this terrible, flaming barney about it. But the interview that Mick gave me afterwards was fantastic.

'On touchdown in Philadelphia, a police escort accompanied us as we sped through the streets to the Spectrum, a huge ice hockey venue which had gained a reputation as the home of the biggest rock names. When I asked Bill Wyman where I might sit to watch, he generously handed me an Access All Areas pass and gestured to the stage: "Sit with us." I did, witnessing a performance from the greats from a vantage point just a few feet behind them. On occasions since, I catch vintage footage of the gig with the camera panning round to catch my young face sandwiched between Mick and Bill.

'After the concert,' remembers David, 'it was onwards to Pittsburgh, from where take-off was delayed. Given this was a private plane, airport procedures were a little less formal and we disembarked for the wait. Killing time, one of the guys got out a football and the band invited me to join in a kickabout on the runway. A career in radio offers many surreal experiences, but little compares with playing football with the Rolling Stones at midnight at a Pittsburgh airport.'

It was the flight after that one that caused the controversy. Heading from Pittsburgh to New York for their four shows at Madison Square Garden, the final performance scheduled for Mick's twenty-ninth birthday, some of the roadies indulged in an in-flight gang bang. They were cheered on enthusiastically by many of those on board, including Keith and Mick. The very young girl engaged in the exercise may not have taken part of her own accord.

'I was aware of what was going on at the back of the plane,' admits Jensen. 'Walking up the aircraft at a very quick pace were Bill Wyman and Charlie Watts, the rhythm section. I looked round and saw a lot of people leaning forwards over the seat in front of them. I realise now that it was to get a better view. And it suddenly occurred to me why Marshall Chess was so anxious that they should not have any press or promo on the plane. Truman Capote, his friend Princess Lee Radziwill (the sister of Jackie Kennedy) and Andy Warhol were also with us. Capote was writing a piece for *Rolling Stone* magazine and Warhol was capturing everything on his tape recorder. I've often wondered what they made of it. Some of the band members had children with them. Certainly Bill was trying to shunt his little boy Stephen up to the front, away from what was going on. And I can tell you exactly what I saw: Keith Richards and his doctor pouring cartons of orange juice over two naked girls; and Keith having sex with another man.'

This was all being filmed, alarmingly, for a fly-on-the-wall documentary following the Stones on tour. Directed by lauded art photographer Robert Frank, one of whose images graced the cover of the *Exile* album, it was intended for cinema release. Frank's *vérité* approach involved the use of several cameras which were left lying around, so that members of the entourage could lift them at random and start shooting whatever was going on. As well as the sex scenes, the footage features Mick Taylor smoking marijuana with some roadies, Jagger snorting cocaine backstage, a sequence in which he films himself getting ready to masturbate, and a young groupie injecting herself with heroin in a hotel bedroom.

'One of the rules when making the movie was that none of the people in the Rolling Stones could say no,' explains documentary director Paul Justman, who was an editor on the film. 'If they said no, then Robert put the camera down and he left. There wouldn't be any anger or anything. It would be like, "OK, you guys have given up and said no to me. Get someone else."'

Once they'd come down off their cloud and had a chance to review the footage, the band were appalled. Not in anyone's imagination was such a film going to enhance their image and repair the damage done by Altamont and *Gimme Shelter*, as it had been intended to do. They wanted it scrapped. Frank disagreed, insisting that his film be released. Thus, so the story goes, did they find themselves immersed in a legal scrap. A court order was said to have been awarded, preventing the film from being screened unless the director himself was present – because the film had to be viewed in the context of *his* work, not that of the Stones. Frank died in September 2019, aged ninety-four. Does his estate have a say? What now?

Many claim to have attended screenings, including one during the mid-1990s at the Anthology Film Archives in New York. It was also shown at London's Tate Modern in 2004, as part of a major retrospective of Frank's photography and film work, entitled 'Storylines'.

'It's such a time capsule of what life was like behind the scenes in 1972,' commented the film's editor Susan Steinberg. 'I've always wanted to get it released and seen. What was controversial at the time is now history.'

A bootleg of the film is available on the internet. My most recent search turned up as US DVD for seventeen US dollars, with the following description:

'The Rolling Stones 1972 tour on film. Whew, wild movie! Sex, drugs and rock'n'roll! Songs: "Cocksucker Blues," "Brown Sugar," "Midnight Rambler," "Uptight" (with Stevie Wonder), "Happy," and "Street Fighting Man." Keith and Mick snort up and hit the stage. Sin and debauchery. Girl shoots up. Keith tells Mick it's best to snort coke through a rolled up dollar bill. Bobby Keyes [sic] and Keith toss a TV off their hotel balcony. Dick Cavett asks Bill Wyman, "What's running through your nervous system right now?" Many, many amusing scenes!

Cast of "characters" includes: Bianca Jagger, Tina Turner, Stevie Wonder, Dick Cavett, Truman Capote, Andy Warhol, Ehmet [sic] Ertegun, Marshall Chess. Once you see it you'll know why the Stones decided to stop its theatrical release!'

'Other bands played at being rock stars,' muses David Jensen. 'The Stones always had the edge. They were doing it for real. Not all of it was admirable, much of it was hedonistic and downright debauched, but you take the rough with the smooth in this game. Standing in the wings onstage with the Rolling Stones, you *felt* like a Rolling Stone. Their energy was all-pervasive and addictive. Going to the gig with all the outriders, sirens going, lights blazing, thousands of kids screaming, eating their rider food backstage for several nights in a row, it was all amazing and it didn't get better. Maybe I considered things a little differently once I had kids.

'It struck me at one point that they weren't the most handsome band in the world, and that this was actually a major breakthrough. Suddenly, you didn't have to be a pretty boy to make it. In that respect, they did rock'n'roll a great service. No one really talks about this. I wonder if they ever realised.

'You'd have to say, though, that things were much more cavalier in those days. The extreme lifestyle, the excessive drug-taking, the underage groupies, they would never get away with all that now. But you know what? The Stones, right? Wow. I breathed the same air as them. Great band, great music, they've stood the test of time. Mick Jagger seems younger now than he did twenty years ago. They have grown old disgracefully. It all adds to the allure.'

But when he thinks about them from this vantage point, sixty years after they began, David finds them an unlikely set of people: 'As bandmates and as friends. Can they even *be* friends, at this stage in the game? And you have to ask, in 2022, at what point does the corporate gig lose its appeal? Five hundred pound tickets going for thousands on some of these secondary ticket broker sites. You get there and the band are stick men a mile away on a barely visible stage. There's a delay in the sound. A bottle of water costs ten quid. You're not getting home any time soon, maybe not even until the early hours of tomorrow, because the traffic jams out of the venue are so bad. What's it about? Isn't corporate rock the very definition of the Emperor's New Clothes? And in any case, are they a band any more, or are they only a memory? Do they even exist, or is what we see when we go to the show all in our minds? Personally, I try to think of them as they once were, a bunch of young musicians who were dedicated to the preservation of the music they had chosen to play. Especially Brian Jones, so young and so idealistic. Who once sat in my radio studio in his Afghan coat. He was experimenting with Arabic music, and he impressed me no end with his knowledge. They were unruly and uncontrollable, but they did live the dream.'

Are they still living it?

'Yeah, I think so. I'm sure Mick Jagger still goes to bed at night thinking, "What do we do next?" As mature as they are (or are they?) they continue to flirt with their legend and their reputation, and they keep on taking risks. I can't help but find that admirable. We know that nostalgia sells because people want to re-live their youth. The Stones exploit that, and we let them. They are rock'n'roll mercenaries with a legacy that is so deep, so widespread and so exciting that you have to hand it to them. Thanks to them, old age is cool. It's getting a second wind.'

*

At a party at impresario, rock manager and film producer Robert Stigwood's house in November 1974, Mick Taylor told Mick Jagger he was leaving the Stones. Did anyone quit the Stones of their own volition? the latter had the temerity to ask. The man in Keith's Bentley beside him had no answers ... especially not to the invitation to replace him. Ronnie Wood was spoken for.

Prospective substitutes came and went during the first few months of 1975 before the Faces plucker came aboard as a temp, ahead of their 1975 Tour of the Americas.

'It was such a shame that Mick Taylor left the band,' commented David Ambrose, former head of A&R at EMI. 'It happened because he and Jagger were having sex. Their relationship destroyed him, and he left quite suddenly. Whatever he says now, and they are going to deny it, aren't they, that was the reason. Jagger must have feared for the future of the band at that point. Who were they going to get who was as good as him? Because Taylor was as good as Eric Clapton in his day. Taylor completed the Stones' sound.

'Ronnie Wood was never up to it, not in my opinion. He's one of these people who is *quite* everything. Quite a good artist. Quite a good guitarist. But he doesn't do it with the love, the passion that the others have. I've always felt he's just going through the motions. You can replace Ron Wood, he is the master of none. He can put his hand to something, but he's a terrible songwriter. He wrote 'It's Only Rock 'n Roll'? With Jagger, yes. I rest my case. He is dispensable. The only ones who are not are Mick and Keith. Only they are the Rolling Stones. Without them, it dies. The reason they keep on going is because Jagger has a lot of wives, girlfriends and children to support. They don't sell any records to speak of. They get PRS off the radio, but it's pennies. Like PPL.[2] Touring is about merchandising money, mainly. It's not ticket sales. Twenty pounds for a T-shirt costing fifty pence to make: that's where the dough is.'

*

It was during the mid-seventies that rumours began to surface of drug-addled Keith getting his blood changed at a clinic in Switzerland. Ambrose remembers it well. 'It was true,' he insists, 'but it didn't start in Switzerland. I used to go to a guy on Seymour Place near Baker Street, right near the swimming baths, where they did blood transfusions routinely. Everyone went. It was Ken Lawton's practice. He was a psychiatrist. He also did psychoanalysis and faith healing, the laying of hands, on me. I got really hooked on it. He said I had a massive Oedipus complex. He was probably right. It was one of his colleagues who did the transfusions there. A number of my close friends were in there all the time having it, and I heard that Keith Richards had his done there too. It made sense. I mean, why do you have to go to Paris or Geneva all the time when you can get it done down the road on Seymour Place? This was the pre-eighties, pre-AIDS era, remember, when you could still do such things safely and cheaply. Get rid of all the heroin in your body and start again.

'I hear that Keith goes to church now, and that he has a good relationship with God. I'm sure he talks to Keith Richards the way he talks to anybody else. God does have a choice.'

*

Beaky, crow-coiffed, pleat-faced Ronnie had to thrash guitar for the Stones for more than a quarter of a century before they stopped referring to him as 'the new boy'. The former art student, Faces and Jeff Beck Group guitarist who co-wrote 'Gasoline Alley' and 'Every Picture Tells a Story' with Rod Stewart, and who composed and recorded extensive solo work, would not become a full-blown partner until Wyman called it a day in 1993. Formerly married to model Krissy Findlay, he took Jo Karslake as his second wife in January 1985.

Left: Altamont: the death of the sixties. This is what a crowd of 300,000 to 500,000 people looks like from above the Californian speedway. © *Getty / Bettmann*

Right: Audience members looking on as Hells Angels beat a fan with pool cues. Tragically, it was not to be the last, or the worst, of the violence that day. © *Getty / 20th Century Fox*

Left: Mick Taylor and Jagger can be seen onstage between the shoulders of two of the burly Hells Angels who were tasked, disastrously, with security for the concert. © *Getty / Icon And Image*

Top: Mick, and the woman who thought she was his wife: Jerry Hall, mother of four of his children. © *Getty / Antoinette Norcia / Ron Galella. Middle*: Bill Wyman with his bride-to-be, Mandy Smith – now last over 18 and, in theory, presentable to the world. At Bill's restaurant in Kensington. May 1989. © *Getty / Mirrorpix. Below left*: Jerry and the pacemaker. © *Getty / Neil Mockford. Below right*: The author with Mandy Smith. Taken at a promo shoot for Wyman's fund-raising all-star album, *Willie and the Poor Boys*. Fulham, 1985. *Author collection.*

Above: 5 June 1989, the day Bill married eighteen-year-old Mandy Smith, thirty-four years his junior. © *Getty / Dave Hogan*. *Below*: If a picture is worth a thousand words, Mandy's glance to camera here as the world's politely incredulous media crowds in on them authors a book of its own. © *Getty / Mirrorpix*.

Left: Keith and one of his iconic five-string Telecaster perfect for the open-G tuni he favours on so many class Stones songs. © *Getty / Christopher Simon Sykes*

Right: Keith, Anita and their son Marlon, pictured at Nellcote, their villa above Villefranche-sur-Mer – where the Rolling Stones served their famous 'exile'. © *Getty / Mirrorpix*

Left: The thousand-yard stare. © *Getty / Gijsbert Hanekroot.*

Above: Mick Taylor: elegant, fluid, bluesy – the finest guitarist the Stones ever had. Discarded lover of Mick Jagger. © *Getty / Michael Putland. Below*: Another, rather more famous, of Mick's historic conquests. Chemistry still crackles. © *Getty / Denis O'Regan.*

Right: Keith Richards reclining, acoustic in hand, in the beautiful library of his Connecticut home. © *Getty / Christopher Simon Sykes..*

Left: Producer Jeff Griffin and presenter Andy Peebles interviewing Mick Jagger about the Stones' *Undercover* album. Savoy Hotel, London, 4 October 1983. © *Malcolm Hill*

Below: Peter Myers, New York grocer and personal friend of Keith Richards, samples his stash of Stones Cabernet Sauvignon 2016 back home in Keswick, Cumbria. *Author collection.*

Above: The author (*centre*), with (l-r) Chris Jagger (Mick's brother), his wife Kari-Ann Muller, Maxene Harlow and her late partner, the Who's bassist John Entwistle. *Author collection.*

A page for Charlie: ever the antithesis of peacocking Mick Jagger (*left*), eternally keeping the beat in the shadows (*middle*) and, now, looming large over what remains of the Stones today (*below*). © *Getty / Christopher Simon Sykes / Fiona Adams / Ethan Miller*

Above: Even Covid-19 couldn't stop the Rolling Stones juggernaut, as evidenced by their participation in an online concert at the height of lockdown, in aid of frontline healthcare workers. 18 April 2020. © *Getty*. *Below*: The Stones, complete with new boy Steve Jordan on drums (and relative new boy Ronnie Wood on guitar!), doing what they do best: strumming, strutting, sneering and selling out arenas. Get off of their cloud. © *Getty / MediaNews Group*.

'I got the world exclusive on their engagement,' remembers former journalist turned publisher John Blake. 'I was having lunch one day with Ronnie and Jo at Joe Allen's when I was on the *Sun*. While I was in the loo, Ronnie took my tape recorder and said into it, "I've just asked Jo to marry me, and she said yes." I didn't know about it until I got back to the office and found this revelation on there, which of course was a great scoop.

'They then invited me to the wedding. It was at Marylebone Register office, then off to some weird church in Buckinghamshire for the blessing. I remember they were all ducking down behind the pews, doing coke. Photographer Brian Aris was there doing the pictures, and I was going to write something. All the Stones were there except Keith, who they were expecting, because he was his old mate Ronnie's best man. He arrived late, with a face like thunder. Then he spotted me.

'"*John Blake?*" he raged. "What *you* fuckin' doin" ere?" "Ronnie invited me," I said gingerly. He was not what you'd call pleased to see me, because I'd done a book with his dealer, "Spanish" Tony Sanchez [*Up and Down with the Rolling Stones*). "I've got a Derringer in my boot, and I'm gonna fuckin' kill you," he growled. I was so scared, I just burst out laughing. "Don't fuckin' laugh at me, boy. I'm gonna kill you!" he insisted. What can I say, I lived to tell the tale.'

John landed yet another Stones scoop two years later, when Mick's 'wife' Jerry Hall was charged with possession of marijuana in Barbados. The then thirty-year-old model had only asked her butler at their home in Mustique to send her over a few personal effects. When she went down to the airport to pick up her package, she was arrested. The drugs must have been a plant, but there was panic.

'A load of us jumped on a plane and went out there,' said John. 'I went for the *Sun*, and Baz Bamigboye came for the *Daily Mail*. It was February, the weather was shit back home, the judge kept adjourning the bloody court case so we had to stay there. What a drag. The case being *sub judice*, we couldn't write anything, so we had to try and amuse ourselves in other ways. Which I did, by learning to scuba-dive. In the end, the judge dismissed all charges and Jerry was free to go. Mick had supported her in court throughout the ordeal, which was good of him. Afterwards, Mick gave me his exclusive interview, because I got on well with him, and Baz got the interview with Jerry. So it all worked out, we got what we came for.

'It was at that point that Mick told me all about the problems he was having with Keith. "There he was, staggering around on smack for years, and now he's clean and he's telling me what to do," said Mick. "Having carried him for years and years, he's now trying to boss me around." It was the root of all the trouble between Mick and Keith, that would resurface regularly well into the future.'

Mick preferred it, it seems, when he had the shop to himself.

*

After twenty-three years together, the Woods' marriage hit the rocks. Ronnie, a former heavy drinker, turned to the bottle again towards the millennium. He suffered a major mid-life crisis in 2008 at the age of sixty-one, leaving Jo for Kazakhstani-born Russian model and waitress Ekaterina Ivanova. The twenty-year-old was forty-one years his junior. They met in the London club Churchill's, and played out their tempestuous relationship across the tabloids. She kissed and told of their cocaine binges, claiming that he first gave her the drug only hours after they met; that he was sucking fifty fags a day and guzzling litre bottles of spirits, more often than not rum. Was this a man on a mission to do himself in? He clearly didn't like what he saw in the bottom of his glass. Her attempts to get him to AA meetings, she lamented, were in vain. The dishevelled pair traded accusations of assault and acrimony. Ronnie entered rehab. The so-called 'evil Goblin King' and his 'cute little gold digger' eventually went their separate ways, but Ronnie never went home to his wife. Jo divorced him. Reality television claimed the coquettish Russian, who entered the Big Brother house for series seven in 2010, the year of contestants Stephanie Beacham, Vinnie Jones and Alex Reid. It was a predictable descent after that for 'Katia'. She did a few topless spreads for girlie mags, then faded away.

'Going out with an older man can be quite different,' she said in 2012, 'but [Ronnie] had the mentality of a fifteen-year-old. He didn't even teach me to sing.'

There was Brazilian model Anna Araujo and shop assistant Nicola Sargent before Wood pulled himself together. He met and fell for theatre producer Sally Humphreys, a sensible former head girl and drama school graduate only thirty-one years his junior, and made her his third wife at the Dorchester Hotel in December 2012. Ronnie had two best men, Rod Stewart and Paul McCartney. Sally's new husband was two years older than her mother and a year younger than her father, both retired classical musicians. She herself is only a few months older than Ronnie's daughter Leah. Their twin daughters were born in May 2016, making Ronnie a father of six. A cancer survivor who still paints and draws prolifically, who has written three autobiographical books and bred racehorses, he has kept himself busy. He announced with pride in 2021 that he has been sober for ten years.

*

'Woody's fabulous,' Bill Wyman told my late friend the journalist and producer John Pidgeon in 1978, just after the Stones' 'farewell' US tour. 'He's made this band come back to life again, more than anybody else, I think. Mick Taylor was a fabulous musician, he really was. So quick and clever at inventing something or learning something … as far as I was concerned, he was the best musician in the band. Technically brilliant. But when [he] was in the band, it became three groups of people … he's been away from the band for a long time now, and he hasn't got his shit together. That happened to Stevie Winwood a bit too, but now he's making great music.[3]

'[It] will last as long as we have fun, as long as it's worthwhile, as long as it doesn't become a drag and a bore and an obligation … as it was getting to be for me, three or four years ago. Now I've got a new lease of life, a second wind, and it doesn't cross my mind ever to leave the band or that [we're] going to break up. And touring, doing shows, getting on the road – Keith thinks that's the most important thing, and he's probably right …The more you work on the road, the better you play, and the better the next session gets, and the next tour …'

But going on the road is exhausting, as Bill concedes. 'A lot of people get really fucked up … [they] can't handle it without getting into something else to manage to do it. Some people can, some can't. Living in suitcases, living on bad food, not getting laundry done – all them stupid things that have to be part of living, getting your bloody jacket pressed or your socks washed, sitting in these boring rooms when you'd rather be at home; but then the next day knowing the reason was because you're just having a great time on stage for two hours and you're glad you're not at home. Fortunately we can now afford to live in better hotels, in nice suites, and have a video machine and a good sound system and friends popping by, and it becomes a bit more like home and life. But if it didn't – like those early days, man, you really had to be dedicated to get that together, to go on the road for forty-six cities and stick to it, manage to stay on the road with bad hotels and bad organisation. When you're big, you can sort it out and make it a lot easier – have days off and eat better food – but you can become very wasted on tour. Mick loses pounds. I haven't got many to lose, but even I lose pounds and I don't even sweat on the stage.'

*

Ronnie wasn't the only Stone to suffer a devastating midlife crisis. Charlie Watts, the abstemious one, became so heavily addicted to booze and drugs during the eighties that Keith took it upon himself to intervene. Pot, kettle? It was rich, coming from the junkie who had dodged so many scrapes and life-threatening scenarios; who had been hanging around death's door for the past twenty years, boozed to the hilt and smacked to the nines to the point that *NME* had voted him 'Most Likely to Die' ten years in a row during the seventies; who was fond of taking tequila on his cornflakes; who, when asked what was the strangest thing he had attempted to snort, snapped back, 'My father. I snorted my father.

'He was cremated,' Keith revealed of Bert, Richards Snr, who, er, snuffed it in 2002 at the age of eighty-four. 'I couldn't resist grinding him up with a little bit of blow (cocaine). My dad wouldn't have cared, he didn't give a shit. It went down pretty well, and I'm still alive.'

As he added, almost slyly, 'Keith Richards has got to do everything once.' He was, he admitted, really disappointed when he fell off the 'Most Likely to Die' list: 'Some doctor told me I had six months to live, and I went to their funeral.'

But did the snorting his dad thing really happen?

'There were headlines, editorials, there were op-eds on cannibalism, there was some of the old flavour of Fleet Street indignation at the Stones … There were also articles saying this is a perfectly normal thing, it goes back to ancient times, the ingestion of your ancestor,' reflected Keith in

Life. 'So there were two schools of thought. Old pro that I am, I said it was taken out of context. No denying, no admitting.'

So was it true?

When the story looked in danger of going too far, Keith penned a memo to his assistant to explain the scandal's genesis. Having kept his father's ashes in a black box for six years, he said, because he couldn't bring himself to scatter him – the longer you keep them, the harder to let go – he eventually got around to planting an English oak tree, with the intention of committing Bert to the soil underneath.

'And as I took the lid off the box, a fine spray of his ashes blew out on to the table. I couldn't just brush him off, so I wiped my finger over it and snorted the residue. Ashes to ashes, father to son. He is now growing oak trees, and would love me for it.'

But Charlie was something else. Charlie was the sensible one, the voice of reason, the one upon whom the others could count. The backbone, the metronome, the one who was there when all else failed. Now here he was, heavily addicted to alcohol, amphetamines and heroin. No one saw that coming.

'It got really bad,' admitted Watts, remembering the day he passed out in the studio. 'I lost consciousness, and that was so unprofessional. Keith was the one who dealt with me. Keith, of all people. Who I saw go through every state doing anything and everything. He was kind. He said to me, "That's the kind of thing you do when you're sixty". Looking back, I think it was really a midlife crisis. I became a completely different person in 1983, and didn't leave until 1986. I nearly lost my wife and everything over my behaviour.

'After two years of speed and heroin, I felt very sick. My daughter told me I looked like Dracula. I almost killed myself. I wasn't that badly affected, I wasn't a junkie, but giving up [drugs] was very, very hard,' he told the *Observer* in 2000. He also said that falling drunk down the steps of his cellar and breaking his ankle while trying to retrieve yet another bottle of wine 'really brought it home to me how far down I'd gone. I just stopped everything – drinking, smoking, taking drugs, everything, all at once.'

Charlie was diagnosed with throat cancer in 2004. After a course of radiotherapy, he recovered. The clock ticked on.

Chapter Sixteen

JUGGERNAUT

In October 1983, a month ahead of the release of *Undercover* – the Stones' seventeenth UK album, their nineteenth in the States – Jeff Griffin, the award-winning BBC producer who recorded the Stones live many times for the *In Concert* series and other programmes, accompanied distinguished Radio 1 presenter Andy Peebles to London's Savoy Hotel to record interviews with Bill Wyman and Mick Jagger.

'We did Mick in Mick's room,' recalls Griffin, 'and we did Bill … somewhere. We then flew to Paris to do Keith at the Warwick Hotel. We had to go to him because Keith was doing a tax year out. We went with EMI executive Wally Slaughter. We go in the room, everyone introduces themselves and we get ready to set up. Sherry Daly from the Stones office is in the anteroom, while Keith is waiting for us in his room. "Don't ask Keith anything about drugs," Sherry warns us. I turn and stare at her. "I have to say to you," I said, "that I do not accept any pre-conditions. I have interviewed Keith many times. I have known him for years. If *he* says that, I will take it from him, but I am not going to take it from you." Wally's looking at me like he's about to drop dead or kill someone. He's terrified that I've just blown the entire interview.

'Anyway, we're in there with Keith, we're having the preliminary chat, and I look him in the eye and say, "By the way, Keith, about these things you don't want to talk about." And we start discussing all the bad publicity he's attracted over the years because of taking hard drugs. It had been in the news recently, so it was relevant. But it's always preferable to get it from the horse's mouth.

"Ah, well, man, let's just see how things go," Keith nods at me. He smiles. He's relaxed. I glance at Andy. Who is brilliant, he knows exactly the way I want things to go. We sit down and switch on. We've picked two or three tracks from the *Undercover* album to discuss during the interview, and everything is simmering nicely. At which point, I nudge Andy, and on cue he comes out with the relevant question.

'Well. Keith totally opens up about it. He says how glad and relieved he is to have got himself off the hard stuff. He tells us about his New York apartment down on Fourth and Broadway, about going out at night on those mean streets to meet his dealers. "I'd be down there with a wad of money in one hand and a gun in the other," he says. "I could have been killed. Many times. The positions I put myself in, it seems unreal to me now." He was so candid, it was unbelievable.

'Back in London, I told Derek Chinnery, the then controller of Radio 1, that I wanted to use this. "I think it was much better for him to get it all out," I said. To my amazement, Derek agreed. He was absolutely fine about it. It was unheard of at that time for the BBC to broadcast such shocking material. The only other time I can recall something similar happening was when we went to interview Ozzy Osbourne. He'd not long given up taking drugs as well. When you've got a rock superstar revealing past weaknesses and really opening his heart, it makes for compelling radio. And it was just one of the reasons why I loved working with Andy Peebles. He is so talented. He had a knack for winning the trust of these people and putting them at ease, so that they lost their fear and said what they needed to say. I would call it a form of psychotherapy.'

*

Something happened during the 1980s that knocked rock'n'roll off its trajectory, divorcing it from its roots and changing it so profoundly that it would never be the same again. It started with the pounding vibe that heralded a certain single towards the end of 1984 that not only deprived my friend Jim Diamond of a Christmas No. 1,[1] a robbing he actively encouraged, but which set the wheels in motion for a global fundraising extravaganza the following summer that would both save lives and ring a death knell. To call it the day the music died is no exaggeration.

Live Aid was regarded at the time in some quarters as evidence of the rockerati snatching back control, having expunged punk and got the hang of hairspray. Umbrage was taken at the sight of millionaire musos banging out fifteen minutes of fame, I mean tunes, in the name of feeding the world. Bob Geldof's 'Give us your fucking money!' message stuck in the craw, given that these fat cats could have clubbed together to solve third world hunger from the comfort of their own bank accounts. So who was the giant gig for, really?

When the 'Global Jukebox' subject arises nowadays, it is usually in the context of Queen having stolen the day, using the occasion to relaunch themselves after a couple of bumpy episodes (a ban from the Musicians' Union for playing Sun City, South Africa, during apartheid, wrecking their reputation in America with their single 'I Want to Break Free') to go again as world-beaters. This rejuvenated force soared from strength to strength on the back of it, unaware at first that Freddie Mercury was on the way out. So solid was their Live Aid performance that their name has become synonymous with it. It misses the point. That benefit gig was for famine relief, not for the benefit of Queen.

Prompted by the success of the Band Aid single 'Do They Know It's Christmas?' Live Aid has long been hailed as 'the day that rock'n'roll changed the world'. On the contrary – and those of us who got this at the time would have been lynched for saying so – it was the day that the world changed rock. Not just because the sight of Princess Diana in a baby-blue frock, clapping politely, and the Prince of Wales in an unsuitable suit, looking bewildered by it all, made some of us feel uneasy about proceedings. It had to do with something more momentous, which we sensed but couldn't quite put our finger on. It was this: that by donating their time and music to raise funds for the starving millions of Ethiopia via a concert broadcast on an unprecedented scale, the cream of the planet's rock stars were giving the money men big ideas. How about this as an under-tapped force to be harnessed?! Prised open with all the ease of an artist flipping the top off a tin of paint, the lid to Pandora's box was never going back on.[2]

On seemingly innocuous moments has the world long turned. Just as the advent of all-seater stadiums, the abolition of standing terraces and the subsequent fall in violent behaviour between clashing fans led to an explosion in the popularity and influence of football; just as the England team's devastating exit from the Italia '90 FIFA World Cup semi-finals made a money mascot of blubbing midfielder Paul Gascoigne, fetching hundreds of millions of pounds' worth of investment into the beautiful game; just as the Premier League stole its essence and point, making the focus about transfer fees, ludicrous wages and extortionate broadcasting deals; and just as football sold its soul to the advertising industry, rock'n'roll post-Live Aid sold out on a boggling scale.

Its creators, Bob Geldof and Midge Ure, would disagree vehemently. But even they would have to concede that music was changed irrevocably, because it was hijacked after that by the corporate world. Not only that, but this would lead to an eruption of musical talent shows on television that turned rock and pop into karaoke, from the relaunched *New Faces, Search for a Star* and *Stars in their Eyes* to *Popstars, Pop Idol* and *The X Factor* to the travesty called *The Voice*. The sight of Queen guitarist Brian May thrashing the Red Special[3] on *Strictly Come Dancing* during the 2011 ninth series, in which his wife Anita Dobson (former Queen Vic landlady Angie Watts on *EastEnders*) was a contestant, was the moment I almost hung up my pen and went home.

Those not born when it happened or too young to remember or care will not regard 13 July 1985 as significant. Their field of reference extending only as far back as the bands who were big during their childhood, it is of no concern to most of them that the music industry was reconfigured during the eighties; nor that what came before had had such bearing on the sounds with which they grew up. They will be blissfully unaware that MTV launched on 1 August 1981 in New York, or that it became available in the UK on the same date in 1987. If they have heard of weekly television chart show *Top of the Pops*, they probably have no inkling that its once massive influence began to decline during the late 1980s, thanks to a demise in the show's association with BBC Radio 1. It began to be perceived as uncool, sending viewing figures into decline. There was no longer any central, cohesive judgement of the pop music released each week. MTV, while mopping up its viewership and projecting promotional videos as of equal importance to the songs, failed to provide a barometer. As for football: unaware or uninterested in the fact that there was a time when soccer did not dominate every aspect of our lives, particularly the media and especially television; when most women never watched it; when its players would have fallen about laughing at the idea of being Rolex-and-designer-clad style icons and entertainers; and when WAGS,[4] the future influencers of the shopping habits, hair, make-up, nail styles and even values of young girls (thanks, Victoria Beckham, Coleen Rooney and Becky Vardy) had not yet been invented, they are similarly unruffled by the thought that genuine rock breathed its last in Wembley and Philadelphia that long-ago day. The Premier League, stupid money and the music industry coalesced during the early nineties, adding weight and wealth to the growing phenomenon of celebrity culture ... which was itself a triumph of style over substance, of publicity, marketing and merchandise over authenticity, and of the validation of the vicarious thrill.

*

The Stones did not perform at Live Aid. As a group, that is. Mick's recorded jaunt and video with David Bowie, lively and successful though they were, and Keith's and Ronnie's inadequate, best-forgotten accompaniment of Bob Dylan, hardly count. The band did not rock up as a collective, as a contributing live act. The irony is that they have benefited beyond imagining, above and beyond everyone else, from the global celebrity culture that ensued. They would overcome their differences, conclude their estrangement and capitalise on their worth on the back of it. They became mainstream celebrities and tabloid fixtures from that point on. Their private lives, spending habits and especially their women were now pored over, dissected and gossiped about by folk who had little to zero interest in the music they were making. Should I say, *made*. Because the Stones had peaked creatively during the seventies and early eighties. There was nothing innovative or outstanding beyond *Exile on Main St.* (1972), with the exception of 1973's *Goats Head Soup* and 1981's *Tattoo You*. The second of those, despite being a No. 1 album, disappointed the critics and is widely considered to have marked the start of the band's creative decline.

Pause to reconsider these three great Stones albums. *Exile* is famous for 'Rocks Off', 'Tumbling Dice' and 'Sweet Virginia'. Mick said that it reflected the band as 'runaway outlaws, using the blues as its weapon against the world'. It scored a No. 1 in the UK, America and Canada. Remastered and re-released in 2010, the upgrade featured a bonus disc offering ten new tracks. It hit No. 1 in the UK and No. 2 in the US.

Goats Head Soup also sailed to the top in the UK, the US and around the world. It spawned 'Angie' and 'Star Star', the latter better known as 'Starfucker'. That track's subject matter, inventive sex with a groupie, is reckoned to be Mick's riposte to Carly Simon for her tongue-lashing, 'You're So Vain'. There are blatant lyrical echoes. Either way, the song encapsulates the extreme excesses of the seventies in ways that make for fun or uncomfortable listening, depending on what floats.

'With *Exile on Main St.*, we were ready to go, we just lived in my basement and did what we did,' Keith told Paul Sexton in 2020. 'We were still on each other's backs. But by the time we got to cut *Goats Head Soup*, Mick and, well, all of the band, had separated over the world for a while. So we had to figure out how to write songs, not being in each other's pocket.' Of the remastered expansion, Keith informed the music writer, 'Sometimes by listening in a different time and in a totally different space, whole different areas come to mind.'

Before *Tattoo You* came *Black and Blue*: the mostly forgettable album that nevertheless stormed to No. 1 in America, No. 2 back home, and which spawned 'Fool to Cry'. Not that the critics jumped all over it. Its general reception was lukewarm. Yet as is so often the case, one reviewer's vanilla ice cream is another fan's red-hot chilli.

Tattoo You was their last album to top the US charts. It arrived during the year when the band signed a new four-album deal with CBS worth a staggering $50 million. At the time, it was the biggest recording deal in history. What exactly did CBS believe they were going to get for this? That was some blind faith. By 1986, Mick and Keith would barely be talking to each other, let alone in the mood to record. While each immersed himself in his own solo albums, the Stones were not recording anything at all.

I confess to a soft spot for *Tattoo You*. It's the album that gave us 'Start Me Up', with its 'bathroom reverb', stark beat, trademark riff and classic groan, 'You make a grown man cry'. The one that they so often open live shows with, it is the last great Rolling Stones song. It also gave us 'Waiting on a Friend', one of my all-time favourites. Its searing sax appeal courtesy of legend Sonny Rollins[5] helped it to No. 13 in the US. What a shame it passed Europe and the UK by. It is notable for its portrayal of Jagger, who was now pushing forty, as a man who at long last sees sense. Even though, as it turns out, his Damascene conversion was short-lived. Eschewing women and other distractions, he reawakens to the value of lifelong friendship. Which is ironic, given the permafrost that would set in between him and Keith during the eighties.

Check out the video, which might be the coolest Stones footage of all. It sums up, for me, what they were about at that time. There's Mick looking all camp in an edgy East Village doorway,[6] and laid-back Keith making his way along the street. They meet, and Keith bends to kiss his old school chum. They sit for a moment before sauntering off in the direction of a downbeat bar and grill. Propping up the bar is a backcombed Ronnie, three sheets to the wind by the look of him. His presence is interesting, given that he doesn't play on the track. Bill and Charlie are seated behind, grinning self-consciously. The four indulge in an inebriated sing-song before meandering down the back, taking up their instruments and launching into an inevitable jam, of which no one else in the place takes a blind bit of notice. It's simple and nostalgic, and was a big MTV hit at the time. It was who we wanted the Stones to be. It was who I believed they were.

*

While we are in this zone, let's take a moment to ponder the modern trend for remastering, reworking and re-releasing every little thing. 'Bonus tracks', 'previously unreleased material' and 'stuff we didn't know was in that box behind the freezer in the garage' saturate the market with alarming frequency. Much of it feels mercenary. We either like it or we don't. Because I was immersed in the originals when I was young, I find the variations challenging to listen to. Such 'new', 'improved' releases diminish the worth of what artists created in the first place. They seem somehow disrespectful to the millions who paid good money for them the first time round, at least some of whom must feel short-changed. Granted, technology has moved on. Songs, like teeth, deserve a polish. Just as everyone should get a second chance (never a third), music is allowed a new lease of life. The record industry is only following Hollywood's lead, with its remakes of classic motion pictures.

For my money, it's a rare effort indeed that lives up to its predecessor. Take Baz Luhrmann's 2013 interpretation of F. Scott Fitzgerald's *The Great Gatsby*, featuring Leo DiCaprio and Carey Mulligan. The reviewers raved, bully for them, but how could it eclipse Francis Ford Coppola's seminal 1974 piece starring Robert Redford and Mia Farrow? They shouldn't go messing with *Breakfast at Tiffany's* either (it's coming), *Lawrence of Arabia*, *The Sound of Music* or *Gone With the Wind*. The fact that Spielberg couldn't leave *West Side Story* alone is irksome enough. Pretty and lively *but*. You know. If it ain't broke.

Besides, there is much to be said for rudimentary recording techniques. They are an important element of retro charm. That music was made then, not now. It reflects the times during which it was written and laid down, and should therefore still sound like 'then'. The commercial incentive to reach younger fans who couldn't have heard it in antiquity, and whose skin-so-soft ears are accustomed to digital finesse, is understandable. Reworkings and re-releases allow new generations to discover vintage music for themselves. Music must live and breathe if it is to survive, and therefore to a certain extent must change. But the fashion for upgrading and improving can go too far. How does the painter know when his work is done? He decides.

*

Back to the records. When the post-Live Aid Stones became a touring circus, a magnificent happening and a very monument to their own divine majesty, the impact of their music, ironically, seemed to recede. Do people really attend rock gigs simply to gaze at the objects of their fascination, the way they might crowd around Borneo elephants, four-eyed turtles or Bahama Nuthatches in a zoo? You'd be amazed. The Stones experience had reached a stage at which it was less about the songs, more about the spectacle … as well as the opportunity to purchase the spenny logo'd T-shirt, hoodie or hat that you couldn't buy anywhere else. Forget band, the Stones were now a *brand*: the greatest rock'n'roll brand in the world.

And they believed their own mythology. At least, Mick did. The music had become a means to an end, and it showed. Their *raison d'être* now seemed avaricious. At which point, many went off them. Millions more, who of their dark, distant history knew little and could care even less, switched on.

'But all the rebellion, their anti-Establishment stance, had melted away,' remembers former journalist Stuart White. 'There was not a trace of the anti-Fab Four who excited us in the first place. All that energy, the strange Mars bar-eating shenanigans (myth though that was, we loved it) and weirdness had gone. They no longer pissed on forecourts outside South London petrol stations, infuriating local burghers and getting themselves nicked. Now, it was multi-million-dollar tours, Jagger in a blazer watching cricket at Lord's, Keith in a mansion in Switzerland. *Switzerland?* Land of eternal neutrality, yodelling and the cuckoo clock? That was like Satan taking a bijou bolthole in the Vatican City. Go get a pad down in Haiti, Keith, mate. Don't play at it, do it for real. Rum, drums and voodoo, get the picture? *Switzerland?* Say it ain't so. At least he made it to Jamaica and based himself there for a while, which was much more his speed and where Anita could misbehave until the coneys came home, far from the prying eyes of Fleet Street.

'There was talk,' Stuart remembers, 'of Jagger laying down pipes of port in a cellar somewhere.[7] *Port!* Rumour had it he was after a knighthood. Well, the sword did tap his shoulder eventually. Up yours to the world and now we want to kneel before Her Non-Satanic Majesty? At least, Jagger did. How Keith must have howled. We were told that Richards was disgusted by his bandmate's official acceptance by the Establishment. This is what so repelled our parents? This was who we were warned not to be, because if we aped them we would 'never get on'? *O tempora! O mores!*[8] They were now in a nosedive from groundbreaking rock'n'roll down, deeper and down to a plateau of corporateness. As Clinton didn't say, "It's the money, stupid."[9] Okay, maybe not for Krazy Keef, the rock'n'roll Hells Angel. But Charlie Watts, great drummer though he was, looked like a lad from the Land of Perpetual Boredom throughout all those lucrative tours. One could almost hear him thinking, "Right, Montreal tomorrow … Vancouver and then home. Ker–*ching!*"'

Their rogue spirit had clearly deserted them. Thus, as Stuart implies, did the Musical Marx Beat Bolsheviks make it, turning from little Lenins into latter-day Roman Abramoviches … he of the private jets, and another oligarch casualty of Russia's war on Ukraine.

'What next, one wondered: "Rolling Stones PLC"? A Royal warrant: "Purveyors of Fine Rebellious Songs to Her Majesty the Queen"? They should have broken up while the legend was still alive and kicking, as the Beatles had the courage to do. Instead, Mick Jagger became Bill Gates and the band became Microsoft. An admittedly amazing global corporate enterprise – but to misquote Thunderclap Newman,[10] they were not suggesting that anyone "Get out the arms and ammo, because there's something in the air." Reimbursement was now the R-word, not revolution. My dear, late mum and dad, who regarded the Stones' "awful racket" as aural anarchy and the band as sex-maniac drug addicts, would have been delighted to see how those scruffy lads turned into model citizens with distinct conservative and Conservative values.'

The other key contributing factor was the unofficial abolition of age constraints. While the so-called 'older generation' tended to disconnect from youth culture at around thirty-five or forty latest, as my father's record collection (which I still own) testifies, there now prevailed a number-blind defiance. People no longer felt obliged to 'settle down' and become adults until they were well into their thirties. Although the law regarded you as fully mature once you reached the age of eighteen, the pressure from above to 'act your age' was off. We had the scientists to thank. Professors engaged in the study of the brain and nervous system were just beginning to find that the age at which humans achieve full maturation is not uniform, but different for everyone.

We now knew that this was an infinitely more nuanced transition than originally thought, which takes place over several decades. No longer expected to transform overnight from caterpillars to butterflies before being sucked into the cyclone and shrivelling to dust, we could take our time over it. This would lead to us making big-birthday statements such as 'thirty is the new twenty' and sixty is the new forty'. Which boiled down to a communal acceptance that we were now hitting middle age 'later'. The point at which we thought people were 'old' shifted too. The healthy were now living longer and the numbers could be adjusted, taking into account the extra time that we might expect to live.

The knock-on effect on rock stars was magnificent. Where once the idea of them doing it beyond the age of forty or even thirty had seemed ridiculous, the game was now gloves off and no holds barred. Likewise, people could now decently remain rock fans beyond their forties. Observers no longer batted an eye; or if they did, they kept their opinions to themselves. Tina Turner in a fanny pelmet shrieking 'Nutbush City Limits' into the gods[11] was still flinging into her dotage. She gave her last live performance in 2009, aged seventy. Lulu's still out there shaking a thigh bone at seventy-four, as is Suzi Quatro at seventy-two. Macca, Neil Diamond, the Who, Aerosmith, the Beach Boys, Rod Stewart, Iron Maiden and Def Leppard were still at it, last time we looked. No one is telling these groovy grandads (in some cases, great- or even *great-great*-grandads) that it's time to slow down. It's rock-'til-you-drop from here on in.

It can be uncomfortable, in that case, to recall that the rock that emerged after Live Aid was a parody of itself. Those who slam rock-themed stage musicals – *Rock of Ages* (eighties classic rock by Bon Jovi, Poison, Pat Benatar et al), *Bat Out of Hell* (Meat Loaf numbers), Queen's *We Will Rock You*, *Tina* (the Tina Turner story, featuring songs by the artist who has sold more concert tickets than any other solo performer in history, and who oversees this production personally) – as a diminution and betrayal of the original music overlook the fact that corporate rock/arena rock/stadium rock (whatever you want to call it) did precisely the same thing. It changed it into something that challenged its integrity. Contemporary fans don't want to hear that rock'n'roll died during the eighties, or that the Stones did their share to kill it off. If rock music in general seems to have become a sub-genre of musical theatre, at least it is part of something passionate and thrilling that captures every art form: not only acting, singing and dancing but songwriting and storytelling, with set-, costume- and make-up design, staging, spectacle and special effects, and orchestral and band accompaniment. Most of which we don't get when we attend a Rolling Stones gig? *Au contraire*, we get the lot!

Purists who bog down in categorisation are inclined to miss a simple truth: that the arts are not about categories. They are bigger than that. They are cross-categorisational. They also allow us to experience, to remember, to touch base, to feel alive. Go to a show, check your problems and preoccupations at the door, immerse yourself in the adventure and let the tidal wave wash over you. For the next two hours or however long it lasts, you are on a ride through surreality and on a dance through sheer abandonment, in which you get to live life through others' eyes. Your heart and soul are stretched to bursting. You can actually imagine yourself as Mick or Keith, up there on stage, giving it welly. You are re-energised by the wildness, and wrung out by the time you head home. Without even realising, you have just taken part in a mass celebration of creativity. Which is in itself a manifestation of hope. Because, though life is short, human art can last forever. If this is as close as we'll ever get to experiencing immortality, I'm in, baby. Who says it's no good unless it's cool? As the kids say, 'it hits different now'. What is 'cool' anyway, but a beatnik relic kept on life support by marketeers?[12]

*

'When hell freezes over' is a common trope in rock'n'roll. As in, 'We'll get back together like never.' The Eagles looked as though they might properly kill each other when they fell out so badly in 1980 that they swore never to go near one other again. The chiller retort was apparently made by Don Henley. Following which, the singing drummer, lead guitarist Don Felder and frontman Glenn Frey went off to wallow in successful solo careers, and we never imagined that we would see them on stage again. But anger fades, and bank accounts dwindle. In May 1994 they reunited for the first time in fourteen years, to embark, in Burbank, California, on their ironically entitled Hell Freezes Over tour, promoting the album of that name and proving beyond doubt that fans will pay whatever it takes if they want to see something badly enough. That tour grossed more than $63 million. The Eagles went down in history as the first rock band to charge a hundred smackers per person, at a time when tickets to Midwestern shows were selling for between twelve and twenty dollars top whack. Life in the fast lane if you like. Play the scalpers at their own game and take the punters for mugs, let's do this.

Picture the poor sweaty guy over at CBS Towers, who must have felt like he'd bought the Stones with his life. Would there ever be anything to show for it, beyond compilations and re-releases? The world had to wonder. At least the band's comeback wasn't as tardy as that of those Eagles. Our boys only took eight years. *Voodoo Lounge*, their twentieth British offering, twenty-second in the US and their first without bassist Bill Wyman, put smiles on the critics' faces and took the Grammy for Best Rock Album the following year. But it set not a turntable alight, nor did it frizz a single airwave.

Its most prominent song, 'Love Is Strong', was not that memorable. Disagree? Sing it to me. The album fell short of a Top 40 hit. Despite which, the tour to support it grossed $320 million, making it the world's highest-grossing tour of all time. The man at CBS breathed and took a toilet break. The Damoclean sword moved not a millimetre. Then 1997 was the year of the *Bridges to Babylon* album, though how hard was that to make? Because, oh, boys, Mick and Keith were not speaking again, and could barely bring themselves to be in the studio at the same time. The single 'Anybody Seen My Baby?' seemed symbolic. By the time they went out to promote it, they were managing to squeeze past each other in corridors without slashing each other to bits. The tour was another massive success. Who said that rock'n'roll stars don't know how to act?

Another eight years on, they celebrated their fortieth anniversary in 2002 with a double greatest hits album, *Forty Licks*. The one in everybody's collection scored them a No. 2 at home and in America. Three years later, their two-year Bigger Bang tour in support of *Licks*, their last clutch of original songs, broke their own extraordinary 1994 record. The single 'Streets of Love' fell short of the American chart, but landed at No. 15 in the UK and performed decently around the world. Their compelling documentary *Shine a Light*, directed by Martin Scorsese and the one that everybody has seen, is the film of that tour.

February 2006 saw them perform their biggest-ever free concert to more than a million Brazilians in Rio. You had to wonder whether Hyde Park and Altamont crossed their minds that heaving night. Come a long way there, boys. They were hardly off the road thereafter for the next fourteen years. Which by anybody's standards is remarkable for men of the twilight zone. Kerching, and thrice ker-*ching*.

Yet another decade flashed by in a beat. The older we get, the quicker it zaps. Out came the *Blue & Lonesome* covers album in 2016. Their twenty-third in the UK and twenty-fifth in America, this was the first Stones album for eleven years. But they could beat even that: when it took the Grammy for Best Traditional Blues Album, it was their first award from the US Recording Academy in twenty-three years.

*

All the old rumours resurface, with the predictability of infectious disease outbreaks. Jagger's undergoing a sex change operation – this story actually ran, in the *Daily Express*. (What the fuck is going on? It was a *joke*! I think you'll find that Mr Altham was just pulling your leg, sir.) It's 'let's get them in the papers for any reason we can think of' to begin with, then suddenly it goes the other way. They build up a wall, so people write on the wall. Don't take it so seriously, folks, it's only rock'n'roll. They cooked a dog in a microwave? Not that one again. I mean, I could have sworn it was a cat.

'They are spent, in terms of new music, and have been for a long time,' muses their former publicist Keith Altham. 'But I don't see why some of their old music won't last forever. Which is true of only a chosen few. Elvis will always be Elvis. The Beatles, Charlie Parker, Miles Davis, Jimi Hendrix. That's it. The rest are forgettable.

'The fact is, there is something remarkable about the Rolling Stones,' he concedes. 'Especially Jagger. He is certainly a showman who never completely runs down. He has established a unique position in popular music history. But there was a price to pay for that. He used to be fun. It's gone out of him. I wish I'd never become his PR. I would like to have preserved the memory of the keen-to-please young guy with the coconut smile, and with all that vitality. I got too close. It's like seeing your dad dressed up as Father Christmas, or going backstage. Once you've witnessed it at point-blank range, you can never again bring yourself to believe in magic.'

*

None of which deterred anybody. Once Mick and Keith patched up their differences, bought new pants and hauled the show on the road, it was just like the good old days. The ghouls are back on the ghost train. Fill the smoke machines, tweak the mirrors – these guys are *cool*, they still have twenty-eight-inch waists, they're wearing eyeliner! Keith's looking a whole lot better since he got his teeth fixed, right? He's still got fish hooks in his hair! And that's his real hair, right? None of your implants, fake bangs or hair dye for the Human Riff. I bet he still cuts it himself, too. Always did, back in the day. I ever tell you 'bout the time he did mine?

'... Keith Richards *cut your hair*?'

'... with a *cutlass*. Out on the terrace at his place Point of View in Jamaica, that old house in Ocho Rios, used to belong to some dude by the name of Steele.'[13]

Which just goes to show. There are few who've never indulged in the Rolling Stones fantasy.

The past forty years have been all about what the Stones represent rather than who they actually are. Haven't we known this all along? Stuart White insists so. 'When you think about it,' he reasons, 'all the good stuff on the Stones happens before 1976. I look back and I note, why yes: after that, it becomes a plateau of wealth and corporateness. Same old, same old. What distinguishes the eighties from the nineties, the two thousands from the twenty-tens and the dozen years after that? Not a lot. It all rolls into one. There's an immutability about it. For which, read boredom. They've been going through the motions for so long now that it's no longer possible to get excited about them. There's nothing to keep you awake at night, panting for your next fix of them. The vast majority of their younger fans don't feel that way, of course. Maybe it's us who got old, not them.

'Maybe they have portraits in the attic after all.'[14]

*

You can't help wondering when the cynicism crept in. We know, and we know they know we know, that we the paying punters are just another date ticked off, another bunch of money banked, another step along the road towards the end of yet another tour. Which in some ways can't come soon enough, they're a bit sore and queasy these days. But they will miss it like hell as soon as it's done. Which makes them slaves to it. They have no choice but to start planning the next outing, and so it goes on. They might have overcome the narcotics and other evils, but the road remains the most threatening addiction of all. Every artist experiences this, whether they admit to it or not. That's show business. The brighter the light, the deeper the shadow.

'Believe what?' asked Shadow. 'What should I believe?'
'Everything,' roared the buffalo man.[15]

He's behind you. Oh yes, he is. Just as every cop is a criminal, and all the sinners saints.

Chapter Seventeen

MANDY

I can't remember the first time I heard a Stones song, nor which one it was. I remember with terrifying clarity the first time I met a member of the band.

Some memories torment us in perpetuity, despite our best efforts to forget them. All the if-onlys, the why-didn't-I?s and the wish-I-never-hads can be ignored, most of the time. We park the poor choices and the lapses of judgement. We might wince occasionally when something uncomfortable returns to haunt us, but most things are easily brushed aside. Others are not. Wounds are silent. Left untreated, they fester. 'The only thing necessary for the triumph of evil is for good men to do nothing,' goes the old adage.[1]

My guilt is hinged to the things I did not say. I knew a grown man who was having sex with a child. He was, in those days, my friend. His girlfriend was under the age of consent. British law on this subject is crystal clear: if an individual over the age of eighteen engages in sexual activity with a person below the age of sixteen, he or she may be charged with a criminal offence which could result in a fourteen-year prison sentence. I knew what was going on. I should have told someone. But the thing is, even if I had done so, not a thing would have been done. Even now that the whole world knows, nothing has changed.

Hollywood feigned surprise when movie mogul Harvey Weinstein was exposed as a sex abuser. As if Hollywood didn't know. It opened floodgates. Actresses, models, ordinary women, and men, rushed to join the movement that sheds light on the sexual misconduct of powerful males, declaring #METOO and #TIMESUP. When Kevin Spacey was exposed, his fabulous career disintegrated. Bill Cosby, media icon, father figure, philanthropist and world-renowned paragon of virtue, who for decades had used the power of television to influence millions of his fellow Americans on the subjects of class, race, morality and his own importance, was found guilty of sexual assault after a year-long trial during which he challenged the accusations of sixty-odd victims. He was convicted of aggravated indecent assault against his accuser Andrea Constand in 2018, and was imprisoned. In 2021, the Supreme Court of Pennsylvania voided his conviction.[2]

How many would-be starlets have been conned onto the casting couch down the years? How many millions in myriad other industries have yielded to predators who were in pursuit of only one thing, because they didn't know that they were allowed to say no? How many Roman Polanskis still roam the earth?[3] How many Bill Wymans does it take to change a light bulb? Only thirteen? I know, but the thing is she *looks* twelve.

I agree, it is no laughing matter. But such gags still do the rounds. When they hear them, the vast majority laugh at them. They would laugh on the other side of their faces if the girl in question had been theirs.

*

Though we have grown accustomed to the sight of his paunch, sagging chins and thin silver hair, there was a time when the former Stones bassist was physically attractive. This stooping old man was once rock's most prolific shagger. Three or four a night on the road, he was wont to boast. Three at a time, sometimes. He wasn't fussed. Bring it on. He couldn't help it, could he, women threw themselves at him. He'd have been an idiot to say no. He was always boasting about his conquests, which made us feel uncomfortable. Too much information, not to mention inappropriate conversation with young girls. I realise only now how insecure he was. He was selling himself to us. As William Perks from Penge, as we have seen, he'd done National Service in Germany and was married with a son when he found himself caught up in the fledgling biggest band in history. He was unhappy at home. He nipped out for a few halves. It was the sixties. Bill and I had dinner a couple of times at the original Ivy. On 21 February 1984, we attended the British Rock & Pop Awards at the Lyceum Ballroom off the Strand, sharing a table with Midge Ure. Bill accepted an award on behalf of late bluesman Alexis Korner, who had died of lung cancer the previous month. 'If Alexis hadn't been there, we wouldn't have been there,' he said in his short acceptance speech, referring to the Stones', should I say Brian's, first enabler. Bill seemed distracted by a couple of identical young blondes on the dance floor, prompting Midge to lean over and whisper in my ear, 'I think you've just lost him.' 'Not mine to lose,' I retorted, 'and I'm not his.'

Despite which, a friendship emerged. It was all it was, and I didn't dwell on it. I hadn't heard from Bill for a few weeks, and had been too busy to care, when he called to invite me to accompany him to the 30 May opening night of a West End revival of the Broadway musical *Little Me*, starring comedian Russ Abbot and actress Sheila White, at the Prince of Wales Theatre. He arrived wearing an odd tan leather two-piece suit that reminded me – I had an old sofa like that once.

The after-show party was at the Ivy. Bill and I shared a table with the actors Jill Gascoine and Alfred Molina. The next time I saw him was at a dinner at Thierry's, the French restaurant below his Kings Road office/pied-à-terre. Also present were his PA Karen, a couple of her girlfriends and the songwriter Ken Gold.[4] The vivacious waitress that night was Lou. She and Ken became an item, and the gang that gelled that night continued to go around together. Our group soon expanded to include Bill's son, Stephen. And there were two sisters I was sure I'd met before, Nicola and Mandy Smith. Bill had apparently introduced them to a friend of his, who ran the agency Models One. They were accompanied by their middle-aged mother, Patsy. Later, the penny dropped: they were the girls by whom Bill had been mesmerised at the Lyceum pop awards back in February.

Mandy soon emerged as the ringleader. She was fun, and always up for anything. She tended to be the one to choose which restaurant we would eat in, and which club or party we would go on to afterwards.

Though we always offered, Bill insisted on picking up the tab every time. Mandy's favourite club was Tramp, the exclusive haunt on Jermyn Street. Bill was friendly with its founder, Johnny Gold, whose business partner was Oscar Lerman, then married to author Jackie Collins. Lisa Vanderpump and her husband Ken were part of the throng too. We knew Lisa from the ABC videos. They called Tramp 'the office'. The dance floor was a handkerchief. You sat around chatting most of the time, getting drunk on champagne.

They didn't call Bill 'the quiet one' for nothing. He'd survey the scene as though peering through binoculars. He didn't draw attention to himself, nor did he schmooze other celebrities. They came to him. None of the other Stones ever came out with us. He rarely socialised with 'the others'. Bill said: 'They keep themselves to themselves, and so do I. We're not family.'

So far, so what, doesn't it sound? What I have to remind myself is that it *was* rather magical to sit listening to him talking about being in the Rolling Stones. In us, he had a captive audience for his tales about the songs, the band's escapades and their exploits on the road. He didn't know how Keith went out there and did it some nights, he said, because he was more often than not off his head. Charlie and Bill were allies. Mick was the boss, and never let anyone forget it. Ronnie was the bridge, between the two camps. The band had evolved into something different after Mick Taylor left and Ronnie joined, he told us. It had a whole new vibe. His most surprising revelation, if you could call it that, was that he, Charlie and Ronnie were effectively employees of Mick and Keith, at that point. Their pay was salary. Mick and Keith wrote the songs and banked the royalties. It was a situation that would not change during Bill's tenure.

His punctuality and reliability impressed me. These are not, as a general rule, rock star qualities. He chain-smoked, which was annoying, but at least he was never a diva. I have known a few in my time. If you stopped to think about it, I suppose we thought it *was* rather odd, being friends with a Rolling Stone. But there was never anything 'us and them' about it, because we were a diverse and lively bunch in our own right. I think Bill found us entertaining. He struggled to keep up, half the time.

He had seen the world, but through a narrow angle lens. His views on most subjects were limited. But he was always willing to lend his name to one of our projects. When music journalist Robin Eggar, radio producer Phil Swern and I wrote the best-selling *The Sony Tape Rock Review* (Rambletree, 1984), Bill contributed the foreword and a fetching, recently shot photograph of himself. 'Tit for tat,' he said.

'What does that mean?'

'You are my friends.'

Were we, though? I didn't give it much thought at the time, but I get it now. Even celebrities had to find friends from somewhere. Most of us who hung together at that point had relatively normal jobs. We lived regular lives and did everyday things. Perhaps Bill identified with us because he hailed from humble himself. He rarely felt comfortable, he confessed, among toffs and superstars, whereas Mick actively courted the great and the good. Bill didn't because such people made him feel uncomfortable, he said. He never knew what to say. He liked the fact that Mandy and Nicola lived on a London council estate. They spoke his language. Maybe he saw all of us as a refuge of normality. Who was deluded: him, or us?

Only years down the line could I admit to myself that Bill had gathered our clan to conceal his affair with Mandy. It is glaringly obvious now. When his limo approached our chosen restaurant, he would ask one of the boys, usually the tall, dark, good-looking one who grew up to be a famous broadcaster and writer, 'Would you mind walking Mandy in?' He would then take my arm and beam for the photographers, snuggling close as we got out of the car. At the end of the night, when the driver dropped us home one by one, it would always be Bill and Mandy left in the back. Just the two of them.

We knew about their relationship. It was never discussed. What we didn't know – genuinely didn't know, initially, was how young Mandy was. We assumed she must be nineteen or twenty-ish. We had no idea at the time that Bill was paying for her education and had transferred her from her former North London state secondary to an expensive private school within walking distance of his flat. We might never have known that Mandy was a schoolgirl under the age of consent had Bill not thrown a party for her birthday. The whole gang was invited. There was only one candle on her cake. Our tall, dark, handsome broadcaster-and-writer-to-be couldn't help himself.

'Go on, then, Mand, how old are you today?' 'Fifteen,' she said. She had been dating Bill by then for more than two years.

'After that,' recalls the broadcaster, 'we all just fucked off as fast as possible, didn't we. We knew it was wrong. We didn't do anything about it. We never told anyone. We didn't dare. We were unwittingly used to disguise what was going on. As far as the press were concerned, we were just the walkers. The moment we learned the truth we scarpered, we were dust. We never challenged Bill about it. We never talked to anyone else about it. The media were never the wiser. But *we* knew. Knowing that he was abusing Mandy but saying nothing made us as bad as Bill. I feel foolish and guilty now, for having been dragged into it. The guilt doesn't go away, does it.'

The last time I saw them together was when Bill took Mandy and me to lunch at Langan's Brasserie. He ordered bread pudding for 'afters', and Mandy turned up her nose. 'What?!' said Bill. 'I can't marry a girl who doesn't know how to make bread pudding!' The first inkling of the tinkling of wedding bells. I failed to hear them.

I went to Fleet Street, started travelling, and shoved them to the back of my mind. I remember hearing that they'd split up, then that they were getting married, and eventually that they'd tied the knot. Mandy had turned eighteen by then, while Bill was fifty-two: thirty-four years her senior. I wasn't invited, nor had I expected to be. Like everyone else, I read about the lavish nuptials in *Hello!* magazine.

The ritzy Wyman church 'wedding' that followed Mandy's and Bill's register office nuptials in June 1989 – the summer of Michael Keaton's Batman and Jack Nicholson's Joker, of the New Kids on the Block, of Richard Marx's 'Right Here Waiting' and Bette Midler's 'Wind Beneath my Wings' and of the Rolling Stones' Steel Wheels tour, the third highest-grossing of the decade – was the 'most memorable event of the year'. Was it? If you didn't count the end of the Cold War and the tearing down of the Berlin Wall, the slaughter in Beijing's Tiananmen Square, the Hillsborough football stadium disaster and the sinking of the Thames pleasure cruiser the *Marchioness*. Still, at least the Stones took it seriously. They turned up and presented Bill with a zimmer frame. The happy couple then headed down to Bill's villa in St Paul de Vence in the South of France. As did Mandy's mother Patsy, some cousins and her sister Nicola. Call that a honeymoon? Outnumbered Bill called his secretary Karen and begged her to come over and keep him company. Rock'n'roll.

*

I was surprised to hear that Mandy's mother Patsy, forty-six, and Bill's son Stephen, thirty, had become engaged. That didn't seem right. But why? Because Patsy was so much older than Stephen? The age gap was only about half that between Mandy and Bill. It was an on-off relationship, however. I later heard that Bill had threatened to cut Stephen out of his will if he refused to dump Patsy. His son was his best friend, he said, and he was heartbroken by the 'betrayal'. They married, but threw in the towel after two years. Perhaps the surreal nature of their relationship caught up with them. Because that marriage made Stephen the husband not only of his own stepmother's mother, but of his own father's mother-in-law. It also made him his own grandfather. As for Mandy, her ex-husband became her step-grandfather. Confused?

*

I still see, and occasionally work with, the famous broadcaster and a couple of the others. Now and then, we talk about the past. We wonder, what on earth were we thinking? We conclude that we were not. Neither was Bill. Do I believe his defence: that he had no idea Mandy was only thirteen when he met her? He acknowledges her age at the time they met in his autobiography. Despite which, he insists, she was 'a woman'. To look at, perhaps. But not emotionally. And certainly not in the eyes of the law. Although it is no defence, you could see where he was coming from. He couldn't help himself. There was nothing 'thirteen' about her. There being nothing to reveal that the girl was still a child, it never occurred to any of us to question it. Mandy was mature and *soignée*, and so beautiful. Total strangers would stop and stare when she walked along the street with us, or made her entrance in a club or at a do. She knew how powerful she was. She was Bill's personal Brigitte Bardot, and he was helpless. So were we, to an extent. Mandy was stunning. We adored her. We were content to bask in her limelight.'

The age of consent exists to protect children from themselves, as well as from predators. The minute that Bill discovered Mandy's age, he should have manned up, controlled himself, taken legal advice, assessed the consequences, and have run several miles if not left the country. He did none of these things. He would later shrug off the whole tragic episode as a 'mid-life crisis'. He got away with it. How?

I asked a High Court judge, whom I know personally, and whom we shall call The Hon. Mr Justice X Kt. Who shrugged and shook his head. 'I cannot answer you,' he said.

'Can't, or won't?'

'What I mean is that I simply do not have the answer. This lady says she was fourteen when the relationship was consummated. If that is true, a crime was committed. The matter ought to have been brought to trial. Had guilt been established beyond reasonable doubt, it is possible that it would have concluded in a prison sentence.'

'Even though they were married?'

'No defence. Makes not a scrap of difference. A crime is a crime. It is a criminal offence in the UK for any kind of sexual activity to take place between two people where one or both participants is or are under the age of sixteen. This, like it or not, is paedophilic behaviour.'

Furthermore, stated His Lordship, 'Anyone over the age of eighteen in such a relationship is dealt with more severely in law. This is because age gaps in relationships can cause power imbalances, which may lead to abusive behaviour. In fact, the older the abuser, the more serious the punishment is likely to be.'

'People have defended Bill,' I remind him, 'on the grounds that Mandy's mother gave her permission to have sex with Bill.'

'Irrelevant,' said the judge. 'It is not up to your parents to decide if you can break the law. Regardless of whether they are happy for their child to become sexually active, it is still illegal for anyone to have any kind of sexual contact with a person under the age of sixteen. Wyman should have been arrested. The law applies to everyone.'

*

Mandy's sister Nicola did call for Bill to be prosecuted. Nothing happened. Years later, amid the furore over celebrity paedophile allegations sparked by the Jimmy Savile, Rolf Harris, Stuart Hall, Gary Glitter and Max Clifford scandals, Bill revealed to the media that he had taken matters into his own hands:

'I went to the police and I went to the public prosecutor, and said, "Do you want to talk to me? Do you want to meet up with me, or anything like that?" and I got a message back: "No".'

The Metropolitan Police refused to comment on Wyman's claims. Allegations of bribery and corruption came to nothing.[5] There was no case for Bill to answer ... because no one had lodged a formal complaint. When the police went gunning for former pop star and producer Jonathan King, comedians Chris Langham and Jim Davidson, DJs Paul Gambaccini and Dave Lee Travis, Nigel Evans MP, Sir Cliff Richard and the rest, turning their lives upside down, it was because formal allegations had been made. Which throws into sharp focus a sizeable elephant in the room: the time limit.

The matter is complex: there is no limitation period for criminal offences. For civil claims relating to historic child abuse, a claimant has had to issue court proceedings within six years of the date of the incident (for trespass) or three years (for personal injury – for psychological injury, three years from when the claimant knew the injury was related to the event) – and if the claimant was a child at the time of the abuse, these time limits generally apply from the date when the claimant reaches the age of eighteen. Of course, survivors of childhood abuse often suppress traumatic memories, and are unable to discuss what happened to them for years afterwards. They may not realise until later adulthood that they had been subjected to grooming, emotional or sexual manipulation. Only one thing is completely clear in all this: things are never simple for any alleged victims of historic abuse.

*

The marriage collapsed in 1991. They were divorced two years later. 'Mandy went off the rails for a while. She had lots of affairs,' Bill said. 'And she got really ill. Really thin. She almost died.'

They did not keep in touch. She went on to marry footballer Pat Van

Den Hauwe in June 1993, but that fell apart too. As did her sister Nicola's engagement to another soccer star, Teddy Sheringham. Shortly after his divorce from his second wife, Bill took a third, Suzanne Accosta, the former girlfriend for whom it is said that he wrote his hit single '(Si Si) Je Suis un Rock Star', and with whom he would have three daughters. He also quit the Stones. Jumped or pushed?

*

After her second marriage folded, Mandy moved to Manchester to escape the pressurised London lifestyle. In 2001, she embarked on a relationship with male fashion model Ian Mosby. When she gave birth to their son Max, the couple were engaged, but it did not last. In 2005 she turned to the church, and began counselling abuse victims. Mandy is now fifty-two: the age, give or take, that Bill was when she married him. In 2010, she had this to say: 'You are still a child, even at sixteen. You can never get that part of your life, your childhood, back. I never could.' She revealed that she *was* questioned by police after the story broke but refused to press charges.

She knows that what Bill did was wrong; that his behaviour was criminal; that putting a ring on her finger did not absolve him of guilt. She fell prey to illnesses both physical and mental after marrying him that have blighted her life ever since. Didn't she want to see him punished?

'What good would it do? He has a family now. What happened, happened.'

To those who accused her of only marrying Bill for his wealth, Mandy points out that her settlement was only £580,000. 'Take off the house and the lawyers' bills and I was left with £50,000, which went on a tax bill. If I had wanted money, I'd have stayed with him.'

*

We are still asking, all these years later: did Bill groom Mandy? Was all that getting to know the mother and the sister and winning a precocious child's confidence part of his plan? Why did Patsy Smith 'sell' her daughter to a rock star? Despite having clearly been neglected, loyal Mandy would never have a word said against her mum.

'She was really ill at the time and thought she was going to die – we didn't know what of – and he looked after me,' she told journalist Caroline Phillips. Wasn't it because he was a rich celebrity? 'No, no. We weren't impressed by people.' Why *didn't* Mandy help the police press child abuse charges? Because, she said, she felt partly to blame.

'It was like it was my fault as well,' she insisted – with the 'classic guilt of an abuse victim', as Caroline observed. 'I fell in love with Bill. I wasn't a little sex temptress. But I'd feel too guilty getting someone charged for sex abuse.' Yet in the opening pages of her autobiography, *It's All Over Now*, written with journalists Andy Coulson and Ingrid Millar and published in 1993, the year of her divorce from Bill, she dedicates it:

> … to every woman and girl who has suffered abuse – sexual, emotional and psychological – at the hands of a man.

It was an illegal and immoral relationship. It was accepted, and blind eyes were turned. The perpetrator was an A-list rock star. It was not until I became a mother myself that things became more sharply focused. It was then that I knew what I had known all along: that I had turned a blind eye too. I am so sorry, Mandy.

*

In 2012, Bill turned up at the opening of Exhibitionism: The Rolling Stones, at London's Saatchi Gallery, to join his former bandmates for their fiftieth anniversary. In 2015, he released *Back to Basics*, his first album in decades, and was diagnosed with prostate cancer. He celebrated his eightieth birthday in 2016 with his own photographic exhibition at Chelsea's Proud Gallery. He also signed up to co-produce an autobiographical documentary, *The Quiet One*. There was much to depict. Not only the endless years rolling with the Stones and his own Rhythm Kings, but Sticky Fingers, his rock'n'roll restaurant in Kensington; his many books, including an arty tome on the work of Marc Chagall, once his neighbour in St Paul de Vence; his obsessive metal detecting; the diaries he has written daily since childhood; and his Rolling Stones archive, said to be worth millions. The ninety-minute film, released in 2019, proved controversial. A number of planned screenings were cancelled after protesters complained.

246 | THE STONE AGE

*

Does Bill ever pause to reflect how lucky he was? Or does he fear that his luck could yet run out? Because that was never a 'love' affair. Whatever he says, it was anything but. In April 2010, journalist Victoria Coren (now Coren Mitchell) wrote about it in the *Guardian*, denouncing Mandy's status as poster girl of the wild-child generation: 'It was never right,' she declared. 'How was I allowed to believe that this relationship – Mandy's life – was glamorous, cool and aspirational? It was child abuse.'

Even if the law never catches up with him, perhaps the greatest punishment imaginable has already been handed down. It cannot comfort Bill to know, as he shuffles towards the abyss, that he will not go down in history for talent and achievement, nor for having been a member of the greatest rock'n'roll band of all time ... but because he had sex with a child.

*

While preparing to film a documentary for an American production company, I read the late Gregg Allman's *New York Times* best-selling autobiography *My Cross to Bear*. The Southern rocker jokes therein about an old road manager whom he cheerfully describes as 'the original dirty old man'. The manager kept a chart in his case, giving the legal age of consent in every US state. He had copies made for every member of the band and the road crew. He would hand them round at the start of each tour, and kept further copies in case of emergencies. It begs all the questions I would like to ask Bill Wyman. It also answers them.

Chapter Eighteen

CLÍODHNA

In October 2005, New York-based journalist Annette Witheridge joined the band in Philadelphia on their A Bigger Bang American tour.

'Backstage at the Wachovia Sports Arena, there was a door with a black sign on it bearing the words "Camp X-Ray" with a burly security guard standing in front of it,' she remembered. 'But it was not the press that they were seeking to bar. This was the entrance to Ronnie's and Keith's shared dressing room and private domain. Their persona non grata was Mick Jagger.'

It was the one that came to be known as 'the tour of bad blood'. The Stones themselves weren't calling it that, of course, but word gets around. Mick's willowy six-foot-three 'girl-fiend' L'Wren Scott, a thirty-eight-year-old West Coast fashion designer who towered above him (she was known to bend discreetly at the knee when they were about to be photographed, so that the difference in their heights would not be apparent), and who had been decorating his arm for the past four years, somehow became the object of spite and speculation.

They had met at a fashion shoot, and she had been 'throwing her weight around' ever since. The beautiful brunette with hip-length hair and the grace of a prima ballerina had a knack, according to rumour, for rubbing people up the wrong way. It was claimed that the rest of the band hated her and that the entourage were always bitching about her behind her back, calling her 'the First Lady' and making fun of her superior demeanour. Keith Richards allegedly called her 'Le Man' and teased her relentlessly about her gigantic feet. Others referred to her spitefully as 'the apostrophe', and took exception to the ways in which she was always trying to influence Mick's decisions. He was no fun when she was around, they complained.

Communication between the boys and Mick was said to have almost ceased because of her. It was L'Wren, Ronnie and Keith had allegedly decided, who was to blame for recent dissent. She was exerting too much control over Mick. The delicate rhythm of the band, which had worked fine for years, didn't need her or anybody else's interference. There were whispers that Mick had changed; that the man who had always called the shots with women, subtly treating them with kind contempt and obliging them to cower to *his* rules, was now her subordinate. Poor L'Wren stood accused of throwing her weight around. Nobody liked her, they said, least of all Ronnie and Keith. How dare she tell them that they couldn't smoke in her presence, that they shouldn't wear those embarrassing stage clothes, that they should listen to her when she offered her advice about what they should be wearing.

'She wasn't even there in Philadelphia with them,' said Annette, 'but all the talk was about her. A member of the crew even said to me, "I've been with the Stones for ten years, and it's never been this bad before. They get around by private jet," he said. "Mick boards last and doesn't even acknowledge the others. There isn't even eye contact between them. But L'Wren's not the real problem. It's the Stones. Each of them has his own drug, and with Mick, it has always been women. But the bottom line is that Keith and Mick hate each other. Ron sides with Keith, and Charlie keeps his head down. Rock'n'roll. L'Wren hasn't done anything wrong. This accusation that she is 'the Stones' Yoko Ono', trying to bust up the band, is the most offensive thing I've ever heard. Yoko didn't break up the Beatles, Paul McCartney did. If the Stones call it a day, it won't be L'Wren or any other woman who makes that happen. It will be the band themselves."'

*

Things calmed down. Mick and L'Wren remained an item. They lived happily ever after for the next nine years. L'Wren designed outfits for the Stones' Glastonbury performance, and launched her own high-end fashion label. Her clothes were worn by Sarah Jessica Parker, Michelle Obama, Renée Zellweger and Nicole Kidman. Then, in March 2014, when she was forty-nine years old, she killed herself. She left no note.

L'Wren and Mick had just returned from a holiday at his glorious Stargroves Villa in Mustique, the beachside home where Jerry Hall had long been the lady of the house. It's a stunning place, I have been there. Only the night before she died, she had hosted a dinner party in her own New York apartment.

Having pored over the details, it is hard not to feel baffled. What was going through her mind, that she felt she had no choice but to end her life? On Monday 17 March, the morning of her death, she texted her assistant Brittany Penebre at eight thirty in the morning, and asked her to come over to her apartment. When Brittany arrived around ninety minutes later, she found her boss's fully clothed, lifeless body flumped on the floor. L'Wren had hanged herself with her own black silk scarf. How could this by all accounts caring, thoughtful woman do such a thing to a valued assistant of whom she was personally fond? She must have realised the trauma that Brittany would experience on finding her employer dead in her flat. The poor girl managed to dial emergency and to get an ambulance round, but her efforts were too late. L'Wren was beyond help. By the time her body was ready to be removed, a gaggle of photographers had gathered around the entrance to her apartment block.

None of the guests who attended her dinner party the previous night had felt cause for concern. If she seemed 'quiet' or maybe a little 'troubled', they ventured, it could only have been because she had been having a few business niggles. It was also hinted at that she was experiencing financial difficulties. There might have been something in that. The British division of her design company, LS Fashion Ltd, which she had launched eight years earlier, had deficits of £3.5 million. Production delays had forced her to cancel her London Fashion Week show. While she was known for styling and dressing numerous celebrities, many of whom she counted as personal friends, they were unlikely to have paid for the garments she made for them, because that is how the fashion industry works: you make me free gowns, I'll lend you my celebrity profile by wearing them in public to red-carpet events, I'll be photographed and interviewed everywhere, I'll drop the name of my designer, and you get the benefit of all the publicity because it will drive up the value of your brand. That's the general idea.

L'Wren's clothes were not the kind one sees in department stores. They were beyond the budget of all but the elite. Some even suggested that she was about to cut her losses and call time. Others refuted this, insisting that, not only were her projections positive, but also that she had entered into co-brand deals with a number of partners including Banana Republic and the make-up range Bobbi Brown. In any case, if her financial predicament had been too great to bear, wouldn't her rich-as-Croesus boyfriend have stepped in to bail her out? I wonder if she asked him.

Mick wasn't there that night. Not that his absence was a portent. He just happened to be Down Under with his band. The day that his partner's body was found, they had just arrived in Perth for the start of their tour of Australia and New Zealand. At least they did the right thing and swiftly cancelled. This apparently kind, thoughtful girl who was such a mover and a shaker on the fashion scene, who had a huge circle of friends, many of them rich and influential, and about whom few had a bad word to say, clearly had demons. But what could they have been, and what had activated them? Not even Mick could fathom it. And the consequence of not letting her nearest and dearest know why she did it, so that they will always wonder and suffer … Perhaps this was a simple, tragic case of extreme depression, which deprived her of reason and left her feeling that she had no choice. But the manner in which she took her life was such a violent thing to do. The image of that will haunt her loved ones forever.

'Still struggling to understand how my lover and best friend could end her life in this tragic way,' Mick made known. His extended statement on his Facebook page added the following: 'We spent many wonderful years together and had made a great life for ourselves. She had great presence and her talent was much admired, not least by me … I have been touched by the tributes that people have paid to her, and also the personal messages of support that I have received. I will never forget her.' They were perhaps the most tender words that Mick had ever shared publicly about any of the women with whom he had lived his life.

Her funeral service was held at the Hollywood Forever Cemetery. One of the oldest in Los Angeles, many celebrity ghosts stalk its lawns. Judy Garland's remains lie there, as do those of Mickey Rooney and Rudolph Valentino. This was not a celebrity burial, however, but a subdued and private affair, with only about seventy guests in attendance. Mick's daughter by Marsha Hunt, Karis Hunt Jagger, read a poem. His daughter Jade by Bianca Jagger read Psalm 139. His grandchildren by Karis, Mazie and Zak, read Psalm 23: 'Yea, though I walk through the valley of the shadow of death, I will fear no evil ...' This was clearly a woman who had forged close personal relationships with her partner's family, and by whom she was greatly loved. Long-serving Stones backing vocalist Bernard Fowler sang the Christian hymn 'Will the Circle be Unbroken'. He was accompanied by Eurythmic Dave Stewart on guitar.

A memorial service was held in May at St Bartholomew's Church on Park Avenue, New York, at which extended family, friends and colleagues paid tribute. She was a 'girl's girl', she was 'warm and funny', and she 'made people feel special', they said. She was also 'a good listener,' 'considerate of others', 'never a diva' and 'serene and happy'. As one might expect of a woman with the world at her feet, a global superstar partner, a loaded, privileged lifestyle and access, through Mick as well as via her own high-profile contacts, to virtually anyone in the world she wanted to meet. Not only all that, but she was wealthy and successful in her own right, despite the fact that her business was in deficit. She owned her $6 million apartment on 11th Avenue, and had recently paid off its outstanding mortgage. She and Mick shared homes in London and in Paris, on the Left Bank, boasting a bathroom tiled with Lalique glass. They also just happened to have Mick's French home to hang out in; the one that he and Jerry purchased in 1982 for a couple of million pounds. The majestic sixteenth-century château La Fourchette[1] stands on the outskirts of Pocé-sur-Cisse, a tiny village in the Loire Valley. Mick calls it his 'haven of peace in the valley of kings'. The Stones have recorded there. He is said to be fond of mountain biking in the vicinity, and also of fishing and cooking. As well he might be.

All this, it seemed, was not enough. *Sex and the City* star Sarah Jessica

Parker spoke at L'Wren's memorial service of 'a mysteriousness' to her that was impossible to pin down, marked by 'silent boundaries' that her friends knew never to cross. What could be behind such detachment and coldness? Perhaps the answers were to be found in her distant childhood, which had been hallmarked by rejection and a sense of standing out like a sore thumb. Yielded for adoption shortly after her birth, she landed in the lap of a good family and was much loved while growing up. Even so, she may never have overcome the need to know her true identity. Many adoptees feel this. Some are driven to search for their birth parents, and are often bitterly disappointed by what they find. We do not know whether L'Wren went down this route. But there were questions, the answers to which she presumably never found.

She was raised as Luann Bambrough in Roy, Utah, one of three adopted siblings. Her father Ivan served in the military during the Second World War, and was subsequently employed by an insurance company. The family were Mormons, and kept a modest but comfortable home. By the time Luann was twelve years old, she had literally outgrown her childhood. Already six feet tall, she was being taken for and treated like an adult. In 1985, when she was eighteen, the striking teenager happened to be spotted by fashion photographer Bruce Weber during a visit to the state. He was later to shoot her for a Calvin Klein commercial, for which she was paid $1,500. That was it, she knew what she wanted to do. She upped and left the backwater behind for glamorous Paris, where her modelling agency restyled her 'L'Wren'. While she was far too tall for the catwalk, she was perfect for photographic work, especially her forty-two-inch legs. David Bailey famously photographed her for a Pretty Polly hosiery ad, in which her pins were portrayed as the hands on a clock.

She moved to Los Angeles during the mid-nineties, and left modelling behind to work as a photographers' stylist. Shoots on which she worked for Helmut Newton, Herb Ritts and Mario Sorrenti graced the pages of the glossies, including *W* magazine and *Vanity Fair*. She got married in 1993, to the property entrepreneur Anthony Brand. The union lasted only three years and did not produce any children. Four years later she met Jagger on one of her photo shoots. They rapidly became involved. It was he who would encourage her to establish her own fashion label.

Her parents having died, and her relationships with her siblings having thinned, there were fewer and fewer reasons to return to Utah. Mick's family became her family. She forged and tended close relationships with every one of his children: he had seven by four different mothers, as well as four grandchildren. His first great-grandchild would be born around the time of his girlfriend's memorial service. The Jagger grandkids called her 'Glammy', a nickname she loved. The one she was way less keen on was the one by which she was far better known. 'Mick Jagger's girlfriend,' she would say, 'is what I am, but it is not my name.'

Could she have feared his infamous propensity for infidelity? Did she worry that he would dump her for a much younger model, just at an age when she was too old to give him her own baby? Not that she said much to her friends about wanting one. Besides, Mick didn't want any more, he was into the great-grandkid phase now for heaven's sake! But fifty is fifty. She was about to turn that age in April 2014, a month after her death. Even the thought of that birthday is enough to shake confidence and strike fear into the heart of the most desirable woman. It just is. She had also undergone knee surgery a few months earlier, to repair a torn meniscus. Hobbling around on crutches was hardly her style. It must have reminded her of her frailty, and of the inevitable ageing process, while her partner still had what it took to attract younger and younger females. Oh, she knew all about his diversions. Most of the time, she turned a blind eye. But was this the thing that threatened her? Did she know of someone in particular who was already hovering in the wings?

After her death, it came out. Humping Jack Flash had become close to Melanie Hamrick, a twenty-seven-year-old dancer with the American Ballet Theatre. It was claimed that they had met during the Stones' tour of Japan, only a few days before L'Wren was found dead. Any impropriety was furiously denied. A picture on a balcony told a story.

*

'I chased this very pretty, very tiny, incredibly graceful ballerina across an underground car park at the Lincoln Center,' said journalist Annette Witheridge. 'We'd been sure for months that something was going on between her and Mick. It struck me how uncannily similar to L'Wren Scott she looked in the flesh. Same colouring, same look. She was in her late twenties at the time, but looked about ten years younger. Like a schoolgirl. I found out where she lived: in a grotty first-floor walk-up, one of those non-elevator tenement blocks that you see all over old New York. It was shabby. Soon afterwards, I got to know a couple of people at her ballet company. Although it was considered a great honour to be a member of that company, they clearly weren't earning very much. One of them told me that Melanie had been engaged, but that she stopped wearing her ring after stories about her and Mick began to leak. 'She must have seen an opportunity and ran with it,' he said. 'Who can blame her?' It was obvious to me, from the way they talked about her, that she was highly ambitious and not that well liked. 'She wasn't even a principal, just a member of the corps de ballet,' her colleague told me. 'The rumours started, and she called in sick. When she returned, she had become a prima donna. You could tell because she was wearing Jackie O sunglasses. At night.'

On 8 December 2016, thirty-two months after L'Wren Scott died, Melanie Hamrick gave birth to Deveraux Octavian Basil Jagger in a New York hospital. Mick was present for the arrival of his eighth child. In 2019, his partner retired from the American Ballet Theatre after fifteen years, to focus on choreography and to mother her son. Both of them.

Chapter Nineteen

RESONANCE

In the dwindling days, there is restlessness. The fear that it has all been for nothing. Dismay at the dawning that what lies ahead could be void. It keeps them awake at night, when sleep is all they crave. It causes them to slumber during precious daylight hours, when there are not so many of those left. Though we all fear death, many make their peace with it via faith or other means. For all of us, but especially for those who have lived exceptional and privileged lives, who have 'been someone', who have gone everywhere and done everything they never set out to do, the thought of no longer existing is unbearable.

'It's the reason why the Stones keep doing it,' says rock manager, songwriter and film-maker Simon Napier-Bell, who made stars of the Yardbirds, Marc Bolan, Wham! and George Michael as a solo artist. 'It's the reason why we all do it: because nobody likes to die. So that we don't have to face the inevitable. It's no use sitting around worrying about how long you've got left. You do the thing that you do to stay alive. Because they need to feel relevant, they can't just give up. It's worse for superstars like the Stones, worshipped by millions all over the world and richer than they could ever have imagined when they were spotty young oiks. The hardest thing they have to swallow is that they are so powerful they practically own countries, they can buy absolutely anything they want, but they can't buy their own immortality. The moment they realise this, when the end is nigh, it all begins to feel pointless. Yet they can't stop, retreat, go into hiding and be just like any ordinary old person.

'If being a rock'n'roll star is what you do in your life, you do it forever. They have to keep on, fighting back time, getting the steroid injections and the vitamin shots, being who they are and doing what they do until the last. Why keep recording and performing when they don't need the money, when they could easily sit back and enjoy an easy life pottering in the shed and playing with their grandchildren? Because they *wouldn't* enjoy it. It would be anathema to them. The last thing any star wants to be is a has-been, a whatever-happened-to? So they keep on, hoping for the best that it lasts as long as possible. It's what I'm doing.

'Mick is no fool. He's quite interesting. He was also very honest when he gave Lord Weidenfeld back his million-pound publishing advance in the early eighties, because he found he didn't want to write his autobiography. "I lived it," he told me. "I didn't want to go through it all again. When I started to think about everything, it made me very unhappy. Some people seem to get off on living the past, but it wasn't for me. I prefer to look forward, not back."'

*

The past is a foreign country. They do things differently there.[1] The way we remember it is not how it was. The memories we carry are obscure and untrustworthy. Our true stories avoid us, as if they can't abide having been that dull. They rewrite themselves, embellishing wildly, trying to convince us of alternative versions and parallel universes. The past being anathema to the Stones, especially to Mick, the last thing they want to hear is that their songs are the soundtrack of it. They would rather we didn't go dredging it up, either, because it reminds them of something uncomfortable: that their claim to fame, and to some extent their legacy, is as much about their personal lives as about their music. You can see why. Who in history, with the exception perhaps of King Henry VIII, ever wove a more festering, noxious tapestry of betrayal, infidelity, abuse, neglect, addiction, criminality and destruction? You couldn't make it up. Nor did they. The phrase 'sex, drugs and rock'n'roll' in this context is almost cartoon.

But it's not all bad. At least the Stones will not go down in history as 'mythomaniacs', the stinging term coined by travel writer and novelist

Paul Theroux to describe U2's Bono, actors Brad Pitt, Angelina Jolie and the rest who are, in his eyes, 'people who wish to convince the world of their worth'; which they do primarily by interfering in the social politics of other countries, notably African ones. Nor could they be denounced as 'ego-warriors', having never been into activism, give or take the odd fundraiser. They do not flaunt beliefs, nor dabble in politics. They readily declared themselves tax exiles rather than continue to live in and support the Treasury of the mother country whose NHS saw them into the world, and whose education system schooled them. The curiosity of Jagger's knighthood for services to popular music in Her Majesty's 2002 Birthday Honours is not that he accepted it (he had long craved that gong), but because he had turned his back on the land of his birth.

'The Rolling Stones are actually a number of businesses: touring, recording, publishing, sponsorship, synch and so on,' reported the *Guardian* in 2014. 'As *Fortune* magazine explained in 2002, these businesses are headed by a partnership of the core members of the band. To feed into that, they created separate companies to handle each aspect of the business – Promopub, Promotone, Promotour and Musidor – which were based in the Netherlands for tax reasons.'

Nor is it just the Stones' companies that depend on tax efficiency. 'The whole business thing is predicated a lot on the tax laws,' Keith himself informed *Fortune*. 'It's why we rehearse in Canada and not in the US. A lot of our astute moves have been basically keeping up with tax laws, where to go, where not to put it. Whether to sit on it or not. We left England because we'd be paying ninety-eight cents on the dollar. We left, and they lost out. No taxes at all. I don't want to screw anybody out of anything, least of all the governments that I work with. We put 30 per cent in holding until we sort it out.'

*

And they do whatever it takes to stay ahead. They headline the Isle of Wight in June 2007, at the invitation of John Giddings, my pal of forty years who owns the show. This is their first festival fixture for more than three decades, the kind of thing that calls for the Red Arrows. 'Start Me Up' brings them kicking like kung fu fighters: kohl-eyed Keith in lurex pinstripe, Ronnie in floral black leather, requisite fag dripping from his gob. Mick's in red satin and Charlie sports a clean white tee. Full brass, keys and BVs are all revved. Phenomenal sound, superlative energy, and nobody's chanting 'When I'm Sixty-Four'. Mick's taking us places we've barely been and can hardly imagine, fang queue very *m-u-u-u-ch*. 'Sympathy for the Devil' generates mass woo-woos and returns Jagger in a red sequinned tailcoat. 'Ain't Too Proud to Beg' brings Amy Winehouse, tippy-toe tiny in satin ballet slippers, hair as high as herself. She smiles broadly, exposing the gaps in her teeth. She flirts with the old man, all attitude and beehive, out-grooving Mick and giving him a run for it. She is sensational.

If she knew then what we would all too soon be grieving, that she had only four years left to live. Amy was found dead in her London flat in July 2011, poisoned by alcohol. The Stones kept rolling. There was a lesson there somewhere. If only we could work out what it was.

*

Six years later they make their Glastonbury debut, on the world-famous Pyramid Stage. Prince Harry is there too, somewhere in the crowd. Imagine that, now. Mick makes out that the band have been sitting around for years, awaiting the call from Michael Eavis. It wasn't quite like that. The festival organiser has been pleading with them for decades. They weren't available or didn't respond. What happened? The Stones' fiftieth anniversary happened, in 2012. It must have thrown the remainder into sharp focus. As if galvanised by the realisation that time really is running out on them, they give what they've got. As one observer puts it, 'Keith seems to be running out of steam but Ronnie's picking up: I'd call that a positive outcome.' Mick teases with a silly song called 'Glastonbury Girl', which he tells us he penned last night. Forget that, though, because Mick Taylor's back. You heard. Have the old feuds been forgotten, or is there acrimony yet to come? Not tonight there isn't.

An orchestra of guitarists rearrange themselves on stage, Taylor posing alongside Ronnie, his replacement. If the delivery at first sounds hesitant, it's because it is. He puffs his cheeks and slides into 'Can't You Hear Me Knocking' with all the mellow of a warm Black Velvet. Skinny minny Mick does the dislocation dance and sweats a bit. He sidles down one of the three specially erected catwalks to shake his booty at wide-eyed fans. His hips look narrower than his ankle measurement, and his legs are so thin that he seems knock-kneed. Keith gets the giggles now. He turns his back.

The special bit, the one they haven't all been waiting for, is Taylor's guitar solo. He hasn't come all this way for nothing. At last he loses his inhibitions and comes alive. Less chubby geography teacher giving it a go on the axe at the end-of-term disco, more paid-up rocker playing for the past. Jagger maracas away in the back there, squinting. Either his face sinks in or it must be a trick of the light.

Most of the mostly young crowd look blank. Who did you say that is again? Couldn't tell you. Not bad though, izee. If you like that sort of thing. The night heaves, as rock'n'roll nights tend to. Taylor takes no notice, just gets on with the job in hand. He's not milking it. He doesn't have to. He is suddenly the only grown-up on stage. Charlie's loving it.

'Fang *queue*, Mick!' roars Jagger. 'Fuckin' great, we love yew.'

No Adele. No Springsteen. Both had been rumoured. But we do get 'Sympathy for the Devil' in its entirety, during which flares scarlet the sky and a scrap-metal phoenix pops out of the top of the Pyramid like a cuckoo from a clock, raising its wings and spurting fire. A little red rooster might have been funnier, but this is symbolic. 'Our passions are the true phoenix,' said Goethe.[2] 'When the old one is burnt out, a new one rises from its ashes.' In other words, long live the Stones. Did they get it, down in the front? Did Harry?

As the fireworks light up Worthy Farm, Mick turns to the crowd. 'We've been doing this for fifty years or something,' he says. 'And if this is the first time you've seen a band, please come again.'

The festival loves the Stones, all right. It is official. Glasto boss Michael Eavis calls them 'The high spot of forty-three years of Glastonbury. They finally did it,' he enthuses, 'and it was fantastic. My God, did they deliver.'

'You Can't Always Get What You Want', straight in, followed by a psycho thrashing of 'Satisfaction'. Beat that, little'uns.

*

On an end-of-summer sojourn in the Lakes, I am staying with my friend Peter Myers. The former mountaineer and member of the Keswick Mountain Rescue Team lives half the year here, the other half on Hudson

Street in MePa, as they call downtown New York's Meatpacking District. He opened a shop there in 1985, naming it 'Myers of Keswick' after his dad's old butcher's shop in the town of his birth. He made sausages, pork pies and sausage rolls in his kitchen there, and imported British grocery items such as Heinz beans, Jacob's cream crackers and Marmite. He once supplied Princess Diana with bangers at the Upper East Side's Carlyle Hotel. Not a euphemism. The December queues for his homemade mince pies and Christmas puddings stop traffic for several blocks.

Pete still supplies thousands of ex-pats throughout New York and across the US of A. He and my late sportswriter father Ken Jones became pals in the way back, when Pete ran a pub at 105 West 13th Street near Union Square called The Bells of Hell. He bought it from a gold smuggler, Malachy McCourt, brother of *Angela's Ashes* author Frank, who later became a famous writer himself. Pete turned the watering hole into a heaving think tank of journalists, musicians and activists. By importing all the daily British newspapers and weekly singles releases for his jukebox, inventing Happy Hour with free pork pies and sausage rolls on the bar and presenting live bands, he ensured a feisty Blighty clientele. Mick Jagger was said to frequent the Bells, though nobody could remember ever seeing him in there. Bill, Keith and Charlie would rock up from time to time too. Dad frequented Madison Square Garden throughout the golden era of heavyweight title fights, when the world's best boxers were the rock stars of their game. From Pennsylvania Plaza, it was only a ten-minute walk down 7th Avenue to the Bells. Dad and Pete became best friends, and here we are … chewing cud while gazing over breathtaking hill and dale, swallowing our way through my Cumbrian chum's fine wine cellar.

The next bottle that Pete fetches up bears the Rolling Stones lip and tongue logo. I take a closer look. It's a bottle of Washington Cabernet Sauvignon 2016, emblazoned with the words 'The Rolling Stones 50 Years'.

'Where did you get *that*?!'

'Keith gave it me.'

'Keith Richards?'

'Of *course* bloody Keith Richards. Who else would brew their own plonk with the Stones logo on the label?'

'You never told me you knew him! How do you know him?'

'Because I am the corner shop for English folk in New York. The kind of folk who still want to eat sausage rolls and pork pies. When I started out, there were a hundred and fifty thousand Brits living in the city, and another hundred thousand in the tri-State area. That's like being the only butcher in Carlisle. Anyway, I opened, in 1985, and shortly afterwards a woman came in calling herself Jane Rosen, Jane Rose as she is now. Works for the Stones. She places an order for "HP Sauce for Mr Richards", and says, "You know who that'll be for." Keith was living on East 3rd Street above Tower Records. He was with Patti by then.

'I delivered the HP Sauce, a bloody case of the stuff, to "Mr Richards". I sent a delivery boy over there, I didn't have the time to go myself. He came back and said, "It's fucking Keith Richards's house!" Forever after that, I made sure it was me who took it round. You can't have these upstarts salivating over the customers. It's not hygienic. I'd go up, I'd hand it over to Patti, and over time we became quite friendly. One Saturday afternoon, Patti calls the shop. "Can you send over another case of HP ..." – what's he doing, bathing in the bloody stuff? – "and some kippers, please, Pete?" "We don't deliver on Saturdays," I informed her. "Oh, *Peter*," she says. "You can have a drink with Keith when you come over, if that makes a difference." That was it. Out came the motorbike and off I went. Lug it over there. Knock, knock. Go upstairs, go in the kitchen, put the kippers in the fridge, which is heaving with bottles of Heineken and Beck's. Patti pours me a beer. "Keith's waiting for you in the front room," she purrs.

'I go in the front room. It's pretty sparse, there's not much furniture. Just a huge couch in front of the window, looking all the way uptown. And there on the couch is Keith, unconscious, with beer bottles rolling on the floor all around him. I look round at Patti and she is giggling her head off. This is her idea of me having a drink with Keith Richards.'

Peter's first face-to-face encounter with the guitarist happened not long afterwards.

'He flew in from Sydney early one morning, and instructed his driver to bring him straight to Myers of Keswick on Hudson Street. He walks in the shop. He's wearing a beautiful snakeskin jacket, and he looks as though he could do with a cup of tea. No big deal, I greet him like I greet everyone else. "Hiya, Keith. Welcome. Siddown. Want a cup of tea?" I sit him down, pour him a cuppa and hand him a sausage roll. It is then that I notice the two huge bodyguards, one of whom stands blocking the doorway. It's Keith Richards. Even though he is sitting with his back to the door, the python jacket is a dead give-away. Other customers come in and out. One or two of them slide bits of paper in front of him to sign, which he does, ever so graciously. But nobody really bothers him, and he's not bothered by anybody else. It's all very relaxed.'

What made him come there?

'Nostalgia. He's an old-fashioned man, and a very homely one. I'd gone round to his place a few times. I once found him and Ronnie Wood and his dad playing dominoes. He wanted to see the shop for himself. It took him back. It was the grocery shop of his childhood. It still is.'

Shortly before the Steel Wheels tour of North America kicked off in August 1989, the phone rang in Peter's shop. 'It was Patti. They are now living out in Connecticut with their daughters, they are regular customers and we are on first-phone-number terms. "Keith wants to speak to you," she said. She put him on. "Hiya, Pete. How ya doin'? How many people work for you?" 'Five,' I said. "Here's the deal," he replied. "I've got five tickets for Sunday night, Shea Stadium. I want five sausage rolls, five pork pies and five steak and kidney pies in return." "Well, Keith," I said, keeping a straight face, "this is quite a lot of stuff. Any chance of another VIP ticket for my daughter?" I had some bloody cheek, me. Needless to say, he obliged.'

Peter went to the gig with Jenny, his daughter who now co-runs the business and who at the time was a little girl. 'We go to the VIP room, which is a bit basic. Jenny and I are sitting in the middle of this room, all on our own, when Robert De Niro walks in. Talking Italian, yeah. More people start to trickle in, they all look shiny and important. I'm thinking, what the fuck am I doing here? Then Patti walks in, looking bloody marvellous, her leather skirt held together with safety pins. She peers over the top of these important heads and shouts, "*Pete!* Did you bring the stuff?!" Every head in the place turned, true as I sit here.'

At which point, the Myerses were upgraded. 'We are sent into the

VVIP room, which is reserved for band members and family. There's a table to one side with a roast turkey centrepiece, surrounded by roast chickens, ducks, smoked salmon and caviar. In front of the table watching American football on telly is Keith's dad Bert, smoking a bloody great spliff. And directly opposite me and Jenny stands Jagger. Who is staring at me.

'I knew why. I was the only person in the room who he didn't know. It wasn't that many years since John Lennon had been murdered uptown, and every rock star was wary in New York. Mick starts heading towards me and opens his mouth to speak when I am saved by the bells of hell. A gorilla comes in and starts shouting at everyone: "Will everyone in this room who is not, repeat NOT in the band, please get out now!" Jenny and I oblige. We make our way down this walkway in front of the stage. At the end of which a huge Mercedes rolls up, the back door opens and Keith falls out of it. The bloody *back*! The arms are flailing, the eyes are going, and he beams me a dirty great smile: "*Ha*-llo, Pete!" and I'm thinking, there's no way they'll let this bugger on stage tonight. Twenty minutes later the Stones are up there giving it 'Satisfaction' and there's Keith coming on like an eighteen-year-old, more energy than a planeload of Russian gymnasts and going like a good'un.'

Keith sent Peter tickets to all the shows after that.

'And what a nice guy he turned out to be. Contrary to what I'd been expecting, having read about the shenanigans, the drugs and the drink. Almost a gentleman. He'd never want to be called a complete one. And we became friends. People thought we were chalk and cheese. They couldn't be more wrong. He and I are not dissimilar. Not only are we the same age, but we have our childhood in common. We both grew up on Colman's mustard and Branston Pickle, on all the things that I sell in my shop. His Britishness, his roots, are very important to him. I remember an occasion when I had my mate Jack in, a good old East Ender whose son is Keith McNally, 'the restaurateur who invented Downtown' and owner of Balthazar, all that. Jack loved to come and sit in my shop and drink tea. This particular evening, getting ready for closing at about ten to seven, I've got Jack in the corner and the door bursts open.

In walk Keith and Patti. Keith is wearing the most ridiculous bloody outfit I've seen in my life. Slate grey leather trousers, a three-quarter-length jacket and a bowler hat. In they breeze, and Patti and I sit and get chatting. Keith's parading back and forth, picking up all sorts of shit. Caster sugar, self-raising flour. He's fascinated. Patti tells me he likes going out to restaurants but he never eats in them. He goes home and cooks something afterwards. I say, "Here, Keith, this feller here, I think you and him are from the same neck of the woods." They practically fell into each other's arms. I opened a few beers, as I tend to after closing time, and these two get stuck in, talking about old London.'

Not long after Keith fell off the branch in Fiji in 2006 and wound up having brain surgery, the then sixty-two-year-old came down to Myers of Keswick for another cup of tea. 'I asked him how he was feeling after landing on his head,' remembers Peter. "Peter," he replied, looking me straight in the eye, "I've been falling on my head for most of my life. It's the only thing that ever knocked any sense into me." Which sums him up. He's been a loyal pal. He still sends me presents every year. A copy of his autobiography when it came out. Picture books, all signed. A copy of his first solo album, *Talk is Cheap*, dedicated "To Peter with love." Special box sets with booklets and multiple CDs. A crate of the Stones' wine, the very stuff we are drinking now. A Stones umbrella and a hoodie, very smart. They never forget me, and I never forget them. Keith Richards is standard, a down-to-earth British lad. He always will be.'

*

'People can laugh at the Stones and call them ridiculous,' says David Ambrose. 'But that's just ageist, and it doesn't wash these days. Besides, unlike the Beatles, the Stones *rock*. It's like being in an octuple scull, an eight-man rowing boat, and everyone's rowing beautifully in unison. Jagger knows, and Richards knows, that they are as good as it gets. No one has bettered them. Yes, others have lasted as long. The Who have always been brilliant, but they never really rocked. The Stones have got it down to a fine art. The chords fall in the right place at the right time, and take you perfectly into the choruses with these great grooves. It doesn't do to dissect the elements, you have to consider it as a whole. Mick's not a real singer, for example. He's a character singer. His voice hits highs and lows, like a teenage boy's. It sounds unique, but is easily impersonated. It's an affectation. But look how far they have come on it.

'I do believe that the Beatles, had they continued, would have mattered in this way too, at this stage in the game,' mulls EMI's former head of A&R. 'But they quit, they created a vacancy, and the Stones stepped straight in. They are the seminal act. But how much longer can they go on for? Not long now.

'Who succeeds the Stones? It's the big question. U2? Not sure. Bono's a bit boring now. We've kind of gone off him. My guess is that Lindsey Buckingham will come back to Fleetwood Mac. That they'll take the Stones' ball and run with it and be the next forever band.'

Chapter Twenty

SO LONG

20 September 2021

Back on the road, ahead of the official first night of their resumed *No Filter* trek in St Louis, Missouri, in six days' time, the Stones pre-open 1,000 miles away in Foxborough, Massachusetts. Such distances are so-what to those who 'fly private' and pick their own departure times. This invitation-only gig, in a giant tent that appears to hover above the field of the grand Gillette Stadium, is hosted by billionaire businessman and New England Patriots American football team owner Robert Kraft. It is a major-league night, to which the band of bands rises unfazed. They would anyway. What do they play? 'Let's Spend the Night Together', 'Tumbling Dice', 'Under My Thumb'. 'Troubles a-Comin' – an old Chi-Lites favourite getting an airing on the soon-to-be-released, expanded fortieth anniversary re-issue of 1981's *Tattoo You*. They recorded the track forty-two years ago, in 1979. It is one of nine previously unreleased gems on *Lost & Found*, the bonus disc of newly completed songs and rarities that light up the latest package.

They also bring out 'Living in a Ghost Town', their reggae-infused chanson written in 2019 and completed in 2020, updating the lyrics in the spirit of Covid awareness; 'You Can't Always Get What You Want', 'Midnight Rambler' and 'Miss You' bring up the rear. The icing is the first appearance in sixteen years of '19th Nervous Breakdown', sprinkled with

'Start Me Up' and 'Gimme Shelter'. '(I Can't Get No) Satisfaction' closes. It's the one that they want.

What's this, Keith, Mick and Ronnie arm-in-arm downstage, looking like Lost Boys?

'I must say,' says Mick, addressing the audience. Say what? He hesitates, swallows, gets a grip. 'It's a bit of a poignant night for us, and it's our first tour we've done in fifty-nine years that we've done without our lovely Charlie Watts. And we all miss Charlie so much. We miss him as a band, we miss him as friends on and off the stage, and we've got so many memories of Charlie … I'm sure some of you that have seen us before have got memories of Charlie as well, and I hope you will remember him as we do.'

He swigs neatly from a bottle of beer. 'We'd like to dedicate this show to Charlie. Let's have a drink to Charlie.'

Who might have grinned his chumpy, jaw-set grin and muttered, 'Get outta here.'

*

Bernard Fowler, the gracious, gifted vocalist who started out singing on street corners as a fourteen-year-old while working evenings in a Harlem nightclub; who has made music with many favourites: Robert Plant, Def Leppard, Ivan Neville, Bonnie Raitt, Jerry Lee Lewis, Alice Cooper, Duran Duran; whose first ever record was the Stones' 1964 US album *12 X 5*, which was given to him by his father; who has spent literally half his life on the road and in the studio with this band, collectively and individually. He has seen it all. When I ask him how much longer they can go on, he bursts out laughing.

'Keith told me he intends to die on stage, playing his guitar, and I believe him,' he says. 'That could be the way it is. He also says he'll stop when Charlie wants to stop, and that ain't happening. The point that we are at now, I reckon they'll rock 'til they drop. Music is ageless and timeless. The Stones have proved that beyond all doubt, and they have nothing left to prove.'

He has been in a lot of bands, has Bernard. He knows first-hand that keeping a band together is the most challenging aspect of rock'n'roll, because there are so many personalities, agendas, obstacles and supporting casts involved. And the older it gets, the more complicated it becomes, because each member of the band has an entire dynasty to consider. Never mind all the extracurriculars.

'The biggest stars are just normal guys wanting to do normal things, but having to go out night after night and be anything *but* normal,' he says. 'I must have spent years of my life playing dominoes with Keith Richards in hotels, and listening to music with him. Walking the streets of strange cities with him in the early hours, listening to him talk. I know the guys in this band better than I know my own family. I've spent more time with them. And I can tell you, it hasn't been easy for them. People look in from the outside and go, "It's OK for you." But they know nothing.

'You don't get to become artists like these guys unless you have suffered. The lives and careers of most artists flourish out of dysfunction, deprivation and abandonment. I have recognised it in the backgrounds of so many. John Lennon, David Bowie, Michael Jackson, Freddie Mercury. You name them. They become artists because music is the antidote. It's as simple as that. You don't see the dysfunction in Mick and Keith? I'm telling you, the damage is there. You don't even have to look too deep. They keep it hidden, most of the time, but you get to know the signs. It erupts, they suppress it, but it informs everything they do. There is deep-rooted pain, the frustrations of a lifetime, the addiction to the road, to keep on rolling, which of course is a form of getting away from yourself. You can reinvent yourself every night on stage, leave the last version of yourself and all your troubles behind in the last hotel room. But those guys check out too. Every version of yourself that you have ever been will always be following you around.

'You don't get to compose songs like they did, to write lyrics like theirs, unless there is pain. It's stored deep down in your soul, and it is summoned to do the business. And people relate. People all over the world relate to what they have come to represent, to what unites us as humans.'

'How do they still do it, at their impossible ages?'

'Hey, man. They got some great people looking after them.'

'Medical people?'

'Yeah, and shit. And they don't do stuff the way we all did stuff when we were young. I had to give it all up, just like them. The booze and the powder just stopped working. But I'm not giving up on the Rolling Stones. I've been hanging with these boys a long time, and I've got to see it through. Which is something I don't look forward to. I get lumps in my throat if I think about it too long. People have been asking me for years, "Is this gonna be the last tour?" I hear someone say, "*Another* last tour!" and I get a little defensive. They'll do it as long as they want. We've never seen something like this before. And when they do decide, we'll never see anything like it again.'

'But what,' I ask him, 'is "it"?'

'Shit, Lesley-Ann, do *they* know what it is? And they live it, day in, day out. It's just a thing. It is the soundtrack of many, many lives. Just look into a Rolling Stones audience, any night, and just wow at it. There's people their age, my age, the next age. People carrying babies. Toddlers and teenagers walking around the stadium. They've been hearing that music in their homes and their hearts since the day they were born.

'Everyone has a Rolling Stones story. At this point? Everybody has one. And everyone has their Rolling Stones song. I can't explain it better than that. But it tells the story.'

*

6 December 2021

When you think about it, where else? Ronnie Scott's was Charlie's favourite jazz club. It may not be much to write home about, but take the long way round and it is home. This tucked-away Soho dive crammed with ghosts is where he soaked up and feasted on many of his musical heroes. Where he hid himself away and licked his wounds when he couldn't take any more. When all seemed hopeless and life felt pointless. During the down years, the wilderness years, in a fug of drugs and booze, when he lost the plot and when his only salvation was the music that had first turned him on.

Ronnie Scott, the late tenor saxophonist, opened his first club in 1959 with a £1,000 loan from his stepfather. Not in this location but across Shaftesbury Avenue in Chinatown, where a Gerrard Street tearoom got them started. He and his business partner, fellow sax player Pete King, moved it over here six years later. The current premises were once a dance hall. Its drab, gloomy interior with chewing gum for carpet lent itself blithely to after-hours larks, and even joined in the fun. You could get up to no good in its shadowy corners and no one would notice, because they were all mischiefing too. The Stones looked in, the Beatles hung out, and so did Princess Margaret. No tiara in place to indicate who she wasn't. Nina Simone, Buddy Rich, Ella Fitzgerald, Sarah Vaughan and countless musicians have performed here for as long as the Stones have existed. Princess Diana found it convenient when in the throes of one of her flings. If walls could talk. But these walls can. If not in decipherable language that can be converted into written words, they ooze with stories.

It is Charlie's night tonight. His wife Shirley, daughter Seraphina, wider family and faithful friends had to wait a while to pay fitting tribute, because the Stones were on the road across America. But they're back, for the celebration some months overdue. Less than three weeks before Christmas, with nippy, fairylit London once again on a threat of lockdown, the vaxxed and the boosted flock, invitation only, to give him the send-off he might have loved.

Perky pianist, bandleader and television host Jools Holland is in charge of proceedings. He leads the house band into an aural smorgasbord, delighting an audience that includes former Stones bassist Bill Wyman, his wife Suzanne, and Steve Jordan, Charlie's replacement in the touring band. Watts's childhood chum Dave Green, who played cheek by jowl with him down the years in numerous jazz line-ups, together with Axel Zwingenberger, Ben Waters and their bandmates from the group the A B C & D of Boogie Woogie, set the pace. The Americans are in: Stones stalwarts, backing vocalists and duettists Bernard Fowler and Lisa Fischer, and saxophonist Tim Ries, who delivers 'Blues for Charlie', composed to commemorate his friend. Feisty Lisa, once an integral part of the Stones' troupe but glaringly absent lately, floors the room with 'Trouble in Mind'. Summoning the spirits of Otis Spann and Lonnie Johnson, she stirs in some Nina for good measure.[1] She won't be blue always. She welcomes Bernard to join her in a rendition of 'Up Above My Head'. Gospel magic. Sister Rosetta leans down from heaven, thrashing her Gibson Les Paul.[2]

Nobody wants to go home. They gotta. There's only one way to make them leave. C'mon, up you get, Mick, Keith and Ronnie. Do what you came for. No way are this lot leaving without a jam. Oh go on then, if we must, if you wouldn't mind holding my Bud. They dive into 'Shame Shame Shame', echoing the vigour of their hero Jimmy Reed; and 'Down The Road Apiece', written by Don 'Boogie Woogie Bugle Boy' Raye[3] and recorded more than half a century ago for *Rolling Stones No.2*.

And sixty years fall away like fruit off a flatbed. Hitting the tarmac and bouncing through time, they juice all the way back to the start line. Back and back to a bunch of kids looking like they're playing truant. Here they are, captured in mono and preserved for all time. Bill chewing, Charlie poker-facing, Mick shimmying, Brian strumming. Keith's acing it, he is game as a bagel on lead guitar. A jug-eared boy chuffed to bits just to be there. Look at me now, Grandad Gus, are you listening? Doris – Mum! – were you watching? Keith'll be pinching himself when he wakes. They all will. Even Mick. From such innocence and hope are legends made.

ROOTS

What did they know, the rock'n'rollers, of the more than six hundred thousand Africans who were enslaved and shipped between 1619 and 1808 to what is now the United States? Would they have cared that so many had been ripped from their homelands, places of diverse cultures and multiple languages, and then separated on arrival from those with whom they shared family, roots and tongues? They might have reacted with mild indignation at the thought of those people having been deprived of an essential feature of their heritage: the playing of drums.

Slave owners, fearing uprising and rebellion, took away those vital tools of communication. Slaves improvised. They fashioned percussive instruments from sticks and bones. They used spoons, washboards and their own bodies, clapping hands, stamping feet and 'slapping' or 'patting' juba: hitting legs, chest and cheeks to create sounds and rhythms, later known as 'hamboning'. They also sang, to drown the suffering of body and soul. From the mists rising over vast plantations drifted the haunting sounds of field hollers: unaccompanied songs without set form or steady beat. These mournful moans and vocal shifts and bends echoed both West African music and the adhan, the Muslim call to prayer, because many slaves were adherents of Islam.

Forced by their owners to abandon their faith in order to be 'civilised' as Christians, they kept their religion and traditions alive secretly through song. Call-and-response work-songs also found across African cultures were sung together by groups as they went about tasks dependent on precise timing, such as the adjustment of railroad tracks. Later came the spirituals: Christian songs chorused by African Americans before and after slavery. Although hymns were mainly composed by white Americans and Europeans, they were customisede by distinctive African performance styles. Other songs highlighted the conditions they endured. 'Negro spirituals' served up biblical stories recounting the plight of the Jews under slavery in Egypt, as well as David-and-Goliath-type tales of triumphant underdogs. From the late nineteenth century, blues ballads celebrating the lives of heroes and villains combined European-influenced native American ballads with African American music, giving rise to the slow, sentimental songs we know as ballads today.

By 1860, there were still close to four million enslaved black people in America. Slavery officially ceased in 1865, at the end of the Civil War, when ownership of other humans became illegal. But life remained miserable for survivors and their descendants. The rights of African Americans were severely restricted. Racial segregation persisted until the mid-1960s, when discrimination based on race, colour, religion, sex and national origin, and later sexual orientation and gender identity, were outlawed. Little wonder that the blues emerged among people for whom segregation, isolation and hopelessness were a way of life, and for whom the railroad was a symbol of opportunity and escape.

Most were sharecroppers: agricultural labourers working somebody else's fields in return for a share of the profits, with housing and basics provided. The system was corrupt. Isolated rural Americans could purchase goods from mail-order catalogues, if they had the money to buy. But by the end of most months, most sharecroppers were in debt to the owners of the land they toiled. Many made music to remain sane, and to survive. The blues were rooted in their plight. Rueful reflections and soul-baring laments evolved to solve, soothe and sustain.

They accompanied themselves on the barest instruments: the diddly bow, also known as the 'one-string', the 'jitterbug' and the 'mono chord zither', a rudimentary one-stringed guitar harking back to basic single-stringed African instruments; the washboard, played by rubbing sewing thimbles or other metal pieces against its ribbing; the harmonica, the free wind instrument common in American folk music, known variously as the mouth organ, the blues harp and the Mississippi saxophone; and the banjo, often played with a metal or glass slide usually fashioned from a broken-off bottle neck. Improvised bass instruments included household jugs, blown into to create low sounds. Jug bands featuring improvised instruments alongside stringed instruments became popular in the 1920s, particularly in Memphis. Acoustic guitars gained widespread popularity during the early 1900s when mass production made them cheap and available by mail order.

Maybe the birthplace of the blues, as the dusty cobalt sign at Dockery Farms in Cleveland, Mississippi admits, is long lost to time. But that humble former cotton plantation boasts a sturdier claim than most. For almost three decades it was the home of Charley Patton, the most important of the early bluesmen. Patton himself was taught by his Dockery neighbour Henry Sloan. They influenced many other musicians who drifted into their midst, guys like Howlin' Wolf, Willie Brown, Tommy Johnson and Roebuck 'Pops' Staples. But who started it? When was it first heard? What are the features that make it perhaps the most vital musical genre of all?

There's a story about an Alabama-born African American musician, songwriter and bandleader W.C. Handy (1873–1958), William Christopher to his friends, who called himself 'the Father of the Blues'. He wasn't, exactly, although he was among the first to promote and popularise it. He claimed to have happened upon it one day at the train station in Tutwiler, Tallahatchie County, played by an anonymous itinerant guitarist. 'The weirdest music I ever heard' was how Handy described it. Adopting aspects of the sound that had caught his attention into his own compositions, Handy delivered it to the masses across the Mississippi Delta and other parts of the South by publishing sheet music. By the 1910s, thanks to sales of Handy's scores, the music had become a national craze. Within the blues, to all who listened with the right ears, throbbed the field hollers and work songs of slaves of yore. The blues gave voice to a silent, mostly illiterate group with little to their name and less to hope for. They told of what it was like to be an African American. They sang their songs to live audiences, and made records to reach those who might not otherwise get to hear. These recordings are of monumental significance because the music was not taken seriously as an art form in its day. The blues, said the bluesmen, was heaven's way of helping folk with hard times.

Why 'blues'? As a metaphor for melancholy and hopelessness, it leans back to the term 'blue devils' found in English from the 1700s. Folk would later speak of 'having the blues' when they felt sad. Thus, the blues is both an emotion and a musical form. It is also the perfect paradox. Musicians play the blues in order to expunge the blues.

'The blues' is at once a state of mind and the soundtrack thereof. It's about a good man feeling bad. Sing the blues and feel better about yourself. Overcome your negative feelings by listening to somebody else expressing them through music. Purge your emotions through art. Find a way out of your loneliness and frustration. It's easy to understand why the music, sung mostly in the first person, was so appealing back in the bleak, and why it took hold. Blues songs describe feelings both personal and universal, instead of telling specific beginning-middle-end stories. Without a set plot to stick to, blues songs can be lengthened and improvised upon during performance and recording. They can take you anywhere you want, if you feel so inclined.

Ever heard the 'blue note', the 'secret ingredient' of the blues? You have: in the Stones' '(I Can't Get No) Satisfaction' ('the one with the fuzz box') and in the Beatles' 'Can't Buy Me Love', bending every blue note possible (the verses use a twelve-bar blues progression, unusually for them, and get George's cheeky guitar solo). Audible proof that the blues is not only about vocal brilliance or depth of emotional expression, but also about the notes being sung. Not just notes that we are accustomed to and expect to hear, but a range of out-of-key others that rise from elsewhere. Also known as the 'outside note', the elusive blue note is the hallmark of the blues. David Temperley, Professor of Music Theory, Eastman School of Music at the University of Rochester, New York, has long been fascinated.

'As musicians, we're always taught there is an octave divided into twelve pitches,' he says. 'Now, we're finding evidence that it's not so simple, and people sometimes deliberately fall between one pitch and another for expressive effect.' For example, he says, a melody in C major might be sung with a note that is halfway between E and E-flat, or a C minor blues might feature a tasty F# note for instant down-home effect. 'Blue notes arising in systematic ways suggest to me there is some kind of intentionality at some level, though that could be unconscious,' Temperley reflects.

In 2017, the team at Eastman developed algorithms and used automatic pitch-tracking software to extract and analyse the pitches within vocal tracks. Pitches were then examined in context of the entire song, to determine whether the tuning deviated from conventional pitches of the chromatic scale, and whether the deviations appeared to occur in intentional ways. Their work is ongoing.

*

Although the genre is widely regarded as the male guitarist's domain, the earliest blues stars were female. The first African American blues song ever recorded was by **Mamie Smith** from Cincinnati. Born Mamie Robinson (1883–1946), she was a vaudeville pianist and dancer who had toured with a white dance troupe from the age of ten, later dancing herself into the clubs of Harlem, New York City, where she began to sing. In February 1920 she recorded 'That Thing Called Love' and 'You Can't Keep a Good Man Down' against fervent racial opposition. Months later, she scored her biggest hit with the first blues recording, 'Crazy Blues'. A million copies sold in under a year, most of them purchased by African Americans. Thus began the era of so-called 'race records'. Record companies went looking for more female blues singers, giving rise to the age of classic female blues.

The 'Queen of the Blues' was soon eclipsed by **Bessie Smith** (1894–1937) from Chattanooga, Tennessee, who as an orphaned child had sung for pennies on street corners. She became not only the most important female blues singer of the Jazz Age, but also 'Empress of the Blues'. **Clara Smith** (1894–1935) from South Carolina was 'Queen of the Moaners'. She mentored thirteen-year-old dancer **Josephine Baker** (1906–75), the pair becoming 'lady lovers'. This risqué future spy and siren of the French Resistance married several times but was openly bisexual. She was awarded the Croix de Guerre and the Légion d'honneur.

Ma Rainey (1886–1939), born Gertrude Pridgett in Russell County, Alabama, took up performing in her teens, becoming known as 'Ma' to match her husband Will's nickname 'Pa' Rainey. They featured in black minstrel shows, toured with the Rabbit Foot Minstrels and formed their own group. Ma recorded more than a hundred songs including 'Moonshine Blues' and 'Ma Rainey's Black Bottom'. Her fierce, soul-baring, defiant work was a stark portrayal of the real lives of African Americans. But she did not betray them, as has been suggested, with her materialistic lifestyle and extravagant wardrobe. Decked out in her twinkling tiaras, gold-dollar jewellery, ostrich feathers and satin frocks, her glamour gave hope to downbeat women.

The 'Mother of the Blues' was visible, audible proof that there were ways out. In this sense, she was an important proto-feminist icon. Her deep, gritty, powerful voice and subtle phrasing inspired the likes of Louis Armstrong, with whom she would later record, and Janis Joplin and Bonnie Raitt. A forerunner of the LGBTQ cause, she was rumoured to be romantically involved with Bessie Smith. Her 1928 song 'Prove it on Me' is notable for daring allusions to her bisexuality. A poster for the record featuring Ma in drag with a cop hovering close by may well have inspired George Michael seventy years later, when he released his 1998 single 'Outside' after his arrest for engaging in lewd behaviour in a Beverly Hills public toilet. The tongue-in-cheek video for the smash hit featured heli-cops, bathroom arrests, kissing policemen, stripping patrolwomen and al fresco fornication.

Ida Cox (1888 or '1896–1967), born Ida M. Prather in Toccoa, Georgia, first stepped out in touring troupes including the Rabbit Foot Minstrels, like her idols Ma and Bessie. A charismatic, comedic and expressive singer, she was known at the height of her career as the 'Sepia Mae West'.

Alberta Hunter (1895–1984), a lesbian blues singer, was born in Memphis and moved to Chicago to sing in brothels and bars. She developed a talent for improvising lyrics. On tour in Europe in 1917, she visited Paris and London. She took the role of Queenie in 1928 in *Show Boat*'s first London production, at the Theatre Royal Drury Lane, opposite Paul Robeson, and sang a 1934 season at the Dorchester. In later years she worked with Louis Armstrong, abandoning her career after the death of her mother to work for twenty years as a nurse. Music lured her back when she was in her eighties, and she enjoyed an unexpected revival.

Her albums were certainly popular among London students in the early 1980s. I was one of them.

Memphis Minnie (1897–1973) was born Lizzie Douglas, probably in Tunica County, Mississippi, and gained fame as 'the Most Popular Female Country Blues Singer of All Time'. Gifted her first guitar at the age of eight, she also learned to play the banjo, and spent most of her teens singing and playing on street corners. She joined a circus in Memphis, supplementing the music crusts with sex work – as many female artists had to back then, when the dough ran dry. She performed with a succession of husbands, toured the South extensively, and had established herself in Chicago by 1935. As a blues guitarist, singer and songwriter, she recorded some two hundred songs over her thirty-year career. Her biggest hit was 'Me and my Chauffeur Blues'. One of her greatest fans is Bonnie Raitt, who cherished her memory and paid for her headstone. Minnie could sing and play as well as any man. So can Bonnie.

Billie Holiday (1915–59), born Eleanora Fagan in Philadelphia, worked as a brothel maid and began singing in Harlem nightclubs in her early teens. She made her recording debut at eighteen with Benny Goodman in 1933, and later worked with Count Basie and Artie Shaw. Her relationships with bad men, booze and heroin made a lag of her, and ultimately destroyed 'Lady Day'. She was dead by the age of forty-four, a grotesque shadow of her once glistening self. Her 1956 autobiography *Lady Sings the Blues* was adapted for the screen, starring Diana Ross.

The blues were the first medium via which African American women could express their social, political and personal problems publicly. Ladies who sang the blues spoke for their kind, and were inspirational. But the Great Depression threw a fire blanket over the age of the female blues artists. By the end of the 1930s, they were on the wane. The blues became a male-dominated domain.

Henry Sloan (1870–1948?) was a plantation worker who lived at Dockery Farms. One of the earliest blues musicians, Sloan taught Charley Patton to play guitar and was a friend of Robert Johnson. Patton, Tommy Johnson, Son House and others named him as their teacher, as well as the originator of what flourished as the Delta blues. He may have migrated north to Chicago after World War I. He left no recordings.

Charley (also spelled Charlie) Patton (1891–1934) was born in Hinds County, Mississippi. The 'Father of the Delta Blues' and one of the most important American musicians of the twentieth century was so light-skinned that his appearance provoked speculation. He was a popular showman and all-rounder with a distinctive gravelly voice. His 1929 song 'Pony Blues' is preserved in the US as a work of cultural, historical and aesthetical significance.

Son House (1902–88), born Edward James House Jr in Lyon, Clarksdale, Mississippi, was a man of the cloth who gave in to the blues when he was twenty-five, pouring the passion of his preaching into music. He also became an exquisite slide guitarist. Under the patronage of Charley Patton he recorded from 1930, but the Great Depression thwarted his quest for national fame. He inspired Robert Johnson and Muddy Waters, but was disappointed by the lack of personal recognition. He moved to Rochester, New York in 1943, turning his back on music to work as a railroad porter and chef. Rediscovered twenty years later when he was sixty-two, he was coaxed out of retirement and became a folk blues singer for predominantly young white audiences. Several albums and live concert recordings ensued.

Big Bill Broonzy (1903–58) was born Lee Conley Bradley, probably in Arkansas, Mississippi Delta. He made his first fiddle from a cigar box when he was ten, and learned to play spirituals and folk songs. Starting out as a country blues musician, he became a leading light in the American folk music revival. He moved north in 1920, took up the guitar, and became a pioneer of the Chicago blues. This suave, sharp-suited jazzman would sport the overalls and hat of the field hand for his folk performances, attracting praise for his authenticity. Many of his influential songs drew on his personal rural-to-urban metamorphosis.

T-Bone Walker (1910–75), born Aaron Thibeaux Walker in Texas, was a pioneer and creator of jump blues and electric blues. He performed professionally on the blues circuit from the age of fifteen. Known for songs such as 'Bobby Sox Blues' and 'West Side Baby', his most famous number is the desolate 1947 release 'Call It Stormy Monday (But Tuesday Is Just As Bad)'.

Howlin' Wolf (1910–76) was born Chester Arthur Burnett in White

Station, Mississippi, to Native American and African parents. The Chicago blues guitarist, singer and harmonica player is known for songs such as 'Smokestack Lightnin'', 'Spoonful' and 'Killing Floor'. He was a major influence on subsequent artists, including the Stones.

Robert Johnson (1911–38), born in Hazlehurst, Mississippi, was a blues guitarist and singer-songwriter. 'The King of the Delta Blues Singers', his following increased massively after his death, allegedly from poisoned whisky. He became an icon of the British blues movement, Eric Clapton describing him as 'the most important blues singer that ever lived'. Keith Richards, Bob Dylan and Robert Plant have all recognised him as a major influence on their work. His best-loved recordings include 'Me and the Devil Blues', 'Sweet Home Chicago', 'Cross Road Blues', 'Hell Hound on My Trail', 'Come On in My Kitchen' and 'Love in Vain'. The master.

John Lee Hooker (1912 or '1917–2001) landed in Tutwiler, Tallahatchie County, Mississippi. The blues singer-songwriter and guitarist performed an electric guitar variation of the Delta blues, e.g. on 'Dimples', 'Boom Boom' and 'One Bourbon, One Scotch, One Beer'. He collaborated with many artists in later life, including The Doors, B.B. King and Van Morrison, which earned him a wide and appreciative next-generation audience.

Sonny Boy Williamson (1912?–65), born Alex/Aleck Ford, later Miller, was a distinctive blues harmonica player, singer and songwriter who went by a variety of stage names including Rice Miller and Little Boy Blue, the latter inspiring the name of Mick Jagger's starter band. He settled on Sonny Boy Williamson, a name already taken by a better-known Chicago blues singer and harmonica player. Historians therefore sometimes refer to him as Sonny Boy Williamson II. When he moved to Memphis, he lived with Howlin' Wolf, taught him to play harmonica, married Wolf's half-sister Mae, and ran his own radio show. He began recording in 1951, and rose to prominence as a member of Elmore James's Chicago-based band.

Recording for Chess Records, who had inherited his earlier contract, he achieved fame and relative fortune from some seventy songs. He toured Europe during the 1960s, recording with the Yardbirds and the Animals. A pre-Led Zeppelin Robert Plant is rumoured to have stolen one of Williamson's harmonicas during one of those British shows. He's not going to tell us, is he. Famous numbers include 'Don't Start Me Talkin'', 'One Way Out' and 'Bring It On Home'. Notable is Chess's 1972 compilation of his work, *This Is My Story*.

Muddy Waters (1913–83) was born McKinley Morganfield, somewhere in the state of Mississippi. Accounts vary. He acquired his nickname as an infant, being fond of playing in the mudslide-y Deer Creek. He added 'Waters' in his teens when he started performing. The good Baptist blues singer-songwriter and musician rose to fame as 'The Father of Modern Chicago Blues'. Hailed for his recordings of blues classics 'I Just Want to Make Love to You', 'Hoochie Coochie Man' and 'I'm Ready', he shocked trad jazz and folk enthusiasts on his first visit to England in 1958 with his squealing electric guitar and rocking blues. He inspired the UK and European blues revival, and remains a major influence on rock'n'roll. When he returned to Britain four years later armed with an old acoustic, it was to find that his followers had gone electric and were in the process of outdoing him.

The Rolling Stones named themselves after Muddy's 1950 recording 'Rollin' Stone', a variation on the Delta classic 'Catfish Blues'. As Keith remarked, Muddy's was 'the most powerful music I had ever heard – and the most expressive … When you think of some dopey, spotty seventeen-year-old from Dartford who wants to be Muddy Waters – and there were a lot of us – in a way, very pathetic, but in another way, very heartwarming.'

Willie Dixon (1915–92) started life in Vicksburg, Mississippi. The blues musician, singer-songwriter, producer and arranger is reckoned to be the most influential musician in the shaping of post-World War II Chicago blues. He played double bass and guitar. His most famous songs 'Hoochie Coochie Man', 'I Just Want to Make Love to You', 'Spoonful' and 'My Babe' influenced artists all over the world. 'Little Red Rooster', a blues standard first recorded by Howlin' Wolf for Chess in 1961, was covered by the Stones as their fifth UK single in 1964. It gave them a No. 1 and was the first blues song to top the British charts. The Stones' cover left the world in no doubt as to what the blues are really about. Clue? Three across. Dixon remains a significant figure in the transition from blues to rock'n'roll.

Elmore James (1918–63) was born Elmore Brooks in Richland,

Holmes County, Mississippi. He started out with a diddley bow, the one-stringed instrument so pivotal to the evolution of the blues sound. A blues guitarist, singer-songwriter and bandleader, he was known as 'the King of the Slide Guitar' and for songs such as 'My Bleeding Heart', 'The Sky's Crying' and 'Stranger Blues'. James was a massive influence on the Stones. When he first heard him, Brian Jones said 'it was like the earth shuddered and stopped on its axis'. Bill Wyman confirmed that James was 'the single most important reason for the formation of the Rolling Stones', while Rod Stewart named him as a major influence on his singing style.

Elmore admitted to having picked up his 'Dust My Broom' lick from Robert Johnson himself, electrifying and injecting it with more muscle. He customised amps in order to wring distortion and feedback from them, chasing 'a sound louder than God'. Sonic manipulation was in. Keith Richards must have had Elmore in mind when he plugged in Nashville engineer Glen Snoddy's Gibson Maestro FZ1 Fuzz-Tone and played 'Satisfaction'.

Jimmy Reed (1925–76), originally Mathis James Reed, arrived in Dunleith, Mississippi. He started out busking and found his way to paid engagements in Chicago, before serving in the US Navy during the Second World War. This popular electric blues musician gifted the world many cherished songs, including 'Honest I Do', 'Big Boss Man' and 'Bright Lights, Big City' – the title being borrowed by author Jay McInerney for his seminal, second-person 1984 novel about life in New York during that decade. Reed toured Europe in 1968, as part of the American Folk Blues Festival.

The Stones performed Jimmy's hits during their earliest outings, for example 'Ain't That Lovin' You Baby', 'The Sun is Shining' (which they also performed at Altamont), 'Bright Lights, Big City' and 'Shame, Shame, Shame'. They recorded 'Honest I Do' for their debut album *The Rolling Stones* in 1964. Their 2016 covers-only *Blue & Lonesome* album featured a sublimely soulful rendition of Reed's 'Little Rain'. It has been said that they felt the presence of Brian Jones while they were in the studio recording it. The song was one of Brian's all-time favourites.

Little Walter (1925 or '1930–68) started life as Marion Walter Jacobs in Marksville, Louisiana. The 'king of all post-war blues harpists' and the 'father of modern blues and blues rock harmonica' learned to play the harmonica as a child, left school before his twelfth birthday and was on the road doing odd jobs and busking, from New Orleans to Memphis to St Louis by the time he was sixteen. He learned from the masters, including Sonny Boy Williamson II. Reaching Chicago in 1946, He took guitar work where he could but found himself in demand primarily as a harmonica player. He was one of the first to hold a small microphone in the palm of his hand next to the harmonica, to project his playing. Amplification allowed him to experiment with sonic effects hitherto unheard from the instrument. He joined Muddy Waters's band in 1948, and within two years was playing both acoustically and amplified electronically on Muddy's recordings.

His first No. 1 hit, 'Juke', remains the only harmonica instrumental ever to top the chart. Many hits followed. An angst-ridden alcoholic, he was often in trouble, and his popularity waned towards the end of the 1950s. He toured Europe in 1964 and 1967. But a claim that he had toured the UK with the Stones in 1964 is denied by Keith Richards.

Chuck Berry (1926–2017) was born Charles Edward Anderson Berry in St. Louis, Missouri. The singer-songwriter and guitarist looms large as 'the Father of Rock and Roll' (although Little Richard claimed the distinction). Inspired to pursue a career in music by T-Bone Walker, an early pioneer of electric blues, Chuck met Muddy Waters in Chicago in 1955 and recorded with Leonard Chess at Chess Records. When Chess cajoled Chuck into reimagining the old country fiddle tune 'Ida Red' as 'Maybellene', he had a hunch. 'Roll Over Beethoven', 'Rock and Roll Music', 'Sweet Little Sixteen', 'Johnny B. Goode', 'No Particular Place to Go' and 'My Ding-a-Ling' followed. He did time for trafficking an under-age Apache waitress to work at his St Louis nightclub, and for having sex with her. Sentenced to five years, he appealed, got the sentence down to three and wound up serving eighteen months. His final single ahead of his incarceration was 'Come On', later covered by the Stones. Their and other versions of his songs kept his name alive while he languished behind bars.

He resumed recording on release, and toured the UK to wild acclaim in 1964. His return to Britain the following year was less incendiary. He continued to tour, and performed at the White House for Jimmy Carter in 1979. Then the IRS caught up with him over evasion of income tax. Back to the slammer. Later years were dogged by scandal. He was accused of filming women in the bathroom of a restaurant he owned, and of drug possession. Video footage emerged of him in scatological compromise with an unknown female. On his ninetieth birthday he announced *Chuck*, his first new studio album for thirty-eight years. He died the same year.

The Beatles famously admired him and covered his songs, notably 'Rock and Roll Music', 'Roll Over Beethoven' and 'Memphis Tennessee'. The Stones were more assiduous, pumping out their takes on 'Around and Around', 'Bye Bye Johnnie', 'Carol', 'Let It Rock', 'Little Queenie', 'Talkin' About You', 'You Can't Catch Me' and more, as well as 'Come On'. Though many identify Berry by his 'duck walk' and 'a coupla crackin' toons', his contributions to the genre are immense. For what would a rock band be without a posturing frontman, signature guitar riffs and epic songs?

Bo Diddley (1928–2008), born Ellas Otha Bates in McComb, Mississippi, and later became Ellas McDaniel. His adoptive family relocated to Chicago. His love of music stemmed from his involvement with the Baptist church. He played trombone and violin, the latter so well that he was invited to join the church's orchestra. Inspired by music he came across at a nearby Pentecostal church, he switched to guitar. His performing name remains something of a mystery. Although several individuals claimed to have coined the nickname, 'Bo Diddley' may simply have been a reversal of the name of the old one-stringed instrument the diddley bow.

He favoured African rhythms and a hambone rhythm that were dubbed 'the Bo Diddley beat', and which would later become a hallmark of hip hop, rock and pop. He played an unusual, one-off rectangular guitar of his own design, made for him by Gretsch, which had a rare resonance and sound. As a guitarist, singer-songwriter and producer, he remains an important figure in music's evolution from the blues to rock'n'roll. Many artists admired and were influenced by him, not least Buddy Holly, Elvis Presley, the Beatles, the Animals, the Clash and the Rolling Stones. He performed as part of a 1963 UK concert tour with the Everly Brothers, Little Richard and the fledgling Stones. He regrouped with the latter on their 1994 concert broadcast of *Voodoo Lounge,* performing his song 'Who Do You Love?' Said Mick Jagger after his death, 'He was a wonderful, original musician who was an enormous force in music and was a big influence on the Rolling Stones. He was very generous to us in our early years, and we learned a lot from him.'

*

Music seemed to speed up during the 1950s. Rock'n'roll grew dominant, but the roots were still there: gospel, country, blues. Teenagers and the electric guitar became rock's primary forces. In August 1952, Big Mama Thornton recorded the twelve-bar blues song 'Hound Dog', the work of black culture fans Jerry Leiber and Mike Stoller. Her only hit, it sold more than half a million copies. Elvis Presley's multi-chart-topping effort came four years later, one of the best-selling singles ever. He championed rockabilly, a variation on the rhythm-and-blues-meets-country theme. His uninhibited sexual performances caused outrage. Presley, Chuck Berry, Little Richard, Jerry Lee Lewis, Gene Vincent, Bo Diddley, Big Joe Turner and Bill Haley and his Comets seized the reins. In March 1955, the film *Blackboard Jungle,* showcasing twenty-eight-year-old Bahamian-American future Oscar winner Sidney Poitier, made stars of Haley and his band, and 'Rock Around the Clock' entered the songbook. Clean-cut Pat Boone covered black R&B hits, bleaching them for mainstream radio. Though its pioneers were black, rock'n'roll gained traction as a 'white' genre.

Satellite Records was founded in 1957, later evolving into Stax and its Volt subsidiary. Southern soul and Memphis soul were born. Here was the home of interracial band Booker T. & the M.G.'s and Otis Redding, and later of Isaac Hayes, the Staples Singers, and the Dramatics. Black American entrepreneur Berry Gordy Jr founded Tamla Records in 1959, which evolved into the Motown Record Corporation the following year. Motown's R&B-to-pop-crossover template went down in history as the most important development in sixties American music, performing a vital role in racial integration. But despite becoming the most successful black-owned business in the United States, many of its artists and those of other labels soon stood accused of racial betrayal for 'not being black enough'.

Elvis was drafted into the US Army in 1958, and was never the same again. The music, some of it, died on 3 February 1959 when Buddy Holly, J.P. 'the Big Bopper' Richardson and Ritchie Valens fell out of the sky in a chartered Beechcraft Bonanza in Iowa, soon after take-off from Mason City. They were immortalised by Don McLean in some song.

The Beatles 'invaded' America in 1964, with the Rolling Stones hot on their heels. Both groups promoted the black American sounds they had cut their teeth on. It was the Stones who took the flak for it, finding themselves called out for 'ripping off black music' as a result of their 'white appropriations of black genres'. Criticism was both ironic and erroneous. The Stones implied from the outset that the only distinction among musicians was talent. The scruffy white R&B group was defiant in its carting of coals to Newcastle, a heaving that frequently backfired. Having done more to uphold black musical tradition than any other contemporary act, they were denounced for having become, by default, lukewarm defenders of a heritage they had plundered and restyled for nobody's benefit but their own. Having set out to pay homage to the founders of the blues, they came to find themselves worshipped as the architects of a dimension in which musicians all over the world strove to be them. Take the money and run? Wouldn't you?

*

Pause the 'Honky Tonks', the 'Jumpin' Jacks', the 'Brown Sugars'. Tread back through their more obscure tracks to hear what turned the Stones on in the first place, and what they were getting at: raw, guitar-led blues that throbbed and erupted like sex. You get the picture. A style more rock'n'roll than ever before. Pull up 'Little Red Rooster', their 1964 take on the Willie Dixon standard made classic by Howlin' Wolf three years earlier. Was it phallic or was it farmyard? Jury's still out. The Stones recorded their version at Chess Studios in Chicago, where the original was laid down. That place was a church to these young pretenders. Imagine how overwhelming it must have felt. Listen. Savour blues purist Brian Jones's finest hour, perhaps his greatest-ever slide guitar performance. Sam Cooke did have a hit with a pacier version, but the Stones' rendition was more faithful to the first. Theirs topped the UK chart. 'The reason we recorded "Little Red Rooster" isn't because we want to bring blues to the masses,' insisted Jagger. 'We've been going on and on about the blues, so we thought it was about time we stopped talking and did something about it. We liked that particular song, so we released it.' Fair dos.

Then there's Willie Dixon's evergreen blues number 'I Just Want to Make Love to You'. First recorded by Muddy in 1954, the Stones covered it on their first LP *The Rolling Stones* ten years later. Their version, flogging Keith's frenzied guitar and Brian's flawless harp, serves as a virtual manifesto for the band the Stones would become.

'No Expectations', written by Mick and Keith, the B-side of the original 'Street Fighting Man' single and a track on 1968's *Beggars Banquet,* is as lonesome as they come. Mick's vocal is controlled, sad and accepting. Keith's acoustic rhythm guitar is mournful. The magical tinkling keys are by Nicky Hopkins. But the lament is all Brian's, whose heart-cracking acoustic slide is one of his final contributions to the Stones' oeuvre. Even the lyrics can be interpreted as a shrouded last goodbye to him. He won't pass through here again.

'Midnight Rambler' from 1969's *Let It Bleed* is perhaps better showcased by the live take on *Get Yer Ya-Ya's Out!* of the following year. 'As close to genuine blues as the Rolling Stones ever got'? The statement was hard to disagree with at Madison Square Garden in 2003 when a possessed and dislocated Mick dervished and harmonica'd as if for his life. Keith in blue satin (a back-up green shirt underneath) raised the Mississippi dead, and howled happily. Also on *Let It Bleed*, find their take on Robert Johnson's heart-rending 'Love in Vain'. Controlled and gut-wrenching, it's a little more country than the original. The train left the station, but the Stones are still aboard.

'You Gotta Move' is a traditional African-American spiritual, recorded as a blues song by 'Mississippi' Fred McDowell in 1965. Mick, Keith and the boys went for a more raucous, insistent take with a funereal feel and an alarming closing beat that was otherwise faithful to Fred's, at Muscle Shoals Sound Studio in Sheffield, Alabama in 1969. They included it on 1971's *Sticky Fingers*. 'Right,' said Fred, 'I make the guitar say what I say.' Keith did too.

There's always a favourite. Today, for me, that's 'Ventilator Blues' from 1972's *Exile on Main St.* So Muddy, so so Wolf. Favourite not just because majestic Mick Taylor (on lead) who created the riff is credited as co-writer, for Mick's rare double-tracked vocal, for Keith on slide, for Nicky Hopkins's lightnin' trills or Bobby Keys's weird rhythm which Charlie had to learn by having him clap it; nor for its heavy, seductive, drama-filled, draining tone. This wrings you out. I think it's partly the whole thing of it having been created during the Stones' real-life exile in the dungeons of Villa Nellcôte, Keith's sinister rented mansion in the South of France, where anything went and everything did. That Keith kept a speedboat called *Mandrax* was the size of it.

I wasn't there, of course, but I've been, at times, obsessed with it. The menace and the magic never wane. This song feels like the soundtrack of the entire sojourn; the addictive, hellish vibe of those months captured for posterity on tape. I allow myself a listen sometimes. You don't want to overdo it, it can keep you awake. I wish I'd been there for their only live performance of it, in Canada, on the 1972 North American tour.

*

In October 2015, I flew to Illinois to deliver a lecture at the Fifth Annual Chicago Ideas Week. A break in the busy schedule afforded me a few hours to spend in the city's Art Institute, which houses a masterpiece I'd been longing to see for years. The painting, the first-ever Picasso acquired by an American museum and said to be worth $100 million (it's not for sale) was *The Old Guitarist*: a stark rendition in oils of a decrepit, apparently blind minstrel, strumming his battered instrument on a Barcelona backstreet. It reflects Picasso's own poverty when he painted it, at the age of only twenty-two. Thousands gaze at it each week. They are as enchanted by it as the many who make the pilgrimage to the Paris Louvre to stare at Da Vinci's *Mona Lisa*. I too had contemplated Picasso's guitarist over the years, if only on postcards and in coffee table books. I had never yet set eyes on the genuine article. The painting lured me, for reasons I could not explain. Something told me that once I'd looked at the real thing, I would never feel the same again. In it, I knew, I would find grief and degradation, things that most of us find difficult to confront and process. I was almost afraid to go looking for it. I went anyway.

I found it on the third floor of the Institute's Modern Wing. It was larger than I had expected. I lingered before it for a while, did the rounds and circled back. I was unprepared for its blueness, even though I had known what to expect. I was well aware that it had been painted during Picasso's 'Blue Period', in late 1903/early 1904. I had underestimated the impact that the brownness of the guitar would have – the only other colour Picasso uses here. Which is significant. The lowly instrument leaps out as a symbol of redemption. The picture told me in apparently living oils, in a way that printers' ink could not, that Pablo empathised with the destitute. It also said that the blues would save him. Not the blues of the oils, but the music.

I know now that the painting represents not only worldly poverty, but also emotional dysfunction and hopelessness. By which I mean the dilemma and drive of all who create, including Picasso himself, but especially musicians. It is the perfect depiction of the artist's paradox: art makes him special, but it is the thing that isolates him from the rest of the world. He is incapable of abandoning his art because it is the means by which he survives, the very thing that saves him from doom. He is a slave to it.

I have no idea whether Brian Jones ever got the chance to look at this painting. I'm guessing not. But I think that he of all artists would have identified with Picasso's blue man.

OUT OF TIMELINE

The Stones' thirty studio albums, thirty-three live albums, twenty-nine compilation albums, a hundred and twenty-one singles, three EP singles, thirty-two box sets, forty-eight video albums and seventy-seven music videos, three Grammy Awards and Grammy Lifetime Achievement Award are not all mentioned here. For the sake of simplicity, I have confined myself (give or take) to the thirty studio albums and forty best-known single releases ... with the odd exception of a significant solo album, live recording or compilation. This book being neither Stones encyclopaedia nor definitive work but my personal take, there were no rules. I compiled this chronology as a simple aide-memoire: to give an overview of the sequence, cause and effect of events and occurrences both global and personal, and of significant tours and recordings that shaped the Stones era and underpin their life and times.

*

1930s

24 October 1936   Bill Wyman born William George Perks, Lewisham, South London.

18 July 1938   'Stu' born Ian Andrew Robert Stewart, Pittenweem, East Neuk of Fife, Scotland.

1939–45   World War II.

1940s

2 June 1941   Charlie Watts born Charles Robert Watts, Bloomsbury, London.

28 February 1942   Brian Jones born Lewis Brian Hopkin Jones, Cheltenham, Gloucestershire.

26 July 1943   Mick Jagger born Michael Philip Jagger, Dartford, Kent.

18 December 1943   Keith Richards born, Dartford, Kent.

1 June 1947   Ronnie Wood born Ronald David Wood, Hillingdon, Middlesex.

September 1948   Mick Jagger and Keith Richards enrol at Wentworth Primary School, Dartford. They first get to know each other *c.* 1950.

17 January 1949   Mick Taylor born Michael Kevin Taylor, Welwyn Garden City, Hertfordshire.

1950s

1953   Brian Jones proceeds from his private Dean Close Preparatory School, Cheltenham, to Cheltenham Grammar School.

1954   Mick Jagger passes 11-plus exam, proceeds to Dartford Grammar School. Keith Richards enrols at Dartford Technical School, moving on to Sidcup Art College.

1 November 1955   Vietnam War commences, exacerbated by Cold War hostilities between JFK and Soviet premier Nikita Khrushchev. Direct American involvement continues for eighteen years, until 1973. The war will eventually end in April 1975.

1 December 1955   Rosa Parks, later known as 'the mother of the civil rights movement', is arrested for refusing to yield her bus seat to a white man in Montgomery, Alabama, sparking the Montgomery Bus Boycott.

1960s

1960–73   The era of the sixties counterculture, erupting in reaction to US military intervention in Vietnam, influences songwriters and recording artists for years to come.

July 1960   Mick and Keith renew their acquaintance on a platform at Dartford railway station.

Summer 1961   Armed with seven O Levels and two A Levels, eighteen-year-old Mick leaves school. He later enrols at the London School of Economics to read finance and accounting. Brian Jones, as Elmo Lewis, debuts as a musician at London's Ealing Club. Mick, Keith and Brian become flatmates in a squalid property on Edith Grove in London's Chelsea.

19 March 1962   Bob Dylan releases first, eponymous LP. Initiates anti-war stance, predicting route that contemporary popular music will take.

12 July 1962   Stones' debut gig, at the Marquee Jazz Club, Oxford Street, London.

16–28 October 1962   Cuban Missile Crisis, the closest the world has come to full-scale nuclear war.

21 October 1962   Mick, Keith, Brian, Jimmy Page, Alexis Korner, Paul Jones and John Mayall attend the only UK show of the First American Folk Blues Festival on that year's European tour, at Manchester's Free Trade Hall. This was the first major concert in the UK to feature American bluesmen. They see Howlin' Wolf, Sonny Boy Williamson II and Willie Dixon. Dixon says, 'I left lots of tapes when I was over there in London. I told them anybody who wanted to could go and make a blues song. That's how the Rolling Stones and the Yardbirds got their songs.'

12 December 1962   An early incarnation of the Stones: Mick Jagger Keith Richards, Brian Jones, Ian Stewart, Ricky Fenson and Tony Chapman perform at Keith's alma mater, Sidcup Art College.

12 January 1963   First performance by the classic Stones line-up with Charlie on drums, at the Ealing Club.

2 February 1963   Charlie comes on board as the Stones' staff drummer, the post he will hold for the rest of his life. The Stones' acting manager Giorgio Gomelsky lands them Sunday afternoon residency at Crawdaddy Club, Richmond.

22 March 1963   Beatles' debut LP *Please Please Me* released.

May 1963   Recommended by the Beatles, nineteen-year-old Andrew Loog Oldham becomes the Stones' manager. Gomelsky is backstabbed. After initially trying to copy the Beatles' neat style, Oldham has the brainwave to promote the band as the nasty, dirty antithesis of Liverpool's finest. They sign, favourably, for Decca, famous for having rejected the Beatles. Keith will be billed as 'Richard' on early releases. He later reverts. Stu, an original member of the Stones, is ejected from their line-up at Oldham's behest. He is retained as road manager and pianist.

June 1963   Debut single 'Come On' released.

28 August 1963   Baptist minister Martin Luther King Jr leads a peaceful interracial march in Washington DC of more than two hundred thousand people. On the steps of the Lincoln Memorial in his 'I Have a Dream' speech, he demands equal justice for all.

29 Sep – 3 Nov 1963   Starter British tour, performing Chicago blues and Chuck Berry and Bo Diddley numbers. They are part of a classic 'package tour', this one headlined by the Everly Brothers and Bo Diddley. Little Richard replaces the Everlys along the way. This opportunity to perform alongside some of their earliest idols is priceless. The Stones perform two ten-minute shows at each date. The Pretty Things, an early British R&B group, form at Sidcup Art College. One of its founder members is Dick Taylor, a student at the college and an early Stones bassist.

November 1963   'I Wanna Be Your Man' single, a Lennon-McCartney composition gifted to the Stones, released.

22 November 1963   President John F. Kennedy, thirty-fifth president of the United States, assassinated in Dallas, Texas. He is the eighth sitting president to die in office, and the fourth to be assassinated.

1 January 1964   Stones are the first band to play on BBC's *Top of the Pops* TV chart show, performing 'I Wanna Be Your Man'.

6–27 January 1964   First official British concert tour.

February 1964   'Not Fade Away', a cover of Buddy Holly's Bo Diddley-esque song, released as a single. Oldham, perceiving where the real money lies, directs his boys to write their own songs, which he will produce.

7 February 1964   Beatles touch down in New York for their historic first appearance on CBS TV's *The Ed Sullivan Show* watched by half the population of America. The Stones will soon follow suit, but will make a somewhat different first impression.

8 Feb – 7 Mar 1964   Second British tour.

16 April 1964   Debut LP *The Rolling Stones* released in the UK. The same LP appears in the US as *The Rolling Stones (England's Newest Hit Makers)* on 30 May.

June 1964   'It's All Over Now' released. First UK No. 1 hit. First US tour … in their own words, 'a disaster'. The 5–20 June outing concludes with two shows at New York City's Carnegie Hall. The band appear on The Hollywood Palace variety show, and are mocked by the host, crooner Dean Martin (who might have felt threatened by them).

10–11 June 1964   They record at Chess Studios, Chicago, where they meet some of their idols including Muddy Waters. 'As Tears Go By', sung by seventeen-year-old Marianne Faithfull, released. Written by Mick, Keith and Andrew Oldham, one of their earliest original compositions. Marianne achieves a No. 9 UK hit with it. The Stones later record the song, and perform it live.

2 July 1964   US president Lyndon B. Johnson signs the Civil Rights Act of 1964. To end discrimination based on race, religion, colour and national origin, as proposed by John F. Kennedy in 1963.

1–22 August 1964   Third British tour. They also play one gig in the Netherlands and some concerts in the Channel Islands.

5 Sep – 11 Oct 1964   Fourth British tour.

14 October 1964   Charlie Watts marries girlfriend Shirley Ann Shepherd, a sculpture student at the Royal College of Art. They remain together for nearly fifty-seven years, until his death in 2021.

17 October 1964   Second US LP *12 X 5* released in America only.

25 October 1964   Stones' first appearance on *The Ed Sullivan Show* in the US, following which he bans them. 'I promise you they'll never be back on our show,' declares Sullivan. 'It took me seventeen years to build this show, and I'm not going to have it destroyed in a matter of weeks.' The host re-books them to appear the following year.

30 Oct – 15 Nov 1964   Second US tour.

November 1964   'Little Red Rooster' single released.

1965–67   The Stones' heyday: their singles chart success will have peaked by the end of the decade.

6–8 January 1965   They perform their first Irish dates.

15 January 1965   *The Rolling Stones No. 2* LP, recorded at Chess Studios Chicago and RCA Studios LA, released UK.

22 Jan – 16 Feb 1965   Their first Far East tour is a package featuring Roy Orbison, the Newbeats, and Ray Columbus and the Invaders. They visit Australia, New Zealand and Singapore.

February 1965   'The Last Time' single released, second UK No. 1, US No. 9. It is the first Jagger/Richards composition to make it to No. 1 on the UK chart. The songwriting pennies drop.

13 February 1965   *The Rolling Stones, Now!* LP released US.

5–18 March 1965   British tour.

26 Mar – 2 Apr 1965   Scandinavian tour.

16–18 April 1965   The band play an Easter weekend 'mini-residency' at L'Olympia, Paris. Twenty-three-year-old Italian-born German/ Swedish/Swiss model Anita Pallenberg is living in the city, attends one of their shows, and meets Brian for the first time when a group of beautiful young hipsters goes partying afterwards. In later life, Anita never references that first encounter, preferring to claim that she and Brian first crossed paths in Munich, five months later.

23 Apr – 29 May 1965   US tour.

2 May 1965   Stones' second appearance on *The Ed Sullivan Show*, performing 'The Last Time': the first time they perform a Jagger/ Richards original on the show.

June 1965   '(I Can't Get No) Satisfaction', recorded during the US tour, released. No. 1 UK, US, Germany, Netherlands, Australia; No. 3 France and Canada. Their first international No. 1 hit and a global commercial success. Andrew Loog Oldham brings American manager Allen Klein on board, to re-negotiate Stones' contract with Decca. Oldham has a rock superstar drug habit. Klein gradually assumes control.

15–18 June 1965   Scottish dates.

24–29 June 1965   Further Scandinavian dates.

30 July (UK)/24 Sep (US) 1965   *Out of Our Heads* LP, produced by Andrew Loog Oldham, released.

September 1965   'Get Off of My Cloud' single released.

3–4 September 1965   Second Irish tour.

11–17 September 1965   European tour. At Munich's Circus Krone Bau, the Stones topping bill featuring the Spencer Davis Group and the

Troggs before a riotous audience. Brian officially meets Anita Pallenberg for the first time. The encounter takes place backstage, the model armed with hashish and amyl nitrate.

24 Sep – 17 Oct 1965   British tour.

29 Oct – 5 Dec 1965   American tour.

December 1965   'As Tears Go By' single Stones version released.

4 December 1965   *December's Children (And Everybody's)* LP, produced by Andrew Loog Oldham, released US.

February 1966   '19th Nervous Breakdown' single released.

18 Feb – 1 Mar 1966   Australasian tour.

4 March 1966   Brian, Anita, Mick and Paul McCartney attend the twenty-first birthday party of Irish Guinness heir The Hon. Tara Browne on the family estate at Luggala, County Wicklow.

26 Mar – 5 Apr 1966   European tour.

15 Apr – 2 Jul 1966   *Aftermath* LP released.

May 1966   'Paint It, Black' single released. No. 1 UK, US, Netherlands, Switzerland, Australia; No. 2 Germany; No. 7 France.

24 Jun – 28 Jul 1966   US tour.

July 1966   'Mother's Little Helper' and 'Lady Jane' singles released. The former is one of the first-ever pop songs to address the problem of prescription medication abuse.

September 1966   'Have You Seen Your Mother, Baby, Standing in the Shadow?' single released. The first Stones single to feature brass horns. The original American sleeve shows them dressed in drag, eighteen years before Queen caused controversy by dragging up for their single 'I Want to Break Free' (1984). 'Have You Seen Your Mother …' is supported by one of the first official pop videos (Queen do not have that distinction with 'Bohemian Rhapsody' either), directed by counterculture luminary Peter Lorrimer Whitehead.

23 Sep – 9 Oct 1966   British tour. Opened by Ike & Tina Turner, the Kings of Rhythm Orchestra, the Yardbirds and Peter Jay and the New Jaywalkers.

17 December 1966   Driving his (yellow/turquoise/light blue/white, reports vary) Lotus Elan through South Kensington with his nineteen-year-old girlfriend Suki Potier, father-of-two Tara Browne, who is under the influence, crashes at high speed and is killed. John Lennon commemorates him in the Beatles song 'A Day In The Life'. He will later deny that the song is specifically about the Guinness heir, saying that Tara was 'just in his mind' when he wrote the lyrics.

In October 2021, ahead of publication of his autobiographical two-volume work *The Lyrics*, Paul McCartney again claims that *he* wrote the opening lines, not Lennon. Having previously stated that the song was about a politician, he now supports John's explanation that the lyrics were inspired by Browne. 'I wrote about him in "A Day In The Life",' says Macca. 'He blew his mind out in a car/He didn't notice that the lights had changed'. It later emerges that the car was not Browne's: he worked with Chelsea Lotus dealer Len Street, and the car was one Street had in the garage at the time. Potier escapes unhurt. She will become involved with Brian Jones, moving into his Sussex home, Cotchford Farm. After Brian's death, she will marry Robert Ho and will live in Hong Kong, only to die in a car crash while on holiday in Portugal, when the couple's youngest daughter is only two.

1967   Abortion and homosexuality legalised in the UK. Evolving attitudes lead to various Acts of Parliament. The 1967 Sexual Offences Act, decriminalising homosexual activity between consenting males over twenty-one, and the 1967 Abortion Act, legalising abortion in certain circumstances, will be followed by the 1969 Divorce Reform Act and the 1970 Equal Pay Act. The band's drug use is becoming excessive. British Sunday newspaper the *News of the World* is on their case. The first instalment of a special exposé goes for the jugulars of Pete Townshend, the Moody Blues, Donovan and Ginger Baker. The second instalment, published 5 February 1967, focuses on the Stones. But the paper mistakes Brian Jones for Mick in the feature. Mick sues for libel. American *Rolling Stone* magazine launches, infuriating Mick Jagger, both for stealing his band's name and for putting the Beatles on the cover three times in one year. Mick threatens to sue, but is placated with ownership of a new British edition. It folds within months, after an interview with Bob Dylan is heralded on the front cover with his name spelled 'Bob Dillon'.

January 1967 'Let's Spend the Night Together' and 'Ruby Tuesday' singles released. The latter No. 3 in UK, No. 1 in US.

20 Jan – 11 Feb 1967 *Between the Buttons* LP released. Andrew Loog Oldham's final album as Stones' producer.

9 Feb – 23 Oct 1967 *Their Satanic Majesties Request* album recorded at Olympic Studios, London. Following the departure of Andrew Loog Oldham, the band self-produces. The recording process is a slapdash, disorganised free-for-all that the band later acknowledges.

12 February 1967 Sussex police raid Keith's house Redlands. No arrests during the raid. Mick, Keith and art dealer Robert Fraser later charged with drug offences. Andrew Loog Oldham, terrified of his own likely fate, flees to the US and leaves them to it. The raid becomes infamous as 'The Mars Bar Incident', and for Mick's girlfriend Marianne Faithfull being attired in nothing but a fur rug.

March 1967 Mick and Marianne, Keith, Brian and his girlfriend Anita Pallenberg and friends travel to Morocco. Brian abuses Anita, who switches allegiance to Keith. Keith and Anita become the danger-couple for the next twelve years.

25 Mar – 17 Apr 1967 European tour: the last Stones tour with Brian Jones, and one of the first times a Western rock band performs in Eastern Europe. On 13 April they perform two shows at the Palace of Culture and Science in Warsaw, Poland, where the fans riot. Visiting Soviet officials are not impressed, and the Stones will not return to the Eastern Bloc for many years. Other destinations on this tour include Greece and Italy.

10 May 1967   Brian's house raided by police. Brian arrested and charged with cannabis possession. Three of the five Stones are now facing drugs charges. Mick and Keith are both tried at the end of June. Mick sentenced to three months behind bars for possession of amphetamines. Keith found guilty of allowing cannabis to be smoked in his home, and sentenced to one year. Both are incarcerated, only to be released the next day on bail, pending appeal. *The Times* publishes celebrated piece by editor William Rees-Mogg, headlined 'Who breaks a butterfly upon a wheel?', suggesting that the two Stones had been harshly dealt with because of their fame.

Jun – Jul 1967   Monterey International Music Festival, the world's first official Rockfest, staged over three days in California. The Who and Eric Burdon and the Animals represent the UK. The Beatles and the Stones are conspicuously absent. During the Summer of Love, 100,000 hippies descend on San Francisco's Haight-Ashbury district. The hippie revolution is born.

31 July 1967   Keith's conviction overturned in court of appeal, and Mick's sentence reduced to conditional discharge.

November 1967   Brian tried and sentenced to a prison term. During his December appeal, receives a £1,000 fine, placed on probation for three years, and ordered to seek medical help.

December 1967   'She's a Rainbow' single from *Their Satanic Majesties Request* released.

8 December 1967   *Their Satanic Majesties Request* LP released simultaneously in UK and US. It is panned by the critics. The newly-psychedelic Stones are accused of trying to emulate the Beatles and their *Sgt. Pepper's Lonely Hearts Club Band*. Its cover art is by Michael Cooper, who also created the cover for *Sgt. Pepper*.

1968   Stones create a mobile recording studio in a van, enabling them to record wherever and whenever they want. 'The mobile' is also used by other artists, including Led Zeppelin and Deep Purple. Bavarian aristocrat Prince Rupert Loewenstein (1933–2014) is engaged as the band's new financial manager, acting for them for nearly forty years until 2007. He would later be credited with transforming the Stones into 'a global brand and one of the world's richest bands'. Prince Rupert packs them off into tax exile in the South of France, funnels their earnings through companies in the Netherlands, and persuades them to rehearse in Canada rather than the US to reduce their tax bill. Only in the 1980s will the Stones make 'proper money'. Jagger will be outraged and distraught when Prince Rupert publishes his autobiography in 2013, in which he reveals highly personal details about the band's financial affairs. He dies of Parkinson's disease the following year, aged eighty.

17 Mar – 25 Jul 1968   *Beggars Banquet* album recorded, at Olympic Studios London and Sunset Sound LA. The first Stones album produced by Jimmy Miller, who will reshape their sound into the early seventies, it is also the last Stones album to be released during Brian Jones's lifetime. 'Sympathy for the Devil' is the stand-out.

May 1968   'Jumpin' Jack Flash' single released. No. 1 UK and Germany and on some US charts; No. 2 Netherlands, France, Switzerland and Australia.

Summer 1968   Mick films controversial crime drama *Performance*, co-starring James Fox, Anita Pallenberg and teenage French stray Michèle Breton. Anita, now Keith's girlfriend, performs sex scenes with Mick and a threesome with Breton, which she later admits were consummated. Keith suspects so during filming and is deranged with jealousy, his relationship with Mick suffering as a result. The film's graphic sexual content and violence render it 'too shocking for the sixties', and it is shelved until 1970. It is later claimed that Breton, who is embroiled in a ménage-à-trois with director Cammell and his wife, was under the age of consent during the sex scenes. Anita becomes addicted to heroin during the production. Donald Cammell abandons Breton in Paris. He will shoot himself dead in 1996. Keith never forgives Donald for the betrayal in directing actual sex between Mick and Anita. He will later describe *Performance* as 'the best work Cammell ever did, except for shooting himself'.

August 1968 'Street Fighting Man' single released.

Nov 1968 – Nov 1969 Recording of the *Let It Bleed* album, at Olympic Studios London, Elektra and Sunset Sound LA. Notable for the implosion, collapse and firing of Brian Jones during the album's creation.

6 December 1968 *Beggars Banquet* LP released UK & US. Country and blues-inspired, it represents a return to their roots.

11 December 1968 *The Rolling Stones Rock and Roll Circus* concert show performed and filmed in Wembley, West London, but not released until 1996. A DVD version will appear in 2004.

February 1969 'Sympathy for the Devil' single released.

22 Mar 1969 – 31 Oct 1970 *Sticky Fingers* album recorded in Muscle Shoals Sound Studios Alabama, Olympic Studios and Trident Studios, London, and Stargroves, Mick's mansion, Newbury, Berkshire. Produced by Jimmy Miller.

June 1969 Brian is melting from the band. His drug use is destroying him. He cannot get a US visa. Mick and Keith visit him at his home to inform him that they want him to leave the band. Brian agrees to leave the Rolling Stones.

28 June 1969 Stonewall Riots in New York City denote dawn of modern gay rights movement.

July 1969 'Honky Tonk Women' single released. No. 1 UK, US, Switzerland, Australia; No. 2 Germany.

3 July 1969 Brian drowns in his pool in mysterious circumstances at Cotchford Farm, East Sussex, aged twenty-seven. Conspiracy theories rage to this day, about what was probably not murder but a tragic accident.

5 July 1969 The Stones in the Park free outdoor festival in Hyde Park, London, before an audience of 'between a quarter and half a million'. The pre-planned show is now billed as a tribute to Brian. Guitarist Mick Taylor makes his live debut as Brian's replacement. The Stones are introduced for the first time as 'The Greatest Rock'n'Roll Band in the World'.

20 July 1969   NASA astronaut Commander Neil Armstrong becomes the first human to walk on the moon during the Apollo 11 space mission.

15–18 August 1969   Woodstock Music & Art Fair, Bethel, New York. The Stones are not available.

30–31 August 1969   Isle of Wight Festival, starring Bob Dylan. Beatles John Lennon, George Harrison and Ringo Starr attend, along with Keith Richards and Eric Clapton.

7 Nov – 6 Dec 1969   US tour, supported by Ike & Tina Turner, Terry Reid and B.B. King, substituted by Chuck Berry on some of the dates. Later described as 'history's first mythic rock'n'roll tour'.

5 December 1969   *Let It Bleed* LP released UK and US. Their last album of the sixties and the first of five consecutive No. 1 albums in the UK. 'Gimme Shelter', 'Midnight Rambler' and 'You Can't Always Get What You Want' feature, with choral intro by the London Bach Choir.

6 December 1969   Altamont Speedway Free Festival, Altamont, N. California, marking 'the end of the sixties'. The Stones perform here at the conclusion of their US tour. Black fan Meredith Hunter is murdered, and several other fans die. It will be described as 'the most shameful episode in rock history'. Allen Klein is fired.

1970s

1970   The Stones launch their own company. A legal settlement later grants Klein the rights to most of the band's songs recorded prior to 1971.

30 Aug – 9 Oct 1970   European tour.

4 September 1970   *Get Yer Ya-Ya's Out!: The Rolling Stones in Concert* album released. Widely considered to be the greatest live album of all time.

18 September 1970   Jimi Hendrix dies in London apartment hotel, aged twenty-seven.

4 October 1970   Janis Joplin dies in Los Angeles Landmark Motor Hotel, aged twenty-seven.

4–26 March 1971   UK tour.

April 1971   The Stones relocate to the South of France as tax exiles, all departing before 5 April, the end of the British tax year. There ensues a six-month house party at Keith's rented mansion Villa Nellcôte, the original hazy summer of sex, drugs and rock'n'roll. With the help of their mobile studio, Keith's home from home becomes their recording base. The result will be *Exile on Main St.*, arguably their greatest album. How they got it together to record it at all remains a mystery. The band have been tax exiles ever since. The UK is no longer their primary residence. Their holding company Promogroup maintains offices in the Netherlands and the Caribbean. It is reported that they have paid a mere 1.6% tax on their total earnings of £242 million over the past twenty years.

April 1971   'Brown Sugar' single from *Sticky Fingers* released. No. 1 US, Netherlands, Switzerland, Canada; No. 2 UK.

23 April 1971   *Sticky Fingers* LP released. First album on their own Rolling Stones label. First public outing of the lip and tongue logo: one of the most recognisable logos (not just pop logos) in history, used on everything they have produced (reworked a little) ever since. The first of eight consecutive No. 1 studio albums in the US. Andy Warhol designs the cover, which features a suggestive working zip.

12 May 1971   Mick Jagger marries pregnant Nicaraguan actress Bianca Pérez-Mora Macías in Saint-Tropez, France, in a star-studded bunfight of a wedding that will later prompt the bride to reflect that her marriage ended on her wedding day. In 1978, after seven years, Mrs Jagger files for divorce on grounds of adultery.

June 1971   'Wild Horses' single released.

3 July 1971 On second anniversary of Brian Jones's death, The Doors frontman Jim Morrison found dead in his bath in Paris. He was twenty-seven.

April 1972 'Tumbling Dice' single from *Exile on Main St.* released.

12 May 1972 *Exile on Main St.* album released, on Mick's first wedding anniversary.

Jun – Jul 1972 US and Canada tour: a huge US tour to promote the new album, which becomes known as the 'American STP' (Stones Touring Party). The outing is captured in two films, the never-officially-released *Cocksucker Blues*, and *Ladies & Gentlemen: The Rolling Stones* (released 1974).

July 1972 'Rocks Off' single released.

November 1972 The band begin recording at Dynamic Sound Studios, Kingston, Jamaica, for the album *Goats Head Soup* and material for what will become the *It's Only Rock 'n Roll* album: also recorded at Musicland Studios, Munich, West Germany (November 1973, February–March 1974), and the Wick (Ronnie's house), Richmond, Surrey (December 1973). Produced by Jagger and Richards, aka the Glimmer Twins.

18 Jan – 27 Feb 1973 Pacific tour, which is really an extension of the STP. Thanks to drug convictions, the Stones are refused permission to perform in Japan, and are almost banned from Australia.

April 1973 'You Can't Always Get What You Want' single from *Let It Bleed* released.

August 1973 'Angie' single from *Goats Head Soup* released. No. 1 US, Netherlands, France, Switzerland, Australia, Canada; No. 5 UK and Germany.

31 August 1973 *Goats Head Soup* album released.

1 September – 19 October 1973 European tour.

February 1974 'Star Star' single released.

July 1974 'It's Only Rock 'n Roll (But I Like It)' single released.

18 October 1974 *It's Only Rock 'n Roll* album released. Produced by Jagger and Richards, as the Glimmer Twins. No. 2 UK; No. 1 US.

December 1974 Mick Taylor quits the Stones acrimoniously, to pursue a solo career.

5 Dec 1974 – 4 Apr 1975 The band record their next album *Black and Blue* at Musicland Munich, in their mobile studio in Rotterdam, and at Mountain Studios in Montreux. Various guitarists contribute, including Peter Frampton, Jeff Beck, Robert A. Johnson, Wayne Perkins, Rory Gallagher and Shuggie Otis. Some do not realise that they are being auditioned. Ronnie Wood does, and gets the job, joining the Stones as a salaried employee until the early 1990s, when he is welcomed into their business partnership.

1 Jun – 8 Aug 1975 Tour of the Americas. The production features a gigantic phallus, and Mick swinging out over the audience on the end of a rope. Their first tour with new guitarist Ronnie Wood.

April 1976 'Fool to Cry' single released.

23 April 1976 *Black and Blue* album released.

28 Apr – 23 Jun 1976 European tour, including two dates in Yugoslavia: their second visit to a communist country after 1967. One of the band's most challenging tours to date: in Paris, a boyfriend with an axe to grind runs at Mick with a gun. In Munich, the Baader-Meinhof terrorist group threaten to blow up the Olympiahalle where the Stones are playing; backstage in London, HM the Queen's sister is papped, fuelling rumours of an affair between Mick and Princess Margaret; Keith is on bail for drug possession after crashing his car on the M1 motorway at 100mph. Bets are taken that Richards won't survive beyond Knebworth.

6 June 1976 Keith's third child Tara Jo Jo Gunne dies aged ten weeks. In show-must-go-on denial, Keith performs live on stage with the Stones that night, as scheduled.

21 August 1976   The band play before two hundred thousand fans at Knebworth, a Tudor stately home in Hertfordshire that stages rock concerts. Their gig concludes at 7am the following day.

1977   Mick begins an extramarital affair with American supermodel Jerry Hall, the girlfriend of his rock star friend Bryan Ferry. Mick and Jerry will marry in a Hindu ceremony in Bali in 1990. When Jerry, who has given Mick four children, attempts to divorce him for adultery on discovering that he has fathered a son by Brazilian model Luciana Gimenez Morad, the marriage is declared invalid under British and Indonesian law.

24 February 1977   Keith and family arrive in Toronto to join recording sessions for live album *Love You Live*; detained by customs when drugs paraphernalia is found; Anita later arrested; heroin found in Keith's room. Charged with importation of narcotics, he faces a prison sentence of seven years to life. The prosecution later accept that he had not imported the drugs, but had purchased them locally. The band perform two gigs in Toronto. Scandal erupts when First Lady Margaret Trudeau, wife of the Canadian Prime Minister, is caught partying with the boys into the night. Anita is fined for possession. Keith's case lingers for a year, concluding in a suspended sentence and an order to give two free concerts for the Canadian National Institute for the Blind. It proves a turning point for Keith, who finally resolves to relinquish his heroin habit. It is another nail in the coffin of his relationship with Anita. Ronnie gets together with Jo.

16 August 1977   Elvis Presley dies at his home in Memphis, Tennessee, aged forty-two. Mick is living the high life, becoming a fixture at New York City's legendary nightclub Studio 54. With the rise of punk, the Stones are beginning to be seen as passé dinosaurs.

1978   The tables turn with their new album *Some Girls*, winning the Stones a new young audience.

May 1978   'Miss You' single from *Some Girls* released. No. 1 US, France, Canada; No. 3 UK.

9 June 1978   *Some Girls* album released, No. 1 in US; No. 2 UK.

10 Jun – 26 Jul 1978   US tour, a back-to-basics tour featuring classic Stones and songs co-written with Ronnie Wood. Billed as the 'Farewell Tour', as it was intended to be. Guests and openers include reggae star Peter Tosh, Linda Ronstadt, Patti Smith, Foreigner, Etta James and the Doobie Brothers.

September 1978   'Beast of Burden' single from *Some Girls* released.

22 Jan – 19 Oct 1979   Recording of the next album *Emotional Rescue*, at Compass Point Studios, Nassau, Bahamas, Pathé Marconi, Paris, and Electric Lady, New York City. Produced by the Glimmer Twins (Mick'n'Keef). Recording sessions expose a deep rift between them.

20 July 1979   Seventeen-year-old Scott Cantrell shoots himself dead in Anita Pallenberg's bed in an apparent game of Russian roulette, with a gun owned by Keith, at the South Salem, New York home of the couple. It marks the end of Keith's relationship with Anita, who is unable to quit heroin.

1980s
June 1980   'Emotional Rescue' single released. No. 1 Canada.

20 June 1980   *Emotional Rescue* album released, tops the charts in six countries including US, UK and Canada.

September 1980   'She's So Cold' single released.

8 December 1980   John Lennon assassinated in New York, aged forty.

August 1981   'Start Me Up' single from *Tattoo You* released.

24 August 1981   *Tattoo You* album released, reaching No. 1 in US; No. 2 in UK. This and *Some Girls* become their best-selling albums. The former has been a long time in the making, consisting primarily of outtakes from studio recordings dating back to 1972.

25 Sep – 19 Dec 1981 US stadium and arena tour, their longest, biggest and wildest ever, and the highest-grossing tour that year, earning $50 million in ticket sales. Two million fans attend. The show on 5 December in New Orleans sets the indoor concert attendance record that holds for thirty-three years.

26 May – 25 Jul 1982 European tour: their last for seven years. During the West Berlin gig on 8 June, thousands of balloons are released, prompting Nena guitarist Carlo Karges to write the song '99 Luftballons'/'99 Red Balloons'.

12 July 1982 The Stones' twentieth anniversary. By the end of the year, they will have left Atlantic Records for a $50 million, four-album deal with CBS Records: at the time, the biggest record deal in history. Mick and Keith fall out bitterly over Mick's separate solo deal, also with CBS.

Nov 1982 – Aug 1983 Recording sessions for the album *Undercover*, at Pathé Marconi, Paris, Compass Point, Nassau, and the Hit Factory, New York City. Mick and Keith, aka the Glimmers, are at odds creatively. Chris Kimsey produces, which is just as well. He has long experience of the Stones, having been an engineer on *Sticky Fingers*, *Some Girls* and *Emotional Rescue*, and having assisted Mick on *Tattoo You*. Many guest artists are drawn into the mix. This will be their first release of all new recordings in the 1980s.

November 1983 'Undercover of the Night' single released.

7 November 1983 *Undercover* album released: the final album on Rolling Stones Records to be distributed by Atlantic.

18 December 1983 On his fortieth birthday, Keith marries American model Patti Hansen. The couple will have two daughters.

21 February 1984 Bill Wyman meets thirteen-year-old schoolgirl Mandy Smith at the *Daily Mirror*-sponsored Rock and Pop Awards at the Lyceum on the Strand, London. They become an item.

2 January 1985 Ronnie Wood marries long-time partner Jo Karslake.

February 1985   *She's the Boss*, Mick's solo debut, released, heralded by the single 'Just Another Night'. Both single and album are global hits. Keith later compares the album to *Mein Kampf* (Adolf Hitler's autobiographical manifesto, 1925): 'Everybody has a copy, but nobody listened to it.' The 1987 follow-up, *Primitive Cool*, will disappoint.

Apr – Aug 1985   Recording for the *Dirty Work* album at Pathé Marconi Studios, Paris, and RPM and Right Track New York. Steve Lillywhite produces. Mick is often absent from sessions, and the boys are still feuding. Tom Waits, Bobby Womack and Jimmy Page contribute.

Mid-1980s   Charlie suffers mid-life crisis. While his bandmates have largely overcome their addictions and are now clean-living, Charlie succumbs and goes off the rails with drink and drugs, leading to heroin addiction. His wife Shirley battles alcoholism simultaneously.

13 July 1985   Live Aid global jukebox concert, London and Philadelphia. Mick and David Bowie record and perform for video 'Dancing in the Street', a cover of the Martha and the Vandellas' 1964 hit. Jagger's and Bowie's rendition of this much-covered song soars to No. 1 in the UK and No. 7 in the US. Keith and Ronnie play acoustic guitar for Bob Dylan's set. The world knows that Mick and Keith have fallen out.

12 December 1985   Stu dies of heart attack aged forty-seven, London.

February 1986   'Harlem Shuffle' single released.

24 March 1986   *Dirty Work* album released. With Jagger and Richards barely speaking, Mick refuses to tour to promote the album, and goes out on his own solo tour instead. He inflames the situation further by performing Rolling Stones songs. The Stones remain so in name.

24 October 1986   Bill Wyman turns fifty.

July 1987   For their twenty-fifth anniversary, *25 X 5: The Continuing Adventures Of the Rolling Stones* documentary features archive footage and original interviews with band members. It is broadcast on the BBC's *Arena* documentary series.

October 1988   Keith releases debut solo album *Talk is Cheap*, arising from jam sessions with a non-band band of musicians who will later acquire the moniker 'X-Pensive Winos'. Rave-reviewed by critics and adored by fans, it performs steadily, going gold in the US, and will be re-issued in 2019 for its thirtieth anniversary.

1989   The Rolling Stones, including Mick Taylor, Ronnie Wood, Ian Stewart and Brian Jones, are inducted into the Rock and Roll Hall of Fame in Cleveland, Ohio. Following which, Mick and Keith settle their differences and get to work on a new Stones album, *Steel Wheels*, featuring 'Mixed Emotions' and 'Rock and a Hard Place'.

29 Mar – 5 May 1989   Recording sessions for the *Steel Wheels* album, at AIR Montserrat, mixing at Olympic, London and in Morocco. Chris Kimsey produces with the Glimmers.

2 June 1989   Fifty-two-year-old Bill Wyman marries eighteen-year-old Mandy Smith. The couple separate two years later, their divorce finalised in 1993.

29 August 1989   *Steel Wheels* album released. The eagerly anticipated 'comeback album' reaches No. 2 UK; No. 3 US; and launches biggest tour to date. It is their last to feature Bill Wyman.

Aug 1989 – Aug 1990   Steel Wheels/Urban Jungle tour: the Stones' return to live touring after seven years with their debut 'named' world tour. But it's not like the bad old days. This is their biggest ever stage production – and Bill Wyman's final Stones tour. By 2007, they will have scored four of the top five highest-grossing concert tours of all time (since surpassed by Ed Sheeran, U2 and Guns N' Roses). The band then take an extended break. Charlie Watts releases two jazz albums. Ronnie Wood releases fifth solo album, his first for eleven years, *Slide on This*. Bill Wyman releases his fourth solo album.

1990s
1991   Fifty-five-year-old Bill Wyman leaves the Stones early in '91; Stones will not announce his departure until 1993. He is not replaced in

the line-up, but Darryl Jones, brought in by Charlie Watts, will play bass with the band as contracted session player for the next quarter-century.

2 June 1991   Charlie turns fifty.

November 1991   The Stones reclaim their 'rock's highest-paid band status by signing an estimated 45 million contract with UK's Virgin Music Group, for three new studio albums commencing 1993. Virgin are also to remaster and repackage their entire back catalogue of seventeen albums, with the exception of three live albums.

1992   EMI acquire Virgin Records, and the Stones become an EMI act.

October 1992   Keith releases second solo album, *Main Offender*, and tours to promote it, including Spain and Argentina. Album is well received, but fails to make much commercial impact. Keith will not release another solo album for twenty-three years.

February 1993   Mick releases third solo album, *Wandering Spirit*, featuring Lenny Kravitz and Flea of Red Hot Chili Peppers. Performing favourably, it makes No. 12 UK; No. 11 US.

April 1993   Bill Wyman marries Suzanne Accosta. The couple will have three daughters.

26 July 1993   Mick turns fifty.

Sep 1993 and Nov – Dec 1993   *Voodoo Lounge* album: rehearsals and initial recordings at Ronnie Wood's house in Ireland, then recorded at Windmill Lane Studios, Dublin. Don Was co-produces with Mick and Keith.

18 December 1993   Keith turns fifty.

July 1994   'Love is Strong' single released.

11 July 1994   *Voodoo Lounge* album released: a worldwide No. 1 (No. 2 US). In the UK, their first chart-topper for fourteen years, since 1980's *Emotional Rescue*. It will win Best Rock Album at the 1995 Grammy Awards.

Aug 1994 – Aug 1995   Voodoo Lounge tour: at $320 million, the highest-grossing tour of all time.

8 September 1994   The Stones perform their new song 'Love is Strong' and 'Start Me Up' at the 1994 MTV Video Music Awards, Radio City Music Hall, New York. They receive the Lifetime Achievement Award at the ceremony.

18 November 1994   They become the first major recording artists to broadcast a concert via the internet.

24 October 1996   Bill Wyman turns sixty.

January 1997   Writing and recording sojourn in Barbados.

Mar – Jul 1997   Recording sessions at LA's Ocean Way Recording for the new *Bridges to Babylon* album. They work with a variety of producers including Don Was, Rob Fraboni and the Dust Brothers: E.Z. Mike and King Gizmo. Mick and Keith have fallen out again. They avoid studio sessions together and record their parts separately. By the time they reconvene to tour the album, they have kissed and made up. Attracting mixed reviews but great sales, the album features a global Top 40 single, 'Anybody Seen My Baby?' It leans closely towards k.d. lang's 'Constant Craving'. Heading a lawsuit off at the pass, the Stones credit co-writer Ben Mink on the song. The video for the single stars twenty-two-year-old Angelina Jolie.

1 June 1997   Ronnie Wood turns fifty.

Sep 1997 – Sep 1998   Bridges to Babylon tour kicks off in Toronto. Grosses £274 million, the second highest-grossing tour at that time (behind their own Voodoo Lounge tour, 1994–95). It features a 'web vote', allowing ticket-holders to vote for the song they want to hear performed. Any song selected four shows in a row becomes a permanent fixture on the set list.

29 September 1997   *Bridges to Babylon* album released. No. 6 UK; No. 3 US.

Jan – Jun 1999   The Bridges to Babylon tour is followed by the down-scaled No Security tour: fewer dates and destinations, much smaller venues. The *No Security* album is the live album of that tour.

2000s
2 June 2001   Charlie turns sixty.

20 October 2001   Following the 9/11 terrorist attacks in New York on 11 September 2001, Mick and Keith plus a backing band perform in the Concert for New York City benefit at Madison Square Garden.

19 November 2001   Mick releases his fourth solo album, *Goddess in the Doorway*, immortalised by Keith as 'Dogshit in the Doorway'. With cover photography by fashion designer Karl Lagerfeld and backing vocals by two of his daughters, Elizabeth (then sixteen) and Georgia May (eight) on the concluding track, 'Brand New Set of Rules', his best solo offering hardly troubles the charts. Apart from *The Very Best of Jagger* (2007), it is his last solo release to date.

Sep 2002 – Nov 2003   Licks tour, in support of the *Forty Licks* album. Sponsored by the E-Trade Financial Corporation, it grosses over $300 million, claiming the second highest-grossing tour slot (behind Voodoo Lounge). An additional *Live Licks* album will be released in 2004, a live recording of the tour.

30 September 2002   Commemorating the band's fortieth anniversary, *Forty Licks* double compilation greatest hits album released: along with Queen's *Greatest Hits* and ABBA's *Gold*, the one that 'most people' own today. The album includes four new songs. No. 2 UK and US. To date, it has sold seven million copies worldwide.

26 July 2003   Mick turns sixty.

9 November 2003   The band play their first concert in Hong Kong, for the Harbour Fest Celebration and in support of the SARS-blighted economy.

12 December 2003   Having been honoured for services to popular music in Her Majesty the Queen's Birthday Honours 2002, Mick Jagger receives his gong from HRH The Prince of Wales. But Mick is not seen as deserving, and the award is much criticised. Keith Richards is apoplectic, regarding Mick's acceptance of it as a betrayal of everything the Stones have ever stood for. 'Mick got his knighthood for services to Mick Jagger,' quipped former Stones PR Keith Altham. Whatever: arise, Sir Shagger.

18 December 2003   Keith turns sixty.

November 2004   The Stones inducted into the UK Music Hall of Fame.

Nov 2004 / Mar 2005 / Jun 2005   *A Bigger Bang* album recorded, at Pocé sur Cisse and La Fourchette (Mick's château home) in France; Ocean Way Recording, and The Village Recorder in LA. Charlie diagnosed with throat cancer. Mick and Keith consider delaying the album, but Mick steps in to lay down the drum parts, most of which Charlie re-records later. Don Was co-produces with Mick and Keith.

August 2005   'Streets of Love' single released.

Aug 2005 – Aug 2007   The A Bigger Bang tour, a massive sell-out. A hundred and forty-seven shows will be seen by close to 5 million people.

5 September 2005   *A Bigger Bang* album released: a good back-to-basics hard rock offering that scores No. 2 in UK; No. 3 in US. Their first new album in about eight years, it features 'Streets of Love' and the strongly political 'Sweet Neo Con'.

February 2006   The band play the prestigious half-time show of Super Bowl XL in Detroit, Michigan.

18 February 2006   They play a free concert to more than 1 million people at once on Copacabana Beach, Rio de Janeiro, Brazil: one of rock's largest concerts ever.

April 2006   On holiday with Ronnie Wood and their families on a private island off the coast of Fiji, Keith falls from the low-hanging branch of a tree, sustaining injuries that force the band to postpone further tour dates. A fractured skull and intracranial haemorrhage lead to acute subdural haematoma. Keith makes an emergency flight to New Zealand for treatment. The European leg of the A Bigger Bang tour is delayed by six weeks.

June 2006   Ronnie submits to treatment for alcohol abuse.

Jul – Sep 2006   Mick suffers throat problems. Two shows cancelled.

24 October 2006   Bill Wyman turns seventy.

29 Oct and 1 Nov 2006   Martin Scorsese films the band at the Beacon Theatre, New York City, for his documentary *Shine a Light*, released 2008. At the first show, Atlantic Records boss Ahmet Ertegun trips and falls, hitting his head on a concrete floor. He remains in a coma in hospital and dies on 14 December, aged eighty-three.

November 2006   A Bigger Bang declared the highest-grossing tour of all time.

1 June 2007   Ronnie turns sixty.

10 June 2007   The band perform their first festival gig for thirty years before sixty-five thousand fans at the Isle of Wight Festival. They perform Robert Johnson's 'Love in Vain' with twenty-year-old Paolo Nutini, having rehearsed in a Travelodge hotel room. They are also joined on stage by Amy Winehouse. She will be found dead in her apartment four years later, aged twenty-seven.

26 August 2007   They play the final concert of the A Bigger Bang tour at London's O2 Arena. The tour grosses a record $558 million, and achieves the Guinness World Record.

April 2008   The *Shine a Light* soundtrack album of Scorsese's film is released as an album, No. 2 in UK, No. 11 in US.

July 2008   Ronnie enters rehab for treatment for alcoholism. Meets twenty-one-year-old Russian waitress Ekaterina Ivanova in Churchill's

Bar, London. Sets up home with his forty-years-younger girlfriend. The Stones leave EMI to sign with Universal Music, taking their catalogue back to *Sticky Fingers* with them. New music will be released by Universal's Polydor label. In the US, post-1994 recordings are handled by Interscope, formerly a subsidiary of Atlantic.

4 July 2009   Allen Klein dies.

2009   Ronnie and Jo divorce. Ronnie arrested on suspicion of assault after he and Ekaterina have a vicious public scrap. The couple separate in March.

2010s

19 May 2010   *Exile on Main St.* remastered and deluxe-reissued. Documentary *Stones in Exile* premieres at Cannes Film Festival on 23 May. The reissued album reaches No. 1 on UK chart almost thirty-eight years to the week since the first time they had a No. 1 with it. The Stones are the first act to see a classic album return to No. 1 decades after its first release. In America, it re-enters the chart at No. 2. Prince Rupert Loewenstein recommends that they wind down touring and recording and start selling off their assets. The Stones refuse and they part company. Lawyer Joyce Smyth, long a member of the band's entourage, assumes the position of manager in 2010.

2 June 2011   Charlie turns seventy.

21 June 2011   Maroon 5 with Christina Aguilera release the single 'Moves Like Jagger', a disco/electropop-flavoured number. That band's second No. 1 single (and her fifth), it becomes one of the best-selling singles of all time.

12 July 2012   Fiftieth anniversary of the Stones' first official gig, at London's Marquee Jazz Club, Oxford Street. Mick, Keith, Ronnie and Charlie gather at the venue's original site for a photo shoot, their first together since 2008. They release a book, *The Rolling Stones:50,* and an updated version of their lip-and-tongue logo by American graphic designer Frank Shepard Fairey. *Crossfire Hurricane*, a documentary directed by American Brett Morgen, is released in October. *GRRR!* compilation album released 12 November. It includes two new tracks, 'Doom and Gloom' and 'One More Shot'. The album sells more than 2 million copies worldwide.

Nov 2012 – Jul 2013   The 50 & Counting tour, commemorating fifty years of the Stones, with Mick Taylor as a guest artist throughout the tour. They kick off at London's O2 Arena with special guest Jeff Beck. The second show features Eric Clapton and Florence Welch. During spring 2013 they perform nineteen shows in US.

21 December 2012   Ronnie marries actress and producer Sally Humphreys, thirty years his junior. In 2016, when Ronnie is pushing seventy, the couple are blessed (cursed?) with twins.

29 June 2013   Stones perform for the first time ever at the Glastonbury Festival, Pilton, Somerset. Attended by Prince Harry, their two-hour, twenty-song set is hailed by festival organiser Michael Eavis as 'the high spot of forty-three years'. They extend the world-famous Pyramid Stage with three catwalks. Their special guest, long rumoured to be Adele or Bruce Springsteen, is their old faithful Mick Taylor.

6 July 2013   Almost forty-four years to the day since their first iconic performance they play Hyde Park, the first of two massive gigs there. This time, it's not free.

26 July 2013   Mick turns seventy.

8 December 2013   Keith turns seventy.

15 December 2013   Bruce Springsteen and the Black Keys join the band on stage for the tour's finale.

Feb – Nov 2014   On Fire tour, again featuring Mick Taylor. Dates announced in Australia, New Zealand, Abu Dhabi, Shanghai, Singapore and other territories.

17 March 2014   Mick's long-time girlfriend fashion designer

L'Wren Scott dies suddenly in New York City. Suspected suicide. All Australasian dates postponed.

4 June 2014   Historic first performance in Israel.

24 May – 15 Jul 2015   Zip Code tour of US, in celebration of *Sticky Fingers*, re-released in 2015.

18 September 2015   Keith releases third solo album *Crosseyed Heart*. Great reviews, and the record performs well.

Feb – Mar 2016   América Latina Olé tour, including a historic concert in Havana, Cuba, on 25 March attended by five 500,000 fans – the first time a rock band has played such a huge gig there. A film of the concert, *Havana Moon,* will be released on 11 November, followed by a tour of Latin America, their first in ten years.

14 February 2016   *Vinyl,* a series about the 1970s rock scene and starring Mick's and Jerry's son James Jagger as Kip Stevens, singer of a pre-punk band called Nasty Bits, makes its debut on the HBO channel. Created by Mick Jagger, Martin Scorsese, Rich Cohen and Terence Winter, it runs for ten episodes and concludes 17 April 2016. A second series is announced, then cancelled.

2 June 2016   Charlie turns seventy-five.

24 October 2016   Bill Wyman turns eighty.

2 December 2016   *Blue & Lonesome* album of covers of blues songs by their earliest inspirations – Little Walter, Howlin' Wolf, Jimmy Reed, etc. – released. Featuring Eric Clapton on two tracks, it makes No. 1 in UK and debuts at No. 4 on the US Billboard 200.

1 June 2017   Ronnie turns seventy.

13 June 2017   Anita Pallenberg dies aged seventy-five, of complications from hepatitis C. Survived by her two children and five grandchildren.

Sep 2017 – Nov 2021   No Filter tour of UK and Europe – the band's first UK tour since 2006.

18 November 2017 They announce plans to take the tour around US stadiums in 2019.

26 July 2018 Mick turns seventy-five.

18 December 2018 Keith turns seventy-five.

March 2019 Mick submits to heart valve replacement surgery. The North American leg of the tour is postponed.

30 August 2019 Charlie Watts performs live with the Stones for the last time, at Miami's Hard Rock Stadium.

2020s

March 2020 No Filter tour shows postponed again, due to the global Covid-19 pandemic.

18 April 2020 Mick, Keith, Charlie and Ronnie, each performing from home, are among the headlining acts for Global Citizens' One World: Together at Home on-screen and online concert in support of the World Health Organization and front-line healthcare workers.

23 April 2020 'Living in a Ghost Town' single released. Their first original song since 2012. No. 1 Australia and Germany.

4 September 2020 1973's *Goats Head Soup* album reissued with previously unreleased outtakes, including 'Scarlet' featuring Jimmy Page. On 11 September the album tops the UK chart, making the Rolling Stones the first band to top the chart in six different decades.

April 2021 Four years after his lung cancer diagnosis, Ronnie Wood announces diagnosis of rare, aggressive small-cell cancer. He also says that his doctors have given him the all-clear.

2 June 2021 Charlie turns eighty.

August 2021 Charlie withdraws from the resuming No Filter tour to submit for an unspecified medical procedure. He chooses session drummer Steve Jordan to replace him.

19 August 2021 'Living in the Heart of Love' single released, from the forthcoming anniversary edition of *Tattoo You*.

24 August 2021 Charlie dies in London. No official cause of death is given.

September 2021 Band resumes No Filter North American tour in St Louis, Missouri.

22 October 2021 Fortieth anniversary re-issue of *Tattoo You* released, featuring nine previously unreleased tracks and a live album recorded at Wembley Stadium in 1982.

23 November 2021 No Filter tour concludes at the Hard Rock Live Amphitheater, Hollywood, Florida.

6 December 2021 Family, friends, bandmates and colleagues pay tribute to the late Charlie Watts at a private gig at his favourite jazz club, Ronnie Scott's Soho, London.

12 July 2022 Sixtieth anniversary of the Stones' first official gig, at London's Marquee Jazz Club.

STONES WOMEN

BRIAN JONES

Pat Andrews

Linda Lawrence

Dawn Molloy

Christa Päffgen – who will become Nico of the Velvet Underground

Zouzou

Anita Pallenberg

Suki Potier

Anna Wohlin

MICK JAGGER

An estimated four thousand lovers including these women:
Chrissie Shrimpton, Marianne Faithfull, Marsha Hunt, Bianca Pérez-Mora Macías, Jerry Hall, Luciana Gimenez Morad, L'Wren Scott, Melanie Hamrick.

Cleo Sylvestre

Brigitte Bardot

Tina Turner

P.P. Arnold

Ava Cherry

Lori Mattox

Pat Cleveland

Claudia Lennear

Devon Wilson/'Dolly Dagger'

Linda Eastman (later Mrs Paul
    McCartney)

Valerie Perrine

Janice Dickinson

Monique Pardo

Natasha Fraser-Cavassoni

Patti D'Arbanville

Pamela Miller

Catherine Guinness

Sabrina Guinness

Miranda Guinness, Countess of
    Iveagh

Grace Coddington

Cornelia Guest

Michelle Phillips

Mary Badham

Vanessa Carbone

Twinkle

Claire Verity

Jana Rajlich

Orsolya Dessy

Nicole Kruk

Melissa Behr

Kathy Latham

Linda Ronstadt

Dana Gillespie

Edie Sedgwick

Catherine James

Jane Holzer

Estelle Bennett

Chris O'Dell

Madonna

Anita Pallenberg

Michèle Breton

Carly Simon

Pamela Des Barres

Bebe Buell

Jane Fonda

Fernanda Eberstadt

Jane Ormsby-Gore

Cyrinda Fox

Barbara Allen

Nathalie Delon

Apollonia 'Apples' von Ravenstein

Janice Kenner

Margaret Trudeau

HRH The Princess Margaret,
    Countess of Snowdon

Jacqueline Kennedy Onassis

Uschi Obermaier

Lisa Barbuscia

Peta Wilson

Christina Haack

Savannah

Daryl Hannah

Maryam D'Abo

Janice Dickinson

Carla Bruni

Angelina Jolie

Uma Thurman

Sophie Dahl

Minnie Driver

Mackenzie Phillips

Natasha Terry

Nicole Kruk

Rae Dawn Chong

Luciana Gimenez Morad

Vanessa Neumann

Farrah Fawcett

Masha Rudenko

Luli Fernández

Nia Long

Caroline Winberg

Ortensia Visconti
Peggy Trentini
Noor Alfallah

... plus any number of nameless groupies, and these men:
Keith Richards
Kit Lambert
David Bowie
Helmut Berger
Mick Taylor
Jann Wenner

KEITH RICHARDS

Anita Pallenberg, Patti Hansen
Lil Wergilis, aka Lil Wenglass/Lil Green
Haleema 'Lee' Mohamed
Linda Keith
Uschi Obermaier
Ronnie Spector

CHARLIE WATTS

Shirley Shepherd Watts

BILL WYMAN

His conservative estimate is a thousand. The most significant:
Diane Cory Wyman, Astrid Lundstrom, Mandy Smith, Suzanne Accosta.
Stephanie Bews
Nike Clark
Kelly Winn
Tania Bryer
Stacey Nelkin
Judi Gable
Pamella Bordes/Pamella Chaudry Singh
Wendy Jewels
Emmaretta Marks

RONNIE WOOD
Krissy Findlay, Jo Karslake, Sally Humphreys Wood
Pattie Boyd
Ekaterina Ivanova
Ana Araujo

PAPA WAS A ROLLING STONE
… the greatest rock'n'roll dynasty in the world …

BRIAN JONES
Barry David Corbett (renamed Simon) – May 1959, mother Valerie
    Corbett. Adopted
Belinda – born August 1960, mother Angeline
Julian Mark Andrews (now known as Mark) – October 1961, mother
    Pat Andrews
Julian Brian Jones – July 1964, mother Linda Lawrence. She later
    married folk rock artist Donovan, and the child was given his
    stepfather's surname Leitch. He is now also known as Julian Jones
Paul Andrew Molloy (renamed John Maynard) – March 1965. Adopted.
    Mother Dawn Molloy

MICK JAGGER
Karis Hunt Jagger – November 1970, mother Marsha Hunt
Jade Sheena Jezebel Jagger – October 1971, mother Bianca Jagger
Elizabeth Scarlett 'Lizzy' Jagger – March 1984, mother Jerry Hall
James Leroy Augustin Jagger – August 1985, mother Jerry Hall
Georgia May Ayeesha Jagger – January 1992, mother Jerry Hall
Gabriel Luke Beauregard Jagger – December 1997, mother Jerry Hall
Lucas Maurice Morad Jagger – May 1999, mother Luciana Gimenez
    Morad
Deveraux Octavian Basil Jagger – December 2016, mother Melanie
    Hamrick

GRANDCHILDREN

Mazie and Zak, son and daughter of Mick's daughter Karis Hunt Jagger

Assisi Lola Jackson, Amba Isis Jackson and Ray Emmanuel Fillary, the children of Mick's daughter Jade

Eugene Behlau, son of Mick's daughter Lizzy

GREAT-GRANDCHILDREN

Ezra Key and Romy Key, children of Mick's granddaughter Assisi

River, son of Mick's granddaughter Amba

KEITH RICHARDS

Marlon Leon Sandeep – August 1969, mother Anita Pallenberg

Dandelion Angela – April 1972, mother Anita Pallenberg

Tara Jo Jo Gunne – born 26 March, died 6 June 1976 aged ten weeks, mother Anita Pallenberg

Theodora Dupree Richards – March 1985, mother Patti Hansen

Alexandra Nicole Richards – July 1986, mother Patti Hansen

GRANDCHILDREN

Ella Rose, Orson and Ida, children of Marlon

Ava Melody and Otto Reed, children of Angela

CHARLIE WATTS

Seraphina Watts – March 1968, mother Shirley Watts

GRANDCHILD

Charlotte, daughter of Seraphina

BILL WYMAN

Stephen Paul Wyman – 29 March 1962, mother Diane Cory Wyman

Katharine Noelle 'Katie' Wyman – September 1994, mother Suzanne Accosta Wyman

Jessica Rose Wyman – November 1995, mother Suzanne Accosta Wyman

Matilda Mae Wyman – April 1998, mother Suzanne Accosta Wyman

RONNIE WOOD

Jamie Wood – 1973, son of Ronnie's ex-wife Jo and her former husband
  Peter Greene, and adopted son of Ronnie
Jesse James Wood – October 1976, mother Krissy Findlay
Leah Wood – September 1978, mother Jo Wood
Tyrone Wood – August 1983, mother Jo Wood
Gracie Jane and Alice Rose Wood, twins – May 2016, mother Sally
  Humphreys Wood

GRANDCHILDREN

Rex, son of Jesse and broadcaster Fearne Cotton
Jesse also has two children with model Catherine 'Tilly' Boone
Maggie Dylan and Otis Sonny David, children of Leah Wood

MICK TAYLOR

Chloe Taylor – 6 January 1971, mother Rose Millar
Emma Taylor – born to Susan, an American backing vocalist with
  the Stones

GRANDCHILD

Eleanor, daughter of Chloe

CHAPTER NOTES

CHAPTER ONE: KARMA

1. The marquise diamond cut was originally commissioned in 1745 by King Louis XV of France to reflect the smile of his mistress, Madame de Pompadour.

2. Spencer House is London's finest surviving eighteenth-century town house. Still owned by the Spencer family, its current title holder is Charles Spencer, the 9th Earl and brother of the late Diana Princess of Wales. It is open to the public and is available for weddings and private events.

3. Rupert Murdoch has had four wives. His first was Melbourne flight attendant Patricia Booker. Married 1956, one daughter, Prudence, divorced 1967. Second, Anna Maria Torv, Scottish journalist, married 1967 for thirty-two years; one daughter, Elisabeth, and sons Lachlan and James. Divorced 1999. Third, Wendi Deng, Chinese businesswoman, married 1999, when he was sixty-eight and she thirty; two daughters, Grace and Chloe. Murdoch divorced her in 2013 over unproven scandal of her alleged infidelity with former British Prime Minister Tony Blair. Fourth, Jerry Hall.

4. The phone-hacking scandal of 2005 onwards saw employees of the *News of the World* and other Murdoch papers accused of hacking phones, bribing police officers and breaking the law in other ways as they gathered sensational stories. Royals, celebrities and politicians were targeted. In July 2011, it emerged that the phones of murdered schoolgirl Milly Dowler, victims of the 7/7 London bombings and deceased army personnel had also been hacked, causing executives to resign. The Leveson Inquiry investigated phone hacking and police bribery. Several arrests and convictions ensued. Boycotting by advertisers caused the *News of the World*'s closure after a hundred and sixty-eight years. Murdoch's worth as a newspaper proprietor was called into question.

5. Two Brydges members' club relaunched as Brydges Place in 2020.

CHAPTER TWO: JONER

1. Leukaemia: a type of cancer affecting blood cells, mainly the white cells and bone marrow.

2. Britain's publicly funded healthcare system the NHS was founded in 1948 by Labour Party politician Aneurin Bevan (1897–1960). 'Nye' was the son of a Welsh coal miner.

3. Geraldine Crehan, 'The Surviving Sibling: The Effects of Sibling Death in Childhood', 2004. David E. Balk, 'The Self-Concepts of Bereaved Adolescents: Sibling Death and its Aftermath', 1990.

4. Richard Hughes's references: John Bowlby: *The Making and Breaking of Affectional Bonds*, Routledge Classics, 2005; Albert C. Cain, Barbara S. Cain: *On Replacing a Child*, The American Academy of Child Psychiatry, Elsevier, 1964. The Mimi or 'Mimih' spirits to which Hughes refers are the fairy-like creatures of Arnhem Land in the beautiful Northern Territory of Australia, said to be one of the last remaining areas that could qualify as its own separate country. It is made up of many different Aboriginal countries with

languages, traditions and cultures that date back tens of thousands of years. According to their collective folklore, the Mimi taught the Aboriginal Australians the arts of hunting and cooking kangaroo, and how to paint. The protected region is known for its rock art and bark paintings. Keith Richards may, however, have meant to describe Brian Jones as a 'me, me person': the kind to whom we would refer today as an extreme narcissist. That is, a controlling, bullying, self-absorbed, exploitative, explosive, entitled and impulsive individual given to possessive behaviour and jealous fits of rage; someone who demonstrates a lack of empathy with others, who lacks insight into their own emotions, who is obsessed with the way others see him, who is easily offended, and who often humiliates, ridicules and even hurts their partner(s) and makes contemptuous remarks about others behind their backs. Know who I mean? No moral compass? Bereft of self-control? Lives beyond their means, eating, drinking and even drugging themselves stupid? Get the hell out.

5. Keith Richards probably meant '*delusions* of grandeur'.

6. P.P. Pond, born Paul Pond in Portsmouth, 24 February 1942, rose to fame as Paul Jones, lead singer and harmonica player with the group Manfred Mann, who scored hits with '5-4-3-2-1', 'Do Wah Diddy Diddy', 'Oh No, Not My Baby', 'Pretty Flamingo', 'Ha! Ha! Said the Clown', 'Mighty Quinn' and more. Brian Jones and Keith Richards asked him to front a new group they were putting together. He turned them down, and the part went to Mick Jagger. Paul went solo in 1966. He formed the Blues Band in 1979, and is a member of the Manfreds: a reunion band of former Manfred Mann members (excluding Manfred himself) including Tom McGuinness, of McGuinness Flint fame. Paul also hosted BBC Radio 2's *Blues Show* for thirty-two years until 2018, when the then seventy-six-year-old was replaced by Cerys Matthews. All part of the BBC's misguided drive to lure thirty- and forty-somethings back to radio. We did warn them.

CHAPTER THREE: MICK'N'KEEF

1. Avon was founded in the US as the California Perfume Company Inc. in 1886 by bookseller turned entrepreneur David H. McConnell. He changed the business's name to Avon in 1928, inspired by Stratford-upon-Avon, birthplace of William Shakespeare, whom McConnell adored. He launched what became a vast army of mostly fragrant stay-at-home mothers (a small percentage of their representatives were male), who demonstrated the company's products to other housewives, around their own neighbourhoods. Goods were then ordered from catalogues, with the rep receiving a commission. The company launched in the UK in 1959. In 2010, Debbie Davis from Sunderland became the first British Avon lady to earn over £1 million. Having signed up after being made redundant, she built a sales team of 8,000 reps. Until 2014, when it was overtaken by American health, beauty and homecare company Amway, Avon was the number one global direct sales company.

2. Mick Jagger would rekindle his love for cricket in later years, becoming an enthusiastic spectator, Test match follower and fixture at Lord's Cricket Ground, the 'home of cricket'.

3. 'Love Me Do', the Beatles' debut single with 'P.S. I Love You' on the B-side, was released in the UK on 5 October 1962. It rose to No. 17 on the British chart.

4. Glaswegian Anthony James 'Tony' Donegan, 'the king of skiffle', changed his name to Lonnie in tribute to Alonzo 'Lonnie' Johnson, revered New Orleans blues and jazz guitarist and singer-songwriter.

5. Little Richard, born Richard Wayne Penniman (1932–2020) in Macon, Georgia. Best known for his hits 'Tutti Frutti', 'Long Tall Sally', 'Lucille', 'Good Golly Miss Molly'.

6. Buddy Holly, born Charles Hardin Holley (1936–59) in Lubbock, Texas, inspired and influenced the Beatles, the Stones, Bob Dylan, Eric Clapton, the Hollies (who named themselves after him), Elton John and just about everybody else. He is credited with having established the

'traditional rock'n'roll line-up' of two guitars, bass and drums. He and his Crickets very nearly called themselves 'the Beetles'. A while down the line, the Beatles settled on their name partly in tribute to him. Holly died in a plane crash near Clear Lake, Iowa, on 3 February 1959, at the age of twenty-two. His wife Maria Elena was pregnant with the couple's first child, which she miscarried soon after receiving the news of his death. Paul McCartney later acquired Holly's song publishing rights.

7. The documentary was *Jazz on a Summer's Day*, about the 1958 Newport Jazz Festival in Rhode Island, New England. The line-up included Louis Armstrong, Chuck Berry, Dinah Washington and Thelonious Monk. The film premiered at the 1959 Venice Film Festival.

8. Borstal, part of the English prison system, for young offenders aged between sixteen and twenty-one, who would be trained while kept in custody. Named after an old convict prison bear Borstal, Kent, not far from Rochester.

9. From the Latin poet Virgil's *Georgics*, it means 'To know the causes of things'.

CHAPTER FOUR: DRUM'N'BASS

1. Charlie famously took exception to being called 'my drummer', in Amsterdam in 1984. Mick and Keith had been out on the town. On returning to their hotel in the early hours, an inebriated Mick called Charlie in his room and demanded, 'Where's my drummer?' Charlie did not respond. Twenty or so minutes later there came a knock at the door. Keith opened it, only to find a freshly showered, shaven and fully Savile Row-suited and booted Charlie standing there. He marched past Keith, grabbed Mick by the lapels of Keith's wedding jacket (which Mick was wearing), and punched him in the face, with the warning, 'Never call me your drummer again!' The embellishment, 'You're my fucking singer!' has been added over many years of re-telling, but is not how Keith remembered it in his memoir *Life*. As he recounted it, Mick

fell backwards into a silver salver of smoked salmon and towards an open window, which looked out on to a canal glinting below. Had Mick fallen into it from that height, he would likely have been killed. The thought of which did nothing to dampen Keith's enjoyment of the spectacle, when suddenly he remembered that Mick was wearing his wedding jacket. He lunged for it, saving Jagger at the same time. Keith reckoned that it took a good twelve hours to calm Charlie down. He was only too keen to have another go, and had to be restrained.

2. The backbeat is the second half of the beat. It usually means the snare drum being played on beat two and four (if in a 4/4 time signature). The drums are the foundation of the music. The drummer is the engine driver, with the job of keeping it all together. The rock drummer usually sits at the rear because drums are loud. Positioning him upstage lets the sound fill the stage, and allows the other musicians to play and sing over the top of it.

3. Manny's Music dominated midtown Manhattan's W48th St at two addresses for seventy-four years. Founded by sax salesman Manny Goldrich in 1935 on what became 'Music Row', it started small and grew to meet demand, enjoying a heyday during the British Invasion of bands during the sixties. Incoming musicians could get what they couldn't in Europe, at competitive prices. Its walls were plastered with signed photos of many famous musicians, including Buddy Holly, Bob Dylan, the Beatles and Jimi Hendrix. The store appears in the video for Guns N' Roses' 'Paradise City'.

4. Nearly one hundred and sixty thousand prefabricated homes, known as prefabs, were constructed in the UK from 1945–48. They were built as temporary accommodation to house families made homeless by bombing during the World War II. Although most were later demolished, some were still inhabited decades later, particularly in parts of south-east London.

5. The boys' and girls' Tylers Croft Secondary Modern schools merged to become Kingsbury High School (motto: *Spectemur agendo* – Let us be

judged by our actions) in 1967. Other celebrated alumni include George Michael and jazz saxophonist Courtney Pine.

6. Harrow Art School was later absorbed by the University of Westminster, the alma mater of the author.

7. It was Shakespeare's Hamlet who said, 'I am native here, and to the manner born.' (Act 1 Scene 4 of the *Tragedy of the Prince of Denmark*). 'To the Manor Born', its title a wordplay, was a popular 1979–81 BBC TV sitcom starring the late Peter Bowles, and the ineffable Penelope 'The Good Life' Keith as Audrey fforbes-Hamilton.

8. Daisy Buchanan, the woman with a voice 'full of money', is Jay Gatsby's unobtainable true love in F. Scott Fitzgerald's most celebrated novel *The Great Gatsby* (1925).

9. Bread pudding, also known as 'poor man's pudding' and dating back to the eleventh century; its base is scraps of stale bread into which dried fruit and peel, suet, eggs, sugar, milk, butter and spices are mixed before baking.

10. Beckenham and Penge County Grammar School (motto: *Mores et Studia* – Good character and learning) later became Langley Park School for Boys. The author gained a place to the girls' equivalent of Langley Park, but accepted a place at the Ravensbourne School (formerly Bromley Grammar School for Girls).

11. The Wetherby Arms was located at 500 Kings Road, close to the Stones' flat on Edith Grove. It later became known as the Dean Swift, before closing as a public house in 2004. It passed into commercial use, becoming a Paddy Power betting shop.

CHAPTER FIVE: HUSTLERS

1. Henry the bookmaker's proclamation was perhaps the first of multiple variations on the theme. By 1964, *Melody Maker* was blaring,

'Would You Let Your Sister Go With a Rolling Stone? – asks Ray Coleman, who has been on tour with them.' The phrase was seized upon and redeployed as his own invention by manager Andrew Loog Oldham, when he decided to position the Stones in the market as the anti-Beatles.

2. Murrayfield in Edinburgh, the home of Scottish Rugby Union, is Scotland's largest sports stadium with a seating capacity of just over 67,000.

3. Gomelsky later managed the Yardbirds, and launched his own Marmalade Records, representing Brian Auger's Trinity and Julie Driscoll, Blossom Toes, and Graham Gouldman, Kevin Godley and Lol Creme, who later formed the band 10cc; he worked with various other artists, including Soft Machine.

4. The Stones were at that stage still a six-piece.

5. Bruce Channel, 1940–, American singer-songwriter and one-hit-wonder co-composer with Margaret Cobb of multi-million selling No. 1 hit 'Hey! Baby' (ooh, ah), 1962. The song features famously in the 1987 film *Dirty Dancing*, and has been covered by many including Del Shannon, Brian Poole and the Tremeloes, the Shirelles, Pat Boone, Adam Faith, Jerry Lee Lewis, Ringo Starr and José Feliciano.

6. 'Exit, pursued by a bear' is a stage direction in William Shakespeare's romantic tragicomedy *The Winter's Tale*, published in his First Folio, 1623.

7. Galeano launched his own rock band, Diamante Eléctrico, in 2012. Their sixth album, *Mira Lo Que Hiciste Hacer* (*Look What You Made Me Do*) was released in 2021.

8. Loog Oldham's reference to ECT involves electroconvulsive therapy, used to treat psychiatric patients with severe depression or bipolar disorder that has failed to respond to alternative treatments.

9. By 'Allen Krime', Andrew means the late American music business manager Allen Klein, who became the band's manager after him.

CHAPTER SIX: HEYDAY

1. 'Shuffle off this mortal coil' is a phrase from William Shakespeare's most celebrated soliloquy, Prince Hamlet's 'To be or not to be.' Its meaning is obscure, many scholars interpreting it as the shedding of one's earthly, physical form to prepare the soul for eternal life in the hereafter. It is sometimes compared to the way a reptile shrugs off its dead skin.

2. Originally expressed by Geoffrey Chaucer in the Prologue of *The Cook's Tale* (1390) as: 'Ful ofte in game a sooth I have herd saye!'

3. The Who captured the mods v rockers culture in their 1973 album *Quadrophenia*, leading to 1979's hugely influential cult film of the same name set in Brighton during the infamous 1964 clash and starring Phil Daniels as Jimmy and Leslie Ash as Steph. Toyah Willcox, John Altman and Sting also appear.

4. There would be one last, impromptu performance on the roof of their Apple Corps building at 3 Savile Row, London, on Thursday 30 January 1969 ... a final farewell rather than a full-blown gig.

5. From the author's *Who Killed John Lennon? – The lives, loves and death of the greatest rock star*, John Blake, 2020

6. Henry David Thoreau (1817–62), American naturalist, philosopher and poet.

CHAPTER SEVEN: REACTION

1. Olympic Sound Studios, established during the late 1950s, had moved to a derelict synagogue on Carlton Street by the time the Stones arrived.

They relocated to 117 Church Road, Barnes, a building which had previously been a theatre, cinema and a television studio in 1966. The Stones were among the first clients to record there, creating six albums at Olympic between 1966 and 1973. Among the many A-listers also to record there were the Beatles, Jimi Hendrix, David Bowie, Queen, Led Zeppelin, the Who, Prince, the Eagles, Madonna, Björk and Adele.

2. The Staple Singers (they dropped the 's' from their surname for commercial purposes – see, Keith, there was a precedent) were a Mississippi family group made up of Roebuck Staples, known as 'Pops', and his children Cleotha, Pervis, Yvonne and Mavis. The family moved to Chicago after the birth of Cleotha, where Pervis, Mavis and Yvonne were born. They recorded and performed primarily religious music. As a result of Pops's intense friendship with Martin Luther King Jr, they became the musical and spiritual voices of the civil rights movement. Achieving vast success as 'God's Greatest Hit Makers', their most celebrated hits during the 1970s included 'Respect Yourself', 'I'll Take You There', 'If You're Ready (Come Go with Me)' and 'Let's Do it Again'. All are now deceased, except Mavis Staples, who continues to work well into her ninth decade. When she performed live at the 2019 Glastonbury Festival, she was eighty years old. In an acclaimed 2015 documentary about her life and career, entitled *Mavis!*, she revealed that Bob Dylan had once proposed marriage, but that she had turned him down. They remained close friends, and later toured together.

The Stones clearly plagiarised the Staple Singers' specific arrangement of the traditional spiritual song 'This May Be The Last Time', for which they were never pursued. Having 'gotten away with it', shame on them for later suing the Verve for sampling 'The Last Time' on their release 'Bitter Sweet Symphony'. Because as they say, where there's a hit, there's a writ. Richard Ashcroft and his Britpop band had a worldwide hit with the 1997 recording. The Stones challenged its authorship. Although Ashcroft wrote the lyrics, its melody and arrangement borrowed substantially from the Stones' recording, and also from an orchestral version recorded in 1965 by the

Andrew Oldham Orchestra: a separate project for which Oldham used session musicians to create classical renditions of Stones songs.

The Verve, to their credit, did do things properly and above board. They sought permission from Decca, the label that had released Oldham's orchestral album. They had been granted the right to use a few notes of the string melody, in return for half the Verve's royalties earned by their song. But the applecart was overturned when Allen Klein, who had managed the Stones during the late 1960s and who controlled their copyrights into 1970, sued the Verve for plagiarism after 'Bitter Sweet Symphony' was released. Klein claimed that their use was not fair use; that it infringed the songwriters' rights, and that it could not be classified as a sample.

The Verve settled with Klein in 1997. They gave Jagger and Richards songwriting credits on 'Bitter Sweet Symphony', and released the song's publishing royalties to Klein's company ABKCO Records. Which should have been the end of it. But Oldham then sued the Verve himself, two years later, for $1.7 million in mechanical (songwriter) royalties. The result of the two lawsuits was that Oldham, Jagger and Richards received all royalties earned by 'Bitter Sweet Symphony' for many years. That'll do nicely.

The Staple Singers were all still alive at this point. Pops did not die until 2000. Cleotha departed in 2013, Yvonne in 2018 and Pervis in 2021. At the time of writing, Mavis is still with us. Klein had died in July 2009 at the age of seventy-seven, twelve years after winning the dispute. Perhaps Mick and Keith felt the gentle breath of the faithful Staple Singers on their cheeks at night as they tossed and turned. Perhaps guilt eventually caught up with them. In April 2019, Mick and Keith signed over all publishing rights for 'Bitter Sweet Symphony' to Richard Ashcroft and the Verve. What a pity that they never settled with the Staple Singers similarly.

3. 'Baby, better come back maybe next week/Can't you see I'm on a losing streak?' refers to a girl the singer wants to have sex with, who cannot oblige because she has her period. She invites him to try asking again the following week, when she will be in the parlance *du jour*, 'off the rag'.

CHAPTER EIGHT: MARIANNE

1. The observation that men want more sexual partners than women do is known as the Coolidge effect. The desire for multiple sexual partners appears to increase as men age. It's certainly so in the case of Mick Jagger. Research has established that males soon grow tired of sex with the same female, and are rapidly aroused by a new mate. Some women under some conditions show some evidence of a Coolidge effect, but overall to a lesser degree. Studies have also found that women tend to prefer resources (status, wealth) over a man's looks when selecting a long-term partner, but that they favour looks over resources in casual flings. It is interesting that ageing men appear to become less fussy about their sexual partners' beauty, as long as the females are young. So older men crave more sexual variety than younger men. May we conclude that older men have come to terms with the fact that biology drives them to desire sex with as many younger partners as possible? Or could that be plain old insecurity, coupled with the fact that they are terrified of their own impending doom?

The Coolidge effect is named after Calvin Coolidge, thirtieth president of the United States, 1923–29. American scientist and author Frank Ambrose Beach Jr claimed to have coined the term, which is based on an old joke. You probably had to be there.

See also *Experimental Evidence for Sex Differences in Sexual Variety Preferences: Support for the Coolidge Effect in Humans*: Hughes S.M., Aung T., Harrison M.A., LaFayette J.N., Gallup G.G. Jr.

2. Masochists achieve sexual gratification through being hurt, punished and/or humiliated.

3. Peter Asher's and Gordon Waller's first and most famous hit, 'A World Without Love', was written by Paul McCartney and was a No. 1 million-seller in 1964. Subsequent hits included Del Shannon's 'I Go to Pieces', 'Lady Godiva', 'Woman' and 'Nobody I Know', also written by McCartney; and 'True Love Ways', a cover of the Buddy Holly and Norman Petty song. Asher went on to become a manager and producer, responsible for the careers of James Taylor, Linda Ronstadt and others. Waller died in 2009.

4. 'Wigan Pier' gained fame after the 1937 publication of George Orwell's *The Road to Wigan Pier*. The title is ironic, referring as it does to an inland area of Greater Manchester that is nowhere near the seaside, and has no pier.

5. The UK's Abortion Act, passed on 27 October 1967, did not come into effect until 27 April 1968.

6. *Ned Kelly* was director Tony Richardson's biopic about the son of a transported Irish convict who grew up to become 'Australia's Robin Hood'. Kelly, a bushranger turned bank robber, outlaw and police killer, was hanged for his crimes in 1880, at the age of twenty-six. He became a cult figure, and has had more biographies written about him than any other Australian. The film was poorly received, and Jagger effectively disowned it. It was not the vehicle to celluloid fame that he had imagined.

7. Trident Studios, 17 St Anne's Court, Soho, was a recording business created by the Sheffield brothers, Norman and Barry. It was a working studio for thirteen years, between 1968 and 1981. Trident generated many hit singles and albums. The Beatles recorded 'Hey Jude' there, and Elton John 'Your Song'. Bowie's *The Rise and Fall of Ziggy Stardust and the Spiders from Mars* was a famous Trident album, as were Carly Simon's *No Secrets*, and Queen's eponymous debut album, as well as *Queen II* and *Sheer Heart Attack*. Other artists who used the facility included Genesis, Harry Nilsson, Frank Zappa, James Taylor, Tina Turner, T. Rex, and, of course, the Rolling Stones.

8. Nicholas Dunbar is the author of *The Devil's Derivatives* and *Inventing Money*.

CHAPTER NINE: ANITA

1. *La Dolce Vita* is the charming, seemingly immortal cult masterpiece by Federico Fellini, released in 1960. Starring Anita Ekberg, Anouk

Aimée and Marcello Mastroianni, it charts the adventures of a young magazine journalist as he rips around Rome's Via Veneto and environs in search of love.

2. *Barbarella* is a 1968 sci-fi classic directed by Roger Vadim. It's silly, but it does star Jane Fonda.

3. In *Candy*, also released in 1968, Anita co-starred with Richard Burton, James Coburn and Marlon Brando after whom her and Keith's firstborn (Marlon) is named.

4. https://www.nhs.uk/conditions/sudden-infant-death-syndrome-sids/

5. Many fans around the world were distraught at the apparent destruction in the fire of Keith's 1953 butterscotch Fender Telecaster, nicknamed 'Micawber' after the character Mr Micawber in Charles Dickens's novel *David Copperfield*. But they confused the name 'Macabre' with 'Micawber'. The Fender, a present from Eric Clapton for Keith's twenty-seventh birthday, just as the Stones were getting ready to record *Exile on Main St.*, he uses to this day – for songs like 'Brown Sugar' and 'Honky Tonk Women'.

6. Although South Salem is often referred to as the location of the notorious seventeenth-century Salem Witch Trials, these took place in Salem in the neighbouring state of Massachusetts.

7. See *A Christmas Story*, 1983, a seasonal drama starring Melinda Dillon, Darren McGavin and Peter Billingsley; also, *National Lampoon's Christmas Vacation*, 1989, set in the snowy suburbs, in which the twinkling Griswold house is the star (alongside Chevy Chase); and *The Family Stone*, 2005, with Sarah Jessica Parker.

8. Spoiler alert: in the 1978 war film *The Deer Hunter*, starring Robert De Niro and Christopher Walken, the latter's character shoots himself dead during a game of Russian roulette. It involves loading a bullet into one chamber of a revolver, spinning the cylinder, then pulling the trigger while pointing the gun at oneself. If you're lucky, things don't

line up and you're still alive. 'Playing Russian roulette' has come to mean gambling foolishly on something risky or potentially lethal, e.g. driving under the influence.

9. Anita was once again ahead of the trend. Jaipur was the setting of the 2011 film *The Best Exotic Marigold Hotel* and its 2015 sequel *The Second Best Exotic Marigold Hotel*, starring Bill Nighy, Judi Dench, Celia Imrie and Maggie Smith, which charted the adventures of a group of pensioners who relocate from England to a retirement hotel there. The pictures were based on Deborah Moggach's 2004 novel *These Foolish Things*.

Paul McCartney composed and recorded a tribute to the city, entitled 'Riding into Jaipur'. He included it on his 2001 album *Driving Rain*. Hypnotic and sitar-infused, it features a sparse, chanty vocal that sounds for all the world like the voice of John Lennon.

10. There's a popular bootleg version of 'You Got the Silver' in circulation, with Jagger singing the lead. The album track, featuring Keith's lead vocal, was the last Stones song released with Brian Jones playing on it.

CHAPTER TEN: REDLANDS

1. Lena Mary Calhoun Horne (1917–2010) was an African American actress, singer, dancer and human rights activist. She joined New York nightspot the Cotton Club as a teenager, soon moving on to Hollywood. A popular film actress, she lost faith in the industry after Ava Gardner pipped her at the post for the role of Julie LaVerne in MGM's *Show Boat* (1951). The choice was controversial as Ava Gardner's voice was dubbed. Curiously, Ava sang her two songs herself on the soundtrack album. Miss Horne went on to become an acclaimed variety star, and toured her own one-woman show.

Incidentally, Keith's Bentley was one of only sixty-eight S3 Continental Flying Spurs manufactured, the most expensive model in the Bentley range. Blue Lena's chassis number is BC68XE, and the car was first registered as JLP 400D. Since the 1960s, this car had been the world's ultimate Grand Tourer, able to take you from any capital in Europe to Monte Carlo to play the tables that same night. He purchased it from London dealer H.R. Owen in Mayfair's Berkeley Square. She survived several accidents, including the one that occurred on the way back from Knebworth in 1976, where the Stones had topped the bill alongside Led Zeppelin. Keith dozed off at the wheel and drove the car into a tree. The seven passengers including his little boy Marlon were unhurt. Later that year, driving back down the M1 from a concert in Leicester, Keith tore through a hedge and a fence and wound up in a field. Officers attending found his drugs and arrested him. He sold Blue Lena two years later to an Ascot Rolls-Royce dealer, and promptly bought another one, same model. Bonhams sold Lena at auction for £763,100 in September 2015.

2. As well as Connecticut, New England includes the states of Maine, New Hampshire, Vermont, Massachusetts and Rhode Island.

3. In Greek mythology, Cronus (Kronos, Roman name Saturn), King of the Titans, ruled the cosmos during the Golden Age after castrating and deposing his own father, Ouranos (Uranus). Fearing a prophecy that he would be overthrown by his own son, he devoured each of his children as they were born. Only the youngest, Zeus (Jupiter) was saved. He did grow up to usurp his father.

4. The Who recorded and released 'My Generation' in autumn 1965. The aggressive song that features Roger Daltrey exploding in a furious, exasperated stutter – as if he's so mad, he just can't get the words out – is the definitive encapsulation of rebellious youth. 'Hope I die before I get old' became their mantra. The members of the Who lived on, however, with the exception of their drummer Keith Moon.

5. Preludin: phenmetrazine appetite suppressant pills, consumed to stay awake.

6. Jerry Hall wrote in her book *My Life In Pictures*, Quadrille, 2010, that Mick Jagger told her he dropped acid every day during the 1960s,

and that he gave up smoking heroin for her. Jagger did not sue, nor did he comment.

7. Volker Schlöndorff's film *Mord Und Totschlag* translates as *A Degree of Murder*. It was Germany's entry to the 1967 Cannes Film Festival.

8. 'Who Breaks a Butterfly on a Wheel?' was a quote from English poet Alexander Pope's 'Epistle to Dr. Arbuthnot' (1735). It referenced torture victims having their long bones smashed with an iron bar while strapped to a Catherine wheel.

William Rees-Mogg edited *The Times* from 1967 until 1981. He was the father of Conservative politician Jacob Rees-Mogg and journalist-turned-politician Annunziata Rees-Mogg.

CHAPTER ELEVEN: MOUCHE

1. Borrowdale is in the Cumbrian Lake District of England, about three hundred miles north of London. The town of Keswick lies at the northern end of its lake, Derwentwater, in the shadow of Skiddaw, the sixth highest mountain in England. The highest is Scafell Pike, which can be approached and climbed from Borrowdale. The children's author Beatrix Potter spent summer holidays at Derwentwater. Her stories and drawings were influenced by the surrounding landscape. Ken Russell lived in an exquisite lakeside house, Coombe Cottage, next door to the Borrowdale Hotel.

2. This superb assessment of *Gothic* was made by the American author and critic Harlan Ellison (1934–2018).

3. *Women in Love* (1969) starred Oliver Reed, Glenda Jackson and Alan Bates, and is famous for the first full-frontal male sex scene on film. Ken Russell was nominated as Best Director. *The Devils* (1971) starring Reed and Glenda Jackson, focuses on a French Catholic priest who falls prey to witchcraft. It outraged the censors with its violent and sexually explicit content, and was banned throughout the world. Despite which, Ken

was named Best Director at the Venice Film Festival and by America's National Board of Review. The picture is still listed as one of the most controversial in history.

Ken directed the videos for Elton John's single 'Nikita' (1985); Cliff Richard's 'She's So Beautiful' (1988) from Dave Clark's musical *Time* (it was banned by the BBC … a Cliff Richard video!); and two of the promos of songs from Andrew Lloyd-Webber's musical *Phantom of the Opera*: Sarah Brightman and Steve Harley singing the title number, and Sarah with Cliff Richard singing 'All I Ask of You' (1988). He also directed the video for Bryan Adams's 1993 tribute to the late Diana, Princess of Wales, 'Diana'.

Elton John played the Pinball Wizard in seven-foot-high boots in *Tommy*, and performed the song of the same name.

A father of eight, like Mick Jagger, four times-married Ken suffered several strokes in later life and died in 2011, at the age of eighty-four.

4. The Beatles released *A Hard Day's Night* (1964), *Help!* (1965), *Magical Mystery Tour* (made for television in 1967, a critical flop, although its soundtrack album did well), the *Yellow Submarine* animated fantasy feature and *Let It Be* (1970).

5. John Schlesinger (1926–2003) was the Academy Award-winning director of *Midnight Cowboy* (1969) starring Dustin Hoffman and Jon Voight, father of Angelina Jolie. He also directed 1965's *Darling*, starring Julie Christie, and *Sunday Bloody Sunday* (1971) with Glenda Jackson and Peter Finch.

6. *Peyton Place* was the first popular American TV soap. It aired during the mid–late 1960s, and was broadcast on British television. Based on the 1956 novel by poor young housewife Grace Metalious and the film adaptation of the same name, it charted the dark secrets and sordid goings-on of a small New England town. The principal characters, including Ryan O'Neal as Rodney Harrington, Dorothy Malone as Constance Mackenzie, Mia Farrow as her daughter Allison Mackenzie and Barbara Parkins as Betty Anderson, became household names. Metalious's book, ridiculed by critics, was a *New York Times* bestseller

and an international smash hit. 'If I'm a lousy writer,' said Metalious, 'then an awful lot of people have lousy taste.'

7. Nicolas Roeg (1928–2018) directed *Walkabout* (1971) with Jenny Agutter, *Don't Look Now* (1973) starring Julie Christie and Donald Sutherland, *The Man Who Fell to Earth* (1976) with David Bowie, and *The Witches* (1990), based on Roald Dahl's novel, produced by Jim Henson of *The Muppets* fame and starring Anjelica Huston. He married two actresses, Susan Stephen and Theresa Russell, and died in London at the age of ninety.

8. 'Consent' is when an individual agrees to something or permits something to happen without being bullied or pressurised into it, without being manipulated, and without being given alcohol and/or drugs to make them change their mind.

CHAPTER TWELVE: CHRISTOPHER ROBIN

1. Not only can drugs trigger asthma symptoms, they can also make a sufferer's general condition worse. They affect lung function by narrowing the airways and making them more sensitive, according to asthma.org.uk. Drug use can also lead to stress, anxiety and depression, all of which exacerbate the condition.

2. Lucius Annaeus Seneca (4BC–65AD), best known for his plays *Medea*, *Thyestes* and *Phaedra*, and who influenced William Shakespeare.

3. www.nationalbullyinghelpline.co.uk/about.html

4. Palinacousis or auditory perseveration is, in the non-psychotic, the auditory phenomenon commonly referred to as an 'ear worm' ... when you can't get it out of your head. That tune, those lyrics, that bloody chorus. Drives you nuts. From the Greek *pali*, meaning again, and *acousis*, hearing. It is mostly triggered by external stimuli, e.g. hearing a song repeatedly, or by something that jogs a memory.

5. 'Rock the Casbah' was a 1982 song by the Clash.

6. *The Rolling Stones Rock and Roll Circus* was released on video in 1996, twenty-eight years after it was filmed, and on DVD in 2004.

7. A.A. Milne suffered what is thought to have been post-traumatic stress disorder (there was no diagnosis in those days) after active service during World War I. The *Winnie the Pooh* stories are believed to have been conceived out of desperation to eradicate his horrific memories of war. Christopher Robin Milne, who suffered from Myasthenia gravis, an autoimmune disorder, died in his sleep in Totnes, Devon, in April 1996, at the age of seventy-five.

8. John Lennon was born on 9 October, as was his second son, Sean. He lived at 9 Newcastle Road, was a Beatle for nine years, wrote songs featuring the number – 'One After 909'; 'Revolution 9', a 'sound collage' on the Beatles' ninth studio album (the so-called 'White Album'); and '#9 Dream', on John's ninth solo album, *Walls and Bridges* – which peaked at No. 9 on America's Billboard Hot 100 chart when it was released as a single. There are endless examples: Beatles manager Brian Epstein first saw the band on 9 November 1961; they signed their contract the following year on 9 May; their first appearance on *The Ed Sullivan Show* in the US took place on 9 February 1964 ... all coincidental, of course.

9. *The Murder of Brian Jones* by Anna Wohlin and Christine Lindsjoo, Blake Publishing, 1999.

CHAPTER THIRTEEN: ALTAMONT

1. Marianne Faithfull and Marsha Hunt were oblivious of the fact that they were both there with Mick that day.

2. *Adonais* by Percy Bysshe Shelley (1821); stanza forty.

3. The Battle of the Somme, 1 July–18 November 1916, with World

War I Allied troops against armies of the German Empire. It is named after a river running through Picardy, northern France. Of more than three million men who fought, more than a million were killed or injured. An encounter later condemned as one of 'mud, blood and futility', it was one of the deadliest battles in human history.

4. 'A coupla rocks' in this context is $2 million.

5. A snuff movie is a pornographic film or video recording of an actual murder, and not one created by sophisticated special effects. No conviction having ever been made, the film industry believes such movies to be mythological. The murder in *Gimme Shelter* is not considered by purists to be snuff because it was not pre-meditated. The idea naturally disgusts and terrifies moviegoers, but no evidence of them exists.

CHAPTER FOURTEEN: EXILE

1. The Beatles' *Abbey Road* was released on 26 September 1969. *Let It Be* was released on 8 May 1970. Although *Abbey Road* is generally regarded as the 'last' Beatles album – 'because *Let It Be* was recorded before it' – *Let It Be* does in fact feature the final Beatles song ever recorded. George Harrison's curious, plaintive, multi-tempo 'I Me Mine' was recorded on 3 January 1970, a year after the *Get Back* sessions, and after the release of *Abbey Road*. NB: this was the last Beatles song not counting the two recorded for the Beatles' 1990s *Anthology* series, 'Free As a Bird' and 'Real Love', which were made after John Lennon had been murdered, using material he had committed to tape years earlier.

2. A number of books quote 93 per cent. Maybe this clears it up: 'In the 1970s, the highest rate of income tax on earned income was 83 per cent. Margaret Thatcher's government reduced it to 60 per cent in 1980 and 40 per cent in 1989 (equal to the higher rate). From 1989 to 2010, the highest rate of income tax remained at 40 per cent…'
See LSE blog: https://blogs.lse.ac.uk/politicsandpolicy/the-top-rate-of-income-tax-2/

3. Mick owned the now Grade II listed Stargroves for nearly nine years. He sold it in 1979 for £200,000, four times what he had paid for it. Twenty years later, it was acquired from its then owner by Rod Stewart for £2.5 million. But Rod never lived there. He and his second wife Rachel Hunter separated soon after the purchase, and he sold it again. 'I was a rock star!' he moaned at the time. 'You don't dump a rock star!' The loss of the manor house clearly irked him. 'Instead of getting married again,' he later said, 'I'm going to find a woman I don't like and just give her a house.' In 2012, the house sold again, to a member of the American Sackler family, for more than £15 million.

Mick sold 48 Cheyne Walk later in the decade. He would return to the neighbourhood, purchasing number 98, the grand house once owned by engineer Isambard Kingdom Brunel and his father before him. He obviously missed the stretch of street that ran between Albert Bridge and Battersea Bridge, its blue plaques and famous ghosts. Bram Stoker, Bertrand Russell, T.S. Eliot, Somerset Maugham, Ian Fleming, Laurence Olivier, George Best and Mick Fleetwood had all lived on Cheyne Walk. Ken Follett still did, at 92. Ronnie Wood owned 119, the house in which the Romantic painter J.M.W. Turner had died, and Keith had once lived at number 3. At 100 were Roman Abramovich and family. Was Mick planning on popping round to see his Chelsea FC-owning neighbour, to borrow the odd cup of sugar?

Mick had a thing about the name of his old home. When he built his beautiful beach house in Mustique during the seventies, he christened it Stargroves Villa.

4. Patti D'Arbanville was the inspiration behind Cat Stevens's 1970 hits 'My Lady D'Arbanville' and 'Wild World'. The actress and model was part of Andy Warhol's Factory scene, appearing in his 1968 film *Flesh* and his 1973 flick *L'Amour*. She survived her racy youth to work steadily as an actress, had a child with actor Don Johnson in 1982, and married and divorced three times.

Pamela Miller, 'Miss Pamela', was part of the female line-up Girls

Together Outrageously (Orally/Occasionally/Often/Only) some of whom worked for Frank Zappa as domestic staff. He produced their only album, *Permanent Damage* (1969). Pamela later became the notorious groupie Pamela Des Barres.

5. In 2015, Carly Simon told the *LA Times* that the second verse of 'You're So Vain' is about Warren Beatty, the actor almost as infamous a shagger as Jagger. She added that the other two verses were about two other men, neither of whom is Mick. The contenders could include her ex-husband James Taylor, record producer David Geffen and Cat Stevens. Who also got around. It is rumoured that a recording featuring Carly of the Stones' 'Under My Thumb' lies in a vault somewhere, unreleased. Let's hear it.

6. Gram Parsons (1946–73) was born Ingram Cecil Connor III into a family of wealthy Florida citrus-growers. His father committed suicide by gunshot when Gram was twelve. His mother remarried, the children taking their stepfather's name. His stepfather then ran away with the children's nanny, and his mother died from cirrhosis of the liver on the day of his graduation. Poor little rich boy with a beyond dysfunctional background: the ultimate candidate for rock stardom.

After seeing Elvis Presley in concert in 1956, Gram set his heart on a career in music. He began slowly but surely, co-creating a genre of music that blended folk, rhythm and blues, country, soul and rock that placed him on the same page as the Stones. He recorded with the Byrds and the Flying Burrito Brothers, and started hanging with the Stones during the summer of 1969 when they were working on *Let It Bleed* and their upcoming US tour. He paved his way into their lives with money: they accepted him because he was rich. The Stones did not hang with leeches and gold diggers. Your typical seventies reckless rocker, he shared Keith's heroin addiction and used alcohol and pills like soda and sweets. He became devoted to the Stones, and performed at Altamont as one of the Flying Burrito Brothers. He got out of there on one of the last choppers and tried to pull Michelle Phillips, of the Mamas and the Papas, who was there with Keith.

Gram became a solo artist in early 1970, but his drug addiction hampered his work ethic. He accompanied the Stones on their three-week jaunt around England and Scotland during March 1971, hoping that their new Rolling Stones Records would sign him: he and Keith were talking about recording an album together.

Gram married his long-suffering girlfriend; got off heroin; got in with Emmylou Harris, and started recording with her. They toured the US. In summer 1973, a discarded cigarette started a fire that burned down his Topanga Canyon house, destroying everything except a single guitar and his favourite Jaguar car.

He could afford to pay Elvis's band, and did, to back him on the brilliant solo albums *GP* and *Grievous Angel*, that he recorded towards the end of his life. But he preferred getting zonked, especially while out on the road. An average guitarist, he was a gifted songwriter with the voice of an angel.

Parsons was life-threateningly promiscuous and neglected his daughter Polly. He could be charming company, but was often disloyal to his friends. A fantasist and a rewriter of truth, it was said that no one ever knew him truly. His knowledge of country music was blinding. He made it his mission to contemporise it and expand its appeal. To some extent, he got there.

Gram died on 18 (some say 19) September 1973, from morphine and alcohol overdose. He was twenty-six. His tour manager and friend Phil Kaufman stole his body and conveyed it to Joshua Tree National Park, where he cremated it in the car park. Kaufman later insisted that Gram had asked him to. He got away with it.

7. Gretchen Burrell is listed by IMDb as Gretchen Berrill. Gretchen Parsons relaunched her acting career as Gretchen Carpenter after she remarried.

CHAPTER FIFTEEN: CRISIS

1. Parkinson's disease is caused by a loss of nerve cells in part of the

brain. It causes problems like tremors and stiffness that worsen over time. Physiotherapy and medication can improve quality of life, but there is currently no cure. To support research, visit www.parkinsons.org.uk or call 0808 800 0303.

2. PPL PRS Ltd is the joint venture of the UK's two music licensing organisations. It grants The Music Licence, enabling licence holders to legally play and perform music in public. www.pplprs.co.uk

3. Baby-faced Stevie Winwood started performing in 1956 at the age of eight, and joined the Spencer Davis Group, with his elder brother Muff, when he was fourteen. When the band celebrated its first No. 1 single, 'Keep On Running', a cover of the song written by Jamaican artist and Island Records songwriter Jackie Edwards, Steve was still only seventeen. He left the line-up two years later and went on to great success with Traffic, Blind Faith and Ginger Baker's Air Force. He probably peaked too soon and withdrew from the mainstream music scene for several years. He re-emerged in 1986 at the age of thirty-eight with his album *Back in the High Life*, scoring a hit with the single 'Higher Love'.

CHAPTER SIXTEEN: JUGGERNAUT

1. Glaswegian singer-songwriter Jim Diamond topped the UK singles chart at the end of October 1984 with 'I Should Have Known Better', co-written by his pal Graham Lyle of Gallagher and Lyle. But he threw his No. 1 away, appealing to fans to go out and buy Band Aid's 'Do They Know It's Christmas?', the fundraiser for famine relief that led to Live Aid. Although it is often stated that Frankie Goes to Hollywood's 'The Power of Love' was the Christmas No. 1 in 1984, it wasn't: https://www.officialcharts.com/chart-news/every-official-christmas-number-1-ever-__3618/

Until 1997, 'Do They Know It's Christmas?' was the UK's best-selling single in the UK. It was displaced by 'Something About the Way You Look Tonight/Candle in the Wind 1997', Elton John's double

A-side in commemoration of Diana, Princess of Wales. The Band Aid offering stands at No. 2, followed by Queen's 'Bohemian Rhapsody', 'Mull of Kintyre' by Wings and 'You're the One That I Want' from John Travolta and Olivia Newton-John.

Jim re-recorded his signature song for his solo album *Jim Diamond* (1983). In regular touch for more than forty years, we exchanged texts on 7 October 2015 while I was en route to Chicago to give a lecture. He died the next day, just seventeen days after the death of his mother.

2. In Greek mythology, Pandora was the first human woman, and as such corresponds to the biblical Eve. A 'beautiful evil' whose descendants would 'torment the human race', she was given gifts by each of the gods. She is said to have opened a jar, handed down as a 'box', which contained all the evils of humanity. She thus unleashed them on an unsuspecting world. Only Hope remained contained.

3. 'The Red Special', also known as 'The Fireplace' and 'The Old Lady', is Queen guitarist Brian May's home-made instrument that he created with his father Harold sixty years ago. The wood from which the neck is made came from an old fireplace mantel. Other materials used in its construction were bits and pieces lying around the family home, including from his mother Ruth's sewing box. Brian has played it on virtually all Queen recordings and during live performances since the early 1970s.

4. WAGS is an acronym for 'wives and girlfriends', also known as 'footballers' wives'. Who tend to be young, blonde and leggy with Barbie tresses and killer talons, and usually of the 'Model, Actress, Whatever' variety (check out the song of that name which featured in the film *The Wedding Present*). Having become a British household term during the 2006 FIFA World Cup tournament, thanks to David Beckham's wife Victoria and Ashley Cole's wife Cheryl, it is now in use internationally ('*Les Wags*', '*die WAGS*'). It is also applied to the female partners of high-pro men in other sports.

5. Walter Theodore 'Sonny' Rollins (born 1930) is the legendary American

jazz tenor saxophonist and composer, whose career spans seven decades. A jailbird and heroin addict during the 1950s, he turned himself around and went on to record with Miles Davis, the Modern Jazz Quartet, Charlie Parker and Thelonious Monk, establishing a reputation as the 'Saxophone Colossus' and 'the greatest living improviser'. He plays on three tracks on *Tattoo You*, but goes uncredited. Having travelled the world commanding huge fees for his appearances and having released many albums, he withdrew from public performance in 2012, citing ill health. At the time of writing, he is ninety-one years old.

6. That doorway, on St Mark's Place in the East Village, is known as 'New York's hippest street'. Billie Holiday, Thelonious Monk, Ornette Coleman, Charles Mingus, John Coltrane and Miles Davis played at the Five Spot jazz club at the corner with Third Avenue. Leon Trotsky, Debbie Harry, W.H. Auden and William S. Burroughs all lived there. Andy Warhol ran a nightclub there. Billy Joel filmed a video there – for the track 'A Matter of Trust' from his 1986 album *The Bridge*. The New York Dolls and Led Zeppelin shot album covers there. The Dolls posed in front of the famous news-stand Gem Spa, said to have invented the egg cream (a type of milkshake with neither eggs nor cream in it) for the back of the sleeve of their eponymous first album; while Led Zeppelin photographed number 96 and 98 for their 1975 album *Physical Graffiti* – the same buildings used by the Stones in 'Waiting on a Friend'. Fun factoid: the tea shop Physical Graffitea later opened in the same building.

7. Port production is expressed in 'pipes'. A pipe of port, as traditionally ordered from their wine merchant by wealthy clients, was usually sixty dozen or 720 bottles. A pipe, today, is a unit of liquid volume equivalent to 550 litres.

8. Latin, Cicero: 'Oh the times! Oh the customs!', was famously interpreted by English historian, classicist and cricketer Charles Duke Yonge (1812–91) as 'Shame on this age and on its lost principles!'

9. 'The economy, stupid' was a phrase coined by Bill Clinton's

presidential campaign strategist James Carville in 1992. Their campaign used the US recession to steal a march on George W. Bush.

10. Thunderclap Newman were an English rock band formed by the Who's Pete Townshend and manager Kit Lambert, featuring John 'Speedy' Keen, Jimmy McCulloch and Andy 'Thunderclap' Newman. 'Something in the Air' was a UK No. 1 in July 1969. The lyrics actually read as follows: 'Call out the instigators/ Because there's something in the air/ We've got to get together sooner or later/ Because the revolution's here.'

Scottish guitarist McCulloch, a precocious talent, became a member of Paul McCartney's Wings. He was found dead in his apartment in September 1979, aged twenty-six. Although he was not a known user, cause of death was later given as alcohol and morphine poisoning.

11. 'The gods' are the furthest seats from the stage in the highest tiers of a performance venue: the cheap seats.

12. ... according to writer and reviewer Mic Wright.

13. Tommy Steele, aka Sir Thomas Hicks OBE (born 1936), was the UK's original rock star and teen idol, whose hits included 'Rock with the Caveman', 'Singing the Blues' and 'Little White Bull'. The soundtrack of his 1957 biopic, *The Tommy Steele Story*, became the first British No. 1 album. A major star of stage and screen (see what I mean?) and well into his ninth decade, he performs to this day.

14. 'Portraits in the attic': a reference to *The Picture of Dorian Gray*, Oscar Wilde's only novel, published in 1890/91. It tells of a well-to-do young man who lives a depraved and murderous lifestyle but retains his youthful beauty by selling his soul to the Devil. His portrait, painted by his friend Basil, absorbs his evils. Banished to the attic, the picture reveals the truth about what a grotesque Dorian had become.

15. From *American Gods* (2001), the novel by Neil Gaiman.

CHAPTER SEVENTEEN: MANDY

1. This quotation is usually attributed to philosopher and political writer Edmund Burke (1729–97), but is perhaps more accurately traced back at least in essence to another philosopher, John Stuart Mill (1806–73). He said as much, if not in so many words, during his 1867 address at the University of St Andrews in Scotland: 'Bad men need nothing more to compass their ends, than that good men should look on and do nothing. He is not a good man who, without a protest, allows wrong to be committed in his name, and with the means which he helps to supply, because he will not trouble himself to use his mind on the subject.'

2. At the time of writing, Bill Cosby's new civil trial is pending.

3. Roman Polanski: in May 2018, during an interview with *Newsweek Polska*, the fugitive child rapist denounced the #MeToo movement as 'mass hysteria' and 'total hypocrisy'. He made these comments after the Academy of Motion Picture Arts and Sciences announced that it was at last expelling him and Bill Cosby. Polanski was forty-four years old when he raped thirteen-year-old Samantha Geimer in Los Angeles. She was not, allegedly, his only victim. He admitted part of the crime, and was convicted of unlawful sexual intercourse with a minor. But before he received full sentence, and having spent forty-two days being evaluated by psychiatrists ahead of sentencing, he fled to Paris. He never returned to America, where he could have been sentenced to fifty years' imprisonment. He subsequently won six Oscars: three for *Tess*, starring Nastassja Kinski, and three for *The Pianist*, with Adrien Brody and Emilia Fox. His detractors continue to hope that he will be extradited to face re-trial. Meanwhile, people ask, will Hollywood now obliterate his star from the Walk of Fame? They won't have to. He doesn't have one: https://www.theguardian.com/culture/2018/aug/09/hollywood-walk-of-fame-dark-history-trump-star

4. Ken Gold co-wrote and produced many hits throughout the seventies and eighties, including 'I Can't Ask For Any More' by Cliff Richard, and

'You To Me Are Everything' and 'Can't Get By Without You' by the Real Thing. He also wrote for Billy Ocean and the Nolans.

5. *Untouchables* by Michael Gillard and Laurie Flynn, Abe Books, 2012, exposes countless cases of dirty cops, bent justice, racism and bribery within Scotland Yard.

CHAPTER EIGHTEEN: CLÍODHNA

1. *La fourchette* is French for 'fork'. It also happens to be the name of a small fold of membrane connecting the labia minora in the posterior part of the vulva. Wonder why on earth Mick chose that.

CHAPTER NINETEEN: RESONANCE

1. The opening line of *The Go-Between*, the 1953 novel by Leslie Poles Hartley CBE (1895–1972).

2. Johann Wolfgang von Goethe (1749–1832), German poet, novelist and playwright. Author of *Faust* (1808 and 1832), his play about a man who sells his soul to the Devil. It is widely considered to be Germany's greatest contribution to literature.

CHAPTER TWENTY: SO LONG

1. The vaudeville blues song 'Trouble in Mind' was written by jazz pianist Richard M. Jones. He recorded it with vocalist Thelma La Vizzo in 1924. It was made famous by Bertha 'Chippie' Hill two years later. She also recorded it with Jones, adding Louis Armstrong on trumpet. The now blues standard has been recorded and performed by many, notably Nina Simone, who had a hit with it in 1961, and Otis Spann and Lonnie Johnson, who recorded it in Copenhagen in 1963. Take a minute to find that one, it is sublime.

2. 'Up Above My Head' is a traditional gospel song. It was recorded by the Southern Sons in 1941. Sister Rosetta Tharpe's and Marie Knight's duet of it in 1947 was a huge hit. Tharpe's guitar-playing is a thing to behold.

3. Songwriter Don Raye famously wrote for family singing group the Andrews Sisters, who were hugely popular during World War II for entertaining the Allied forces. They are reckoned to have sold around eighty million records.

QUOTE, UNQUOTE

'The Stones are a great group and I love them. I love what they do. But when I look at their history, they always did what the Beatles did, a year later. When we started writing our own songs, you started to see everyone else doing that. The Stones had always been a blues cover band, but then they realised they had to write their own. You had *Sgt. Pepper* and then *Satanic Majesties*; our initial tour of America and then, six months later, the Stones tour of America. Even people who don't admit to it, and who found their roots in other types of music, couldn't help but be influenced by the success of the Beatles.'

Sir Paul McCartney

'I liked the Beatles but I wasn't mad on the Stones. I always thought they were a slight rip-off of Chuck Berry and some of the old blues people, and they never seemed to change. If people compare me to Jagger and the Stones I would be the one to be put down … I've been far more progressive than any of them.'

Sir Cliff Richard

'It would be awful to be like Keith Richards. He's pathetic. It's like a monkey with arthritis, trying to go on stage and look young. I have great respect for the Stones, but they would have been better if they had thrown Keith out fifteen years ago.'

Sir Elton John

'The reality is that I'm seventy-two now. I still have hair on my head but a lot more on my back. You want to quit and get out while the iron is hot and getting is good. I don't wanna be up on stage at seventy-five or eighty, and that's because we're the hardest working band in show business. I had to wear forty pounds of armor, eight-inch platform heels, wear more makeup and higher heels than any female you know, spit fire, and fly through the air. I mean, I would have been smarter to be in the Stones playing the guitar, wearing a T-shirt and sneakers, and never having to break a sweat. Other than Jagger, of course. So, we are getting out while the getting is good, the health is good, we're rocking it, and we're doing great. Go out when you're on top instead of when you're a sorry mess afterward.'

Gene Simmons, KISS

'Mick Jagger can't even make a successful solo album, and the Stones are the biggest rock group that ever was.'

Don Henley

'My first experience [with him] was when Mick Jagger walked in the dressing room without knocking, and he says, "I love how you girls dance." Often he would come into the dressing room, but we were always prepared because we never knew when he was coming in, but that's how Mick is.'

Tina Turner

'The Rolling Stones are truly the greatest rock and roll band in the world and always will be. The last too. Everything that came after them, metal, rap, punk, new wave, pop-rock, you name it … you can trace it all back to the Rolling Stones. They were the first and the last and no one's ever done it better.'

Bob Dylan

'I got on great with the Rolling Stones. This surprised everyone, including me, because I was "shy Pat" and here I was hanging out with these white rock'n'rollers. And in South Central LA, black girls and white guys definitely did not hang out and party together! While they spoke English here (in UK), it was a different kind of English to what we spoke. And I found the culture completely different. I went from the civil rights revolution in the US to the rock'n'roll revolution in England.'

P.P. Arnold

'I fell asleep at night with dreams of rock'n'roll glory in my head. Here's how one would go: the Stones have a gig at Asbury Park's Convention Hall but Mick Jagger gets sick. It's a show they've got to make, they need a replacement, but who can replace Mick? Suddenly, a young hero rises, a local kid right out of the audience. He can "front": he's got the voice, the look, the moves, no acne and he plays a hell of a guitar. The band clicks, Keith is smiling, and suddenly, the Stones aren't in such a rush to get Mick out of his sickbed. How does it end? Always the same … the crowd goes wild.'

Bruce Springsteen

'There were lots of things I could have done at the age of nineteen that would have been more healthy than becoming Mick Jagger's inamorata. In the end, it doesn't matter that hearts got broken and that we sweated blood. Maybe the most you can expect from a relationship that goes bad is to come out of it with a few good songs.'

Marianne Faithfull

'While Keith was away I'd be starting to get off heroin, really trying, but then he'd return and he'd get me on it just as bad as before. People who used to be friends began to get very bitchy toward me. Keith had this entourage of hangers-on who were always around the house, came for a weekend, stayed on for weeks and months, always a house full of freeloading sycophants. *Yes, Keith, anything you say, Keith,* no private life, no time to talk, the suppliers bringing us the heroin, but that's all we had in common.'

Anita Pallenberg

'Mick was obsessed with the idea of gold diggers. He sees all women as tarts.'

Bianca Jagger

'Mick Jagger and I just really liked each other a lot. We talked all night. We had the same views on nuclear disarmament.'

Jerry Hall

'I'm sorry but in the early 1970s Led Zeppelin wiped their asses with the Rolling Stones. And by 1977 and 1978 Queen would have wiped their asses with the Rolling Stones, too.'

Neal Preston, rock photographer

'Mick Jagger? Mean with money. Still is.'

David Bailey

'The matter of "Would You Let Your Daughter Go With a Rolling Stone?" Did I first say it? No, but I heard someone say it and I repeated it and made it work. It had just been a part of someone else's conversation. I heard it and pushed it into a headline. I had no idea that it would be a byline for life.'

Andrew Loog Oldham

'Mick Jagger's male-to-male sexual attractiveness was a fundamental part of the Rolling Stones' early success. So was Brian Epstein's gayness on the way the Beatles were presented and sold. From the seventies onwards, many artists gained promotional benefits from outing themselves.'

Simon Napier-Bell

'I like it on the road. I don't know what I'd do if I couldn't go out there, I'd go mad.'

Mick Jagger

'Mick's attitude to women is that they are basically cattle. They are goods. That is his basic attitude … I find it quite easy to detach myself from Mick's private life, but then it's ludicrous because it's not private at all. He's intent on being Casanova or Don Juan. He's always looking for it which is cruel to his loved ones, but he has always been like that.'

Keith Richards

'On tour we all get down but Mick can get down lower than most.'

Keith Richards

'When Mick finds out who he is – that will probably be the end of the Rolling Stones.'

Ian Stewart

'The original Rolling Stones band was so incredible, due in great part to Brian Jones. It was initially his band, after all. He was a visionary and creative. I hung out with him from time to time, and one of our favourite things to do was go to eat Indian food. One of the last times I saw him was during the *Beggars Banquet* sessions; we were sitting in a circle on the floor. Keith Richards on my right with an acoustic guitar, Charlie Watts on my left with a snare drum in a briefcase. Opposite me was Brian. We were beating on large Moroccan drums, laying down the basic track for 'Street Fighting Man'.

Dave Mason, co-founder, Traffic

'He ran out of runway.'

John Lennon on Brian Jones

SELECT BIBLIOGRAPHY

Andersen, Christopher, *Mick: The Wild Life and Mad Genius of Jagger*, Gallery Books/Simon & Schuster, 2012

Balfour, Victoria, *Rock Wives*, Beech Tree Books New York, 1986

Bockris, Victor, *Keith Richards: The Unauthorised Biography*, Omnibus Press, 1992

Booth, Stanley, *The True Adventures of the Rolling Stones*, William Heinemann Ltd, 1985

Brown, Mick, *Mick Brown on Performance*, Bloomsbury Movie Guides, 1999

Bullock, Darryl W., *The Velvet Mafia: The Gay Men Who Ran the Swinging Sixties*, Omnibus Press, 2021

Clayson, Alan, *Mick Jagger: The Unauthorised Biography*, Sanctuary Publishing, 2005

Dalton, David and Farren, Mick (compiled by), *Rolling Stones In Their Own Words*, Omnibus Press, 1980

Faithfull, Marianne, *Faithfull*, Michael Joseph, 1994

Glennie, Jay, *Performance: The Making of a Classic*, Coattail Publications, 2018

Greenfield, Robert, *A Journey Through America with the Rolling Stones*, Helter Skelter Publishing, 1974

Hamp, Johnnie, *It Beats Working for a Living: A Lifetime in Showbusiness*, Trafford Publishing, 2008

Hepworth, David, *Uncommon People: The Rise and Fall of the Rock Stars*, Bantam Press, 2017

Hunt, Marsha, *Real Life: The Story of a Survivor*, Chatto and Windus, 1986

Jagger, Mick, Richards, Keith, Watts, Charlie, Wood, Ronnie, *According to the Rolling Stones*, Weidenfeld & Nicolson, 2003

Jensen, David, *Kid Jensen: For the Record*, Little Wing/Mango Books, 2020

Jones, Kenney, *Let the Good Times Roll*, Blink Publishing, 2018

Kent, Nick, *Apathy for the Devil: A 1970s Memoir*, Faber and Faber, 2010

Loog Oldham, Andrew, *Rolling Stoned*, Because Entertainment Inc., 2013

Loog Oldham, Andrew, *Stoned*, Secker & Warburg, 2000

Loog Oldham, Andrew, *2Stoned*, Secker & Warburg, 2002

Mansfield, John and Colin, *As You Were: The true adventures of the Ricky-Tick Club* (self-published), 2019

Milne, Christopher, *The Enchanted Places: A Childhood Memoir*, Eyre Methuen, 1974

Napier-Bell, Simon, *Black Vinyl White Powder*, Ebury Press, 2001

Napier-Bell, Simon, *Ta-Ra-Ra Boom De-Ay: The Dodgy Business of Popular Music*, Unbound, 2014

Norman, Philip, *The Stones*, Elm Tree Books/Hamish Hamilton Ltd, 1984

Paglia, Camille, *Free Women, Free Men: Sex, Gender, Feminism*, Pantheon Books/Penguin Random House, 2017

Paglia, Camille, *Sexual Personae: Art and Decadence from Nefertiti to Emily Dickinson*, Yale University/Penguin Books, 1990

Palmer, Robert, *Deep Blues*, Viking, 1981

Richards, Keith, with Fox, James, *Life*, Weidenfeld & Nicolson, 2010

Sanchez, Tony, *Up and Down with the Rolling Stones*, John Blake Publishing, 2010

Sandford, Christopher, *The Rolling Stones: Fifty Years*, Simon & Schuster, 2012

Schofield, Carey, *Jagger*, Methuen London Ltd, 1983

Smith, Mandy, with Coulson, Andy and Millar, Ingrid, *It's All Over Now*, Blake Publishing, 1993

Swern, Phil, *Sounds of the Sixties*, Red Planet Publishing, 2017

Trynka, Paul, *Sympathy for the Devil*, Bantam Press/Transworld, 2014

Turner, Tina, with Loder, Kurt, *My Life Story*, Viking, 1986

Wells, Simon, *She's a Rainbow: The Extraordinary Life of Anita Pallenberg*, Omnibus Press, 2020

Wood, Ronnie, *Ronnie*, Macmillan, 2007

Wyman, Bill, with Coleman, Ray, *Stone Alone: The Story of a Rock'n'Roll Band*, Viking, 1990

RECOMMENDED

27: Gone Too Soon: Casualties of Rock'n'Roll, A Simon Napier-Bell film, 2017

Crossfire Hurricane, Eagle Rock Entertainment Ltd,

2012 *Gimme Shelter*, Warner Bros Entertainment Inc, 2011, featuring the band on their 1969 US tour, remastered and restored

Ma Rainey's Black Bottom – 2020 musical drama film set in 1920s Chicago, based on the 1982 play by August Wilson, about influential musician Gertrude 'Ma' Rainey, 'Mother of the Blues'. Starring Viola Davis, Chadwick Boseman and Glynn Turman. Boseman was posthumously awarded Best Actor – Motion Picture Drama at the 2020 Golden Globes.

Rolling Stones: The Biggest Bang Boxed Set (DVD), 2007

Shine a Light, Martin Scorsese, Shangri-La Entertainment, 2008. Its highlight is Buddy Guy's performance with the band.

Stoned: The Story of the Original Rolling Stone, Stephen Woolley, 2006. Based on three controversial books, *Paint it Black* by Geoffrey Giuliano, *Who Killed Christopher Robin?* by Terry Rawlings and *The Murder of Brian Jones* by Anna Wohlin.

Stones in Exile, Eagle Rock Entertainment, 2010

Suburban Steps to Rockland: The Story of the Ealing Club – a feature-length documentary about the UK's first rhythm and blues club, launched in 1962.

ACKNOWLEDGEMENTS

I am indebted to my editor, James Hodgkinson, at Bonnier Books, whose idea this book was.

I hope I've passed the audition. Thank you, JH and team, Karen Stretch and Clare Hulton, without whom ...

For recollections, revelations and their valuable time, I thank the following: Keith Altham, David Ambrose, John Blake, Sharon Churcher, Steve Clark of The Kingfisher, Keswick, Paul Endacott, Bernard Fowler, John Giddings, Jason Gore, Roger Gore, Jeff Griffin, Johnnie Hamp, Torben Hersborg, Malcolm Hill, Richard Hughes, Chris Jagger, David 'Kid' Jensen, Gudrun Jensen, Berni Kilmartin, Margaret Kirby, Paul Levett, Andrew Loog Oldham, Zoot Money, Piers Morgan, Peter Myers, Simon Napier-Bell, Sarah Oliver, Denis O'Regan, Andy Peebles, Ed Phillips, John Pidgeon R.I.P., Julia Pidgeon, Jamie Scott, Roger Scott R.I.P., Peter Sheridan, Earl Slick, David Stark, Professor David Temperley, Tommy Vance, Stuart White, Annette Witheridge, Jane Wroe Wright and Alistair Young, and the Ealing Club Community Interest Company

Sam, Chris, Adam and Matthew
Gareth, Beverley, Cleo and Jesse
Bev, Rob, Nick, Alex and Christian
Julie, Karen and Leila
Trevor and Debbie Jones

Suki Yamamoto

Dan Arthure

David Stark, Rab Noakes, Brian Bennett, Clem Cattini,
    Ed Bicknell and all the Scribs

The Revd Canon Dr Alison Joyce and friends at St Bride's Church,
Fleet Street

Mike Parry

David Bolton was the most 'people' person I have ever known. It was said during his St Bride's memorial service on 14 October 2021 that his greatest gift was his interest in absolutely everybody. This book is dedicated to David's memory, and to his grandson Charlie.

For Mum, Henry, Mia and Bridie

LAJ, June 2022

INDEX